Toward
A New Maritime
Strategy

Toward
A New Maritime
Strategy

American Naval Thinking
in the Post–Cold War Era

Peter D. Haynes

NAVAL INSTITUTE PRESS
Annapolis, Maryland

Naval Institute Press
291 Wood Road
Annapolis, MD 21402

Library of Congress Cataloging-in-Publication Data
Haynes, Peter D.
  Toward a new maritime strategy : American naval thinking in the post–Cold War era /
Peter D. Haynes.
    pages cm
  Includes bibliographical references and index.
  ISBN 978-1-61251-852-7 (alk. paper) — ISBN 978-1-61251-864-0 (ebook) 1. Naval
strategy—History—20th century. 2. Naval strategy—History—21st century. 3. United
States. Navy—History. 4. Sea-power—United States—History. 5. Military doctrine—
United States—History. I. Title.
  V165.H39 2015
  359'.030973—dc23
                                                                    2015017477

♾ Print editions meet the requirements of ANSI/NISO z39.48-1992
(Permanence of Paper).
Printed in the United States of America.

23 22 21 20 19 18 17 16 15   9 8 7 6 5 4 3 2 1
First printing

To my lovely wife, Monica

Contents

List of Illustrations   viii

Acknowledgments   ix

    Introduction   1

1   The Cold War   15

2   Maritime Strategy for the 1990s, 1989   35

3   The Way Ahead, 1990   48

4   . . . From the Sea, 1991–92   64

5   Forward . . . From the Sea, 1993–94   87

6   2020 Vision, 1995–96   104

7   Anytime, Anywhere, 1996–97   120

8   The Navy Strategic Planning Guidance, 1998–2000   132

9   Sea Power 21, 2000–2004   148

10   The 3/1 Strategy, 2005   172

11   The 1000-Ship Navy, 2005–6   196

12   A Cooperative Strategy, 2007   213

    Conclusion   239

Notes   253

Index   283

Illustrations

Figure 4.1.   The Manthorpe Curve   69

Figure 4.2.   The Pyramid Slide   76

Figure 10.1. The Bear Paw   185

Figure 11.1. The 2006 Quadrennial Defense Review's Shift of Focus   203

Figure 11.2. The 2006 Quadrennial Defense Review's New Force
              Planning Construct   204

Figure 12.1. Admiral Roughead's Venn Diagram   230

Acknowledgments

First and foremost, I would like to thank my beautiful wife, Monica, the love of my life, for her overwhelming support and love, and our two children, Dallan and Brietta, for their support, love, patience, and humor. They are the center of my world, and the long journey of writing the book would not have been completed without their infinite encouragement. I would like to thank Mom and Dad for being great parents and role models, and Mo for having been a wonderful mother-in-law. I am truly blessed to have such a wonderful family. I would like to thank Dan Moran, a gentleman and scholar of endearing brilliance and patience, for his insights and hard work, and Jim Wirtz for his advice and enthusiasm. I am indebted to Dan and Jim for their support and friendship, and to other professors at the Naval Postgraduate School, particularly David Yost, Anne Clunan, and Jeff Kline. I take great pleasure in thanking Peter Swartz, a former Navy strategist and an analyst at the Center for Naval Analyses, for his insights, friendship, and ever-present support, as well as his dedication to maintain the flame of strategic thinking in the Navy. I am beholden to Randy Papadopoulos, Tom Hone, Paul Nagy, and the Naval History and Heritage Command for their encouragement, as well. Finally, I want to thank the U.S. Naval Institute for its leadership and support, and for the institute's warm and professional folks that I have been privileged to work with, particularly Tom Cutler, Gary Thompson, Emily Bakely, and Claire Noble. During the writing of this book, I have drawn strength from my faith in God, my family, my friends, the United States, and the U.S. Navy. The Navy is an institution that is woven into the fabric of my life and that of my family, one that I am privileged and honored to be a part of.

Introduction

In October 2007 the U.S. Navy released "A Cooperative Strategy for 21st Century Seapower," a strategy that represented a fundamental shift in the Navy's strategic outlook.[1] With it, the Navy sought not only to redefine the terms of its own relevance but also to make a revolutionary argument about where the vital interests of the United States lie and the nature of U.S. naval power in relation to those interests. The Navy argued that those interests should not be seen in terms of the threats to U.S. territory and lives, but rather in light of the relationship between the United States and the international economic and political system. "A Cooperative Strategy" argued that since the United States' "security, prosperity, and vital interests . . . are increasingly coupled to those of other nations, [its] interests are best served by fostering a peaceful global system comprised of interdependent networks of trade, finance, information, law, people and governance."[2] This is not a recapitulation of a rhetorical claim, familiar since the founding of the Republic, that America's interests are humankind's interests: it is, essentially, the opposite of that claim.

This international economic and political system is the source from which the United States draws most of its power, influence, and ability to provide for and defend its way of life, the homeland, and the system itself. The system is the wellspring of U.S. power, which should not be surprising as it was designed by the United States as such. The institutions, regimes, and practices of this system, many of which—such as the Bretton Woods accords—were developed by the United States and its key allies during and shortly after World War II, were

1

designed to privilege U.S. interests and those of its key security and economic partners. By controlling the international monetary and financial structures it designed into the system and providing a nuclear umbrella to its trading partners, the United States fashioned itself into a systemic leader and manager of a highly successful political and economic order that came to be called the free world. The United States engineered the rise of its order in war-torn Europe and Japan and the downfall of imperialism worldwide. In managing the system with and on behalf of others as well as on behalf of its own interests, the United States established a viable alternative to the Soviets' vision of European modernity. In practical terms, then, we might describe this system more accurately as the U.S. liberal political and economic system.

With its "A Cooperative Strategy," the Navy argued that the U.S. Navy, Marine Corps, and Coast Guard—the nation's maritime services—have a uniquely preeminent role in protecting the system and sustaining the United States' leadership of that system. By being deployed around the globe to manage crises, prevent conflict, and deter large-scale war, these maritime services underwrite the political, commercial, and security conditions necessary for global prosperity. In part because they operate in international waters, they knit broader interests with like-minded states in ways that air forces and armies cannot. Since world trade is essentially maritime trade, any compromise of the United States' ability to secure the freedom of the seas—and specifically to ensure the flow of petroleum— threatens the prosperity of the United States, its allies, and its trading partners, all of whom, regardless of rivalries, share a common interest in systemic prosperity, growth, and stability. By advancing a cooperative systemic strategy, one that takes full account of the strategic importance of wealth accumulation and distribution, the Navy acknowledged that its own strategic outlook, and by implication that of the United States, was too militaristic and threat-centric, that it was focused too much on the requirements of operations and warfighting at the expense of thinking about strategic requirements. By advancing such a strategy, the Navy acknowledged that the U.S. maritime services and the United States could no longer afford to separate military goals from economic and political goals.

Ironically, the Navy might have developed "A Cooperative Strategy" at any time since World War II and most certainly since the collapse of the Soviet Union. If one were to take a copy of "A Cooperative Strategy" and replace the word "global" with "free world" or "NATO," and otherwise read it in the context of Cold War geopolitics, one might reasonably come away with the impression that it could have been written at any time since 1945.[3] The Cold War was fundamentally a struggle between two anticolonial great powers striving to prove the efficacy of their respective systemic models. Only one of these models—the free world's—delivered unprecedented increases in the standards of living, met societal expectations, and made up for its political leaders' miscues. Among the reasons why the United States won the Cold War was that nearly all the world's richest states ended up on its side linked by a robust network of trade that was connected and sustained by American sea power. In the final analysis, the strength of the U.S. system proved more instrumental in ending the war than any explicit U.S. military strategy.

After the Cold War the free world expanded into the globalized world, thereby expanding America's responsibilities as well. At this point, one might have expected that the Navy—no longer burdened with having to prepare for great-power war—would redefine its purpose in systemic versus threat-based warfighting terms and restructure the fleet accordingly, focusing on developing platforms more for its constabulary and diplomatic roles and less for its warfighting role.[4] Given its unique relationship to the United States' state-market relationship, no other U.S. military service was more suited to invoke and extend a systemic history of the Cold War (and its role therein) as a basis for a more systemic vision of U.S. postwar strategy. The Cold War had, ostensibly, validated the relationship between global naval power, economic globalization, and liberal political integration. The United States' role as systemic manager had not changed, nor had its geostrategic position astride the trade routes of Europe and Asia, a reminder that sea power is not just about warships.

It is puzzling that the Navy did not advance "A Cooperative Strategy" much earlier, because it is a maritime strategy as classically understood. A maritime strategy is well suited to the interests of a state whose prosperity and security interests have always been linked to and dependent on the vitality of the world economy, and to the free markets, open societies, and democratic policies that have (so far) accompanied sustained economic success. A maritime strategy has always been more directly concerned with the relationship between the state and global markets than with strategies associated with land power or airpower, a statement as true during the Age of Sail as it is today. A maritime strategy ties economic, political, and security interests, and offers a holistic, less militarized, and less threat-centric worldview that, in this case, was free to emerge with the disappearance of the Soviet threat.

The Navy's institutional history speaks of an intimate relationship between U.S. foreign policy, trade, and the Navy. Its history also reflects the exhortations of its own Alfred Thayer Mahan, maritime theorist, political economist, and U.S. naval advocate, who famously related international relations, economic prosperity, and naval power. Despite such a history, however, the Navy did not advance a maritime strategy in an era in which the relative saliency of such should have, in principle, been much more apparent. In short, "A Cooperative Strategy" might have been developed at any time since the end of the Cold War, if not well before. That it was not developed earlier is not because its ideas are new or complicated, but because the forces that shape how the Navy thinks and learns effectively pushed those ideas to the margins of official consideration.

More than twenty-five years have passed since the Cold War ended, and an appraisal of the general trend of strategic thought on the part of the world's only remaining global navy is long overdue. This book seeks to understand how the Navy arrived at its current strategic outlook and why it took nearly two decades for a maritime strategy to emerge. In so doing, it also assesses expectations of how the Navy as an institution will confront equally disorienting changes in the future. This book asks two questions: (1) Why did the Navy not develop a maritime strategy earlier in the post–Cold War era? And (2) What explains why it eventually did develop a maritime strategy?

This book examines U.S. naval strategy from the fall of the Berlin Wall in November 1989 to the release of "A Cooperative Strategy" in November 2007. It links a description and what is at times an unpleasant analysis of U.S. naval strategy in the post–Cold War era to an explanation of the forces that influenced its course. It argues that how the United States and specifically the U.S. Navy adapted to the immense strategic, political, bureaucratic, technological, and operational challenges of the Cold War shaped distinctive national and institutional approaches to strategy that were then applied to the problems encountered in the post–Cold War era. The unexpected passing of the Cold War did little to alter the logic of U.S. strategy or the Navy's institutional ways of thinking, which worked together in shaping the course of U.S. naval strategy away from maritime-systemic ideas during the Cold War, the inertia of which continued well into the postwar era. It argues that it took a peculiar series of sometimes traumatic events for a maritime strategy to emerge. These included the realization among American leaders that the United States faced a generational struggle against Islamist terrorists threats and that it could lose the war in Iraq in 2004–7—events so sobering that they called into question long-standing assumptions about U.S. strategy, threatened the Navy's relevance, and brought about a systemically oriented U.S. strategic approach. These events also included a catalyst for institutional change in the form of two Navy leaders, one of whose late-life conversion to a maritime orientation was as implausible as the other's promotion to a position of strategic leadership.

Why did the Navy not develop a maritime strategy earlier in the post–Cold War era? The logic inherent in U.S. strategy during the Cold War bounded and channeled U.S. naval strategy away from a maritime strategy. In the early years of the Cold War, U.S. civilian strategic theorists implanted a way of thinking that was hyperrationalist, apolitical, and ahistorical. The nuclear bomb had, as Henry Kissinger put it, "turned strategy into deterrence, and deterrence into an esoteric intellectual exercise."[5] Viewed as a cost-effective means of deterring and, failing that, winning a war, the bomb obviated the need for the United States to develop an excellence in systemic management and alliance diplomacy and made the tasks of hegemonic statecraft less complex and far easier.[6] America's Cold War leaders and strategists did not take into account how liberal, alliance-based maritime powers like Great Britain had defeated continental hegemons in the past. Instead, U.S. strategy fixated on the Soviet threat and the balance of military power, and on deterring a hot war, and not on winning a cold one. American vital interests, U.S. strategy, and the U.S. military's purpose were defined in terms of the threat and not of the system.

The U.S. military's adherence to the rationalist tradition of the nineteenth-century Swiss military theorist Antoine-Henri Jomini reinforced the separation between military goals and economic and political goals. The Jominian approach reduces complex problems to apolitical principles that, if followed, would lead to quick and decisive victories. It blithely assumes that the political goals for which a war was to be fought would somehow be realized after the field of battle had been won. Seduced by Jomini's formula of efficiency, the military focused more on how to realize high-tech shortcuts to quick and decisive victory, particularly by applying the nation's preferred mode of warfare—airpower—than on how to use force for greater political effect.

Having been relieved from figuring out how to win a seemingly perpetual cold war, and given constant interservice rivalry and the high cost of modern weapons systems, Congress and the Department of Defense's civilian leaders sought to turn the Department into a well-run business. The Department's civilian leaders imposed a centrally controlled programming and budgeting process and the rationality of the science of management in which the coin of the realm was marginal cost-benefit analysis. In so doing, these civilian leaders shifted the locus of U.S. strategy-making from the ways-means-ends dialectic that is strategy to a myopic focus on determining the means. Mirroring American culture, the outlook of U.S. strategy was scientific-methodological, profoundly pragmatic, and technologically dependent, and the style of U.S. defense leadership was industrial-managerial, not strategic.

The logic inherent in American naval thinking was not any more conducive to the Navy's development of a maritime strategy than the logic inherent in U.S. strategy. The Cold War did not demand much competency in systemic thought on the part of the U.S. government, which meant that the U.S. government did not demand the same of its Navy. Relieved from that task, the Navy was allowed to frame its own rationality, identity, and strategic outlook. These elements of institutional thinking were rooted in the institution's seminal event, the Pacific War against Japan, a campaign that demonstrated the versatility and flexibility of a balanced, aircraft carrier–based fleet.[7] The campaign vindicated how the Navy saw the purpose of its officers, which was to apply an adaptable mindset and technological knowledge to the problems associated with war at sea. The establishment after World War II of lengthy overseas deployments as standard practice meant that the institution's knowledge became almost exclusively operational-experiential. Operations—meaning being at sea (either deployed or training to deploy)—became the lens through which Navy officers viewed the world; to most in the Navy, operations also became the Navy's raison d'être. Given the constant demands of operations and advancing naval technology, officers now had little room in their careers to take up the (potentially) career-damaging task of contemplating the Navy's purpose beyond operations. Given the Navy's pragmatic outlook, what the institution learned and inculcated into its members was limited to what was useful operationally.

The institution's knowledge base narrowed further in the 1960s when Secretary of Defense Robert S. McNamara embedded his programming and budgetary process in the Pentagon. The process became the essential means by which the U.S. military services protected their respective identities, preferred weapons systems, and relevance. The Navy did not view any problem as more critical or long-standing during the Cold War than the need to justify its strategic relevance on a par with that of the Air Force and Army. In terms of U.S. declaratory strategy, neither the Navy's purpose nor the reasons for its force structure were ever self-evident. Consequently, the Navy sent its best, most-promising officers to the Pentagon between sea tours to manage its weapons systems programs. Navy officers assumed leadership positions devoid of anything but operational and programmatic experience and technical-technological knowledge, none of which required a deeper understanding of the Navy's purpose. The Navy thus produced leaders whose intellects were of a peculiar mixture, one that combined brilliance with the narrowness of the institution's rationality and knowledge base. In short, U.S. naval strategy during the Cold War was simply the application of the narrow professional experiences of Navy officers to the solution of problems associated with operating, procuring, and rationalizing a generic and forward-deployed fleet.[8]

Their backgrounds shaped an implicit institutional strategic outlook that was an intuitive expression of how they defined the Navy's purpose and identity. The Navy saw its purpose as being contingent operationally, and not instrumental strategically. The Navy prized being prepared for the unknown over understanding its purpose beyond tactical and operational goals. It sought to maintain the operational flexibility that came with an offensive-minded, forward-deployed, and balanced carrier-based fleet that was central to its identity as a warfighting organization and key to its ability and demand to be prepared to project power across an enormous range of circumstances. Emblematic of its contingent outlook was the aircraft carrier, the ultimate hedge against the unknown. Its versatility allowed the Navy to participate meaningfully in a wide breadth of missions, from nuclear retaliation, full-scale and limited war, day-to-day foreign policy needs, and a myriad of ways short of war, a range unique among the services. Absent a Pearl Harbor–like attack or rapid unexpected technological obsolescence, the fleet's composition could not (and still cannot) be changed overnight. Hence, the Navy balked at attempts to narrow the fleet's capabilities to conform to a White House–mandated vision of war. A carrier-based fleet accommodated shifts in the strategic and operational environs and in U.S. declaratory strategy more readily than a fleet built for specific missions like nuclear retaliation or sea control, for example. Specialization meant operational vulnerability, which meant political vulnerability. Only when the fleet was built to handle just about any contingency and was forward deployed (which cost only marginally more than keeping it tied up) could American sea power be fully realized operationally and rationalized politically.

The Navy's emphasis on operational experience, warfighting skills, technological knowledge, and resource management proficiency on the part of its officers was a reasoned response to the operational, technological, managerial, and political demands of the Cold War. This reasoned response came at the expense of a greater understanding of or a desire to understand the Navy's strategic effects, to redress the inchoate nature of sea power theory, and to grasp the nature of the war between the Soviet and U.S. systems enough to develop the functioning and legitimating ideas behind a maritime strategy. The Navy only dimly understood this state of affairs, and yet casually dismissed the need to redress it throughout the Cold War (and after). The logic inherent in American naval thinking was internally consistent with excellence in naval warfare; indeed, the logic was exquisite given the Navy's superb operational performance over the past seventy years. But what made the Navy arguably the most operationally adaptable of the services made it intellectually weak and uninterested in understanding the Navy's deeper purpose and strategic effects. This was ironic, as no other U.S. military service could claim such a unique and direct relationship with the United States–managed system and lay claim to a central role in the United States' systemic Cold War victory.

The Cold War ultimately taught the Navy how to exploit the trade winds of U.S. strategy and defense policy and the currents of U.S. foreign policy, and to catch the occasional wave of American insecurity and budgetary permissiveness. The Navy came to view changing environmental conditions rather in the way sailors view the wind: something that may only limit their options without necessarily changing their mind about where they want to go. The Navy's goal was to remain a forward-deployed, balanced, carrier-based fleet, and the Navy tacked and wore as needed to maintain that general bearing.

After the end of the Cold War, Congress and the Department of Defense's leaders focused on downsizing the military and optimizing how it fought. The Goldwater-Nichols Defense Reorganization Act of 1986 (Goldwater-Nichols) elevated the stature of the chairman of the Joint Chiefs and the commanders in chief of the unified commands (CINCs) (a term changed to "combatant commanders" in 2002). Goldwater-Nichols demanded that the services integrate, which the U.S. defense establishment termed "jointness." It also empowered the chairman of the Joint Chiefs to mandate a single vision that defined the military's purpose. That vision was concerned with how so-called revolutionary precision strike and informational capabilities would deliver a swift and decisive victory against a generic foe in lieu of (or in support of) ground troops. Many in the defense establishment believed that this vision was vindicated in various operations throughout the 1990s. Goldwater-Nichols also further limited the Navy's ability to influence U.S. strategy, and altered how the Navy's senior uniformed leader, the Chief of Naval Operations (CNO), understood the role of that position. To the CNOs of the post–Cold War era, the White House, the secretary of defense, and the chairman determined the ends, the CINCs determined the ways, while the CNO and the CNO's Pentagon-based staff, the Office of the CNO (OPNAV), focused on the means. These CNOs assumed that they were not responsible for anything other than equipping, training, and organizing the Navy: strategy was someone else's job.

The end of the Cold War found Navy leaders and strategists intellectually unprepared to advance a peacetime maritime strategy. It is reasonable to assume that if such strategy had been developed, which is not likely to have occurred, Congress and the Pentagon's leaders would have rejected it: they would have viewed anything not aligned with the prescribed vision as solipsistic. The need to align in some manner with the prescribed ideas is a reminder that strategic ideas are contingent; one person's strategy depends on everyone else's. Strategy—the relating of military force and political purpose—is an inherently practical endeavor. As Bernard Brodie noted, "The question that matters in strategy is: Will the idea work?"[9] Moreover, Congress and the Department of Defense's civilian leaders had come to see the Navy's purpose in light of the Soviet threat, which the Navy itself did much to bring about because it had rationalized itself, particularly in the late Cold War, exclusively in those terms.

Marginalized by the lessons drawn by the U.S. military from the 1990–91 Gulf War, the Navy was not about to challenge the direction of U.S. strategy. It soon found that direction accommodating enough and aligned itself with U.S. strategy's focus on warfighting, conflict with regional powers including Iran and North Korea, jointness, and strike warfare. The latter was a capability the Navy was well positioned to embrace technologically and conceptually. The Navy's embracing of strike warfare was reflected in its new focus on adversaries on shore as captured in its 1992 " . . . From the Sea," which was the Navy's first post–Cold War strategy.[10] The move protected the carriers, which were now needed in the scenarios facing U.S. forces, scenarios in which the carriers had excelled during the Cold War. The Navy staked its claim on its ability to provide the CINCs with a breadth of capabilities, none more critical than striking targets on shore on very short notice. As in the Cold War, the gravitational pull of advanced technologies and associated concepts was the safest and surest route to budgetary success. A flexible, power-projecting fleet allowed the Navy to justify itself in terms of major combat operations against regional powers, which was the Army's and the Air Force's raisons d'être and the locus of U.S. strategy, as well as an everyday instrument of U.S. statecraft.

Why did the Navy subsequently develop a maritime strategy? The U.S. invasions of Afghanistan in 2001 and Iraq in 2003 were seen as vindicating the direction of post–Cold War American strategy. In short order, however, the failure to counter the Iraqi insurgency exposed as insufficient the American way of war, which assumed wrongly that tactical and operational success would speak for itself. The military had equated a theory of highly planned and precision-enabled destruction with a theory of success in war, and assumed wrongly that political goals like stability and democracy would self-organize in the wake of technology-enabled battlefield victories. This complacent outlook disintegrated in 2005, and with it the importance of jointness, talismanic strike warfare and information technologies, and high-end (i.e., the high end of the spectrum of conflict) conventional capabilities. For the Navy, the winds were shifting unfavorably; the campaigns in Iraq and Afghanistan, which only marginally involved the Navy, promised to elevate the Army's and Marine Corps' standing and to undermine the Navy's relevance for at least a decade. In contrast with previous generational wars, the Navy was unable to catch the wave of societal insecurity and fiscal permissiveness that had sustained the fleet's size and preferred composition in the past.

In 2005–6 two maritime-minded Navy leaders recognized in the confused context a set of trends that promised to buoy the Navy's long-term standing via a maritime strategy. CNO Adm. Mike G. Mullen and Vice Adm. John G. Morgan Jr. sought to shift the national-level debate about the direction of U.S. strategy to one they believed was more appropriate to U.S. interests in a globalizing era. They also sought to start a conversation in the Navy to shift the internal debate about its purpose.

From their perspective, globalization had shifted the security calculus toward a greater emphasis on economics, the central element around which any maritime (as distinct from naval) strategy is organized. Globalization has been driven by a revolution in computer and telecommunication technologies; the spread of

Western rationality, norms, and culture; and the worldwide movement to free-market economies.[11] Globalization, which is the process of increasing interconnectedness between societies that is brought about by the expansive movement of trade, capital, information, and ideas, was reconfiguring political power.[12] Globalization was empowering non-state threats like al-Qaeda and was undermining the ability of individual states to govern and making their prosperity more dependent on the smooth functioning of the system.[13] All of this, Mullen and Morgan thought, required more cooperative governing instruments.

In a more multipolar world, a unilateral, preemptive, and threat-centric approach, which the United States had applied in Iraq with destabilizing effect, was inimical to U.S. interests. A more appropriate approach would be an approach that is collective and defensive minded, that focuses on maintaining the status quo of U.S. systemic leadership—and with it continued global prosperity—by using maritime forces to connect interests, expand markets, and open societies to liberal (as in the political philosophy) ideas. Mullen and Morgan believed that U.S. allies and partners would more readily support such an approach, and thus be more willing to share the United States' increasingly expensive burdens as the systemic security manager.

Apart from globalization, these trends included an emerging U.S. declaratory strategic approach that portrayed the United States as the guardian of the system, a shift that came in 2005 from the sobering realization by American leaders that the United States could lose its war in Iraq. The system's functioning was threatened by al-Qaeda, which not only was collocated with the world's largest supply of petroleum and maritime choke points through which that petroleum and most of global trade flowed, but also, from an existential perspective, was alienated from and hostile to the United States–managed system. A maritime strategy would also place the Army's and Marine Corps' efforts into a wider perspective in a way that did not impugn those efforts, and would assert the Navy's broader strategic relevance without unduly denying the Navy's previous post–Cold War strategic approach. Mullen (whose late-career conversion to a maritime perspective was rather implausible) and Morgan (whose appointment as an admittedly nonpromotable three-star to the upwardly mobile position of deputy CNO for Plans, Policies, and Operations [N3/N5] was equally so) hoped to place the Navy in an advantageous position when the wars in Iraq and Afghanistan were ending and U.S. leaders were debating a new strategic direction.[14] Americans—tired of messy, open-ended interventions that called U.S. leadership into question and indebted the nation to its economic competitors—might welcome a systemic approach, one that sought foremost to extend U.S. leadership over a system that has sustained its preeminence and brought untold prosperity and freedom to ever-expanding parts of the world.

U.S. Navy officers are the product of their experiences, as is, ultimately, U.S. naval strategy, which may be defined as the relating of seaborne U.S. military force to political purpose (and vice versa). The officers acquire these experiences during many years spent at sea operating complex technology and advancing in a meritocracy. During those years they assimilate institutional beliefs (which they generally understand) and assumptions (which are hidden and therefore more difficult for them to understand and question). Immersed in a belief system called the U.S. Navy, these experiences structure how the officers think, what they believe the Navy's purpose and aspirations to be, and how they come to understand naval strategy and define and solve the problems associated with it. As Herbert Simon noted, a person "does not live for months or years in . . . an organization, exposed to some streams of communication, shielded from others, without the most profound effects upon what he knows, believes, attends to, hopes, wishes, emphasizes, fears, and proposes."[15] These officers apply their experiences later in their careers while serving in high-level strategy and policy-making positions.[16] Those experiences and the nature of the Navy's iterative, multilevel staffing and traditional consensus-driven strategy-development approval process mean that U.S. naval strategy is more the product of the institution of the U.S. Navy than it is of individual leaders.[17]

What follows will focus on the Navy's strategy-making process. This process is where Navy officers assemble, negotiate, and reshape ideas in light of a range of exogenous influences—which include, for example, the direction of U.S. strategy, budgetary constraints, and perceived threats—and the competing interests of other domestic political and internal actors. The book focuses on this process because even though the subject of the study is American naval thinking—and in this regard it must be emphasized that the concept itself is somewhat metaphorical as only people can think—that is how real strategy is made.

This book examines how key U.S. naval strategic statements and policies were developed and the documents themselves, which are manifestations of American naval thinking. These statements and policies were developed by

OPNAV and not by the Navy's operational commanders, who answer to the CINCs/combatant commanders and the secretary of defense. In general, the statements are self-generated and episodic. These statements vary in form, substance, and authorship; in the problems the commanders sought to solve; and in their intended audience, which includes the Navy, the White House, Congress, senior civilian and military leaders of the Department of Defense and their staffs, the CINCs/combatant commanders, defense analysts, and American society.[18] These statements provide the CNO with a way to rationalize the Navy and its claims on the defense budget, to establish a conceptual framework to align the activities of a complex warfighting organization, and to provide views on the maritime dimensions of U.S. strategy.

Chapter 1

The Cold War

The Pacific Campaign: The U.S. Navy's Institutional Apotheosis

The seminal event in the history of the U.S. Navy, the one that would most profoundly shape its institutional identity and strategic outlook, was the Pacific Campaign against Japan. Before the war, sea power had been about victory *at* sea. Sea power had been about how the indirect effects of controlling the sea enabled victory on land. By virtue of a balanced, carrier-based fleet that bound the once-separate realms of sea and land warfare, an adaptive mindset on the part of its officers, and the sheer scale of its forces, the Navy revolutionized naval warfare, making sea power a decisive instrument of war *from* the sea. A carrier-based fleet demonstrated enormous versatility across a much broader range of missions than one based on battleships, packing more offensive firepower and offering far more range and mobility. Such a fleet broadened the Navy's purpose far beyond that of destroying the enemy's fleet, a mission that was passé with the end of World War II. The Navy's apotheosis was short-lived, however. Despite the revolutionary nature of its victory, the Navy found its new identity and relevance, if not its very existence, called into question. The advent of the nuclear bomb, combined with the absence of any plausible rival on the high seas, threatened to marginalize the Navy in the post–World War II era.

The Late 1940s: The Navy Establishes the Primacy of Operations

In the meantime, however, Navy leaders, who were already proponents of what would be called containment, in the absence of guidance from President Harry

Truman took it upon themselves to deploy the U.S. fleet around the Soviet Union immediately after the war as a hedge against Soviet aggression. In establishing lengthy overseas deployments, which has remained its modus operandi ever since, the Navy maintained its wartime footing. In time the notion of operations grew exalted as a way of life and an institutional goal. What sailors like to do is to go to sea, with all its romantic and richly textured trappings, and to see the world. "Sailors are meant to be on ships and ships are meant to be at sea," as the saying goes. To the members of the Navy, operations came about as close to the Navy's raison d'être as any. As Fleet Adm. Ernest J. King stated, "The be-all and end-all of the [Navy] is the conduct of active operations by the active seagoing forces."[1] The institution's locus remains these forces, termed the fleet. The requirements of the fleet are never questioned, its importance never rivaled; the purpose of the rest of the Navy is to support the fleet. Like operations, the fleet's salience is supposed to be self-evident.

Operations now provided *the* formative experience in a Navy officer's life. Whereas in the interwar period the career path for promising officers was filled with tours on ships, which went to sea occasionally, and on shore, particularly at the U.S. Naval War College and the materiel-oriented bureaus, a far greater percentage of particularly their early years were now spent at sea. The shift from a seniority-based to a merit-based system in the interwar period reinforced the rewarding of those who spent comparatively more time at sea. Operations became the lens through which its officers viewed the world, the defining element of its narrow and empirically based worldview.

Meanwhile, Truman's and Congress' efforts to unify the services' roles and missions threatened to deprive the Navy of its new identity and reduce it to a supporting role in the emerging Cold War defense establishment. In the internecine interservice debates of 1949, the newly established Air Force argued that with its nuclear bomb–equipped transcontinental bombers it could deliver victory against the Soviet Union more effectively and at a lower cost than could the Navy, whose only purpose now lay in its wartime mission of escorting transport ships, and that task did not require carriers. Even before the Cold War was fully under way, the nuclear bomb, the apparent apotheosis of interwar theories of strategic bombing, was already threatening the Navy's relevance, identity, and preferred fleet structure, and casting doubt on the efficacy of a maritime strategy against the Soviet Union.[2] The Air Force's compelling argument of how to wage war in a cost-efficient manner proved irresistible to U.S. leaders. At this early stage of the Cold War, as Colin Gray noted, airpower became "both the symbol and the embodiment of American preferences in the deterrence and conduct of war."[3]

The Air Force's argument was, ironically, essentially the same one that Mahan had made on behalf of the Navy half a century earlier.[4] Following Jomini's principle to concentrate superior forces at the decisive point, Mahan argued that the most effective way to command the sea, which ensured access to resources via overseas markets and lines of production while severing the enemy's, was to build an offensive, technologically advanced fleet and to destroy the enemy's in a quick and decisive engagement. (Decisive victory, as Dan Moran noted, is "victory that goes beyond the accomplishment of some local tactical goal and achieves results of sufficient magnitude to alter the political conditions that brought the war about in the first place."[5]) The prospect that the balance of power could change in an afternoon demanded a single-minded focus on battle. Mahan had elevated tactics to the strategic level. The Jominian approach, wherein the complexity of warfare could be reduced to a set of simple principles that, if followed, would yield victory, came to embody the U.S. military's approach to war. As Colin Gray noted, "This approach finds a near perfect fit with the promise of victory through air power."[6] The U.S. military's focus on battle essentially relieved it from the difficult task of understanding just how destroying things would lead to the political goals for which a conflict is waged. As John Shy noted, "By isolating strategy from its political and social context, Jomini helped to foster a mode of thinking about war that continues to haunt us."[7]

To the Navy, Mahan had bequeathed much, including an offensive mindset and an entitling identity as the guarantor of American greatness. He had also supplied a strategic rationale that was so universally accepted as truth as to foreclose the need for proficiency in strategic thought. Mahan's formula permitted U.S. naval officers to focus on solving tactical and technological problems associated with war at sea without having to take up the uninteresting and potentially career-damaging task of understanding naval power more deeply. The Naval War College sanctioned the focus on battle. As John Hattendorf noted, it sought to instill in its students "a strict and practical method of problem solving, which correlated ends with means and objectives and directed attention to operational and tactical issues. *It did not attempt an analysis of the assumptions behind the objectives.*"[8] In effect, the Navy believed that Mahan had provided everything that was necessary for Navy officers to understand their purpose and the purpose of the Navy; the kind of historical analysis and theoretical speculation on grand strategy and maritime strategy that Mahan had undertaken, which had provided the basis for his highly influential and widely popular concept of sea power, was discouraged.[9] The purpose of Navy officers was to apply an adaptable mindset and technological knowledge to the problems associated with war at sea, an approach that was seemingly vindicated in World War II and institutionalized thereafter.

The Navy's lack of proficiency in strategic thinking was apparent to some. Former CNO Adm. Arleigh A. Burke, USN (Ret.) (CNO 1955–61), who had organized the Navy's defense during the 1949 debates, noted about the period, "People in the navy did not know very much about strategy. . . . That's why we did not have any organization to lay out the navy's case or defend ourselves. . . . We suffered from a lack of knowledge within the navy of what the navy was all about. . . . [This] was an ingrained attitude, and it had terrible consequences."[10] As Burke implied, Navy officers had assumed wrongly that the lessons of Pearl Harbor and the Navy's revolutionary style of warfare spoke for themselves. "Our understanding and our exposition of the indispensable character of our profession and the undiminished and vital nature of Sea Power," noted the president of the Naval War College in 1951, "have been dangerously superficial and elementary."[11] Having realized Mahan's goal of commanding the sea, Navy officers were now finding it difficult to explain the Navy's purpose.

The Korean War helped. The Navy's virtuoso performance, particularly in the conflict's opening months, provided a concrete lesson of the need for a forward-deployed and carrier-based fleet in a way that theoretical arguments could not, a lesson not lost on the Navy. Demonstrating its worth empirically did much to compensate for a lack of a universal theory of usefulness consistent with the scientific approach of U.S. strategy. The Navy's performance ensured that it would never again be subject to the kind of public grilling by Congress that had plagued it in the late 1940s.

The 1950s: The Formative Years of American Strategic Thinking

American strategy in the 1950s revolved around President Dwight Eisenhower's doctrine of massive retaliation, in which military planning was resolved into a massive retaliatory or preemptive nuclear strike on the Soviet Union. The onset of ballistic missiles and thermonuclear bombs refocused war planning from conventional to all-out nuclear war. That and the desire to avoid messy, costly, and limited wars like the one in Korea made U.S. conventional forces virtually irrelevant.

Eisenhower believed that military spending of the kind required to compete with the Soviets in conventional terms threatened the nation's economic health. The Air Force, whose Strategic Air Command offered a high degree of strategic leverage per budget dollar, received nearly half the defense budget.

The immense conceptual challenges of waging and deterring nuclear war occasioned the rise of the civilian strategic theorists, who profoundly shaped American strategic thinking. As Fred Kaplan noted, these theorists' "wisdom would be taken almost for granted, their assumptions worshipped as gospel truth, their insight elevated to an almost mystical level and accepted as dogma."[12] The disciplinary approaches of these theorists—most of whom were physicists, mathematicians, and economists, and most of whom, at least initially, worked for the RAND Corporation (an Air Force–sponsored think tank)—were well suited to dealing with the abstract problems of nuclear war. These strategic reasoners, almost none of whom had backgrounds in history or international relations, set in motion an apolitical, ahistorical, and hyper-rational style of strategic thinking. They relied heavily on systems analysis, which is a marginal cost-benefit methodology. The bomb ushered in an era where the past was thought to be of little use in addressing the problems of the nuclear age.[13] America's strategists and political and military leaders therefore never really examined how liberal maritime-based alliances had overcome continental enemies in the past.

American economic beliefs also discouraged relating military power to broader systemic goals. As reflected in the 1941 Atlantic Charter, the U.S. concept of economic security rested on the belief that the best way to facilitate international and domestic growth was through trade via an open market. Using military force for selfish economic advantage was onerous to Americans in general; as reflected in the Atlantic Charter, the United States was not about building an empire, but rather about tearing empires down.

Also during the 1950s, the Cold War became a Manichean crusade; in the politically charged "better dead than red" atmosphere, U.S. military and domestic political thought merged and became threat-centric, a quality that has been retained, in varying degrees, ever since. Since Soviet nuclear weapons threatened the United States and Warsaw Pact conventional forces threatened Western Europe, there was little need to relate the military's purpose beyond deterring global nuclear war and preparing for conventional war in Europe. Given Americans' threat-sensitive nature, U.S. politicians who took a comparatively harder line against the Soviets than their opponents generally did better at the polls.[14]

Defining U.S. interests apart from the Soviet threat grew difficult.[15] American strategy became profoundly threat-centric. In short, as Colin Gray noted, "That threat, as variously defined over the years, was not *a* factor helping to define the purposes of U.S. policy, grand strategy, and military strategy. It was *the* factor."[16]

All of this meant that, as Marc Trachtenberg noted, "a broad range of strategic issues, having to do with the way the political and military spheres interact with each other, not just in time of war or crisis, but in more normal times as well, was never really closely examined by mainstream American strategic thought."[17] In other words, it was never really a possibility that the United States would adapt a systemic strategic approach during the Cold War.

Also during this time, the Navy established an unarticulated strategy that is best described as generic operational flexibility. Key to this strategy was forward deployment, which allowed the Navy to keep its forces in critical areas for longer periods, thus reducing the time needed to respond to crises, deterring conflict, or, failing that, enabling the United States to seize control of the seas and transition seamlessly to war. It allowed presidents to demonstrate resolve, seize the initiative, and control escalation without either anticipating or foreclosing more-decisive options down the road. It allowed the Navy to bridge the requirements of preparing for major conflict with the day-to-day needs of U.S. diplomacy in ways that the Army or the Air Force could not duplicate.

The strategy was less the product of explicit strategizing and more an intuitive expression of how the Navy defined its purpose and identity. The Navy saw its purpose as being prepared for a wide variety of circumstances; that preparedness was enabled by forward presence. From that perspective the strategy's means (a flexible multimission fleet), ways (forward deployment and a highly adaptive mindset on the part of its officers), and ends (readiness for almost any contingency and for changes in the strategic environment) were logically aligned. In short, the Navy saw its purpose as being contingent operationally, and not instrumental strategically. Geoffrey Till aptly captured the Navy's outlook:

> Because they operate forces of almost infinite flexibility and because they often cannot find people willing to tell them what to do, sailors have tended to go in for what their critics call "parametric planning." They resist being tied down to one scenario lest it unsuits them for another and prefer to rely instead on the inherent flexibility of sea power to provide the necessary options. The sailor's instinctive aversion to the specific and almost mystical

faith in the capacity of a first-rate balanced fleet to cope with virtually anything can be distinctly irritating to the unsympathetic.[18]

In the 1950s and 1960s the Navy's contingent and implicit outlook contrasted heavily with the reductionist, explicit, prescriptive, and rigid approach of U.S. strategy, a state of affairs that irritated U.S. officials who wanted the Navy to hew to the tenets of declaratory strategy. Navy leaders recognized that the Navy had to align with the administrations' declaratory strategies at least in word, but continually balked at the White House's attempts to narrow the fleet's capabilities to accord with their prescriptive declaratory policies or visions of war. "Sea power," as H. P. Willmott noted, "is a long term phenomenon; ships, design teams, industries, and above all experience, cannot be improvised."[19] Consequently, Navy leaders regarded the strategic environment as more ambiguous and less certain than did the nation's political and defense leaders. Navy leaders saw the Navy as a backstop against the administrations' shortsighted policies and diplomatic miscues. As Capt. J. C. Wylie noted in 1957, "We need not remain always within whatever may be the prevalent opinion of the moment."[20]

The Navy recognized that to survive politically it had to compete with or distinguish itself from the Air Force. The quick and decisive war that was now envisioned subverted considerations of a maritime strategy and the need for an offensive sea control approach to ensure the sea-lanes to Europe remained open. In general, the shorter and more decisive the anticipated clash of arms, the more irrelevant the Navy became. Seeing an opportunity to broaden U.S. strategic thinking and secure institutional relevance, CNO Burke embedded the Navy in the policies of nuclear deterrence by constructing the ballistic missile–carrying nuclear-powered submarine (SSBN) and the submarine-launched ballistic missile, the first of which was called the Polaris. The SSBN's mission became the Navy's primary mission for the remainder of the Cold War. Initially, however, it was a loveless marriage. Institutionally, the SSBN was seen as a political concession to Eisenhower's doctrine of massive retaliation, which came at the expense of more operationally useful platforms. It was only after the idea of nuclear deterrence matured in the era of mutually assured destruction that the SSBN's attractiveness in meeting U.S. and institutional needs became apparent.

With the SSBN Burke established a dual-track approach. The generic flexibility track allowed the Navy to demonstrate its worth across the spectrum of force from coercive diplomacy to general war. The other track was a separate and explicit, strategic-level expression of national needs that located the SSBN at the heart of nuclear deterrence. As the nation's only invulnerable second-strike platform (neither the strategic bombers nor land-based intercontinental ballistic missiles were invulnerable to Soviet attack), the SSBN could threaten to target Soviet society, which served as a maximum deterrent to nuclear war. However, the second track would prove just as generic as the first. Neither pointed toward or demanded a deeper understanding of maritime power.

No period of the Cold War saw the Navy develop technology with more urgency than the 1950s. No generation of U.S. naval officers was better suited for this task. In the interwar period, the Navy's best, most promising officers, which included Burke, did postgraduate work in science and engineering; served multiple tours in the bureaus of ordnance, aeronautics, and propulsion; and worked closely across all the warfare communities and industry. They had attended the Naval War College at a time when only the top officers were sent there as students or instructors. During World War II they gained invaluable experience operationalizing technology. Their experiences helped overcome the immense challenges of fielding a weapons system like the SSBN, which, remarkably, went from blueprint to deployment in less than five years.

However, technological fixation had far-reaching effects: It led to early and intractable career specialization, which further narrowed the institution's knowledge base. It curtailed the cross-pollination of ideas and experiences between the Navy's three major warfare communities—surface ships, aviation, and submarines—that had been characteristic of the interwar Navy.[21] Understanding how to employ complex weapons systems now took up a far greater percentage of an officer's career, particularly of those officers in the aviation and submarine communities, who had to dedicate their first three to five years to that end.[22] Reflecting the fanaticism of Adm. Hyman G. Rickover to ensure no accidents endangered his nuclear propulsion program, submariners were (and still are) considered first and foremost nuclear engineers. They now had little room in their careers for anything other than going to sea and learning how to operate their platforms. As a result, almost none of the submariners who assumed high-level positions in the 1970s, 1980s, and 1990s had backgrounds in international relations or strategic affairs.[23] This group included three CNOs, whose time in office stretched from 1982 to 1994.

Technological demands changed how the Navy educated its officers. Rickover gained control of the U.S. Naval Academy's curriculum and mandated that

80 percent of every graduating class had to major in science, technology, engineering, or math.[24] Career paths changed at this time as well, which compounded these effects. Careers were shortened, which meant less time in each rank and fewer tours. Higher operating tempos (i.e., time spent on deployment) and chronic manning problems meant longer sea tours and less time in shore tours, all of which further constricted the institution's knowledge base.

The institution's dedication to the career paths that provided its officers with a broad knowledge base in the interwar years, which had proved vital to victory in the Pacific Campaign, fell by the wayside.[25] Fewer officers were attending the Naval War College, and fewer still of the Navy's best were sent there. Unlike the other U.S. military services, higher education was no longer required for command. There was little time in officers' careers or inclination by the Navy's Bureau of Personnel to send them to a now potentially career-damaging tour at the Naval War College, where they could place operational experience into a broader perspective. As John F. Lehman Jr., the Secretary of the Navy through most of the 1980s, noted, "We have raised a generation of naval officers who have been well trained in technology and engineering, but of whom a great many are essentially illiterate in the conceptual disciplines and humanities."[26] As David Rosenberg stated, the fixation on technology "served to distract attention from, if not actively discourage serious consideration of, strategic issues and challenges."[27]

In the 1950s the Naval War College established a three-year program to develop a cadre of strategic thinkers, who, the Naval War College's leaders hoped, would reprise Mahan's role as a provider of clarity in a confused period of transition. But the effort was short-lived. In a statement that could have been made at almost any time in the past half-century, the chief of the Navy's personnel bureau, in a letter to the Naval War College's president, noted that he could not send any more officers to the program because "our commitments are already beyond our resources. . . . We are operating . . . with a practical deficit of some 250 line captains. . . . We are . . . faced with the absolute and over-riding requirement to maintain our present forces at maximum effectiveness while striving to ready our personnel for the technological advances they must cope with."[28] Navy leaders in OPNAV did not see the need for strategic education, either. They believed that efforts to justify the Navy's policy arguments were of more practical value.[29]

The Navy's reasoned responses to the Cold War's challenges established early on the rules by which the institution's intellect operated. A conservatism bred from operating advanced technology on, above, and below the unforgiving environs of the open oceans confirmed the institution's confidence in the unique and preeminent value of experiential knowledge. The superior form of knowledge and basis of authority (and promotion) was operational experience and technical and technological expertise. Given the institution's operational and pragmatic outlook, what Navy officers learned was limited to what was useful operationally. Neither historical knowledge nor strategic theory helped to solve the fleet's day-to-day problems.[30] The Navy's pragmatic and operationally focused outlook goes some ways in explaining why the Navy did not seek the help of the RAND-style theorists, unlike the Air Force and Army.[31] This outlook also explains why the Navy did not turn to historical analysis and theory to update Mahan's theories, which Navy officers now viewed as the application of a passé deterministic historical methodology, a contrivance of someone writing in a particular period of history.[32] By decade's end, nothing had changed (nor would it until the late 1970s) since J. C. Wylie's comment in 1951 that "the poverty of contemporary naval strategic thought is, I think, self-evident. The Navy, it would seem, has been unable to successfully educate the American people in the imperatives of modern naval strategy and largely because the Navy has no clear concept of just what its strategic necessities are."[33]

The 1960s: The McNamara Revolution

President John Kennedy's doctrine of flexible response was reflective of a period when a nuclear stalemate was emerging and direct conflict was moving to the margins. Now the Soviet Union had to be contained strategically with nuclear weapons and locally with conventional forces. Kennedy rearmed with a flexible mix of conventional capabilities, which promised to elevate the Navy's standing, but in fact did not. The administration saw the Navy's predominant mission as nuclear deterrence. The SSBN embodied flexible response's nuclear side and was fiscally supported as such, but at the expense of the Navy's aging World War II–era surface fleet.[34] Given advanced Soviet weaponry, the administration thought the carriers would be too vulnerable in a general war and refused to fund any more. After attack submarines and SSBNs became the primary instruments of sea control and nuclear retaliation, respectively, the carriers' missions narrowed to gunboat diplomacy and limited war; this was the kind of war that now appeared in Vietnam, where, as in the Korean War, the carriers proved their worth enough that Congress agreed to fund another class of supercarriers.

In terms of U.S. strategic and naval thinking, the 1960s were a watershed. But this was not because of the Vietnam War, which was essentially a laboratory for the RAND theorists. Instead, it was because of Secretary of Defense McNamara's revolutionary managerial changes. With his centralized Planning, Programming, and Budgeting System, McNamara sought not only to optimize resources by applying cost-benefit-based systems analysis to compare, for example, the marginal utilities of Air Force strategic bombers and SSBNs but also to command the Department of Defense.[35] McNamara noted that his process rectified the "tendency on the part of the services to base their planning and force structure on their own unilateral views of how a future war might be fought."[36]

By embedding the science of management in the Pentagon, McNamara expanded the optimization imperative past the realm of nuclear strategy and into all aspects of U.S. strategy and defense policy. He embedded an intellectual outlook that was obsessed not with understanding, but with providing answers in the form of quantitative analyses, which was the new coin of the realm. His was an industrial-manager's approach, which concerned itself more with the efficient allocation of resources than with the relating of ways, means, and ends. As one high-level Kennedy administration official later noted, McNamara's approach was apolitical: it did not focus on "political problems of the goods of war, but how to marry modes of warfare to conflict dominated by new technologies."[37]

The increasing costs and complexity of weaponry and the services' egregious self-serving behavior demanded some kind of managerial revolution. But the one implemented was nonnegotiable, and for the Navy it was countercultural. The Navy struggled to adapt more than the Army and the Air Force, each of which—unlike the Navy—believed that success in its respective operating medium depended on centralizing authority and the ability of large staffs to devise prescriptive and tightly managed campaign plans. For the Navy, which opposed centralizing authority and large staffs in principle, World War II and the Korean War demonstrated that success at sea depended on a decentralized command structure and considerable delegation of individual responsibility. As CNO Burke noted, "We believe in *command*, not *staff*. We believe we have 'real' things to do. . . . We decentralize and capitalize on the capabilities of our individual people rather than centralize and make automatons of them."[38]

But centralized authority also made it easier for the secretary of defense to organize the military around a certain concept or vision of future war. Reflecting the Navy's contingent outlook, J. C. Wylie noted, "Nothing would be more dangerous to our nation than the comfortable and placid acceptance of a single idea, a single and exclusively dominant military pattern of thought."[39] Instead, the Navy wanted a pluralistic decision-making arrangement that allowed a full airing of the services' viewpoints.[40] Run by civilians whose knowledge of naval matters was sparse at best, a monistic structure would restrict the naval voice.

Navy leaders also scorned McNamara's scientific approach. As noted by Adm. George W. Anderson Jr. (1961–63), who was the CNO when McNamara installed his new structure, the purpose of systems analysis was to moderate experience, and not to replace it.[41] From the Navy's perspective, the purpose of a decision-making structure was to make sound decisions, and not to make it more efficient to decide. Unlike the Air Force, the Navy did not use systems analysis to measure its strategic effects and rationalize its purpose, but rather used it as a tool to solve tactical problems, a discipline, called operational analysis, that the Navy itself had developed during World War II to great effect. The assumption that quantifiable analysis trumped experience stuck in the craw of many Navy officers, particularly Anderson, who publically challenged McNamara and his rationalist approach throughout his tenure as CNO.[42]

The McNamara revolution profoundly changed the CNO's role. In the 1950s the CNO's job was strategic, operational, conceptual, and long term. The CNO assessed the strategic environment, established a strategic approach (however implicit), developed long-term resource plans, and commanded the fleet.[43] The CNO had authority over the main elements of naval strategy: the fleet, OPNAV, and, to an extent, the independent materiel-oriented bureaus. All that changed in the 1960s. The CNO, who had lost much legitimacy institutionally when the 1958 Defense Reorganization Act stripped that position of operational command of the fleet, now had far less control over OPNAV. At this point much of OPNAV answered to McNamara's staff, which was the Office of the Secretary of Defense (OSD), with regard to its constant programming and budget demands. Answers to those demands hewed more to parochial warfare community concerns than to the CNO's guidance, the latter of which could be outlasted given the long-term nature of such programs and the CNOs' relatively short tenures. As Adm. David L. McDonald, USN (Ret.) (1963–67), noted, "When I was CNO, I often felt that I had no more authority than a lieutenant commander."[44]

McNamara's changes meant that the Navy's institutional health was now in the hands of those slide rule–wielding officers in OPNAV whose analyses determined and rationalized the Navy's resource decisions. The Navy had to work

much harder to defend those decisions, as OSD policymakers were highly critical of the Navy's decisions, believing that they had been made without analytical
rigor. As McNamara himself acknowledged, the worth of the Navy's general-
purpose fleet and platforms was much harder to quantify than that of ground
or tactical air forces.[45] Ironically, OSD could not quantify the types of flexible
capabilities that the doctrine of flexible response called for the most.

The CNO's job was now programmatic, administrative, mechanical, and
short term. The Navy had no choice. The essential means to defend the institution's identity, preferred weapons systems, and relevance was through OSD's
Planning, Programming, and Budgeting System. Now a service whose worth
after World War II was rarely self-evident, the Navy had to protect itself where
it had always been the most vulnerable: not on the high seas, but in the offices
where decisions about American defense policy were made.[46] As N. A. M. Rodger
noted, "Foreigners come and go, but the [Navy's] real enemies are always in
Washington."[47] The focus of OPNAV—85 percent of whose billets were now
dedicated to programming and budgeting—shifted as well.[48] As one internal
memo noted, "Practically the entire OPNAV organization is tuned, like a tuning
fork, to the vibrations of the budgetary process. . . . There is a vast preoccupation
with budgetary matters."[49]

McNamara's changes reshaped Navy offiers' career paths as well. In the 1940s
the path to promotion to admiral went through OPNAV's war planning directorate. In the 1950s it went through CNO Burke's long-range strategic planning
directorate. Starting in the 1960s the path to promotion changed to managing
weapons systems programs and personnel, and has not changed much since.
During this period, the already constricted backgrounds of those ascending to
leadership positions began to narrow even more. In the 1960s the aviation and
submarine communities produced their first generation of flag officers, the prod-
ucts of severe career specialization and little or no strategic education. These flag
officers would dominate the Navy's leadership positions in the 1970s, 1980s, and
1990s. As David Rosenberg noted, now "most of the navy's flag officers came
late to the more sublime aspects of their profession, and thus approached strategy
not from a theoretical. or historical perspective, but from a more narrow operational one, based on their own experience at sea in their warfare specialties, and
with a technological and programmatic orientation built on recent Washington
budget battles."[50] The experiences of these flag officers were not the sort that
enabled a deeper understanding of the Navy's purpose.

The 1970s: The Navy's Cold War Nadir

In the 1970s, a decade of détente, U.S. presidents sought to reduce superpower tensions, promote stability, and shape a more predictable relationship with the Soviets. The Soviet Union was at the height of its prestige, power, and global presence. It had reached nuclear parity, and its version of modernity was attracting clients worldwide. With an ever-growing, far-ranging, and highly capable fleet designed for nuclear retaliation and sea denial, the Soviets were challenging the United States for control of the seas. For the first time in the Cold War, the Navy had a bona fide rival at sea, which should have helped its cause—but it did not.

Ostensibly, the United States' de-emphasis of the nuclear option meant an emphasis on general war, which meant the Navy had to be ready to protect the sea-lanes to NATO Europe. But the SSBN-Polaris program and the Vietnam War had devoured the funds needed to replace the obsolescent World War II–era ships that would protect the lanes in the face of a one-to-three ratio of U.S.-to-Soviet attack submarines. The CNO, Adm. Elmo R. "Bud" Zumwalt Jr. (1970–74), bluntly told his superiors that should war come, the Navy would not be able to keep the sea-lanes open.[51] The fleet did not have enough ships. The fleet was poorly staffed, trained, and equipped. Morale was at rock bottom. Zumwalt saw the need and opportunity to reorganize the Navy around the Soviet sea-denial threat. He sought to rebalance the fleet, elevate sea control's standing, and limit the influence of the carrier aviators, who, from his perspective, did not understand that limited wars were now passé. He argued for a high-low mix: high meaning franchised high-end platforms like carriers and submarines, and low meaning large numbers of low-cost, low-tech defensive sea control ships.

To gain support for his vision, Zumwalt, a surface officer, released his "Project SIXTY" action plan in 1970, which represented the Navy's first declaratory strategic statement.[52] With this new tool of governance, Zumwalt sought to regain control over OPNAV and provide a conceptual framework for the fleet. The pedagogic companion to "Project SIXTY," the "Missions of the U.S. Navy," was released in 1974.[53] Its author, Vice Adm. Stansfield M. Turner, who did much to redress the Navy's intellectual shortcomings, sought to get naval officers to think deeply about the Navy's purpose. His was the Cold War Navy's first attempt to address the inchoate state of sea power theory. Turner organized what he saw as the Navy's four principal missions—(1) strategic deterrence, (2) forward presence, (3) sea control, and (4) power projection—into a simple and insightful construct. While it proved influential outside more than inside the service, Turner's theory of naval purpose was simply its practice. Unlike American strategic thinking, American naval thinking did not suffer from excessive theorizing. In fact, just the opposite was true: it was merely descriptive and unanalytical.

But Zumwalt's plan failed. The low-end part fell victim to inflation. Of the four classes of ships proposed, only one, a patrol frigate, was built in numbers. By 1975 the fleet numbered only 512 ships, nearly half of what it had been four years earlier.[54] Zumwalt's plan ignited a fierce, decade-long debate inside the Navy. While the tension between sea control and carrier-based power projection had ebbed and flowed throughout the Cold War, the emerging Soviet naval threat and the need to recapitalize the fleet in a period of fiscal austerity brought about a reappraisal of naval strategy, which meant making hard decisions between sea control and power projection capabilities.

Sea control advocates like Zumwalt saw the Navy's purpose more narrowly in terms of general war and the enormous stakes should world war come again. To those advocates, the Navy's purpose resided in its wartime role of keeping the sea-lanes open, which is how the Army and Air Force, dependent on open sea-lanes for logistical support, saw the Navy's purpose. In essence, these advocates argued against the Pacific War's style of warfare and for the style that had won the Battle of the North Atlantic in World War II, which did not require a broadly capable fleet or Marines to seize territory. From the perspective of Zumwalt and other advocates, a fleet structured along the lines of those that had enabled victory over Germany in two world wars provided the highest quality of deterrence against a Soviet invasion of Western Europe.

In contrast, power-projection proponents like CNOs James L. Holloway III (1974–78) and Thomas B. Hayward (1978–82), both carrier aviators, wanted a fleet with broad and flexible warfighting capabilities designed to deter war and prevail in a wide variety of circumstances across the spectrum of warfare. Zumwalt's vision, which he based on a certain view of the future, promised to narrow the fleet's capabilities. As noted in an unclassified executive summary of Holloway's "SEA PLAN 2000" study, "In planning for the long term, hedges against what is not known cannot be neglected."[55]

The primary hedge was, of course, the carrier, which was the Navy's most versatile instrument. Its repertoire of missions included presence, coercive diplomacy, limited war, local and open-ocean sea control, sea control via power projection, nuclear deterrence, crisis management, and humanitarian relief. With the exception of the SSBN, it was the most powerful warship afloat. It was much faster than its escorts and could carry an enormous amount of just about anything: fuel, bombs, weapons systems, and humanitarian relief supplies, and so on. No task force of surface combatants could match its capabilities or coercive diplomatic impact. The carrier, which has a service life equivalent to twelve presidential terms, was the primary hedge against the political unknown as well. As Colin Gray noted, "Although (say) twenty-five years is a long time for people . . . and modern weapons systems, it is almost an eternity in politics. Changes in the global security environment, and policy decisions in response, can move at a speed not remotely approachable by sympathetic alternations in force structure."[56]

With the carrier's capacious capabilities, the Navy was able to find handholds in the administrations' ever-shifting declaratory strategies and across a range of strategic and general war plans. Serving the day-to-day needs of U.S. statecraft brought front-page empirics, which did much to compensate for the Navy's lack of a theoretical vision or inclusion in those declaratory strategies. A carrier-based fleet accommodated shifts in the strategic and domestic political environs more effectively than did a fleet specialized for sea control, for example. The carrier was the generic flexibility strategy made manifest, the ultimate expression of the institutional demand for operational and political adaptability. However, the debate could not be resolved because national policies did not provide the necessary guidance and funding. Regardless of the Soviet naval threat, for the United States the 1970s was a grim decade in which military sufficiency had to suffice.

Things went from bad to worse under President Jimmy Carter. He did not want to be put in a position in which the United States would have to respond to a Soviet invasion of Western Europe with nuclear weapons, particularly because this might escalate to all-out nuclear war, nor did he believe that such a war would necessarily spread beyond Europe. To deter the Soviets he bulked up U.S. conventional land and air forces in Central Europe to defend what was the locus of geopolitical, military, and political attention in the Cold War: the Central Front in West Germany.[57] Funding a global, power-projecting Navy only undermined the deterrent quality of U.S. European-based forces. Carter demanded the Navy adapt Zumwalt's defensive sea control vision, and cut its five-year shipbuilding program from 159 ships to 70.[58] Carter, a 1946 Naval Academy graduate, elected not to take advantage of the Navy's prominent and unique global power projection capability. Instead, he focused U.S. and allied strategy on where the West's position had always been the weakest: the conventional match-up against the Warsaw Pact army in Central Europe.

Given a foreign policy that eschewed limited war, the Navy's purpose boiled down to escorting convoys in a time of war, and even that purpose was suspect. Few Americans understood that their European allies saw the NATO alliance as more of a political guarantee than a means to organize for actual defense.[59] As Colin Gray noted, "European leaders neither believed that the nonnuclear defense of NATO-Europe was feasible nor wished it to be so. . . . Indeed, the very prospect of relatively early failure on the ground provided the critical fuel for Soviet anxiety over NATO's propensity to exercise its nuclear escalatory options. It is no exaggeration to claim that there was intended to be deterrent success in a Soviet estimation of NATO's failure in conventional defense."[60] If the United States did not answer a Soviet invasion with a nuclear response, Warsaw Pact forces would reach the Atlantic before the bulk of U.S. forces could make the transit. The Navy was irrelevant either way.

Navy officers were despondent over the institution's marginalized status. The Navy had little control over the forces that made all but its nuclear deterrent capabilities irrelevant. But Navy leaders refused to accept Carter's tentative and defensive outlook, and doggedly held on to the institution's more independent worldview. In efforts like Holloway's "SEA PLAN 2000" study (1978) and Hayward's article "The Future of U.S. Sea Power" (1979), the Navy finally offered sophisticated geopolitical arguments that attacked the underlying assumptions of U.S. strategy that had subverted its interests in all but the last decade of the Cold War.[61] At last, the Navy was starting to think strategically. But the Navy's realization that it needed to think more deeply about its purpose was only because American defense policies severely threatened its relevance and institutional identity.

The Navy was vindicated soon enough. In response to the fall of the shah of Iran and the Soviet invasion of Afghanistan in 1979, Carter sent U.S. naval forces into the region en masse, doubling the U.S. naval presence in 1979 and quadrupling it in 1980, which would have been nearly impossible had he obtained the kind of fleet that his administration had demanded.

The 1980s: The Navy's Cold War Zenith

President Ronald Reagan rejected the assumption that the Soviet Union and the Cold War were permanent fixtures. He sought not to contain the Soviet Union or rebalance power, but rather to win the Cold War outright. Since the utility of nuclear weapons had diminished due to their sheer numbers, Reagan's rearmament focused on rehabilitating the capabilities required to support an activist policy of Third World interventions and gunboat diplomacy, supporting a strategy of global and protracted war, and deterring nuclear war. Unlike previous administrations, Reagan's did not assume that Europe was the decisive theater or that war would be short and decisive. All this meant a restoration of the Navy's conventional capabilities and, for the first time in the Cold War, strategic parity with the Air Force and the Army.

The Navy's thinking cohered and was finally made manifest in its Maritime Strategy. The Maritime Strategy, which was articulated in a decade-long series of mostly classified briefs and strategic statements, constituted a body of thought about the Navy's purpose.[62] It was a means both of forging institutional consensus (at which it was highly successful) and of shifting the strategic debate at the national level toward a maritime-based U.S. strategic approach (at which it was less successful). It aligned the Navy's operational, programmatic, administrative, intelligence, and pedagogic activities. It successfully marketed the Navy's strategic approach, weapons systems preferences, and goal of a 600-ship Navy. Under Reagan, the fleet grew from 477 to 566 ships.[63] Moreover, it revived and reenergized the institution.

The Maritime Strategy could not be fulfilled until a set of trends presented an opportunity that the Navy was finally intellectually prepared to seize. To find a way out of its impasse, Navy leaders in the late 1970s had established a cadre of well-educated officers to act as strategic thinkers, most of whom served in OPNAV's Strategy and Policy Division between sea tours, where they developed the Maritime Strategy. They realized that Reagan provided an indulgent budgetary environment and, given the lack of a formalized national strategy, that the Navy could define its own strategic direction. Along with Reagan's assumptions about the nature of a conflict with the Soviets, two developments resurrected the carrier's role in general war and with it an offensive sea control strategy: first, the introduction of high-tech U.S. naval defensive weapons systems on ships, and second, intelligence that Soviet attack submarines would protect Soviet SSBNs in their patrol bastions near the Soviet Union and thus would not sally forth to shut down the sea-lanes.

The Maritime Strategy, which was more a heuristic device than an actual war plan, had three phases: (1) Deterrence or the transition to war saw U.S. naval forces deter war and, failing that, transition seamlessly to global war. (2) Seizing the initiative meant seizing control of the seas by destroying Soviet naval forces. (3) Carrying the fight to the enemy meant attacking the Soviet homeland and destroying Soviet SSBNs. By threatening to turn the conflict into a protracted global war that brought to bear the free world's immense production capabilities, the Maritime Strategy sought to deter Soviet aggression and backstop the decisions of leaders from the United States, NATO Europe, the U.S. Air Force, and the U.S. Army, all of whom never gave much thought to what to do should a U.S.-Soviet clash of arms resolve itself into a protracted conventional war.

The Maritime Strategy was a maritime strategy as classically understood, correctly locating as it did the West's center of gravity off-shore amid a web of trade and capital flows, but it was a strategy that functioned as such only in a time of hot war. Although it focused somewhat on the fleet's peacetime effects, the Maritime Strategy did not escape the verities of American Cold War thinking, to which deterrence, operational requirements, and warfighting were preeminent and the system and its importance were largely ancillary.

In the absence of more-fulfilling victories at sea, the Maritime Strategy was the climactic experience of the late Cold War Navy, the more so because of the abrupt end of the conflict that had inspired its creation, which effectively sent it to the dustbin untested, except at the level of procurement, which, for the Navy, was always the most gratifying phase of any strategic initiative. Viewed in light of the Navy's struggles in the post–Cold War era to understand and rationalize itself, the Maritime Strategy was less a moment of clarity about its deeper purpose and more the arrival of the Navy at a solution to a frustrating, decades-long puzzle brought about by its determination to find a way into the fight with the Soviet Union and into U.S. strategy, from which it was released not by its own further strategic reflection, but simply by the Soviet collapse, which would confront the Navy once more with a blank sheet of paper.

Conclusion

The logic inherent in U.S. strategy worked against a maritime-systemic strategic approach. Even though such an approach was well suited to a state whose interests have always been linked to the growth of the global economy, and to the open societies and policies to enlarge democracies that have thus accompanied sustained economic success, the U.S. approach was more characteristic of a continental power, with the Americans' heavy reliance on airpower to enable victories through decisive battle, than a maritime power. The nuclear bomb had obviated the need for the United States to develop skills in diplomacy, rendered many of the tasks of systemic management much easier, and hindered understanding of how to use its military to manage a liberal international system to greater strategic effect.[64] As Colin Gray noted, the United States "is neither a natural sea power nor does a maritime perspective and precepts dominate its strategic culture. . . . The American way of war has been quintessentially continentalist."[65]

The logic inherent in American naval thinking was not any more conducive to a maritime strategy's development. The Navy had framed its purpose not in terms of the systemic Mahan, who, as a maritime theorist and political economist, had argued that the naval forces of liberal states, most prominently the British Royal Navy, had uniquely shaped the history of nations and peoples by spreading the benefits derived from expanding markets and open societies. Instead, the Navy defined itself in terms of the battle-centric Mahan. The Navy's contingent outlook, adaptable mindset, and flexible fleet structure, which were vindicated throughout the Cold War—imminently designed as they were for the near-constant changes in the strategic, operational, and domestic political environs—may be considered Mahan's legacy. The rationality and assumptions of the battle-centric Navy ensured that its officers were virtuosos in the operational art, always tactically and technologically proficient, and adapting to new scenarios with comparative ease. With that route, however, came a historical naiveté and inaptitude in strategic thought of the kind required to understand the Navy's broader purpose in light of the United States' liberal, open-market system, and to form meaningful arguments in relation to competing forms of U.S. military power, mainly the Air Force and Army. With that embedded worldview, the Navy steamed into the uncharted waters of the post–Cold War era.

Chapter 2

Maritime Strategy for the 1990s, 1989

Bush and the "Vision Thing"

The post–Cold War era dawned slowly in the background of rapidly changing domestic considerations. The fall of the Berlin Wall occurred as General Secretary Mikhail Gorbachev announced the Soviet army was withdrawing from Central Europe, while he simultaneously proposed sweeping cuts in conventional and nuclear arms. President George H. W. Bush, a prudent man, reacted with characteristic caution: he refused, as he noted, to "'dance' on the Wall," but preferred to move incrementally, aware, perhaps, that Russian history abounds with reformers who turned into dictators or were enveloped by revolution.[1] He moved tentatively, in large part to avoid inadvertently subverting Gorbachev's leadership or endangering their personal relationship, which Bush needed to guide a leader who had no real plan where to take his nation. The Bush administration saw its purpose as managing a successful end to the long confrontation with the Soviets, and not as laying out a new strategic approach for the postwar era. Bush and his inner circle were deeply schooled in the ways of the Cold War. They had been students and stewards of containment. They were a profoundly pragmatic group, more comfortable with managing subtle rather than tectonic change. They were in no hurry to look farther, a task for which they were not well suited by both background and temperament. As he admitted, Bush was not comfortable with what he called the "vision thing."[2]

The Powell Revolution

Meanwhile, the new chairman of the Joint Chiefs of Staff, Gen. Colin Powell, USA, was revolutionizing the U.S. strategy-making process. He used the authority established by Goldwater-Nichols to centralize strategy making to a far greater degree, and to ensure that the Pentagon maintained control of the military's draw-down.[3] Powell's priority, broadly speaking, was to ensure that Congress' vociferous demands for a peace dividend did not indiscriminately trample on the dictates of strategic rationality or the existing institutional balance among the services.

To redress the perceived failings of the Vietnam War and interservice rivalry, Goldwater-Nichols had increased the chairman's authority. Congress traditionally assumed that the advice of the service chiefs, who, along with the chairman, made up the Joint Chiefs, was colored by competing organizational interests and obscured by its consensual approach. To ensure secretaries of defense or presidents did not brush aside the advice of the military's top uniformed leader, Goldwater-Nichols made the chairman the principal military adviser to the president. No longer was the chairman merely the member of the Joint Chiefs that conveyed their collective decisions to the White House: the chairman was now a power to be reckoned with.

Goldwater-Nichols also sought to redress the services' dominant role in decisions about force structure and weapons. To ensure the CINCs' operational requirements and war plans were properly resourced, the chairman was made responsible for providing strategic direction and integrating and prioritizing the CINCs' capability requirements. If the services' budget submissions and program proposals did not conform to the chairman's guidance or the CINCs' priorities, the chairman was to submit alternatives to the secretary of defense. In accordance with his new duties, the Joint Staff was expanded, reorganized, and placed under the chairman's direct control.

Even as the Cold War was ending, the Pentagon was already undergoing a profound shift in the balance of strategic influence. The new arbiters were OSD, the Joint Staff, and the CINCs. The services were brought down a peg; their purpose was now understood to be nothing more than providers of capabilities to the CINCs.[4] As one Navy flag officer lamented, "We're going back to the McNamara days. [Secretary of Defense Richard] Cheney is shifting power from the services to the defense secretary."[5]

Powell based his strategy on four elements: (1) deterrence, (2) forward presence, (3) crisis management, and (4) regional conflict (i.e., conflict with regional powers like Iran and North Korea). His force structure plan became known as the Base Force, which amounted to a 25 percent reduction in the military.[6] Powell believed that he could not wait for guidance from the president or the secretary of defense on how to reduce the military.[7] In Powell's opinion, the Planning, Programming, and Budgeting System was too unwieldy and too slow, and the services could not be trusted to respond to rapidly changing strategic and fiscal realities. Powell sought to build consensus among the service chiefs, but with Goldwater-Nichols he did not need their approval.

Initially, Cheney did not agree with Powell's rosy view of the future.[8] He thought the world was still too indeterminate for the massive cuts that Congress and indeed Powell himself advocated.[9] He let the chairman continue, however.[10] Cheney wanted to protect the military from what he derisively called the slash-and-burn budgeting approach that was advocated by congressional Democrats who controlled both houses.[11] To Cheney, the diminishing prospect of Soviet expansionism did nothing to reduce American regional commitments in the Middle East and on the Korean peninsula, for example. At the regional level, however, there was a palpable risk felt in OSD that with cuts to the numbers of ground troops, as Undersecretary of Defense for Policy Paul D. Wolfowitz noted, the "distance between a superpower and an aspiring regional hegemon had been greatly foreshortened."[12] Any such cuts would mean the United States would have to compensate by fielding advanced conventional weapons systems and concepts.

In the end, Powell and Cheney's OSD came together to share a regionally focused strategic outlook and a generic force structure that was flexible enough to address a diverse set of circumstances. Bush approved a single plan in June 1990, which the White House announced that August. For the Navy, it meant reducing the fleet from 540 to 451 ships, which was the size of the fleet in 1977, and the number of carriers from 15 to 12.[13]

Maritime Strategy for the 1990s

Throughout the winter and spring of 1990, the CNO, Adm. Carlisle A. H. Trost (1986–90), did not say much as Powell pitched his strategy and Base Plan to the service chiefs and the more vocal CINCs.[14] As with the other service chiefs, Trost wanted to press his case with Powell in private, although he was certainly annoyed that Powell had not much involved the chiefs in fundamental decisions that clearly encroached on their Title 10 responsibilities to organize, train, and equip their respective service.[15] The process had been anything but pluralistic.

Instead, it was a fait accompli orchestrated by a select few.[16] OSD's vaunted thirty-year-old Planning, Programming, and Budgeting System had proven worthless as a means to organize for the future. As one chief lamented, "the planning for the defense build-down was a case of someone determining in advance what was needed, and then seeing that the result was produced."[17]

Trost sought to assert the Navy's comparative importance in the new strategic framework and defend the fleet's balance and size—this at a time when more than one hundred ships were still under construction—by referring to the Maritime Strategy. Trost laid out his thinking in a lengthy article in the May 1990 issue of the U.S. Naval Institute's *Proceedings*, the Navy's professional journal.[18] The article, entitled "Maritime Strategy for the 1990s," had an assertive if not defiant tone. It befitted Navy leaders who were confident of their ability to manage the Navy's destiny and hold off inevitable arguments by the Army and Air Force—who, with the Cold War's end, had lost much of their primary roles—that they could do the Navy's Cold War missions of forward presence, crisis management, and regional conflict better.

Trost did not share Powell's rosy view of the U.S.-Soviet relationship. "We cannot," he noted, "afford to react precipitously to the euphoria. . . . We must consider a potential enemy's *capabilities* as well as his *intentions*. This is especially true for naval force planning. . . . Political intentions can change overnight, while naval force structure, once relinquished, takes much longer to rebuild."[19] A few months earlier, in October 1989, Trost had visited the Soviet Union and found that the Soviets had not stopped constructing their massive *Oscar II*-class cruise missile–carrying nuclear submarines or their supercarrier *Tbilisi*.[20] While they may have recalled their massive army from Central Europe and were seeking to sign conventional and nuclear ballistic missile treaties, the Soviets were continuing to construct an advanced, albeit smaller, fleet at enormous cost.

In general, Trost agreed with the chairman's strategy and the strategy's goal of global stability.[21] In particular, Trost agreed with replacing the military's immense overseas structure with a forward presence approach, which consisted of deployed forces and smaller, more-mobile, and more-flexible permanent forces. Trost noted the difficulties in obtaining overflight rights and decreasing access to dwindling numbers of U.S. bases overseas elevated the significance of U.S. naval forces since they could demonstrate, in his words, "military power without raising politically sensitive issues of territorial sovereignty."[22]

As reflected in "Maritime Strategy for the 1990s," Trost did not believe the chairman understood the Navy's utility in ensuring international stability and managing crises, roles that continued despite the end of the Cold War. Nor did the chairman or the Joint Staff grasp the scale of naval forces needed for its rotational forces to undertake missions like forward presence, crisis response, and limited (i.e., regional) conflict.[23] Trost, who was not privy to the Joint Staff's analysis, had no intention of accepting its figures for the types and number of ships required.[24] With his article "Maritime Strategy for the 1990s," Trost was seeking to influence the thinking of those that did not grasp or appreciate the Navy's utility in bringing about international stability and managing crises. "I was determined to maintain our posture at a level which would permit us to meet our continuing mission responsibilities," he noted.[25] Powell—an Army general—possessed a rather incomplete understanding of the Navy.[26] None of the operational units that he served in, particularly those later in his career, was a joint unit. In short, he did not acquire his knowledge of the Navy in the context of naval operations, but rather in the context of his student tour at the National Defense University and the bureaucratic battles he waged during his considerable time in Washington.

According to Powell, the Army and the Air Force were in for the greatest cuts, since they had based their rationales on the battle for the Central Front in Europe and on nuclear deterrence. Nor did they possess the invulnerable ballistic missile–carrying submarine. Revealing a rather narrow, Army-centric view of the Navy's role in the Cold War, Powell asserted, "The Navy was next in line for a substantial whack, since its major mission was to protect the Atlantic sea-lanes so that we could get to Europe to fight World War III. Part of the rationale for the Navy's aircraft carriers was to project power ashore against an invading Red Army, a role fast becoming obsolete."[27]

Powell's thinking reflected a lack of understanding of the Navy's day-to-day systemic contributions of ensuring international stability and managing crises. He wanted to establish a new defense structure that consisted of a Strategic Force (i.e., the Strategic Command, which would be established in June 1992), a Pacific Force, a Contingency Force, and an Atlantic Force, which would consist of a European-based Army armor corps and the U.S. Atlantic Fleet. "We need an Atlantic Force," Powell noted, "to help achieve stability and deal with contingencies on and across that broad ocean, in Europe and the Middle East."[28] This was a remarkable statement, prompting Rear Adm. J. C. Wylie, USN (Ret.) to respond,

"This is a task that, except in continental Europe itself, the Navy and Marine Corps have been carrying out quite satisfactorily ever since World War II."[29]

Trost pointed out that despite the end of the Cold War, the proliferation of advanced weaponry posed an increasing threat to the fleet. He noted that 41 Third World nations possessed over 250 attack submarines, a total of 100 of which had antiship cruise missiles, and that many had land-based antiship capabilities as well.[30] Many of these nations were anti-Western and sat astride maritime transit routes and key chokepoints. "Survival . . . requires advanced electronics and weapon systems," he noted, "and does not allow the luxury of 'low-mix' platforms."[31] As examples of proliferation of advanced weaponry, he referred to the British experience during the Falkland Islands War in 1982, when the Royal Navy lost two ships to the advanced Exocet antiship missile; and the attack on the USS *Stark* in May 1987 in the Persian Gulf by an Iraqi jet that launched two Exocets, killing thirty-seven crewmembers and nearly sinking the ship.

To assert the Navy's relevance in the new strategic outlook and protect the fleet, Trost reapplied arguments from the Maritime Strategy, specifically its missions of forward presence and coercive diplomacy. Like its developers, Trost was annoyed by misconceptions about the Maritime Strategy, particularly the assumption among the other U.S. military services and Congress that the Maritime Strategy was nothing more than a campaign plan that addressed the Soviet threat and that the Navy's purpose was conceived solely in those terms. "We must also keep in mind that the Navy's role around the world has a focus that isn't only Soviet-oriented, and never has been," Trost noted.[32] To Trost, the Maritime Strategy was about how the Navy supported U.S. interests across the spectrum of warfare, from presence to global war. The Maritime Strategy was not a strategy or a doctrine-driven, operational-level of war concept—such as the Army's and Air Force's 1970s' and 1980s' AirLand Battle Doctrine—that addressed how to fight a specific battle on a specific battlefield against a specific threat. Trost noted that the Maritime Strategy was not a war plan, but rather a concept of operations based on deterrence, power projection, forward defense, and a global network of alliances.[33]

In essence, Trost asserted that the Navy had a unique and important role in ensuring international stability and the economic benefits derived from it, a role that had not changed with the passing of the Cold War. The Navy—in contrast to the Air Force and the Army—had a purpose that went beyond fighting battles. He noted that the United States was, in his words, "essentially an island nation," and that it was the leader of a global network of maritime-based alliances that linked a vast array of political and economic interests among its allies and trading partners. "Global economic interdependence is a fact of life," he stated, fifteen years before the Pentagon released any strategic statement that admitted to a relationship between U.S. security and the global interdependent system. "The majority of our trade routes, our economic and political lifelines, are oceanic. Over 70% of our total trade by value and 99.7% of our overseas export and import tonnage move by sea. Our economic well-being has been made possible by and depends upon political stability."[34]

The CNO also pointed out the Navy's preeminent role in managing crises. Since Truman, U.S. naval forces had been the presidents' military force of choice. From 1945 to 1990 naval forces had been involved in more than two hundred crises, which amounted to 80 percent of the total for the U.S. military. From 1980 to 1990 presidents had used U.S. naval forces almost fifty times, almost none dealing with the U.S.-Soviet confrontation.[35] Most particularly, he noted the Navy's increased presence in the Persian Gulf, and argued that the movement toward politico-military multipolarity and expanding counternarcotics efforts (a key element of U.S. policy in the late 1980s and early 1990s) would likely increase naval tasking. "Overseas regional powers, terrorists, and drug smugglers would be bolstered rather than deterred were we to withdraw naval forces from forward positions and to operate closer to home ports in the United States," he wrote. "Being present in the immediate region enables naval forces to provide a timely response at the outset of future crises." "Consequently," Trost summed up, "only by maintaining a balanced fleet that is forward deployed and combat ready can we fulfill the role of providing regional stability while preserving U.S. economic and foreign policy interests."[36]

Trost and the Worth of the Maritime Strategy

Trost was not about to jettison the Maritime Strategy. He had seen first-hand the intellectual and material investment that went into its development and operationalization. As the director of Navy Program Planning (OP-090) for almost four years in the early 1980s, Trost had, in real terms, built the 600-ship Navy. As the U.S. Atlantic Fleet's commander, he had worked to operationalize the Maritime Strategy in terms of planning and training, including integrating NATO naval forces. The Maritime Strategy had—like Trost himself—provided continuity through the many changes of civilian leadership that occurred during Trost's tenure, which included two presidents, three secretaries of defense, two chairmen of the Joint Chiefs of Staff, and four Secretaries of the Navy. Trost, who had an imposing intellect (he graduated first in his Naval Academy class of 1953), was a steadying influence. Not unlike George H. W. Bush in his low-key, pragmatic, and prudent outlook, he was a steward of the Maritime Strategy and the kind of naval thinking it embodied.

Admiral Trost was a proponent of the Maritime Strategy, but not the kind represented by former Secretary of the Navy John Lehman (1981–87). Trost had little respect for Lehman after the secretary had contested Trost's appointment as CNO in 1986, and after having seen Lehman's management style in action.[37] Lehman had a unique background: he had a doctorate in international relations, was a Navy commander who flew carrier attack jets in the reserves, and was a protégé of Henry Kissinger. A bureaucratic infighter, Lehman had a background in business and public relations that was well suited to drive his 600-ship Navy program through Congress.[38] Lehman's unyielding demand in his first year in office for a strategic vision to organize the service's activities and to yield six hundred ships had coincided with ongoing work in OPNAV on what would become the Maritime Strategy. For six years Lehman was the face of the 600-ship Navy, and tied that effort to the Maritime Strategy.[39] He was hard set against rationalizing the 600-ship Navy in terms of peacetime requirements. Instead, he justified the fleet in terms of the Soviet threat, but only in terms of the Soviet threat.[40]

Once it became obvious that the Soviets were departing the world stage, however, it was evident that the former secretary had little sense of what those ships might do, a failing that strengthened the impression that the Maritime Strategy was a Cold War relic. In March 1990 Lehman told a congressional hearing that the Navy should place half the fleet into the Naval Reserve and otherwise "stop operating as if we are at wartime tempo."[41] Trost remarked that Lehman's comments were "totally out of touch" with his positions when he was secretary, a post that Lehman had left two years earlier.[42] Unlike the Army, the Navy did not rely on its comparatively smaller reserve component.[43] Institutionally, Navy officers believed that naval reserve forces could not be counted on to be combat ready and, in general, did not serve the interests of operational flexibility, tactical-technical proficiency, and forward deployment. Trost pointed out that the cost savings of Lehman's plan would be only 10–15 percent, and that it would be "almost impossible" to keep part-time sailors trained to operate nuclear-powered ships and carriers. "We need to be able to respond with a properly trained, properly maintained ship," Trost noted, and "not one that would require national mobilization or a presidential order."[44]

After entering office in 1986, Trost tried to separate the Maritime Strategy from the 600-ship Navy. The end of Reagan's defense spending surge threatened the goal of the 600-ship Navy, which threatened the Maritime Strategy. In 1987 Trost noted that the Maritime Strategy "was not—and is not—a force builder, and it was certainly not the origin of the 600-ship navy," a true enough statement.[45] Many in Washington and even a few in the Navy had seen the Maritime Strategy as simply a kind of theater conjured by Lehman to extract the appropriations needed for a 600-ship Navy from the tight fists of Congress and a defense bureaucracy that had fought it at every turn.[46] Trost valued how the Maritime Strategy provided a compelling rationale for the Navy, specifically how it had at once articulated the Navy's purpose and identity, aligned its operational, programmatic, administrative, intelligence, and pedagogic activities, and supported arguments for a large and modernized fleet, all of which was now conceivably at risk with the end of the Cold War.

Like the Navy's strategists, and indeed like Lehman himself, Trost understood the Maritime Strategy as a strategy in the general sense of the word: as a means of relating military power to political goals. In his words, the Maritime Strategy was based "upon a solid bedrock of sound facts and principles that will remain valid even as our political and economic surroundings change."[47] The Maritime Strategy's deterrence or transition to war phase, which was about presence, coercive diplomacy, and crisis management, already contained the rationale that placed the Navy at the forefront of Powell's strategy, whose elements were deterrence, forward presence, crisis management, and regional conflict. Trost also understood the Maritime Strategy as a sublime articulation of the Navy's way of thinking. Reflecting the implicit, pragmatic, and experiential-based nature of American naval thinking, he noted, "Over the years our Maritime Strategy has been very much like the British Constitution—unwritten but thoroughly understood by those who must practice it."[48] In short, there was little to gain and much to lose by jettisoning the cherished Maritime Strategy.

The CNO's thinking, however, changed in the spring of 1990: two powerful senators told him that the service chiefs needed to come to Capitol Hill with a new story this year.[49] One was Sam Nunn (D-GA), chairman of the Senate Armed Services Committee, and the other was John Warner (R-VA), who was also a committee member and former Secretary of the Navy (1972–74). Trost had been the executive assistant to Secretary of the Navy Warner, who had intervened with the Reagan White House to get Trost appointed CNO.[50] The two senators' pronouncement that cuts could not be avoided only reinforced Trost's sense that the Base Force was about all the Pentagon could defend. The CNO's testimony in April 1990, which reflected his "Maritime Strategy for the 1990s," was not well received.[51] Congress saw arguments about the need for a balanced fleet in an indeterminate strategic environment, particularly the Navy's desire to retain sizeable numbers of its attack submarines, whose rationale was undermined by the disappearance of the Soviet threat, as simply bureaucratic politics at work. For one, while consensus between the Navy's warfare communities was intrinsic to Navy strategy making, Congress was not about to let what it perceived as internal Navy politics get in the way of a reduced budget.

After Bush approved the Base Force plan in June 1990, the service chiefs relented, having realized the administration was united behind the Base Force. "We knew if Cheney offered the Congress a 40 percent reduction, it would have been pocketed while they [Congress] asked for more," one chief noted. "Therefore, we supported the 25 percent number."[52] Trost had little choice but to start focusing on how to defend the Navy's share of the Base Force.

Conclusion

The abrupt end of the Cold War created a conceptual whiplash in Washington. The Soviet threat had organized U.S. strategy, foreign policy, and defense policy for over forty years. The disappearance of that threat resulted in a kind of indeterminacy that raised few, if any, questions about what the United States' position of systemic preeminence really meant. Congress did not give much thought to convening hearings on why the United States ultimately won the Cold War. Like the American people, Congress had a narrow, nonsystemic understanding of the military's purpose, which was simply to deter and win wars. With that possibility receding, Congress' goals were to leverage a peace dividend and reclaim its rights in the area of defense planning and spending, where it had progressively been obliged to take a back seat to the executive branch.

Having seen first-hand the ill-conceived effects of Congress' hollowing out of the military in the 1970s, Powell's goal to maintain control of the drawdown was understandable. But to achieve that control Powell manipulated Goldwater-Nichols, which further centralized the strategy-making process, which, in turn, structured the direction of U.S. strategy of the post–Cold War era. The authors of Goldwater-Nichols, whose enactment shortly before the end of the Cold War was coincidental, never intended that the Joint Staff, for example, should become so deeply involved in the resource and strategy-making process. According to them, Goldwater-Nichols was designed for the Cold War, with its stable environment and clearly defined threat, and not for the kind of context in which the United States now found itself.[53] As the nation entered the post–Cold War era, however, these points were lost on the Pentagon's leaders. In a vacuum of systemic knowledge and visionary leadership from the White House, the well-meaning but shortsighted goals of Congress and Powell meant that decisions on defense spending became more dependent on the vagaries of the political process than on the less understood merits of strategic rationality.

The strategy that Powell and OSD had put together, with its emphasis on global stability, was reasonably good given congressional and societal demands. Powell had rejected the CINCs' recommendation to base the strategy on their operational, threat-based requirements.[54] The focus had to be on the types of capabilities needed for an unpredictable strategic environment, not on the range of threats. A threat-based strategy was too inflexible. From their respective studies and intuition, Powell and Cheney's staff each arrived at a generic strategic approach, a contingent outlook, and a balanced set of forces designed for adaptability, flexibility, and forward deployment. This was the Navy's strategic approach all along, of course, a fact that genuinely seemed to escape the notice of U.S. leaders, strategists, and—inexcusably—Navy leaders.

For their part, the Navy's leaders believed the service was well positioned to take advantage of Bush's new strategic approach, whose elements were closely aligned with the Navy's everyday missions in the Cold War. But their attempt to get U.S. officials to appreciate the Navy's Cold War contributions and the diversity of the fleet's capabilities in support of missions like presence, coercive diplomacy, and crisis management made little headway. They were struggling against the inertia of U.S. and institutional thinking. During the Cold War, Congress and Department of Defense officials considered these lesser-included missions to be ancillary to those involving nuclear deterrence and warfighting. The Navy itself never put these missions on par with warfighting and found it more effective to rationalize its weapons systems in terms of general war and nuclear deterrence. As Secretary Lehman noted in 1981, "Every dollar has to be justified by what it can do to defeat the Soviet maritime threat in time of war."[55] Lehman's approach was understandable, given the implacable nature of the Soviet threat and Congress' narrow understanding of the military's purpose, yet regrettable after the Cold War's end. Consequently, these lesser-included missions could not be adequately accounted for, and arguments for their relevance now were met with silence on Capitol Hill and in the Pentagon.

Still, Navy leaders were complacent. On the one hand, the Cold War's abrupt end and Powell's exclusive approach gave them little time or opportunity to devise meaningful arguments in a context other than languid congressional testimony and journal articles. In this marketplace of ideas, abstract notions that related the Navy and international stability, for example, simply failed to find purchase. On the other hand, Navy leaders assumed that U.S. defense officials, Congress, and the American public readily appreciated the Navy's day-to-day systemic contributions during the Cold War and the fleet's utility in the postwar era. Navy leaders did not see anything on the horizon—either in terms of domestic politics or the security environment—that might require rapid, even traumatic change on the part of the Navy. At no time in this period did the Navy's leaders—civilian or uniformed—ask for something to replace the Maritime Strategy.[56] Assuming the Army and the Air Force would take the brunt of the budget cuts, they simply rebranded its existing strategy.

Many observers, some in and some out of the Navy, demanded more-creative leadership. Like Bush, Trost was neither visionary nor charismatic. "The measure of how well you're doing in the job," he noted, "is whether or not you keep your name out of the paper."[57] As Norman Polmar noted, "You either need a persuasive individual who can convert people through logic and reasoning or a leader with a lot of charisma. Trost is . . . a good guy, the right guy but at the wrong time. . . . His legacy will be that he held the fort in a period of controversy and transition." Edward Luttwak was less forgiving: "He is a man of procedure and process, and his forte is making current things work extremely well," he noted. "Is he the type of person . . . who can say, 'Right now is the time to rethink the Navy in terms of the new budgetary reality'? No, absolutely not. That calls for the ability to challenge, to innovate, which is exactly what process-and-procedure people do not do." A harsh indictment, but one more applicable to other post–Cold War CNOs.

In his defense, Trost was handed a difficult problem, one that was full of contradictions that he was quite aware of. With the Maritime Strategy, the Navy had just spent ten years convincing Congress and the Reagan administration that it could make an important contribution in a war with the Soviets beyond the Central Front. During much of the Cold War critics had argued that the Navy was superfluous to that battle, and that funds spent on carriers, for example, should be shifted to the Army and the Air Force. They maintained that the Navy should stick with presence, coercive diplomacy, and limited war. Now, with budget cuts looming, these critics were not about to make the Navy's case for it, even though many saw the importance of such missions increasing in the post–Cold War era.

In the end, Trost's attempt to shift the emphasis toward those elements of the Maritime Strategy that seemed best suited to new conditions proved unconvincing, however genuine its motivation. The Navy's efforts to present its new approach as a natural extension of its previous one (hard-won and much-esteemed though it was within the institution) proved misplaced. Precisely because institutional priorities were about retaining as much legacy capacity as possible, it was important that whatever was done appear new and innovative. The fact that Trost tried to tell Congress and the Department of Defense hierarchy about the importance of presence and crisis management and that his comments had no real impact was not necessarily his fault. The Maritime Strategy was too tainted and too rooted in an era now seen as passé to be of much use in an environment in which only self-proclaimed new ideas could be ensured a hearing. The dawn of what Bush called the New World Order proved a poor moment to trumpet the lessons of the past.

The Way Ahead, 1990

Kelso and the Need for a Policy

In February 1990 President Bush announced that Adm. Frank B. Kelso II (1990–94) would be the next CNO, the third successive nuclear submariner. A 1956 graduate of the U.S. Naval Academy, Kelso had spent most of his career at sea. Like Trost, Kelso did not have a postgraduate degree, nor had he attended the Naval War College. Like Trost, he had a programming background. He served in OPNAV as the director of the Strategic Submarine Division and the program coordinator of the new *Ohio*-class SSBN and its Trident missile. Later, he worked under Secretary Lehman as his director for the Program Appraisal Office, one of the most powerful positions in the Navy Department.

Questions about allegations of sexual harassment, hazing, and exam cheating at the Naval Academy dominated Kelso's confirmation hearing. On other topics, Kelso noted that the Navy needed a balance of forces. It needed carriers, amphibious ships, and surface combatants, and it needed to maintain the size of the submarine force. When asked, Kelso replied that the Navy did not need a strategy: it already had one in the Maritime Strategy. What it needed was a policy. He noted, "Military strategy needs a specific enemy and, though developed in peacetime, is applied during war. . . . I do not expect a global conflict so the issue before us today seems more one of naval policy."[1]

Admiral Kelso was defining strategy as nothing more than an operational plan of action against a specific threat, which is how many in the Navy understood it. In contrast, Lehman, Trost, and the Maritime Strategy's developers understood it as a general way of thinking about relating military power to political goals. Trost and his predecessor, Adm. James D. Watkins (1982–86), had fought to portray the Maritime Strategy not as an operational plan, but as an argument about how the Navy made a strategic difference. Clearly, Kelso, who was intimately familiar with the Maritime Strategy, was distancing himself from the Maritime Strategy and downplaying the need for strategy, and with it the need for strategic thinking.

The lack of a threat in the near future meant Kelso could dedicate considerable time and effort to improving the process by which the Navy's resource decisions were made.[2] Along with the need to realize cost-efficiencies to offset budget cuts, the lack of a threat meant that he could indulge in his supreme passion: optimizing managerial processes, which was the central focus of his tenure. Kelso was an ardent disciple of W. Edwards Deming, the noted managerial consultant and guru of corporate scientific management. Deming, whose approach was called Total Quality Management, was credited with improving Japanese manufacturing productivity. Once in office, Kelso vigorously installed Deming's approach throughout the Navy, renaming it Total Quality Leadership.[3]

Kelso's fascination with finding process efficiencies owed much to his background as a nuclear submariner. Admiral Rickover wanted to ensure no accidents endangered his nuclear propulsion program. To avoid mishaps, Rickover had, as a way of thinking, inculcated into the submarine community the need to assiduously follow and constantly improve processes to prevent accidents with nuclear reactors. It also owed much to his time as Lehman's director of the Program Appraisal Office. There, he viewed first-hand Lehman's strenuous yet successful efforts to overhaul the Navy Department's bureaucracy to realize cost-savings in its weapons acquisition process. Kelso observed how Lehman gained control of the sprawling bureaucracy to oversee OPNAV's most important function: resource apportionment.[4] He observed how Lehman had cut through the stonewalling of the three barons—the three powerful three-star admirals who were the respective program sponsors and defenders of the Navy's dominant three warfare communities—surface ships, aviation, and submarines.[5] As Tom Hone noted, not only was Lehman "the most aggressive . . . Navy secretary since James Forrestal [1944–47]," but he was also the most "organizationally perceptive" as well.[6] Kelso was a protégé of Lehman. It was Kelso, not Trost, whom Lehman had picked in 1986 to be the next CNO, but the White House had overruled him.[7]

Kelso's protégé, in turn, was Vice Adm. Paul David Miller, the deputy CNO for Naval Warfare (OP-07). For four years Miller had been Lehman's executive assistant, an unusually long time to be away from the fleet. Miller, a surface officer, was promoted to admiral without having commanded a ship as a captain, which was a rare feat. Once in OPNAV, Miller turned OP-07 into a powerhouse that rivaled OPNAV's other two centers of power: Program Planning (OP-08) and Plans, Policy, and Operations (OP-06), the latter of which was responsible for strategy and operations.[8] Miller would become the catalyst for Kelso's demand for a roadmap policy that laid out how the Navy would organize to plan for the next decade.[9]

Kelso's Roadmap to Reshape the Navy

During a speech on August 2, 1990, President Bush unveiled the new strategy.[10] He noted that the Iraqi invasion of Kuwait earlier in the day showed that the world still contained serious threats to U.S. interests that were unrelated to the U.S.-Soviet confrontation, threats that could emerge without warning. On August 20, 1990, General Powell told the CINCs and service chiefs that they needed to focus on reshaping the force structure.[11] He noted that the nation still needed to project global power, which was what the military was doing at that moment in protecting Saudi Arabia from invasion while preparing to expel Iraqi forces from Kuwait. Powell also emphasized that regardless of how the crisis ended, Congress still would not fund the services' respective POMs (i.e., their Program Objective Memorandum, a recommendation of how a service will allocate its respective resources), which were based on pre–Base Force funding levels.

On August 23 Kelso and Secretary of the Navy Henry L. "Lawrence" Garrett III (1989–92) released a memorandum that addressed how the Navy Department would start reshaping the force structure. "The way ahead is not as murky as some envision," they stated. "We have a first class Navy and Marine Corps with substantial numbers of new ships and aircraft at sea and in production. . . . We *do* know the force structure . . . in the year 2000. It is with us today or under construction." They noted that the Department had three "overriding challenges": First, "of immediate relevance is the necessity of maintaining an adequate industrial base to ensure efficient procurement of the next generation of platforms and systems."[12] Kelso, who had supported the Base Plan only because he thought it would blunt further predations on the fleet, was worried that reaching the Navy's Base Force level too quickly would threaten the health of its industrial base.[13]

No doubt he was particularly worried about the specialized segment responsible for constructing nuclear reactors for submarines, cruisers, and carriers. Second, they noted, "given the projected fiscal climate, we need to determine how many ships and aircraft we can afford to operate in the decade ahead." Finally, the next step was to "examine the shape and size of the Navy of the 21st century which will replace our present ships and aircraft." Referring to Kelso's Total Quality Leadership, they noted that the Navy "must refocus leadership and management practices in order to maintain our nation's investment at the least cost."[14]

To Kelso, a top-down strategy was not required to determine the fleet's shape and size. Such a strategy would have been developed and overseen by OP-06, which had developed the Maritime Strategy. Instead, the future fleet would be determined by staff processes that Kelso was more familiar and comfortable with— the resource-determining processes that were associated with two of OPNAV's most important functions—programming and establishing the requirements for weapons systems. Programming was the responsibility of OP-08, whereas establishing requirements, which the three barons had dominated, was now overseen by Miller's OP-07.

However, from Kelso's perspective the process that determined the fleet's shape and size needed to be overhauled. Changing that process required a new policy, which is what he meant when he testified that the Navy needed a policy. Whereas Trost saw competition between the three warfare communities for resources as healthy, for example, Kelso saw it as pernicious. Following Deming, Kelso changed the process of how resources were determined to one that generated a collective commitment by decision makers in OPNAV particularly at the one- and two-star admiral level; these were the Navy's most current "operators" and represented the future of the Navy. He wanted a process that was not marked by parochialism and one where the decisions were not made by the barons or lower-ranking program managers, but rather were made by these admirals in the form of collective-minded boards. For Kelso, consensus, and not competition, was the key.

The Navy Strategists and the Drive for a New Vision

Despite the historic events of 1989 and 1990, neither Trost nor Kelso had asked for something to replace the Maritime Strategy.[15] Nevertheless, there was an organized effort under way to do just that. It was not driven (as one might have expected, at least during the Cold War) by the new deputy CNO for OP-06,

Vice Adm. Robert J. Kelly, who had arrived in February 1990. Unlike most of his predecessors who had backgrounds in strategy, Kelly had little interest in the strategy part of the job, and focused, at least initially, on the part he was most familiar and comfortable with—the operations part. It took time for him to get over his lack of interest and his publicly expressed disdain for those twenty officers on his staff who were members of the Navy's strategy community.

Kelly took his lead first from Trost and then Kelso, who, following Powell's guidance, made it abundantly clear that OPNAV's focus should be on force structure, not strategy. Kelly, like most of those who followed him in the billet, understood his purpose as serving the day-to-day demands of the CNO, whose background was operational and programmatic, not strategic. For officers like Kelly who were in positions of strategic leadership, adherence to the CNO's to-do list was the safer, more expedient route to promotion to four-star fleet command, the traditional follow-on assignment, than one whose allegiance was to strategy in general. Such an admiral would not want to get out in front of the CNO with self-generated projects. In short, Kelly was not a strategic visionary, nor was he appointed to be one. Consequently, he never gave much thought to tasking his fifteen-person Strategic Concepts Branch (OP-603), which had developed the Maritime Strategy, to come up with a new strategic approach.

Instead, the unbidden effort came from an unofficial group of Navy strategists. These were mostly mid-level officers (i.e., lieutenant commanders, commanders, and captains), most of whom worked either in the OP-603 or the CNO Executive Panel (OP-00K). The group had a few Marines as well. Most came from Headquarters Marine Corps' Plans, Policy, and Operations directorate, its equivalent of OPNAV's OP-06.

The Navy strategists were members of the Navy's small and (at least then) tightly knit strategy community.[16] Between their tours in the fleet, the members of the community, who numbered around two hundred, served in strategy-related positions. Most of these billets were in OPNAV, specifically the Strategic Concepts Branch, which was considered the locus of the community, or in OP-00K. The rest were in OSD, the Joint Staff, the Naval War College, the State Department, and the Navy's component commands to the CINCs (e.g., the U.S. Pacific Fleet, which was the Navy component command of U.S. Pacific Command). Many were part of what was informally known as the Maritime Strategy mafia. In the 1980s these officers served multiple tours in different, mostly Navy, staffs that kept them in a position to work with each other on developing and testing the strategy. Many had multiple tours in OP-06. This was before Goldwater-Nichols had mandated that most of the services' senior officers had to have tours in joint commands (e.g., the Joint Staff and the CINCs' staffs). Before Goldwater-Nichols, OPNAV had been the key staff, the one that promising officers needed to have served on for promotion.

The development of a cadre of strategic thinkers had been part of efforts by CNOs Hayward and Watkins to improve the Navy's strategic thinking. The investment paid off as this group had led the Navy out of the impasse it had found itself in during the 1970s. Almost all of the members of this intellectually inclined community had master's degrees and a significant number had doctorates. Lehman—a doctor of philosophy himself, who had little patience for the Navy's anti-intellectualism, particularly among its admirals—had a close relationship with the group, one marked by mutual respect. He often lauded the group for, in his words, their "very able minds."[17] These officers considered themselves to be the keepers of the Navy's strategic flame. Their allegiance was not to Navy leaders as much as it was to the strategic well-being of the institution and strategy in general. This was particularly so if their bosses were not from the community, which, unlike during the Cold War, was an increasingly common occurrence in the post–Cold War era. Their niche skills did much to compensate for the Navy's lack of proficiency in strategic thought, of which they were painfully aware.[18]

In February 1990 the informal group began to meet after work to deliberate on two questions. First, how should the Navy use its existing means to fulfill political ends, some of which were familiar, while others needed more definition? They wanted something more conceptual than could be expected from the Navy's component commands and their CINCs. The pragmatic and operational focus of those CINCs was thought to stand in the way of a more holistic understanding of naval purpose, one that fully admitted both domestic political and wider foreign policy considerations. Second, what kind of new strategic concept was needed to fulfill institutional and external political requirements? As noted by Capt. E. Richard Diamond, the new chief of OP-603, "the question was, 'So what do we do for a vision to replace the Maritime Strategy now that the Berlin Wall is down?'" He noted that while the group's members saw the need for a post–Cold War vision immediately after the war, Navy leaders did not. "There was no formal Navy leadership tasker to even ask the question," he noted, "much less provide an answer at this point [February 1990]."[19]

The group organized itself into small teams.[20] On a Saturday in late March 1990, unbeknownst to the CNO and Kelly, they presented their visions to a select audience, which included a few rear admirals who were part of the strategy community. Amid lively critiques, one theme in particular resonated with the group. This was Cdr. Joseph A. Sestak Jr.'s declaration that the Navy–Marine Corps team was the "Enabling Force for Follow-On Joint Operations." The group then formed a writing team to synthesize the themes, which came up with five propositions: (1) The Navy's future was not about just war at sea, but also about supporting the land battle. (2) The expeditionary nature and forward presence of the Navy–Marine Corps team made the naval services (i.e., the Navy and Marine Corps) the "911 crisis response team" and the "enabling force" for subsequent joint operations. (3) The Navy needed more foreign area specialists and cultural awareness. (4) The Navy should cultivate bilateral and multilateral maritime-based alliances. (5) Antisubmarine warfare and anti–air warfare capabilities would still be required, but only for local operations, which would free up funds for more Marine Corps capabilities.

In July 1990 Diamond presented the group's vision to his boss, Kelly, who immediately asked, "Who tasked you to come up with this?"[21] Kelly, however, promptly arranged to have Diamond brief Miller. Miller, the consummate empire builder, was enthralled with the group's work and suggested that their directorates work together. Miller asked Diamond to send him everything they had. Miller also suggested a new title, "Won if by Sea," which was replaced in the fall of 1990 with "Meeting the Challenges of a Changing World: Navy Policy for the Future," which, of course, reflected Kelso's focus on policy. By that time, Miller had his own independent plan, much of which he had based on the material that Diamond had provided. Its title was "Sea Power and Global Leadership: Maritime Concepts for 1990 and Beyond."[22] Unlike Kelly, Miller was a member of Kelso's inner circle, having worked closely with Kelso in Secretary Lehman's office. Using his access, Miller began introducing these ideas to the CNO.[23]

General Gray's Demand for a New Navy–Marine Corps Vision

In the 1980s the Marines' involvement in Navy strategy making was commonplace.[24] The close relationship between OPNAV and Headquarters Marine Corps had enhanced and expanded the Maritime Strategy. Signed in 1985 by CNO Watkins and the Commandant of the Marine Corps, Gen. P. X. Kelley (1983–87), the Amphibious Warfare Strategy was the amphibious component of the Maritime Strategy.

To reduce its political vulnerability after Vietnam, the Marine Corps had redefined its purpose from expeditionary to amphibious warfare, a unique role that set it apart from the Army.[25] Marine leaders saw little merit in joining the Army on the Central Front in Europe. After 1985, however, Marine leaders readopted expeditionary warfare as the institution's core identity in the expectation that such operations would, in practice, call for the kind of agile, light-infantry force that only the Marines could supply. President Reagan's interventionist foreign policy, which saw Marines involved in a variety of mid- and low-intensity conflicts, meant that expeditionary warfare was back in vogue. In 1988 the switch became official: Marine Corps units were redesignated back to "expeditionary" (e.g., Marine Amphibious Forces became Marine Expeditionary Forces).

Soon after, in 1989, the commandant of the Marine Corps, Gen. Alfred M. "Al" Gray Jr., (1987–91), released the seminal Fleet Marine Force Manual 1, "War-fighting," which laid out the Marines' warfighting philosophy of expeditionary maneuver warfare.[26] Although the Marines had been instrumental in broadening the Maritime Strategy, it was "Warfighting" that invigorated the Marine Corps' sense of purpose and brought about the alignment of its operational, programmatic, administrative, and pedagogic activities. But "Warfighting" was not tied to a highly visible programmatic goal like the 600-ship Navy, nor was such a link intended. The Marine Corps' strategic approach was far less about resources and technology than it was about the need for constant innovation in waging war. "Warfighting" did not present its central concepts in the framework of an operational war plan with the Soviets. Unlike the Maritime Strategy, it did not attempt to shift the direction of U.S. strategy or broaden American strategic thought to a more maritime way of thinking. "Warfighting" was simply that—a compelling (and still influential) warfighting doctrine. Its purpose was to inculcate a highly adaptable mindset that could readily deal with and take advantage of the unforeseen changes that occur on the battlefield. For the Marines, doctrine was not prescriptive. It was a shared philosophy about the operational art of war. Because of its nature, "Warfighting," unlike the Maritime Strategy, survived the Cold War, and, given the nature of the emerging environment, it thrived.

The Bush administration's focus on crisis response and regional conflict highlighted the need for the Marines' capabilities even more than the Navy's. Gray—the most vocal of the service chiefs—had convinced Powell not to cut the Marines' end strength (i.e., number of personnel). Gray argued that geography—and not the Soviet threat—had determined its size.[27] Powell agreed, noting, "The Marines were on somewhat firmer ground [than the other U.S. military services]. With justification, they presented themselves as the nation's '911' response force, with or without a Soviet Union."[28]

In this context, Diamond briefed General Gray in September 1990. During the one-hour presentation, Gray brimmed with enthusiasm and provided more ideas and guidance.[29] Gray told Diamond to emphasize two key messages: the power, flexibility, and usefulness of forces projected from the sea; and the need for naval power to be on station overseas. Power projection "goes hand in hand with diplomatic power backed up by the military equation," Gray noted. "This puts teeth into our diplomacy. Make the connection." He continued, "Seapower is designed so the navies of the free world can go wherever, whenever we want! This can't be watered down by rice-bowlers" (i.e., those in the Pentagon who sought to jealously protect their programs at the expense of U.S. interests).

General Gray wanted to use the brief as a springboard to develop a strategy document that both he and the CNO would sign. To Gray the audience should not be just the Navy and the Marine Corps, but the entire defense establishment. "It's not a document that's only the CNO's. [It belongs to] the nation's seapower leaders. . . . [The larger, strategic thrust of maritime strategy] will be included or we'll have two documents," he threatened.[30] Gray told Diamond to highlight the combined nature of naval operations and the ability of the Navy–Marine Corps team to tailor forces at sea. "We want to portray the aggregate usefulness and flexibility of the sea services," Gray stated.[31]

"The Way Ahead"

In the winter of 1990–91, the CNO and the commandant agreed to cowrite a journal article. It was Kelso's first major statement on strategy. Entitled "The Way Ahead," the twelve-page article came out in the April 1991 issues of *Proceedings* and the *Marine Corps Gazette* under the byline of Secretary Garrett, Kelso, and Gray.[32] The article, which members of Kelso's and Gray's staffs had written as the service chiefs were preparing for their annual posture statements to Congress in February 1991, was the first such document drafted, signed, and published with equality between the two services. It was developed by a Navy officer from

OP-603 and a Marine from Plans, Policy, and Operations, edited by some senior officers from OP-07, and finalized by Kelso and Gray.

Unlike the Air Force's highly publicized "Global Reach–Global Power," which had come out in June 1990 and was seen as an indication that the Air Force was well ahead of the other U.S. military services in adapting to the post–Cold War era, "The Way Ahead" was not a comprehensive strategic statement.[33] It was an unstructured, multipurpose, and consensus-driven article that sought to represent the various agendas of its many authors: Miller, Gray, the Navy strategists, and Kelso, who was looking for a way to rationalize the Navy's force structure to mitigate looming cuts in the defense budget.

To the general audience, "The Way Ahead" explained how the Navy and Marine Corps would together meet emerging security needs. For sailors and Marines, the authors were sending a clarion call for change, one that would, it was hoped, reduce institutional resistance to ideas like a Navy–Marine Corps partnership and a much smaller Navy. For the audience of regional CINCs, the article asserted the Navy's and Marine Corps' operational virtues and offered ideas about how the CINCs could package task forces and change deployment routines. For Congress and U.S. defense leaders, it argued that the focus of the administration's new strategy on forward presence, crisis management, regional conflict, and conventional (as well as nuclear) deterrence required capabilities that the Navy and Marine Corps were uniquely able to provide.

The article started by noting that for almost fifty years the United States had focused on global war, which was to be fought primarily in Europe and the surrounding waters. But now the nation "must shift the objective of our national security strategy from containing the Soviet Union to maintaining global stability." However, this evidently did not mean the naval service should focus on how to realize global stability. In a peculiarly worded statement, it meant reshaping "naval force structure, strategy, tactics, and operating patterns *that are wedded too closely* to the concept of an Armageddon at sea with the Soviet Union." The authors were defining naval purpose in terms of what it was no longer supposed to be. In a statement that sealed the Maritime Strategy's fate, they stated that while its "enduring principles" were to be gleaned for current planning, the Maritime Strategy nonetheless "remains on the shelf . . . ready to be retrieved if a global threat should reemerge."[34] Both "Warfighting" and the Maritime Strategy represented their service's respective warfighting philosophy, but only the Navy's strategy was being pulled from circulation, and retained only for reference.

In practice the authors' understanding of the strategic environment differed little from CNO Trost's. The authors left little doubt that the Navy's primary purpose was power projection and asserted that the carrier battle groups and amphibious ready groups made up the cornerstone of U.S. forward-deployed forces. The article noted that, as demonstrated in Operation Desert Storm (the campaign that had begun on January 17, 1991, to eject Iraqi forces from Kuwait), the carrier's strike capabilities were supplemented by the immense distributed firepower of surface combatants and submarines that launched conventionally armed Tomahawks into Iraq.

To Garrett, Kelso, and Gray, jointness meant understanding, respecting, and applying the services' respective "functional capabilities" and core competencies in a complementary fashion. "When each service fulfills its respective role," they noted, "we can capitalize on synergistic capabilities that stem from decades of organizational focus and institutional ethos."[35] Their definition was thus about coordination between and not integration of the services, a key distinction in a period when jointness was still being defined and a joint climate had not yet been established.[36] In the article, jointness was always used in conjunction with combined (i.e., allied and coalition forces), and both terms were discussed in the context of collective security, which was noted to be a central element of U.S. policy.

The article offered some creative operational concepts. These, no doubt, came from Miller, who would advance similar innovative concepts later in his career. For example, carrier battle groups and amphibious ready groups could be tailored before or during deployment for specific regions, types of crises, or missions. The authors also highlighted the increasing importance of new missions, which included "humanitarian assistance; nation-building; security assistance; and peacekeeping, counternarcotic, counterterrorist, counterinsurgency, and crisis-response operations."[37] These missions, which gained prominence in the post–Cold War era, would later come to be known collectively in doctrinal documents as "military operations other than war."

The authors noted that given a smaller fleet and the CINCs' requirements for naval presence, the fleet needed focused forward presence. In other words, the fleet needed to ascertain and achieve specific instrumental effects in support of the CINCs' goals, something more than just steaming around deterring regional threats and being in a position to respond immediately to crises. The authors also argued that the fleet needed the capability to surge its forces out of its bases in the United States.[38] This was another innovative idea, one that the Navy would successfully squash until operational requirements after 9/11 demanded its acceptance. Until then, "surge" was a dirty word: it undermined arguments for forward deployment and the numbers of ships needed to support the CINCs' presence requirements. As the authors noted, the newer ships' improved capabilities could not make up for the lack of numbers; both quantity and quality were needed to ensure the credibility of U.S. forward presence. Gaps in presence, they argued, could bring regional instability and conflict.

The authors saved their most emphatic language for detailing the risks of narrowing the fleet's capabilities and reducing its size by 25 percent. A smaller fleet meant that it would be "harder to maintain the wide balance of capabilities required to counter sudden, unexpected geopolitical challenges and newly emerging threats or capabilities." They continued, "High-tempo operations will be even more difficult to sustain. Smaller forces will be less well-balanced, will have less surge capability, and will be less able to respond in a timely manner."[39] Clearly, the authors sought to maintain a balanced force, which included attack submarines, whose relevance Congress and Powell, among others, were now sure to question.

In the end, "The Way Ahead" proved about as ill-timed as Trost's "Maritime Strategy for the 1990s." It had been submitted during Operation Desert Storm, which had started in mid-January 1991 and for all practical purposes ended in late February, and was published a month later, in April 1991. Consequently, the article could not take into account the U.S. military's so-called revolutionary victory over Iraq, which many believed finally demonstrated American airpower as decisive. Nor did it defend the Navy against growing accusations that it had been ill prepared to fight in a truly joint—meaning integrated—manner. Because the article's ideas were not pegged directly to the conduct of the war, it appeared that the Navy's leadership was either supremely out of touch or that it was more concerned about saving its force structure than understanding what many considered to be the profound lessons of the Gulf War.

From their perspective, the Navy's superb performance in the Gulf War gave its leaders little cause for concern. Within days of Iraq's invasion of Kuwait in August 1990, two carriers had steamed to within striking distance of Kuwait, a well-publicized move that many believed had deterred Iraq from continuing into Saudi Arabia. By the end of the month, 15,000 Marines had arrived in Saudi Arabia, which represented the coalition's first armored force. Within weeks four carriers and two Tomahawk-armed battleship groups were on station. Until the

Air Force was finally able to deploy its forces in the late fall of 1990, these naval forces made up the bulk of U.S. tactical airpower. To enforce United Nations sanctions, Navy-led coalition forces began interdicting Iraq-bound merchant ships in August 1990, an effort that subsequently crippled Iraq's economy and denied its military the parts and supplies necessary to wage war. In the largest U.S. naval armada since 1945, strike aircraft from six U.S. carriers, which represented 23 percent of the total U.S. strike force, flew 23 percent of the overall combat missions.[40] The performance of the Navy's expensive Tomahawk cruise missile exceeded all expectations.

Navy strategists shared their leaders' sense of optimism about the Navy's ability to prevail in the upcoming budget wars. As Diamond noted, "At the time we thought that we could construct a rationale for preserving most of the Navy while transferring the brunt of the inevitable cuts to the Army . . . and Air Force . . . despite . . . [their] triumph in the Iraqi desert."[41] By the summer of 1991, however, any optimism had faded, replaced by growing trepidation about the Navy's ability to make itself relevant.

Conclusion

In the final analysis, "The Way Ahead" indicated only that U.S. naval leaders were coming to grips with emerging realities. Not surprisingly, given his operational and programmatic background, Kelso was not focusing on strategy. From his view, Powell and OSD had already figured out what the new strategy should be. Instead, he focused on finding efficiencies in the processes that determined the fleet's shape and size, particularly efficiencies that promised cost savings. In this regard Kelso's narrow focus, which was only marginally more acute than the focus of most of the CNOs who followed him, was manifestly representative in institutional terms. Edward Luttwak's observation about Trost and his lack of creativity and strategic sentience is more appropriately applied to Kelso, whose forte really was making things work.[42] Such skills are indispensable in running a large industrial organization and bending an immense bureaucracy to one's will. Kelso was comfortable with the "vision thing," but only in the corporate management sense.

In contrast, the ever-agile General Gray saw a real need for strategic leadership in a period of fundamental change. He recognized early on that changes in the political and military environment promised to bolster the Marine Corps' standing and move the Navy closer to the Marines' way of thinking. As a result, he saw to it that Marines were involved in the Navy's strategy-making process.

For his part, Miller did not focus on strategy either. Looking through the lens of operations and programming, he focused on determining naval requirements by envisioning the future of naval operations and abstracting operational- and not strategic-level goals. Still, Miller's ideas were remarkably prescient. These included his thoughts about tailoring naval forces as well as his ideas about addressing the regional CINCs' naval presence and foreign security assistance requirements; about the need for a surge capability; and about the growing importance of missions like humanitarian assistance, nation-building, peacekeeping, counterterrorism, and counterinsurgency. But Miller could not cohere all these ideas, destined to be vindicated, into a comprehensive vision of what naval forces do.

Navy strategists farther down the chain of command were palpably uncomfortable with the silence emanating from their leaders about the need for a new conceptual framework. They picked up on the Marine Corps' new thinking to broaden the way the Navy represented its capabilities while still retaining a global vision.

From the interaction of these agendas, two trends emerged. The first was the increasingly intimate Navy–Marine Corps collaboration. The Marine Corps had always been the junior partner in the Navy Department. Few admirals at any time had ever envisioned anything resembling strategic or even rhetorical equality with the Marine Corps. During the Cold War, for example, the Navy had to deal with a wide variety of complex, mostly technology-intensive warfare areas. These included antisubmarine, antiaircraft, antiship, electronic, and strike warfare; nuclear deterrence; intelligence gathering; and so on. However, only a few of these required a relationship with the Marine Corps. In terms of sea control, the Navy's primary concern, the Navy did not require a relationship with the Marine Corps at all. As Peter Swartz noted, from the Navy's view the Marine Corps' mission of amphibious warfare represented "one half of one-eighth" of these global warfare responsibilities.[43] To the Navy, the Marines, with their peckish demands on the Navy Department's budget, were themselves "rice bowlers."[44]

In the emerging post–Cold War environment, however, the Marine Corps strengthened the Navy's institutional flanks. The Marine Corps helped the Navy, which had lost the Soviet navy, to define a new threat, one that was now on shore. Power projection (i.e., naval strike warfare and amphibious assault) became the name of the game. For the Navy, this meant above all an emphasis on naval strike warfare as an essential element of the expeditionary operations that the Marine Corps claimed as its own. As evinced in "Warfighting," the Marine Corps' way of thinking held a certain methodology, a certain theoretical basis of understanding about how to approach open questions that Navy officers lacked, and that made Marines particularly valuable and, as in this case, influential in times of conceptual confusion.

However, one wonders if the Navy had done due diligence in partnering with the Marine Corps. It meant hewing to the Marines' narrow focus on the battlefield and the operational art of warfare, neither of which required a deeper understanding of the Navy's strategic purpose. In practical terms, consummating the partnership was none too easy. The Marine Corps was, in the words of a former commandant, a profoundly paranoid institution: paranoid that the government or the other U.S. military services would stamp out its existence.[45] Its history was all about adapting to ensure its survival, sometimes despite the Navy's best efforts to squash it. While the other U.S. military service leaders worried about their relative stature and budget share, the Marines' imperative was to survive. There were always plenty of voices prepared to argue that the United States does not need a Marine Corps; few other nations have a marine corps let alone one on a comparable scale. It was the Marines' imperative to get the nation to want a Marine Corps.

The Navy's strategists would have to deal with another element of the Marines' institutional culture. As the Marines' saying goes, there's a right way, a wrong way, and the Marine way. Dogmatically inclined, Marines make every effort to spell out and advance their peculiar way of thinking, which is all about the battlefield, the operational art, and operational concepts, and not looking too deeply at the assumptions behind them. For Navy officers, who preferred the Navy's looser, contingent, and largely unarticulated way of thinking, this meant that achieving consensus with the Marine Corps would invariably be a tortuous, frustrating, and drawn-out affair.

The other trend that emerged was the Navy's desire to put the Maritime Strategy behind it. As Trost found out, the problem lay in the way Americans understood or, more precisely, remembered the Cold War. As Trost noted, Congress did not concern itself much with how the Navy employed its forces in peacetime or how it realized systemic benefits. The Navy's purpose was understood in terms of its wartime roles, which meant that the safest and surest avenue to success in the budget wars was to justify its weapons systems in the context of war with the Soviets. After the war, Trost had tried to defend the fleet's size and structure by explaining the increased relevance of the lesser-included missions like presence, coercive diplomacy, and crisis management, which the Cold War Congress and Department of Defense officials had considered to be ancillary to those involving warfighting, but Congress would have none of it. As with "Maritime Strategy for the 1990s," Congress used only a Cold War metric to judge the Navy. To Congress the threat's disappearance meant that the Navy no longer needed as many ships or types of weapons systems, and attempting to justify them with these lesser-included missions was taken as mere stonewalling.

By the time Kelso took over, the Maritime Strategy had in his eyes become an albatross. It was doomed, along with the 600-ship Navy to which it was inextricably linked. "The Way Ahead" declared the Maritime Strategy to be, for all intents and purposes, a Cold War relic; it was on the shelf, and destined to remain there. The apparent ease with which the once dearly held Maritime Strategy was dispatched said much about the imperative to adapt politically regardless of the risk to the Navy's institutional cohesion. To gain distance from the Maritime Strategy, Kelso may have purposefully downplayed the need for a replacement strategy. Keeping one's head down and focusing on the details may have seemed the path of least resistance. The 1990–91 Gulf War, however, rendered all such temporizing calculations irrelevant. After the war had been fought and won, the Navy would again be weighed in the balance, and again obliged to explain itself.

Chapter 4

. . . From the Sea, 1991–92

The Gulf War: Catalyst of Distraction

Operation Desert Storm began on January 17, 1991, with a massive round-the-clock air assault that lasted forty-three days. The advent of twenty-four-hour cable news and real-time satellite communications brought the conflict into the living rooms of Americans like no other. What they saw foremost was the advanced technology of the U.S. military at work. In rapt fascination, they watched in-flight footage of Air Force jets destroying Iraqi aircraft bunkers, command and communications facilities, dug-in tanks, and narrow bridges with laser-guided bombs. They marveled at how the Air Force's F-117 stealth fighters flew over heavily defended Baghdad with impunity to deliver their laser-guided bombs with pinpoint accuracy, and how the Army's modern tanks and attack helicopters decimated the Iraqi army in a three-day ground offensive.

For the Army and the Air Force, whose ways of war the enemy had taken to task in the Vietnam War, the Gulf War was a redemptive victory like no other, further amplifying the lessons that the two services and the rest of the defense establishment drew from the conflict. Summing the belief of many, Richard Hallion stated that the Gulf War "confirmed a major transformation in the nature of warfare: the dominance of air power. . . . Simply (if boldly) stated, air power won the Gulf war."[1] Airpower had at last become decisive.

The Gulf War was also viewed as Goldwater-Nichols' first test, which it was seen to have passed with flying colors. The war validated Goldwater-Nichols' empowerment of the chairman and the CINCs. General Powell emerged as the administration's representative for the war: he was polished, articulate, and clearly in the know. In contrast to the Vietnam War, the field commander, Gen. H. Norman Schwarzkopf Jr., USA, the head of U.S. Central Command, did not suffer a micromanaging president or secretary of defense and was free to control every aspect of the war effort. Centralization continued in the management of the air campaign. To plan and execute it, the Air Force installed a rigid centralized planning and execution process that forced the services to integrate operationally. To Congress and the Pentagon, the integration was seen as a key to victory and a validation of Goldwater-Nichols.

The Gulf War also validated President Bush's focus on regional threats as the center of his strategic outlook and Paul Wolfowitz's belief that high-tech weapons could offset the manpower advantages of aspiring regional powers. For its part, Congress, as result of the victory, did not put up a fight to adjust the Base Force's numbers of ships, Army divisions, Air Force air wings, and active personnel. In short, the victory essentially ended the debate with Congress on the direction of U.S. strategy.[2]

The war showcased the abilities of the Army and the Air Force to wage war against regional powers. This was good news for the Army and the Air Force, which had lost most of their rationale with the end of the Cold War. The Navy, on the other hand, to all appearances had merely played a supporting role in a conflict that was now viewed as the template for how the U.S. military would be designed and used. Given its all-too-familiar marginalized status, the problem for Navy leaders was how to rerationalize the sea service and reassert the institution's relevance.

. . . In the Meantime

There was, however, little interest among Navy leaders to solve that problem, much of which was owed to gaps in critical positions.[3] During the Gulf War Vice Adm. Paul David Miller, deputy CNO for OP-07, and Vice Adm. Robert Kelly, deputy CNO for OP-06, were promoted to four-star rank and took command of the U.S. Atlantic and Pacific Fleets, respectively. Miller took with him many of his key officers from OP-07, whose influence waned after his departure. Kelly's replacement, Vice Adm. Leighton W. "Snuffy" Smith Jr., another carrier aviator, was not arriving until July 1991, a gap of seven months. Kelly's deputy was reluctant to initiate anything as he too was transferring. In June 1991 Gen. Al Gray retired and was replaced by Gen. Carl E. Mundy (1991–95). In the spring of 1991 Captain Diamond's boss, Rear Adm. Edward "Ted" Baker, the director of the Strategy, Plans, and Policy Division (OP-60), arranged to get Diamond on the CNO's calendar in mid-July 1991, ostensibly to provide a strategic introduction to Navy programming assessment. Baker thought correctly this would be the right time and vehicle to unveil the vision that the group had been working on for over a year in a way that created imperatives for discussions on the Navy's programs and budget.

In the meantime, the Navy was coming under increasing criticism about its wartime performance.[4] Defense writers noted that its aircraft had difficulties hitting targets because the Navy, unlike the Air Force, did not have enough precision-guided munitions; its aircrafts' in-flight visual recorders were either incompatible or too old for use by the television networks.[5] As another reporter noted, defending the ships in the Persian Gulf had taken up 30 percent of its total sorties.[6] The Navy's commander in the war, Vice Adm. Stanley R. Arthur, did not join Schwarzkopf and the other U.S. military services' commanders in Riyadh, Saudi Arabia. In accordance with Navy tradition, he stayed on his command ship in the Persian Gulf. Arthur's absence irritated Schwarzkopf, who held little interest in the conflict's naval dimensions. He pointedly ignored Arthur's one-star representative in Riyadh and did not trust the Navy much to follow orders.[7] Navy communications were not well integrated: Desert Storm's daily Air Tasking Order, which contained the day's operational tasking for U.S. and coalition aircraft, had to be flown out to the carriers each night.[8] The Navy did little to redress the perception that the Air Force, Army, and Marine Corps had won the war. "We just got lost in the overall picture," noted one spokesperson.[9] All of this served notice that the Navy was neither prepared for modern war nor was it on board with jointness, which the Pentagon and Congress were now implicitly defining as the Air Force's and the Army's way of doing business.

The day finally arrived when Diamond was able to present the group's vision to the CNO. Within minutes, however, the CNO flew into a rage.[10] He cursed and attacked every recommendation, particularly the one about cutting the submarine fleet. Things went from bad to worse when Diamond presented a slide entitled "The Coming USN Budget Train Wreck." Overnight, however, Kelso had a change of heart. The CNO called Diamond into his office the next day and agreed that the Navy needed to head in the direction that Diamond had recommended, which was to frame the two services' purpose in terms of expeditionary warfare in the littoral environment and as the nation's crisis-response team.[11] After the CNO thanked him for telling him what he needed to hear, he told Diamond that Kelly's relief, Snuffy Smith, who had just arrived, would oversee the development of a new vision. When Diamond relayed the message to Smith, the admiral noted, "We'll have to wait and see, but based on my thirty-five years of experience I can assure you that this here 'littoral warfare' stuff ain't never gonna fly in this man's Navy." He would be proven correct.

The Naval Force Capabilities Planning Effort

The project to develop a new strategic concept was one of the Navy's most organized and lengthy such efforts in the post–Cold War era. It started in October 1991 and ended in March 1992 and was known as the Naval Force Capabilities Planning Effort. Its purpose was to produce a report that, in "simple" and "direct" terms, defined the "strategic concept" for how sea power would be employed and the capabilities required to realize that concept.[12] The report was to lay the groundwork for a strategic statement that would be signed by the Secretary of the Navy, the CNO, and the commandant of the Marine Corps.

In the Navy, the term "strategic concept" has a special meaning. Samuel Huntington defined it in his "National Policy and the Transoceanic Navy," a 1954 article that was popular among Navy leaders throughout the post–Cold War period.[13] Huntington defined a strategic concept as a statement of a service's fundamental purpose or role, which, he asserted, is to implement national policy. He warned that if a service lacks a well-articulated strategic concept, "It becomes purposeless, it wallows about amid a variety of conflicting and confusing goals, and ultimately it suffers both physical and moral degeneration. . . . [And] the public and the political leaders will be confused as to the role of the service, uncertain as to the necessity of its existence, and apathetic or hostile to the claims made by the service upon the resources of society."[14] In short, Huntington's strategic concept was about rationalizing the Navy for political purposes and providing the fleet with a compelling conceptual framework to maintain the cohesiveness needed by a fighting force. But it did not constitute a strategy.

The Naval Force Capabilities Planning Effort was to be a bottom-up review: Nothing was sacred. The participants were encouraged to think creatively and not to parrot the positions of their respective warfare communities and staffs.[15] To encourage creative thinking, the discussions were on a not-for-attribution basis.[16] The effort was conducted at the Center for Naval Analyses, which was located a few miles south of the Pentagon. Smith and his counterpart, Lt. Gen. Henry Stackpole, USMC, led the effort, which was overseen by a committee of five senior officers. The Gang of Five, as it was known, consisted of two Marine generals and three rear admirals.[17] Of the three admirals, one was a carrier aviator who headed the powerful Assessment Division in OP-08, one was a submariner who headed the Programming Division in OP-08, and one was a surface officer; the surface officer was Ted Baker, the head of OP-60. Several Center for Naval Analyses' analysts were also involved, notably Thomas P. M. Barnett, who had a doctorate. He participated in all three phases.

The participants, mainly Navy commanders and captains and Marine Corps lieutenant colonels and colonels, were not limited to those who worked in the strategy shops or the Marine Corps Combat Development Command, where the Marines developed their doctrine and concepts. They also came from their respective programming and budget offices, and, in Phase II, from the operational staffs. "There was a conviction," as noted by Capt. Edward A. Smith Jr., an intelligence officer with a doctorate who participated in the first two phases, "that the answers sought needed to spring from those most familiar with the capabilities and limitations of naval power—experienced naval officers."[18] That conviction spoke to the institutional assumption that operational experience, and not historical knowledge or theory, was the superior form of knowledge.

Phase I: The Transitioneers, the Big Sticks, and the Cold Worriers Cannot Agree

The Phase I participants were to assess changes in the strategic environment and what those changes implied for the roles and missions of U.S. naval forces.[19] Phase I started in late October 1991 and ended in late December 1991. The eighteen officers came from OPNAV, Headquarters Marine Corps, and the Marine Corps Combat Development Command.

Almost immediately, the Phase I group divided into three camps, the result of a brief given by William H. J. Manthorpe Jr., the deputy director of the Office of Naval Intelligence.[20] Manthorpe, a retired Navy captain, had determined that historically the interval between the end of one threatening global empire and

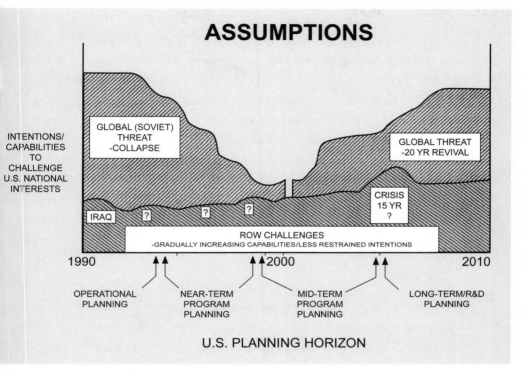

ASSUMPTIONS

INTENTIONS/
CAPABILITIES
TO
CHALLENGE
U.S. NATIONAL
INTERESTS

GLOBAL (SOVIET)
THREAT
-COLLAPSE

GLOBAL THREAT
-20 YR REVIVAL

CRISIS
15 YR
?

IRAQ   ?   ?   ?

ROW CHALLENGES
-GRADUALLY INCREASING CAPABILITIES/LESS RESTRAINED INTENTIONS

1990   2000   2010

OPERATIONAL
PLANNING

NEAR-TERM
PROGRAM
PLANNING

MID-TERM
PROGRAM
PLANNING

LONG-TERM/R&D
PLANNING

U.S. PLANNING HORIZON

Figure 4.1. The Manthorpe Curve
Source: Courtesy of Capt. William H. J. Manthorpe Jr., USN (Ret.).

the rise of another was twenty years, which meant the next one would materialize around 2011. If not the Soviets, it would be some Eurasian power. Independent of that cycle, there was a continuous low level of conflict brought about by the rest-of-the-world threats that periodically precipitated crises for the great powers. Extrapolating from Korea (1950–53), Vietnam (1965–75), and the Gulf War (1990–91), Manthorpe calculated the interval between crises to be fifteen years, which meant the next one would be around 2005. Manthorpe's analysis implied that the United States had some breathing space before the next global threat emerged and could therefore focus on the rest-of-the-world threats for a while.

Each of the camps claimed an area on Manthorpe's curve (see figure 4.1) that it thought was the most important, while the curve itself became the Rorschach test by which all of the effort's drafts were tested. According to Barnett, the camps were the Transitioneers, the Big Sticks, and the Cold Worriers.

THE TRANSITIONEERS

The Transitioneers focused on the curve's left side, where the rest-of-the-world threats, no longer restrained by superpower pressures, were expanding and, in the aggregate, threatening the United States' ability to manage a safe transition out of the Cold War to construct a new order, which would prevent the onset of the next global threat.[21] The Transitioneers were the cops on the beat. They believed strongly in the importance of day-to-day constabulary and coercive diplomatic missions. In terms of force structure, they believed in larger numbers of lower-cost twenty-first-century equivalents of the Victorian gunboat. The Transitioneers were predominantly Marines and surface officers, whose outlook reflected how they operated, which was at a more local, hands-on level than the levels of the Big Sticks and the Cold Worriers.

THE BIG STICKS

The Big Sticks (as in "speak softly") believed that the versatile capabilities of the carriers, Tomahawk-armed cruisers, and amphibious assault ships made them relevant across Manthorpe's curve regardless of the threat. The Big Sticks were more selective. They believed in forward presence, but not in tackling the rest-of-the-world threats en masse, which would exhaust their forces and erode their assets. Instead, they would handle select rest-of-the-world threats, notably regional powers; pummeling these would deter other regional threats and prevent these threats from becoming global threats. Big Sticks were mainly carrier aviators, but included a few Marines and surface officers as well. The Big Sticks held in high regard the carrier's ability to deter and wage war. The Big Sticks were willing to accept the inefficiencies involved in using high-end platforms for low-end missions to keep the fleet's capabilities within the sweet spot of preparedness for general war.

COLD WORRIERS

Finally, the Cold Worriers saw only the right side of the curve, where the specter of the next Soviet Union loomed large. They argued that rest-of-the-world threats did not pose an existential threat to the United States (i.e., a threat that could destroy the nation). Only global threats posed an existential threat, and the rise of those threats was inevitable, which meant the United States needed to make hay technologically. These officers, so-named because they worried about

the next global threat, wanted the nation to focus on sharpening the military's technological edge, developing revolutionary high-end "silver bullets," and maintaining the industrial base. The United States needed to keep its powder dry and
resist the temptation to remake the world. Pursuing the rest-of-the-world threats
would only divert the military's attention and squander resources in quagmires
of dubious strategic value that would be better spent on the military's future.
The Cold Worriers were, for the most part, submariners. For the first time since
the early 1960s, the submariners were faced with losing their dominant position
in the Navy and were clearly not happy about it.[22] The Cold Worriers worried
about that, too.

Throughout Phase I, a steady stream of visitors stopped by to offer advice.[23]
These included officials from intelligence agencies, Congress, defense industry,
academia, and research organizations, as well as Army and Air Force planning staffs,
the CNO, the commandant, and Secretary Garrett. For their part, congressional
staffers wanted to ensure the Phase I group fully appreciated the importance of
the emerging phenomenon of globalization, which they said would be a transformative force. They asserted that the network of interests and trade resulting from
interdependence would become central to U.S. economic power, whose strategic
importance would rival if not exceed that of U.S. military power. However, the
participants had difficulty relating the U.S. military to U.S. economic goals. As
Ed Smith pointed out, "The military or naval connection to national economic
security, however, was not made clear in contemporary policy or academic writings."
It was a revealing statement, one that noted not just the long-standing gap in
political thinking and academic research on the topic, but also the fact that Navy
officers did not think it their responsibility to articulate that relationship.

To their credit, however, the participants tackled the problem. At first they
explored the application of direct military action to achieve U.S. economic goals.
Interdependence meant that states were more vulnerable to outside economic
pressures such as blockades. Securing access to resources and markets in a time
of war was one thing, but, as Ed Smith noted, "securing peacetime access carried
unsavory connotations of gunboat diplomacy of the nineteenth century, something that would have no place in the twenty-first."[24]

The Phase I group came to relate U.S. naval operations to economic security
in terms of regional stability, which highlighted the importance of deterrence
and crisis response missions. Noting that U.S. naval forces have an indirect but
important effect on U.S. economic interests, the group called for a subtler U.S.

overseas presence. But there was little understanding of what forward presence meant apart from being in a position to respond to a crisis or to deter, which is what it effectively had meant during the Cold War. Nor was there much understanding of how forward presence worked to bring stability, if it worked at all. Overall, the range of instabilities that could upset the U.S. economy was thought to be too broad and the naval services' resources too few to operate effectively as a global police officer.[25] In effect, the group saw no reason why the Navy's warfighting and diplomatic roles should not remain preeminent over its constabulary one.

The effort's final report reflected only a marginally clearer understanding of the relationship. The authors of its global economic section, Barnett and Jack Mayer, agreed that global integration needed to be factored into U.S. strategy, but offered only generalities.[26] The authors noted that U.S. naval forces played an important practical and symbolic role in demonstrating how the United States was committed to ensuring stability in the Middle East and Asia and maintaining the flow of trade that originated from and passed through these regions. They noted that there was a clear link between regional stability and U.S. business investment. In the end, however, Barnett and Mayer also conceded that the military's impact in bolstering regional stability was largely indirect. "It is not possible to gain a firm grasp of how big a naval force is needed to generate clear benefit to the U.S. economy through the promotion of regional stability," they noted. Instead, they asserted that "the clearer argument for the U.S. maintaining its forces remains in mitigating the effects of political fragmentation rather than encouraging economic integration."[27] The authors were struggling to understand just how the Navy realized systemic benefits. In terms of conceptual understanding and theoretical constructs, they were operating in virgin territory; during the Cold War, neither the RAND-styled civilian strategists, political scientists, economists, nor the Navy for that matter had ever addressed the Navy's systemic effects.

Phase II: The Warfighters versus the Policy Wonks

Phase II's job was to develop a draft strategic concept.[28] It started in early January 1992 but ended in late February in a deadlock, which necessitated an unplanned third phase. Consensus was difficult to achieve, not only because of the size of the Phase II group, which doubled to forty, but also because of its composition. The newcomers, only a few of whom were members of the Navy's strategy community, came from the numbered fleet staffs (e.g., the U.S. Sixth Fleet) and the Navy component commanders' staffs (e.g. U.S. Naval Forces Europe) and the Marine equivalents. In short, the newcomers' more warfighting orientation counterbalanced the Phase I participants' perspective, which was more about strategy and the need to rationalize the Navy in political terms.

The arguments in Phase II were about warfighting versus peacetime requirements, and just how to justify forward deployment. Unlike warfighting, there was little clarity or consensus about nonkinetic naval purposes, which had not taken center stage in the Maritime Strategy. Consequently, as Ed Smith noted, "there was a strong tendency . . . to focus solely on the familiar aspects of 'warfighting' and to treat all other peacetime functions as lesser-included cases, operations any force equipped for war would surely be able to undertake."[29]

On one side were the Navy operators and Marine warriors. They found it incomprehensible to relate the Navy's purpose in terms of peacetime missions and argued that any attempt to base it on anything but warfighting would jeopardize the fleet's acceptance of the strategic concept. On the other side were, in Ed Smith's words, the "Washington political-military wonks," which included most of the Navy's strategists and Barnett.[30] The wonks sought to build a consensus about the importance of peacetime requirements like presence, crisis response, and coercive diplomacy, and how such missions influenced and deterred threats and rationalized forward deployment.

The wonks were swimming upstream. Discussions with staffers from the House Armed Services Committee as well as white papers written by its chairman, Congressman Leslie "Les" Aspin Jr. (D-WI), revealed that few in Congress understood the worth of naval missions short of war.[31] "The primary reason Americans want military forces," Aspin noted, "is to have the option of fighting when other means fail."[32] Newcomer Capt. Bradd C. Hayes noted, "The working group wrestled with ways to convince Congress and the public of the importance of tasks short of conflict conducted by forward-deployed forces."[33]

However, congressional staffers and the Army and Air Force did understand the merits of forward deployment in terms of one kind of peacetime mission: crisis response, a mission in which the Army and Air Force conceded that naval forces played a leading if not preeminent role. But as a whole, the Phase II group lacked conceptual understanding about that as well. As Ed Smith noted, "There was no broad understanding even inside the Naval Service of the peculiar capabilities maritime forces brought to an unfolding crisis or, indeed, of why they seemed to be the instrument of choice for political leaders dealing with overseas crisis." He continued, "Indeed, there was a vigorous debate even among the naval officers in the group over how, if at all, 'presence' contributed to deterring crises and conflict."[34]

Clearly, the group suffered from a profound lack of theoretical knowledge about the relationship between naval forces and crisis response and how presence deterred conflict.

To help its thinking, the Phase II group had the Center for Naval Analyses update its study on U.S. crisis responses.[35] The update revealed that of the 325 times the military responded to crises between 1946 and 1991, only 12 percent of the responses directly involved Soviet reactions. Eighty-three percent of the responses involved naval forces. Since 1977 carriers have been involved in 70 percent of the responses, the Marines in 59 percent, and surface combatants in 17 percent. In short, the Phase II group realized that the day-to-day focus of U.S. naval forces was not on open-ocean threats, but on local land-based ones.

Given the Bush strategy's emphasis on presence and crisis response, the group sought to leverage crisis response as a unique capability that justified forward deployment. Forward presence brought access, influence, and a swift response during a crisis. As the updated study revealed, the crises generally involved forces already in the immediate vicinity. If a regional conflict was unavoidable, naval forces could kick in the door to secure and otherwise protect the access required to insert ground- and land-based air forces.

Unfortunately, the Phase II group could not reach a consensus. Amid eighteen-hour days, tempers flared and patience wore thin as the deadline for the completion of Phase II loomed. As Barnett noted, "The atmosphere was incredibly tense. . . . As the weeks dragged on without resolution, each of the Gang of Five would anoint his own personal best boy to go off on his own and try writing the magnum opus all of us knew would eventually have to be written. In each and every painful incident, the resulting personal vision was summarily rejected by the congress as a whole."[36] Disagreements revolved around how much to invest conceptually (and therefore fiscally) across Manthorpe's curve and across the spectrum of warfare. The Navy's high regard for consensual decision making and operational experience had hamstrung the process. In the end, there were simply too many views and too little conceptual understanding beyond personal experience to structure the debate.

The final brief to the Gang of Five was a disaster. The five moved to another room and much yelling was overheard.[37] The following week saw Rear Admiral Baker replaced by Col. Thomas L. Wilkerson, the assistant chief of staff for

Plans, Policies, and Operations, Headquarters Marine Corps, a participant who had recently been selected as a brigadier general. In the 1980s Wilkerson had helped Navy strategists draft early versions of the Maritime Strategy, an experience that, no doubt, provided an understanding of Navy thinking and the skills to reconcile differences.[38] He formed a core group of renegade thinkers, who had two weeks to reach consensus and come up with something.[39]

Phase III: Consensus Is Finally Reached

One obstacle involved changing the definition of the fundamental purpose of naval forces from achieving command of the seas to using command of the seas. Particularly to submariners, achieving command of the seas was an end, not a means. Wilkerson found consensus, which required assuring the Phase III group, whose ranks were depleted as many had to return to their commands, that sea control capabilities would not be abandoned because the Navy still needed to achieve local sea control in the littoral.[40] Now that the United States had command of the seas, the real question for the Navy was what to do with it.

The other obstacle was the warfighting-peacetime problem. The Army and the Air Force had cornered the market on regional conflict and major combat operations. Going that route, however, was to deny the unique capabilities of naval forces to operate across the spectrum of warfare and leave unclaimed the remaining elements of Bush's strategy—that is, presence and crisis response. So, the Phase III group decided to stake out everything but the major conflict portion of the spectrum, as represented by an inverted pyramid in a slide from the Naval Force Capabilities Planning Effort's brief (figure 4.2).

This meant shifting the justification for naval power away from the centrality of warfighting, a risky move. To many, the decision was not just unpalatable, but incomprehensible. Given Congress' and the public's understanding of the military's purpose, justifying the naval services in terms of more abstract notions of crisis management, deterrence, and stability was problematic. The tried and true route to success in the budget wars was to justify weapons in the context of war, not peace. No less important was the belief that the shift away from warfighting was too countercultural for the fleet to accept.

Consequently, the Phase III group redefined the threat.[41] As noted in the *National Military Strategy* of 1992, the threat was "instability and [the risk of] being unprepared to handle a crisis or war that no one predicted or expected."[42] In other words, the threat was not defined in terms of traditional confrontation

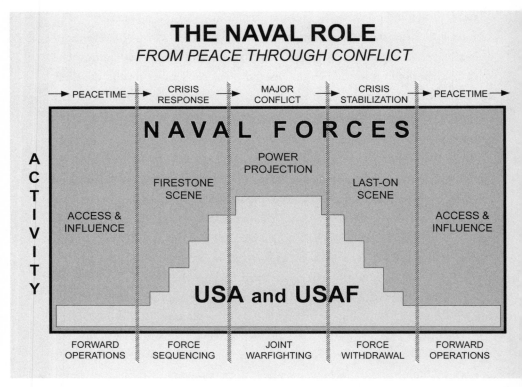

Figure 4.2. The Pyramid Slide
Source: "Final Report": Enclosure (2), slide 32.

and rivalry. Instead, it was defined in terms of a systemic geoeconomic and geo-political abstraction—instability—in which a general sort of risk was ostensibly apparent, and in which the threat, both military and political, arose from a fail-ure of preparedness. The military's ability to act swiftly, made possible by good preparation, was intended both to deter crises and to reassure allies and partners that any instability that might arise would be contained and not allowed to escalate in ways that threatened everyone's interests. As reflected in the *National Military Strategy*, the greatest threat to stability was thought to be regional war, which placed a premium on the deterrent value of forward-deployed forces to prevent conflict and manage crisis response.

The Phase III group's new and finally agreed-on line of thinking was reflected in the Naval Force Capabilities Planning Effort's core statement: "The fundamen-tal purpose of Naval forces is to use command of the seas: to *protect* U.S. citizens and territory; to demonstrate U.S. commitment overseas and *promote* our interests through forward, sea-based operations; to *deter* or *contain* crises through the ability to respond rapidly with credible and sustainable sea-based forces; and, when necessary, to *project* U.S. combat power *ashore*."[43] This approach leveraged the broad and flexible capabilities of U.S. naval forces across the spectrum, and in support of warfighting as well as broader diplomatic and economic interests. The Phase III group argued that although U.S. naval forces are structured primarily for war, free access from the sea means those forces are well suited to influence events in times of peace. It argued that naval forces must conduct forward-deployed operations and focus on the coastal or littoral areas.

In war, U.S. naval forces would strike targets, seize and defend ports and airfields, and otherwise enable access for the introduction of land and air forces.[44] They would provide maximum influence with minimum intrusion. They were the first on scene and the last to leave and did not need permanent forward bases to undertake the missions associated before and after major combat operations. The group noted that all future military operations will be joint, and that joint warfare is essential to victory. The group also asserted that the Navy and Marine Corps team, with its sea-air-ground forces, was inherently integrated and would coordinate with the other U.S. military services.

The Phase III group's vision had five elements: (1) operating forward, (2) responding flexibly and rapidly, (3) enabling joint operations, (4) maneuvering from the sea, and (5) sustaining from the sea. These drove four operational capabilities: command and control U.S. naval forces, dominate the battlespace, project power, and sustain forces.[45]

To facilitate the shift from war at sea to war from the sea, the group recommended establishing commands to develop and integrate Navy–Marine Corps warfighting concepts, doctrine, and training.[46] It recommended reorganizing naval forces into expeditionary fleet and task forces that were tailored to facilitate sharing of naval capabilities by the regional CINCs. A standing expeditionary strike fleet would be the primary naval warfighting organization in a region and would be commanded by the theater's principal naval operational commander. Its subordinate command would be the naval expeditionary task force, an air-surface-ground task force comprising a carrier, amphibious assault ships, and Tomahawk-armed ships. Commanded by a single officer, it would be tailored to specific regions where it would disperse for presence operations and mass for exercises or conflict.

Perhaps because it ran out of time, Phase III did not identify the capabilities its vision required. Its desires were clear, though: "Because of their flexibility and mobility, [U.S. naval forces] are perhaps our most versatile military assets for the spectrum of operations from forward presence through crisis response. Therefore, *naval forces should be sized and shaped to optimize their usefulness in the littoral area.*"[47] This did not mean focusing on the next global threat. At the least, it implied some kind of gradual reduction in open-ocean sea control assets.

In all, the conclusion of the Naval Force Capabilities Planning Effort's final report revealed the scars and victors: "Although reasonable men can disagree, indications are that the threat of global war has been pushed off the screen into the next century. This shift in the strategic landscape allows naval forces to concentrate on littoral warfare—*a major shift from 'blue water' to shallow water.*"[48] Clearly, the Cold Worriers lost their case. The Phase III group advocated not for a high-tech fleet designed for high-end warfare, but for a fleet that was forward deployed, focused on local operations close ashore, and balanced (to what extent was to be determined) more to the requirements of naval power projection. In other words, the Transitioneers and the Big Sticks had prevailed.

" . . . From the Sea"

Meanwhile, the world had continued to change. In December 1991 the Soviet Union was disestablished. Beyond that cardinal fact, however, Bush's New World Order was proving to be more rhetoric than reality, devoid of clear purpose or plans as far as concrete actions were concerned. Wielding immense influence, Powell refused to support plans for military interventions overseas unless they passed an impossibly strict set of pragmatic criteria, the most notable of which was a positive answer to the question "Are vital national security interests threatened?" This was of course the problem throughout the 1990s: absent the Soviet threat there was no consensus on what constituted a national security interest, apart from petroleum and homeland defense.

After the Naval Force Capabilities Planning Effort ended in March 1992, Capt. Howard "Rusty" Petrea, the head of Wilkerson's renegade thinkers, and Capt. Ed Smith began developing a draft white paper, which they had based on the Naval Force Capabilities Planning Effort's final report. They had provisionally entitled the draft "Power from the Sea," which was later retitled " . . . From the Sea" to highlight that naval forces brought not only kinetic force but also influence, deterrence, and enabling support.[49]

Throughout the summer of 1992 the two captains managed the traditional time-consuming process of sending out versions of the draft white paper to the four-star (and many of the three-star) admirals, incorporating their inputs, receiving guidance from Vice Admiral Smith on how to incorporate them, sending it over to Headquarters Marine Corps, and then incorporating the Marines' inputs before sending the penultimate draft around again for approval. The new Secretary of the Navy, Sean C. O'Keefe (1992–93), and his special assistant, Cdr. James G. Stavridis, a member of the strategy community who had a doctorate in international relations, completed the final drafts.

Meanwhile, as the drafts circulated around OPNAV, a few Navy leaders realized something was amiss. As noted by Vice Adm. William A. Owens, the deputy CNO for OP-08, "Internal Navy assessments, comparing the thrust of the white paper drafts with the Navy's fiscal year 1994 program . . . indicated significant discrepancies between what the Navy would formally pronounce as its operational concept and the way it would propose to allocate resources." Something had to give. Either the Navy's POM or the white paper had to change. Owens pointed out, "What we needed was a new consensus on what the new Navy should be. The basic problem that summer [1992] was an absence of consensus."[50] In other words, there were already doubts among at least some senior Navy leaders that the Naval Force Capabilities Planning Effort represented a consensus real enough to influence resource decisions.

Finally, in late September 1992—six months after the end of the Naval Force Capabilities Planning Effort and close to three years after the fall of the Berlin Wall—the Navy unveiled its first post–Cold War strategy. It was called " . . . From the Sea: Preparing the Naval Service for the 21st Century" and was signed by Secretary O'Keefe, CNO Kelso, and the commandant, General Mundy. " . . . From the Sea" appeared as a four-page article in *Proceedings* as well as a news release and later as a glossy pamphlet.[51]

" . . . From the Sea" had much in common with the Naval Force Capabilities Planning Effort's white paper. It was more comprehensive and polished, and its arguments were more cogent, which should not be surprising given its high level of attention. Both highlighted the unique capabilities of U.S. naval forces to operate across the spectrum of conflict. " . . . From the Sea" noted that the Navy and the Marine Corps were full participants in Bush's strategy of strategic deterrence and defense, forward presence, crisis response, and reconstitution. In an overview statement, it noted, "American Naval Forces provide powerful yet unobtrusive presence; strategic deterrence; control of the seas; extended and continuous on-scene crisis response; project precise power from the sea; and provide sealift if larger scale warfighting scenarios emerge. These maritime capabilities are particularly well tailored for the forward presence and crisis response missions articulated in the President's National Security Strategy."[52] Both highlighted the Navy's operational virtues, and how those virtues were well aligned to national policy; and both focused on the littorals.

However, somewhere between the Naval Force Capabilities Planning Effort and O'Keefe's signature, " . . . From the Sea" had become a different animal. Gone were arguments about U.S. economic interests in a more interdependent world. The word "trade" appears nowhere. Likewise, the words "stability," "commerce," and "transport" are absent. The word "global" is mentioned only once, unlike "regional," which is mentioned numerous times. Naval leaders had deleted discussions of a systemic nature that had animated the Naval Force Capabilities Planning Effort's final report and drafts of the white paper. Despite the belief among congressional staffers that economic and political integration would profoundly change the world, " . . . From the Sea," as Maj. Frank G. Hoffman, USMC Reserve, noted, "studiously ignores presence and peacetime tasks in support of political and economic objectives."[53] In short, " . . . From the Sea" had become more politicized, more attendant to the realities of domestic politics.

" . . . From the Sea" focused on major combat operations, high-tech power projection, and warfighting. Naval leaders were not about to yield the field of major conflict to the Army and the Air Force. The Navy and the Marine Corps were more than just door keepers or crisis managers. Undoubtedly, O'Keefe and Kelso worried that defining the Navy in terms other than major combat operations was politically dangerous. Regional conflict was the centerpiece of U.S. post–Cold War strategy. The lessons of the Gulf War were being applied in terms of expensive, high-tech weapons systems, which accorded with how Congress understood the military's purpose. In this milieu, the safest, surest route to asserting the Navy's relevance was to justify it in those terms.

Reflecting the changes wrought by Goldwater-Nichols, " . . . From the Sea" catered to the CINCs, who now had a hand in determining the requirements that ostensibly shaped the services' resource decisions. " . . . From the Sea" was about how U.S. naval forces provided the regional CINCs with a greater range of options than could the other U.S. military services. With forward deployments and a balanced fleet, U.S. naval forces promised a wider, more responsive repertoire of generic capabilities that would obviate the need for the regional CINCs to turn to the Army and Air Force, with their ponderous build-ups, sovereignty issues, and societal debates about their deployment. Since the purpose of the services was seen as providing capabilities to the CINCs, " . . . From the Sea" was predicting (or, more precisely, betting on) a fluid and chaotic future in which the regional CINCs would demand the kinds of capabilities that the naval services were offering.

Naval power projection now reigned supreme at the center of the Navy's strategic vision. The end of the Cold War meant the Navy no longer had to attend to the requirements of global sea control. Achieving local sea control in the littorals would not be easy, however. Layered coastal defenses and advanced weaponry posed formidable challenges. Mine warfare had never been a Navy priority and would now have to become one. Shallow-water antisubmarine warfare against quiet diesel submarines was problematic, as was ballistic missile defense. Achieving local sea control meant retaining large numbers of attack submarines. It meant leveraging technology in an environment that demanded a balanced set of capabilities. In other words, to be effective in supporting the landward side of the battlespace and surviving the dangers of the seaward, the Navy needed technological-tactical solutions, which is to say that it needed once more to solve the kinds of problems it liked best.

Despite the changes, " . . . From the Sea" still fully represented the Marines' core thinking. " . . . From the Sea" represented a strategic concept in Huntington's sense of the term, which meant it not only rationalized the naval services but also provided a conceptual framework compelling enough to maintain the cohesiveness needed by a fighting force. To Marines, the concept of warfighting, like the implicit notion of operations to the Navy, was a consecrated one. It was central to the Marines' identity as a fighting force. In many ways, the focus of " . . . From the Sea" on littoral and maneuver warfare and warfighting in general reflected the contributions of Marine officers and the Marine Corps' rising influence. The littoral was not a new environment for them.

For the Marine Corps, " . . . From the Sea" represented a fundamental change in U.S. naval strategy and the Navy–Marine Corps relationship. The absence of a naval threat meant the fleet would become the primary facilitator of the Marines' expeditionary focus. In other words, the focus on the littoral reversed the Navy–Marine Corps relationship, which was already changing because Goldwater-Nichols had shifted operational control of Marine units from the Navy's fleet commanders directly to their respective regional CINCs.[54] To the Marines, they were now the supported force, and the Navy was the supporting force. To them, " . . . From the Sea" was about getting the Navy to adapt materially, conceptually, and culturally to expeditionary warfare, a concept alien to most Navy officers.

To the Marine Corps, the concept of "expeditionary" was an institutional imperative, an outlook, and a mission that had shaped its organization and force structure. The Marine Corps was a harmonious, tightly integrated force that could operate on land, at sea, and in the air, but it was not a force designed to dominate any of these battlespaces. Within the terms of the Marine Corps tradition, "expeditionary" meant using only what you had in your rucksack and possessing a certain joie de vivre to secure success in trying conditions with limited resources. It meant getting your hands dirty and fixing the thorniest of problems on the periphery of Americans' attention. It meant focusing on skills and speed, and not being dependent on technology. To Marines, the technological-centric approach hindered effectiveness in small and limited conflicts where cultural and political factors dominated. Shifting the Navy's institutional focus onto the Marine Corps' operational space did not, in itself, ensure that these gaps in understanding and attitude would be bridged. As " . . . From the Sea" noted, "'Expeditionary' implies a mind-set, a culture, and a commitment."[55] The term "commitment" reflected the expectation that the Navy would shift the fleet's balance toward capabilities required in the littoral and otherwise absorb elements of the Marine Corps' outlook and culture. It meant integrating doctrine, training, and command structures. But "doctrine" was a pejorative word in the Navy. It was a major concession for the Navy to accept the Marine Corps' approach, as reflected in the promise to establish a naval doctrine command that would alternately be commanded by a two-star admiral and a Marine general.

With the Navy's emphasis on high-tech naval strike warfare as a freestanding expedient and high-tech solution on one side and the Marine Corps' emphasis on low-tech expeditionary warfare in the littoral and doctrinal integration on the other, one can already see the cracks in the Navy–Marine Corps partnership. Navy leaders had reengineered the white paper and now wanted a high-tech fleet that reflected the thinking of the Cold Worriers, but they wanted to use it for the missions envisioned by the Transitioneers. For the Marines, nothing had changed between the draft white paper and " . . . From the Sea." For them, the future was not so much about major combat operations as it was about as the messy crises that percolated under the radar, and the sort of nearly constant operations that required naval expeditionary force. The Marines were essentially Transitioneers, and wanted a fleet to match, which, as will be seen, they did not get.

One wonders if the Marine Corps had done due diligence in selecting its post–Cold War partner. The Navy was an entitled institution that thought about strategy in terms of resources, advanced technologies, and generic capabilities, and in terms of balancing its warfare communities. But of course the Marines knew all that. They knew that it would take much to get Navy leaders to adapt to the Marines' fundamentally different way of thinking. For their part, few admirals had contemplated what the Marine Corps might require of the Navy to consummate the relationship.

Conclusion

The timing of the Gulf War at the beginning of the post–Cold War era was fortuitous. Its lessons were made indelible by the redemptive victory, which many believed had finally exorcized the demons of Vietnam, and by the need to defend the force structure against demands for a peace dividend.[56] The Gulf War was viewed as a template rather than for what it was, a sui generis conflict that reinforced long-standing tendencies of the American approach to strategy while obscuring its limitations behind a penumbra of tactical success. Bush's goal was to move Iraq's army out of Kuwait without leaving Iraq prostrate and unable to balance Iran. Strategic goals were essentially operational goals, which is to say they were achieved primarily by virtue of the way the war was fought.

And that way did not require the application of nuanced force or the need to occupy the country or otherwise understand cultural differences. The lack of cover and the large temperature differential at night made it easier for U.S. airborne infrared sensors to destroy Iraqi armor with laser-guided bombs. The open deserts and the lack of Iraqi sensors enabled rapid maneuver by large-scale armored forces. The theater's numerous port complexes and airfields were among the largest and most modern in the world. The Gulf War was, in essence, a scale-model of the Cold War's Central Front in Europe manned on the other side by an inept and inert foe. The advanced weaponry applied during the war facilitated the development of a reductionist theory of discrete destruction that promised a quick, efficient, and painless mode of warfare, one that did not unduly stress the patience of U.S. society as had the protracted and attritional-based mode of warfare that had been employed in Vietnam.[57]

In other words, one would be hard pressed to find a scenario more suited to showcase the Air Force's and Army's Cold War capabilities and doctrine and reinforce the American way of war. It was the victory in the Gulf War, and not in the Cold War—a war where most of the action was hypothetical and the reasons for victory too ambiguous to support any service's claim of preeminence—that provided the Army and the Air Force with a strong measure of claimancy on the direction of U.S. strategy and a solid foundation on which military theorists viewed the future. The tactical lessons derived from a forty-three-day operation essentially eclipsed the more opaque strategic lessons of a fifty-year war. In Congress and throughout the U.S. military, most particularly in the Pentagon, there was a profound lack of reflection on why the Cold War was won. Few in those institutions had any interest in understanding the nature of that victory and in applying any lessons drawn from it to the problems of the post–Cold War era. As Colin Gray noted, "In retrospect, the Gulf War of 1991, while arguably the first war on behalf of a new world order, was a huge distraction for American statecraft at a moment of historically rare opportunity for creative policymaking."[58]

The debates of the 1990s on how to conceptualize warfare were consequently viewed exclusively from a land- and strike-warfare perspective, in which naval forces were cast either in a supporting role or as platforms from which strike operations and amphibious assault operations could be mounted. In truth, the Gulf War was a benign reality that would be repeated only once in the post–Cold War era: in the brief and shining moment of the United States–led invasion of Iraq in spring 2003. After that, the protracted insurgency revealed to many the perils of reductionism and doctrinal rigidity, which forced the Army and the Air Force to embark on their own post–Cold War crises of confidence.

For its part, the Navy again found itself unprepared to lay out its case or defend itself in the aftermath of the Cold War's abrupt end and then again after the Gulf War. How the Navy handled such problems in the years immediately after World War II and the Cold War is striking. In each case, it assembled an ad hoc team of promising officers to solve what the Navy's leaders saw as the short-term problem of how to secure its relevance and preferred weapons systems. Admiral Burke's comment about the state of American naval thinking in the post–World War II years is equally applicable to these years: "People in the navy did not know very much about strategy. . . . That's why we did not have any organization to lay out the navy's case or defend ourselves. . . . We suffered from a lack of knowledge within the navy of what the navy was all about."[59]

Given the paucity of research, the Naval Force Capabilities Planning Effort's participants had little time to understand the effects of the Navy's nonkinetic Cold War missions of presence, crisis response, and coercive diplomacy, which, ironically, were the types of missions that now more than ever filled the day-to-day operational lives of Navy officers. Despite decades of operating across the full spectrum of warfare with far less prejudice to the lesser uses of force than was manifest by the other U.S. military services, these Navy officers, even those from the strategy community (which ostensibly did represent an organization that laid out the Navy's case), had little understanding of how naval power actually worked beyond a superficial and elementary basis.

Institutionally, it should not be surprising that the Navy did not turn to the Naval War College for insights. As noted by John Hattendorf, Ernest J. King Professor of Maritime History at the Naval War College, "In contrast to officers in other branches of service, naval officers, by and large, have tended to ignore the value of and advantages to be found in historical insight."[60] Such insights might have provided the participants with a clearer understanding of the relationship between U.S. naval operations and U.S. economic security, for example.

Once in the hands of Navy leaders, the draft of the white paper, which had been based on the Naval Force Capabilities Planning Effort's final report, changed. Given their backgrounds as CINCs, naval operational commanders, and programmers, one should not be surprised that they took a more operationally focused and politically expedient route, one that addressed how sea power would be employed, not why. To preserve its preferred force structure and style of warfare, the Navy aligned itself with the general focus of U.S. strategy on warfighting, regional conflict, jointness, and strike warfare. Strike warfare was a capability the Navy was well positioned to embrace technologically and conceptually, and was not incongruent with the Marines' focus on expeditionary warfare and warfighting. Such a move protected the carriers, which were needed in the scenarios in which U.S. officials now found themselves, scenarios in which the carriers had excelled during the Cold War. The Navy staked its claim on its ability to provide the regional CINCs with a breadth of capabilities, none more important than striking targets on shore on exceptionally short notice. As in the Cold War, the gravitational pull of advanced technologies and associated operational concepts was proving to be the safest and surest route to budgetary success.

The responsibilities of understanding how operational goals realized global U.S. interests and strategic goals were handed to the regional CINCs, OSD, and the Joint Staff with little protest from Navy leaders who were bent on seizing opportunities to demonstrate empirical evidence of naval worth. Their acquiescence facilitated the "acceptance of a single idea, a single and exclusively dominant military pattern of thought," as J. C. Wylie had forewarned in 1957.[61] And, coming out of the Gulf War, the U.S. military's dominant pattern of thought was now all about jointness, warfighting, and how "revolutionary" precision strike and informational capabilities promised to deliver swift and decisive victories against regional threats.

The changes wrought by Goldwater-Nichols, Powell, and the Gulf War essentially relieved the Navy from the more difficult task of understanding how achieving operational goals would lead to systemic results. Such changes allowed the Navy to focus on its priorities, which included making up ground lost to the Air Force and the Army in terms of relevance and tactical and technical proficiency on the joint battlefield. It was a task the Navy subsequently did very well, but it distracted it from exploring its deeper purpose.

With " . . . From the Sea," the basic course of U.S. naval strategy was set. The Navy had spent an extraordinary amount of time and resources to find what a few saw was a commonsense answer to the question of where to turn now that the naval threat had disappeared: the answer was that it would turn to threats on shore, a fact that seemed to escape the notice of Navy leaders who were busy heralding " . . . From the Sea" as revolutionary. Having solved its basic problem, the Navy made only minor course changes over the next dozen years. But even as " . . . From the Sea" was being published, Kelso was changing the process by which the Navy's force structure decisions were made, which undermined the expectation that " . . . From the Sea" would reshape the fleet.

Chapter 5

Forward . . . From the Sea, 1993–94

Kelso and the Reorganization of OPNAV

W hile naval leaders were finalizing " . . . From the Sea" in the summer of 1992, CNO Frank Kelso was busy overhauling OPNAV. Ostensibly, this was done to implement " . . . From the Sea," but in fact he had been contemplating it from the time he entered office.[1] Kelso was making the Navy's resource decision-making process more consensual, integrative, and efficient, all of which were tenets of W. Edwards Deming. Reflecting the CNO's thinking, Vice Adm. Bill Owens stated, "It was necessary to incorporate new standards, or criteria, for deciding program priorities, a new vocabulary to the debates over how to allocate the budget, and a new style of decision making." He explained, "These were required, in part, to break up the old categories and compartments consistent with the earlier strategy [i.e., the Maritime Strategy], and in part to develop quickly a new corporate sense of direction within the Navy."[2]

By reorganizing OPNAV, Kelso also sought to strengthen the Navy's position inside the Pentagon to account for the increased power of the chairman and the Joint Staff and the need to cater to the CINCs, something the other U.S. military services had not yet considered. Kelso's forte was in understanding how bureaucracies worked and where power resided. He was innovative, but only in a bureaucratic sense, which in the Pentagon may take one a long way, as it did here.

In the summer of 1992, Kelso renamed OPNAV's directorates to match the Joint Staff's. The OP codes were changed to N codes, "N" meaning Navy. OP-06, for example, became N3/N5, meaning it combined the functions of the Joint

Staff's Operations (J3—"J" for joint) and Strategic Plans and Policy (J5) director-ates. OP-07 was subsumed into Owens' OP-08, which was renamed Resources, Warfare Requirements, and Assessments (N8).[3] OP-07 had been both the inte-grator of requirements and arbitrator of priorities. The requirements were defined by the barons, that is, by the three-star admirals in OP-08 that presided over their respective warfare communities' programs.[4] Over time, the process had, as Owens noted, become a "bureaucratic drill" that preserved the power of lower-ranking officers to determine the fleet.[5] To break up these fiefdoms, the barons (whose billets had already been demoted to two stars) were placed under the vice admiral in charge of N8, who was Owens, Kelso's new point man.

Two months after Owens arrived in July 1992, Kelso instituted a new pro-cess to help the Navy rationalize its resource decisions to OSD, the CINCs, and the Joint Staff. Instead of basing priorities on naval warfare areas such as anti-submarine or strike warfare, the program sponsors had to base them on the joint warfare areas, of which there were seven: joint strike, joint littoral warfare, joint surveillance, joint space and electronic warfare/intelligence, strategic deterrence, strategic sealift/protection, and presence.

Each of these seven Joint Mission Areas had a chairman; all but two of the chairmen worked directly for N8, which prioritized the Navy's programs within their respective areas. After that, Owens chaired a series of review boards that decided the Navy's programmatic and budgetary priorities. The boards consisted of one- and two-star admirals, most of whom worked in N8, and a few Marine generals. Considered the Navy's most current senior operators, Kelso saw the one- and two-stars as the Navy's future leaders. As three- and four-stars, their decisions would be shaped and bounded by their own decisions years earlier. Kelso's iterative and consensual process decreased the need for the CNO to resolve conflict among OPNAV's three-star admirals and promoted a spirit of collective commitment among Navy admirals. For the next nine months, Owens' boards met three times a week for hours at a time. As Owens noted, "It became the most demanding, in terms of time and concentration, of all the tasks facing the senior members of the Navy staff."[6]

Owens reconfigured the Navy's resource decision-making process, and now largely controlled it. His rationale was striking: "The assessment process's most important contribution was to provide *the* forum and framework for the discus-sions that led to the *first full consensus* on the questions raised by the end of the Cold War: what the role of naval forces was to be in the future, and how those forces were to be sized, shaped, and structured."[7] In other words, for Owens and other programmers, neither the Naval Force Capabilities Planning Effort nor " . . . From the Sea" represented a full consensus. " . . . From the Sea" was not a top-down strategy as the Marines assumed, but a piece of paper that rationalized the Navy and its weapons systems and provided a conceptual framework for the fleet. Owens' process, the process that determined the Navy's budget and the fleet's shape and size, was the real strategy.

Owens' Plan for the Fleet

Kelso had centralized OPNAV to an unprecedented degree and handed Owens unprecedented control over its primary task of strategic programming. As the authors of a RAND study noted, Owens was now responsible for no less than "the integration of concepts, requirements, budgets, resource strategy, priorities, CINC liaison, and program and resource plans." In their words, Kelso's reorganization had "fundamentally changed the Navy's resource decision model from decentralized planning and programming to centralized decision-making and centralized execution."[8] Kelso ensured that N8 had the power and resources it needed. N8 had a three-star admiral (Owens), five two-stars, a dozen one-stars, and four hundred officers and civilians. In contrast, N3/N5 had a half-dozen admirals, including a three-star admiral, a two-star deputy, and a two-star admiral that led its one-hundred-person N51 (formally known as OP-60). OPNAV's resource side had always been bigger in terms of numbers (and now was bigger still), but more important, Kelso's changes shifted the balance of power in OPNAV. N8 was preeminent, while the once powerful OP-06 (now N3/N5) was marginalized, and would be increasingly so as the 1990s wore on.

The fleet that emerged from the new process conformed to Owens' strong views. Owens was the first of a handful of brilliant bureaucratic managers and visionary techno-strategists that would come to dominate American naval thinking in the post–Cold War era. A 1962 Naval Academy graduate, Owens was a submariner. Unusual for a submariner, he had two master's degrees, one in politics, philosophy, and economics from Oxford University and another in management from George Washington University. Owens, like another brilliant officer, Vice Adm. Arthur K. Cebrowski, had been a key member of the first Strategic Studies Group in 1981–82 that helped develop the Maritime Strategy. Owens was another programmer, who, like Kelso, had been the director of the Program Appraisal Office in the Office of the Secretary of the Navy.

Owens, along with Adm. Paul David Miller, had been prominent in the final drafting of " . . . From the Sea." Owens helped overrule the Transitioneers' vision of a fleet based on greater numbers of littoral-appropriate ships that relied on current technologies. Instead, he advanced a Cold Worriers' approach of finding high-tech solutions to operational problems. This route proved to be the ticket to consensus among the Navy's leaders, who opted for a smaller, more balanced, and more high-tech fleet. In short, " . . . From the Sea" was simply a means for Owens to explain the kind of fleet he had already determined and was already attempting to realize through the new process.

Released in the spring of 1993, Owens' plan for the fleet of the year 2001 was entitled Force 2001. It had been based on the Clinton administration's first budget estimates, and it also anticipated the results of the administration's five-month-long "Bottom-Up Review," which, in its words, was "a comprehensive review of the nation's defense strategy, force structure, modernization, infrastructure, and foundations."[9]

The review was an ambitious, no-holds-barred look at the military. It was supposed to address sensitive topics such as the role of the Army versus the Marine Corps in expeditionary operations, and the role of the Air Force and the Navy in long-range strike warfare. The "Bottom-Up Review" was the second review after the Base Force and the first to declare that the Soviet/Russian threat was no more. As noted by new Secretary of Defense Aspin, it promised "a lean, mobile, high-tech" military.[10] Aspin—a former McNamara Whiz Kid—promised to root out duplication and redundancy in the services.

The "Bottom-Up Review," which would be released in the fall of 1993, promised unequal cuts among the services. That expectation only exacerbated interservice tension. During the 1992 election, Clinton had proposed to cut another $60 billion over five years, on top of Bush's $50 billion.[11] Once in office, Clinton cut an additional $60 billion with further cuts on the horizon. Adjusted for inflation, defense spending promised to decline by 40 percent. Based on the fiscal year 1990 budget, the "Bottom-Up Review" reduced the military by a third, compared to the Base Force's one-fourth, this at a time when the number of the military's overseas operations was skyrocketing.[12] The fleet's size went from the Base Force's 451 (later changed to 416) to 346 of the "Bottom-Up Review," and the carrier fleet from 12 to 10.[13]

By hashing out the fleet's shape and size and proposing cuts well in advance, however, Owens pleased Congress and OSD's leaders. It seemed the Navy finally had its act together. As Ronald O'Rourke noted, "The Navy now shows every sign of being ahead of the other services."[14] As Vice Adm. Snuffy Smith conceded, however, the proposed cuts were motivated in part by the need to protect the twelve-carrier fleet.[15] Owens was not about to let the Joint Staff dictate the fleet's make-up. Still, Secretary Aspin, whose undisciplined management style was alienating many in the Pentagon, regarded Owens as what Aspin referred to as a "new thinker" and developed a close relationship with him.[16] In March 1994 Clinton promoted Owens to vice chairman of the Joint Chiefs of Staff, the second-most-senior officer in the military behind only Gen. John M. Shalikashvili, USA, who was Colin Powell's successor.

To the dismay of the Marines, who were expecting a more littoral-oriented fleet structure, Force 2001 did not much alter the fleet's composition. A reduction in the number of attack submarines was the only indicator that the Cold War had ended. The number of amphibious ships did not grow comparatively, but took its share of cuts as well.[17] In short, Owens and other Navy leaders believed that " . . . From the Sea" and Force 2001 were not about amphibious operations or expeditionary warfare in general, but rather were about leveraging technology to make naval strike warfare decisive and the fleet more effective across the range of missions.

The Rise and Fall of Interventionist Enlargement

The 1992 presidential election marked a generational change in U.S. leadership. Americans sought to put the Cold War behind them and turned to a young and optimistic president who innately understood their concerns but had little experience or interest in national security. As a candidate, Clinton had shifted the terms of the election to the economy. His message "It's the economy, stupid" had resonated with Americans, who were increasingly indifferent to foreign affairs. Once in office, Clinton hoped his national security advisers would handle inherited problems in Somalia, Haiti, and Bosnia and allow him to focus on his domestic agenda. He spent little time with this group; Powell, who was still the chairman at this point, thought the group was chronically disorganized and that it presented a weak image.[18] They were less experienced than Bush's team, which was not surprising since Democrats had held the White House for only four of the previous twenty-four years. In Powell's opinion, Clinton's national security team was not up to the challenge. More thinkers than administrators, they did not understand how to use military force. Yet they had few reservations on its use, which frightened Powell.[19] Aspin's comment that he would use force "even when vital interests are not at stake" was indicative of the administration's early interventionist view, and worried Powell as well.[20]

Administration officials wanted something to replace containment. They sought a compelling conceptual framework that would rebuild consensus and organize U.S. security and foreign policy efforts. Bush's New World Order had proved too abstract and unpersuasive. They wanted a coherent approach to guide their actions and secure domestic support, something with a simple idea and a catchy title.[21] From their perspective, the policy had to be blanketed in the rhetoric of ideological values like democracy, human rights, and free markets rather than in a more abstract realpolitik rationale.[22]

In the summer of 1993 the concept of enlargement was unveiled as the successor to containment. It was not about containing threats, but rather about expanding market-based democracies. In a more interdependent world, U.S. security would be improved by promoting America's core concepts of democracy and market economies, and by making defense cuts to enhance America's economic power.[23] For the administration, the new battleground was the international economy, which was now the focus of U.S. foreign policy. Secretary of State Warren Christopher summed up the new approach:

> In an era in which economic competition is eclipsing ideological rivalry, it is time for diplomacy that seeks to assure access for U.S. businesses to expanding global markets. . . . For too long we have made economics the poor cousin of our foreign policy. . . . We will not be bashful about linking our high diplomatic goals with our economic goals. . . . Support for democracy and human rights abroad can and should be a central strategic tenet in improving our security.[24]

Economic security and competition were now at the forefront of U.S. foreign policy, and one had good reason to believe they would be at the forefront of U.S. strategy as well.

Multilateral efforts with the United Nations or NATO, for example, were key, as was the use of force. As Aspin noted, the Weinberger-Powell Doctrine "might set the threshold for using force too high for many of the problems the United States will face in the post-cold war era."[25] National security adviser

W. Anthony K. "Tony" Lake noted, "We should not oppose using our military forces for humanitarian purposes simply because these missions do not resemble major wars for control of territory."[26]

The new approach was termed "multilateral intervention." In an exchange in early 1993 about sending U.S. forces into Bosnia, Madeleine J. K. Albright, Clinton's ambassador to the United Nations, asked Powell, "What's the point of having this superb military you're always talking about if we can't use it?"[27] Powell later remarked that he almost had an aneurysm at the question; in his words, he "patiently" explained to Albright that those U.S. soldiers "were not toy soldiers to be moved around on some sort of global game board."[28]

This was a revealing answer. It belied Powell's assumption that the military had only one purpose—to win wars (that have a clear political objective) with overwhelming force in a quick and decisive manner, which precluded the possibility that American society would turn against the war as it had in Vietnam. To think otherwise was to admit ignorance even on the part of a woman who held a doctorate from Columbia University and most recently had been a professor of international relations at Georgetown University. Powell, the most politically influential military leader in a generation, one who shaped the course of U.S. strategy in the post–Cold War era, had little capacity to envision the military as a more nuanced and less kinetically oriented instrument of a liberal, free-market American empire. As Colin Gray noted, "Powell . . . for all his political astuteness did not have a sophisticated view of how and why force may need to be exerted (he could not transcend his Vietnam experience)."[29]

Powell shared the outlook of the Bush administration, including its lack of creative conceptual skills that were necessary to develop an organizing vision about the United States' role, particularly as the manager of the global system. These skills would have come in handy to guide a new administration that was unsure of how to relate force with political ends. They also would have been useful in understanding how to move multilateral concepts of engagement and enlargement beyond mere missionary sentiments to strategic advantage.

By the summer of 1994 Clinton's interventionist enlargement was in tatters, the victim of mismanaged crises, hapless diplomacy, and multilateralist tensions. Clinton's attempts to broker a deal in Bosnia using air strikes to stop Serbian atrocities fell apart. The press excoriated the president, painting him as indifferent, his team indecisive, and his Bosnian policy flip-flops as ineffective.[30] On October

3, 1993, armed street gangs overwhelmed a U.S. search-and-seizure mission in Mogadishu, Somalia, which was part of a larger United Nations effort. Eighteen U.S. soldiers were killed. Americans recoiled at images of cheering crowds dragging dead American soldiers through the streets. It was a fiasco and a geopolitical knockdown for Clinton, whose domestic initiatives hung in the balance. Americans extended the lessons of Vietnam to Somalia, places where there were no clear and vital interests.

A week later, rioting Haitians turned back a U.S. warship delivering a thousand U.S. troops as part of a larger United Nations nation-building project. The ship sat offshore for days as the White House debated whether to send in the troops or recall the ship. (It opted for the latter.) In April–July 1994 genocide in Rwanda saw almost a million Tutsis hacked to death by government-backed Hutus. The world looked to the White House for action, but it was too late. Two months before, Lake had laid down the new policy: "Our armed forces' primary mission is not to conduct peace operations but to win wars."[31]

Discredited were efforts to spread democracy and free-market values and protect human rights. Early in the post–Cold War era, Americans developed a jaundiced eye for multilateral cooperative affairs in general and humanitarian and peacekeeping missions in particular. The assumption that an overarching grand strategy was needed or could be supported domestically proved mistaken. Thereafter, Clinton adopted a more measured and flexible strategic approach, one based on selective engagements and confronting regional powers such as North Korea and Iraq. Regional conflict once again assumed a place at the center of the United States' strategic vision.

Boorda and the Catastrophe of Tailhook

It is against this background of strategic uncertainty that the calamitous events at the Tailhook Association's annual symposium in the summer of 1991 must be understood.[32] The incidents at Tailhook that year shocked the public and shook the Navy to its core. The Tailhook scandal brought about a national discussion on sexual harassment and a high-profile referendum on the role of women in the military. The scandal was the focus of an unremitting media frenzy that kept the Navy in the glare of a spotlight for five years and in a state of penance for another five. The scandal dizzied Navy leaders, dismantled their credibility, and dominated their attentions for years. At the Tailhook Association's annual symposium held in a Las Vegas hotel in September 1991 that was attended by then–Secretary of the Navy Lawrence Garrett, CNO Kelso, and thirty-three other admirals, drunken Navy and Marine Corps carrier aviators sexually assaulted ninety women. The Navy's investigation was a whitewash. The scandal forced Garrett to resign in July 1992.

The Department of Defense's Inspector General took over in what was to be a no-holds-barred investigation, which had all the makings of a witch-hunt.[33] The investigation determined that the head of the Naval Investigative Service, the Navy's Judge Advocate General, and the Navy's civilian Inspector General had manipulated the Navy's investigation to protect senior leaders and avoid publicity. The Inspector General's report came out in April 1993 in a blaze of publicity. It accused 140 naval (i.e., Navy and Marine Corps) officers of misconduct and the Navy of leadership failure. In October 1993 the Clinton administration's Secretary of the Navy, John H. Dalton (1993–98), publicly called for Kelso's resignation, but Aspin refused.

In February 1994 a Navy judge ruled that Kelso had lied about his activities at Tailhook and manipulated the investigation. Kelso denied the accusations, but retired two months early. In all, thirty admirals received administrative punishment, which ended many of their careers. Taking into account also the ten or so who were preemptively retired before the report's publication, the Navy lost 15 percent of its admirals, including some three- and four-star admirals, within a two-year period.

To replace Kelso, Clinton selected Adm. Jeremy M. "Mike" Boorda (1994–96) to restore the Navy's image, rebuild morale, and reestablish relations with Congress. Boorda was a skilled politician with close ties to many in Congress. He had impressed Clinton as the commander of U.S. Naval Forces Europe and NATO Forces Southern Europe, where he successfully fused the activities of forces from the United Nations, NATO, and the United States in Bosnia. Boorda was a manpower expert, having served four tours in the Bureau of Personnel, the last as its chief. Officers with backgrounds in personnel management were in ascendancy. The challenge of overseeing the massive post–Cold War personnel cuts as well as managing skyrocketing personnel costs, which amounted to two-thirds of the Navy's portion of the Navy Department's budget, had increased the power of the Bureau in Navy decision making. The route to advancement now went through either OPNAV N8 or the Bureau of Personnel.

Boorda was a charismatic leader and a sailor's sailor, not the skills for which CNOs were normally selected, but the skills that those who selected him now thought were necessary. In general, the White House, the secretary of defense, the Secretary of the Navy, and the outgoing CNO select CNOs for the expertise and experience they bring to the Navy's problems, which in this case was the Tailhook scandal. Like all the CNOs in the post–Cold War era, Boorda was successful in solving the problems for which he was hired, although the manner in which he eventually solved the problem of Tailhook was, as will be seen, rather unorthodox.

Boorda was a surface officer, the first to serve as CNO since Admiral Zumwalt in the early 1970s, and his tenure would prove just as controversial. Boorda, who had entered the Navy in 1956, was not only the first non–Naval Academy CNO but also the first to rise from the enlisted ranks. As one reporter noted, the Navy had enough of the submariner CNOs, whose engineering backgrounds were said to diminish their people skills, leaving them unprepared intellectually for the kinds of problems the Navy was now facing.[34]

The Task to Update " . . . From the Sea"

In early June 1994 Secretary Dalton directed CNO Boorda, the commandant, General Mundy, and Undersecretary of the Navy Richard J. Danzig (Secretary of the Navy 1998–2001) to develop a new strategy. As he noted the following August, Dalton liked " . . . From the Sea" but wanted a strategy that was aligned with Clinton's first national security strategy, which was released the same month he tasked the strategy's development.[35] Clinton's strategy left intact the administration's pillars of security, economics, and democracy, but noted that military engagement would be selective.[36] Dalton wanted the new strategy to focus on forward presence.[37] Otherwise, Dalton's problem was straightforward. Capt. Sam Tangredi, USN (Ret.), who was Dalton's special assistant and speechwriter at the time, noted that Dalton "supported the concepts of ' . . . From the Sea,' but . . . was embarrassed trying to defend a strategy to [the Secretary of Defense] and the White House that was signed by a Republican. Finally, he gave me the task of 'get me a strategy I can sign.'" As Tangredi later pointed out, "Critics would say that 'Forward . . . From the Sea' was really no different than ' . . . From the Sea' (except emphasizing forward presence). They were right. It was not meant to be different, it was meant to be signed."[38]

Boorda, for one, was not about to pass up an opportunity to place his own imprint on the new strategy. To an extent, he shared Owens' technological fascination and emphasis on future weapons, but not necessarily at the expense of current needs.[39] More important, he thought the Navy had gone too far in letting itself be defined in terms of the littoral, the more specialized mission of amphibious warfare, and, implicitly, the Marine Corps.[40] While he supported the idea of a Navy–Marine Corps team, Boorda did not want to be hemmed in by the perception that the Navy was now all about fighting small wars in the littoral. He sought to emphasize the fleet's ability to operate globally and across the spectrum of warfare, particularly regional war. "Even though we are concentrating our efforts on the capabilities required in the complex littoral environment," he noted, "we retain those blue-water tools required of a global naval force—the tools necessary for maintaining a forward presence and achieving victory in a major regional conflict."[41]

Boorda's emphasis of the Navy's global capabilities and regional conflict was also in response to the administration's shift in foreign policy from interventionism to regional conflict. The CNO stated that the Black Hawk Down event in October 1993 had "changed things," referring to genesis of the shift, as did a case of brinkmanship with North Korea in the summer of 1994.[42] In that light, Boorda sought to highlight the fleet's ability to deter war and manage crisis and, failing that, its strike warfare and sea control capabilities, which would be critical in a conflict on the Korean peninsula.

For his part the commandant could neither forsake expeditionary maneuver warfare in the littoral, which was the Marine Corps' traditional operating area, nor deprecate the kind of small-scale interventions, embassy evacuations, and so on for which the Marine Corps was uniquely qualified and that it was now encountering at an alarming rate. Such operations provided the Marine Corps with empirical evidence that its capabilities were still indispensable regardless of the direction of U.S. strategy. General Mundy was not one to believe that the partnership's focus should be on regional war. Instead, it should be on either side of regional conflict, where the naval services dominated; where their speed, presence, and flexibility were uniquely suited to forestall crisis and, failing that, to buy time as politicians debated, military leaders planned, and the Army and Air Force mobilized.

Meanwhile, the newly redesignated Strategy and Concepts Branch, formally OP-603 (the Strategic Concepts Branch) and now N513, had been searching for a high-profile document to buttress the weak arguments of " . . . From the Sea" about forward presence. The branch was supporting N8's project to use forward presence rather than major regional conflict as a basis for sizing the fleet.[43]

Unlike the Navy and Marine Corps, the Air Force and the Army had not argued that their presence and crisis management requirements should result in larger force structures, which were sized only for regional conflict. As the authors of a RAND study noted, "The Air Force does not appear to have pressed the case that peacetime presence and contingency operations should also be considered in sizing the U.S. Air Force—an argument that the Navy had profitably used to justify a 12-carrier force."[44]

The Air Force and the Army were attempting to overturn the Navy's victory before it gelled into the budget. They pointed out that " . . . From the Sea" had not emphasized presence, which, in their view, was a concept that the Navy was defining as too narrow.[45] For the Army, the ultimate deterrent was the threat of boots on the ground. Warships off a threat's coast offered little leverage, unless, that is, there were Marines on board, in which case Army paratroopers would be more effective than those Marines. The Air Force argued that the deterrent value of a massive precision-guided strike was greater than that offered by U.S. ground forces or warships. The Army's and the Air Force's understanding of presence and crisis management was more kinetic and less nuanced. Neither their experiences nor their capabilities lend them the ability to apply nuanced force across the spectrum of conflict as could the Navy and Marine Corps, which was not about to stop the Army and Air Force from staking out areas on either side of major conflict to bolster their force structures.

For his part, Rear Adm. Philip A. Dur, who had replaced Ted Baker as the head of the N51, hoped to produce an enduring and far-reaching document that drove the direction of post–Cold War naval strategy, as did the head of his N513, Capt. Joe Sestak.[46] Sestak, like Dur, had a doctorate in political economy and government from Harvard and was a highly ambitious officer from the surface warfare community. The desire to pen the next maritime strategy and reap the career-enhancing laurels that would come with it remained strong in the strategy community throughout the 1990s even as the community's influence waned; the desire to be the author of the next maritime strategy was not surprising, as many had participated in its development.

"Forward . . . From the Sea"

The new strategy was called "Forward . . . From the Sea."[47] It was drafted in late 1994 by the N513 and then sent to Dur and his counterpart in the Marine Corps, Maj. Gen. Tom Wilkerson. The two flag officers worked closely in writing major portions of what was to become a four-page document. It differed from " . . . From the Sea" in several respects: It had a global perspective, not a regional, littoral, tactical, or expeditionary focus. Terms like "broad oceans," "transoceanic," and "highways of the sea" conveyed a global perspective that had been missing in " . . . From the Sea." "Forward . . . From the Sea" noted, "The vital economic, political, and military interests of the United States are truly global in nature and scope."[48] Yet, that is about as close as the document came to relating naval capabilities to systemic goals such as those represented by the two pillars of Clinton's national security strategy: first, a strong U.S. economy and the growth of a more interdependent global economy; and second, the enlargement of democracy and free-market values.

An interesting, if not glaring, omission, "Forward . . . From the Sea" did not embrace the technologies associated with the emerging revolution in military affairs. One might have expected such language because Owens, whose enthusiasms for such technologies knew few bounds, was the vice chairman, the military officer who held more sway over the services' resource decisions than any other. "Forward . . . From the Sea" also lacked the strong language in " . . . From the Sea" that naval forces could be decisive on their own. It was also more conciliatory about the need for jointness. "Forward . . . From the Sea" used the term "decisive" in terms of a joint campaign.[49]

If " . . . From the Sea" focused on dominating the littoral, stand-alone strike capabilities, and expeditionary warfare (too much on the latter for many Navy officers), then its update was, as "Forward . . . From the Sea" noted, about how "naval forces are particularly well-suited to the entire range of military operations" and "are an indispensable and exceptional instrument of U.S. foreign policy."[50] The document also contained budgetary charts that offered evidence that the Marine Corps was not being short-changed in terms of the Navy Department's budget. One such chart displayed a history of the Navy's and Marine Corps' shares of the Navy Department's budget since 1980. It showed that while the Navy's share started to plummet in 1986, the Marines' had remained steady through fiscal year 1998. In 1986 the Marine portion was one-eleventh of the Navy's. By fiscal year 1998 it was one-sixth.

Finally, as expected, "Forward . . . From the Sea" elaborated on the presence mission. It pointed out that the "Bottom-Up Review" had "emphasized the importance of maintaining forward-deployed naval forces and recognized the impact of peacetime operational tempo on the size of Navy and Marine Corps force structure." "Forward . . . From the Sea" reiterated that "naval forces . . . are the foundation of peacetime forward presence operations and overseas response to crisis."[51] As a way of gaining support for the presence mission, it quoted the administration's 1994 *National Security Strategy*: "Presence demonstrates our commitment to allies and friends, underwrites regional stability, gains U.S. familiarity with overseas operating environments, promotes combined training among the forces of friendly countries, and provides timely initial response capabilities."[52] Presence, in other words, was key to maintaining a forward-deployed fleet and to justifying the numbers of ships needed to fulfill the regional CINCs' presence requirements because, in general, it takes three ships to keep one deployed.

Overall, "Forward . . . From the Sea" was more explanatory and measured than its more didactic and expository predecessor. "Forward . . . From the Sea" explained how naval forces would support at least a selective Transitioneers' agenda without embracing the approach unreservedly. Nor did it display the Cold Worriers' tactical-technological enthusiasms. It fused the agendas of the Secretary of the Navy, the CNO, and the commandant while concealing the seams more successfully than most of the Navy's and Marine Corps' joint strategic documents. The logic of its arguments flowed from peacetime to crisis deterrence to crisis management to seizing the initiative to large-scale conflict. In its structure and tone, it was more like the Maritime Strategy than any other of the Navy's post–Cold War strategic statements.

Not surprisingly, however, "Forward . . . From the Sea" did not resonate with Congress, whose concerns had always focused on wartime requirements and, in their absence, on economizing. Moreover, the deemphasis on decisive naval power and focus on cross-spectrum and enabling capabilities had inadvertently opened the Navy up for attacks from the Air Force and the Army.[53] The Air Force and Army derisively called "Forward . . . From the Sea" "Foyer . . . From the Sea," arguing that the document merely confirmed that the naval services were really just crisis managers and door keepers, as they had been in the 1990–91 Gulf War. They argued that because the Navy's and Marine Corps' forward forces were so small, they simply were not combat credible.

In addition, the Air Force and the Army successfully had the Joint Staff redefine the concept of presence to include almost any form of military activity outside the continental United States, which implied that Army and Air Force contributions in this area were as important as those of the Navy and the Marine

Corps. The Army's and the Air Force's arguments were bolstered by contending that the naval services' claims about their exceptional and indispensable capabilities were parochial and contrary to the spirit of jointness, an argument that resonated with the Joint Staff.

"Forward . . . From the Sea" enjoyed wide circulation in the defense establishment for about a year. Its arguments were used in the Navy and Marine Corps posture statements, congressional testimony, and speeches, and it had considerable influence on allied and foreign naval thinking.[54] However, those in N8 had never envisioned it to be much more than an instrument for short-term gain anyway, and in that sense it met its needs well. For the strategy folks, it was successful in the sense that it buttressed forward deployment and elevated presence as a central tenet. But it was not the Maritime Strategy, nor did it restore the prominence of N513, which, by all accounts, was not well regarded by Boorda.

Conclusion

Clinton's enlargement strategy was about the closest the United States came to a systemic approach in the 1990s. That is not saying much, however. As an intellectual framework to build consensus and organize American efforts, enlargement was largely rhetorical. It was meant to build domestic support for interventions and fell short of considering how exactly military force would expand free markets and democracies or otherwise realize American long-term goals. The fault, however, simply cannot be laid at the feet of Clinton's thinkers, whose efforts to reorient thinking away from threats and toward greater goals was not without merit. Strategy is the bridge that connects political goals with military force (and vice versa).[55] Success nevertheless depends on the presence of real people able and willing to cross the bridge. Neither Aspin nor Powell was up to the challenge of determining how military force could contribute to the realization of systemic goals. They simply balked. They thought about how force would be used, and when and where, but not ultimately why.

So while Clinton's foreign policy focused on enlarging the number of free-market democracies and vindicating human rights, his defense policy remained preoccupied with finding efficiencies in warfighting through revolutionary technologies to defeat regional foes. In short, enlargement and the "Bottom-Up Review" were utterly misaligned. While Clinton pursued a Transitioneers' approach, the military, which viewed his administration with skepticism if not outright hostility, focused on the next Gulf War and spent its declining funds on building a futuristic Cold Worriers' force at the cost of current capabilities and resources. Botched interventions in turn deprived the Clinton administration of the initiative required to establish a lasting vision for the post–Cold War era.[56]

For its part, the Navy was not about to climb onto the bridge alone and offer a systemic grand strategy. The admirals that structured Navy strategy in the early 1990s were nuclear submariners. These engineers focused on advanced technology and believed in process; this was a psychological legacy, perhaps, of Admiral Rickover's fixation on adhering to procedures and redesigning processes to avoid nuclear reactor accidents. Once established, the correct process would yield the correct answers. In the 1980s the consensual process had been controlled by the strategists in OPNAV OP-603, the mechanism of which was a tightly held secret-level brief that laid out the Maritime Strategy in its various forms. In the 1990s Kelso and Owens had ensured that OPNAV's resource managers now controlled almost the entire process. The new structure ensured that the operational, programmatic, and manpower backgrounds of most admirals trumped the too few admirals with strategy backgrounds.

Motivated by the need to redress the Navy's vulnerability in the wake of Goldwater-Nichols, Powell's changes, and the Gulf War, the decisions of Navy leaders were shaped by the need to meet the joint operational needs of the regional CINCs whose perspectives were regional, not global. This focus allowed the Navy to fixate on solving the technical problems associated with catering to the CINCs and spared it from understanding how operational goals would lead to greater political ends, which was now, ostensibly, the CINCs' responsibility.

Nevertheless, the Navy's nonkinetic missions were attracting attention and were encompassed in its official outlook for the first time since the end of the Cold War. The "Bottom-Up Review" had recognized the relationship between the Navy, foreign presence, and Clinton's foreign policy goals. The Navy had successfully translated presence and crisis response requirements into force structure requirements. The Navy's success raised the ire of the Air Force and the Army, which were jealous of the Navy's ability to demonstrate its relevance across the spectrum of conflict by emphasizing the flexibility of naval forces. Measuring the effectiveness of presence outside of crisis response remained problematic, but even so, the post–Cold War world was not short of crises. Only when a balanced fleet was forward deployed could the possibilities of U.S. naval force be fully exploited. For the Navy, presence and crisis response necessarily went hand in hand.

Meanwhile, the Navy–Marine Corps partnership was wearing thin, strained by different needs and beliefs. They would go their separate ways after "Forward . . . From the Sea," which was the last cosigned strategic document until 2001's "Naval Power 21."[57] The drive for a consensual Navy–Marine Corps view left the Navy vulnerable to attacks that naval power was not decisive in large conflicts and was more suited to serve as an enabling force. In contrast to the Navy, the Marine Corps' future looked comparatively bright, given its warfighting focus, a balanced force structure protected by law, and its indispensable niche capabilities in the kinds of small-scale interventions that seemed to have no end. The Navy was not a niche service, but rather the opposite: it was a global service. The Navy continued to struggle with its own understanding of what this meant and to search for concepts and language to defend its interests in competition with the other U.S. military services, and against countervailing elements of its own traditions.

With " . . . From the Sea," Force 2001, and "Forward . . . From the Sea," the Navy believed it had sufficiently solved the problem of how to refashion its raison d'être, reassert its relevance, and redesign the fleet; now it only had to work out the details. Strategy was placed on the back burner as the Navy spent the rest of the 1990s focused on securing a new strike aircraft, keeping a low profile, and trimming its sails to account for the defense establishment's newest conceptual fads.

Chapter 6

2020 Vision, 1995–96

The Clinton Foreign Policy in Transition

The Clinton administration was transitioning to a new strategic approach. The goals were still to enlarge free-market democracies, and sustain U.S. economic strength, on which American power depended. But the attempt to develop a single crystallized idea—containment's successor—to align military, economic, and political effort was abandoned. In a turning point in U.S. foreign policy, Clinton eschewed a reductionist outlook and adapted a more flexible approach.[1] The post–Cold War era was proving too complex; it was too difficult to define U.S. interests, and Americans were too uninterested in foreign affairs to support an ideologically grounded policy. The administration would address each international issue narrowly on its own merits. This was a complicated way of running foreign affairs, one prone to muddling pragmatically from one problem to another. However, Clinton's emphasis on flexibility and adaptability and weighing Americans' moods perfectly matched his considerable political skills. Clinton was castigated for not having a cohesive approach.[2] But he was not a visionary: he was a consummate politician who understood the fluid link between foreign policy and society in a manner more reminiscent of Franklin Roosevelt than any of his immediate predecessors.

Clinton's new defense team helped. William J. Perry, who had replaced Secretary of Defense Les Aspin after the Somalia debacle in 1993, was widely respected in the Pentagon. The chairman, General Shalikashvili, was another low-key member of the team. Unlike his predecessor, Shalikashvili was not a permanent roadblock in the use of force. His knowledge of European and NATO politics helped parlay Clinton's most intractable foreign policy problem into his first major foreign policy success. This problem was Bosnia, which had bedeviled the Bush and Clinton administrations and was the site of the worst violence in Europe since World War II. The fall of Srebrenica, a small mountain town in Bosnia and Herzegovina, in July 1995 and the subsequent massacre of seven thousand Bosnian Muslims at the hands of invading Serbs galvanized the administration into action despite a lack of interest among Americans.[3]

In August 1995 the United States played a preponderant role in a three-week precision air campaign by NATO forces. An exercise in coercion based on economy of force, Operation Deliberate Force had few equals. It saw strikes from U.S. carriers and surface combatants launching Tomahawk cruise missiles, whose unnerving accuracy proved intimidating to Serbian leaders.[4] The campaign brought about the successful Dayton Agreement and with it an end to the war in Bosnia and Herzegovina. As U.S. State Department official Richard Holbrooke noted, "One of the great things that people should have learned from this is that there are times when air power—not backed up by ground troops—can make a difference."[5] Precision strike warfare had proved, if anything, even more decisive than in Desert Storm.

The success in Bosnia restored America's prestige and bolstered Clinton's fluid foreign policy approach. As John Harris noted, Clinton "emerged from the fall of 1995 as a vastly more self-confident and commanding leader."[6] Clinton followed up his success in September 1996 by launching a massive cruise missile attack against Iraq that stopped an Iraqi offensive in Iraq's Kurdish regions. This was another demonstration of the link between coercive diplomacy and precision strike weapons, whose capacity to limit risk (and casualties generally) cast the use of force in a new and more promising light.

Jointness and the Revolution in Military Affairs

Meanwhile, Shalikashvili and Owens were busy developing a new vision for the U.S. military and the processes to realize it.[7] Goldwater-Nichols, the bottom-up assessments, and the lessons drawn from U.S. victories in the Persian Gulf and the Balkans highlighted the need for jointness, the definition of which was beginning to crystallize. It had always meant fighting as a joint team. After the 1990–91

Gulf War and events in Bosnia, however, it moved from coordination to integration. In short order, jointness became an officially mandated imperative. "It has become politically incorrect to question jointness as *the* preeminent way for the military to do business as a whole," as one Navy officer noted. "Jointness has also become a panacea for Congress and others in reprioritizing declining defense budgets." Consequently, he noted, "civilian officials and military leaders are accelerating this already fast-moving concept."[8]

One of the chairman's primary means to operationalize the new vision and understanding of jointness was through joint doctrine. Shalikashvili's views on doctrine were aptly summed up by his successor, Gen. Henry H. "Hugh" Shelton, USA: "Because doctrine undergirds everything we do, it is the logical beginning for our efforts to translate our vision of joint war fighting into reality."[9] Goldwater-Nichols handed to the chairman the responsibility to develop joint doctrine and guide joint training and education. In short, the chairman held sway over the direction of joint doctrine, whose influence was ubiquitous. "The utility of joint doctrine extends beyond the employment of joint forces," stated Douglas Lovelace Jr. and Thomas-Durell Young. "It affects virtually all of the Chairman's strategic planning activities."[10]

Another means to realize the vision was the Joint Resource Oversight Council, which was created and led by Owens. The council gathered the services' vice chiefs of staff to examine military requirements holistically, air out differences in a candid manner, and arrive at a consensus. It was a corporate board where the vice chiefs could be educated and coaxed to put aside parochial interests and endorse programs and concepts that supported the chairman's vision and the CINCs' requirements. The council institutionalized the chairman's authority over planning and procurement and became one of that position's primary vehicles for advancing budget and program recommendations.[11] Much as he had in OPNAV, Owens had reconfigured the military's resource decision-making process and now largely controlled it (on behalf of the CINCs and chairman).

The council's discussions, which averaged an extraordinary ten hours a week, revolved around how to leverage technology in three areas: precision force; intelligence, surveillance, and reconnaissance; and command, control, communications, and intelligence networking.[12] Owens was, in effect, using the discussions to flesh out and support the new vision.

With their vision, Shalikashvili and Owens were attempting to realize a revolution in military affairs, which Jeffrey Cooper has defined as "a discontinuous increase in military capability and effectiveness."[13] As Shalikashvili noted to Congress, "What we set in motion is an entirely new era in warfare. . . . What is changing is the very nature of modern battle."[14] Owens embraced Information Age technologies and sought to insert them at the heart of joint doctrine to enable a smaller but higher-tech military to secure swift and decisive victory on the battlefield with comparatively few casualties. As the post–Cold War rendition of the traditional U.S. bent toward reductionist theories in warfare, jointness and the revolution in military affairs in information and precision-guided technologies had now fully emerged as the principal big ideas that drove defense thinking in the 1990s. Inevitably, their advancement soon became an end in itself.

The Rise and Fall of Naval Doctrine

The Navy's problem in the first half of the decade had been how to reassert its relevance and restructure the fleet in light of a new mix of international threats, a shrinking budget, a partnership with the Marine Corps, and an emphasis on jointness and technology. From late 1994 through 1997 Navy strategists occupied themselves with the problem of how to tie these considerations together. One way to integrate the partnership was through the development of naval doctrine, which would also serve to shape joint doctrine. In March 1993 CNO Kelso established the Naval Doctrine Command, thereby fulfilling a commitment made in " . . . From the Sea." As that document noted, the goal was to integrate naval forces into joint operations and, reflecting the Marines' emphasis, "above all . . . *build doctrine for expeditionary warfare.*"[15]

Written doctrine had not loomed large in the Navy. Historically, it eschewed authoritative doctrine, which it believed restricted the ability of its officers to react in combat.[16] Success at sea was not thought to depend on adherence to doctrinal norms, but rather on the problem-solving ability of the Navy's officers, its decentralized command structures, and its willingness to delegate authority. Doctrine for the Navy was like the British constitution: it was an unwritten set of convictions, principles, and understandings that were acquired experientially and passed down more or less orally, all of which its practitioners thoroughly understood.

To soldiers and Marines, however, written doctrine is fundamental. It fuses their operational planning, organizational structure, training, tactics, and resource decisions. It coordinates artillery, infantry, armor, and air units, creating the reality of combined arms. For ground forces in particular, written doctrine remains the essential starting point for all forms of functional integration. This was how Shalikashvili understood doctrine, and he wished that understanding to become general.[17]

In July 1994 the chairman changed the statement found in all joint publications, from "This publication is authoritative but not directive" to the more emphatic "The guidance in this publication is authoritative."[18] Navy officers bristled at the move.[19] To them, it was another indication that jointness was being defined as the Army's way of thinking. As Rebecca Grant pointed out, "Joint doctrine perpetuates a 'land-centric' focus because it is largely based on Army concepts."[20] Because they were vindicated in the Gulf War, the Army's AirLand Battle and the Air Force's strategic bombing doctrines were forming the basis of joint doctrine. Nevertheless, doctrine was becoming the lingua franca of the joint world, the common language used by the services to understand each other.

The Naval Doctrine Command consisted of a rear admiral and fifty officers and civilians.[21] The command was in Norfolk, Virginia, home of the Navy's largest base, which ensured close contact with the fleet and with its counterparts in other U.S. military services and in the joint arena, all of which were located nearby. Most of the command's officers came directly from tours in the fleet. Of those that were tasked to develop doctrine, almost none had experience writing strategy, operational concepts, or doctrine (few Navy officers did) or had attended the Naval War College. The pressure for the new command to produce the first of six doctrine publications was immense.[22] The staff spent months first defining what doctrine meant to the Navy. In contrast to their counterparts in the other U.S. military services, the three-officer writing team was starting literally with a blank sheet of paper. The team's efforts were constrained by the command's well-meaning philosophy, which intentionally did not seek to outsource its development, which allowed the team to maintain control of the document's flow and emphasis. As noted by Cdr. Robert M. Zalaskus, the primary writer, "The command's general feeling was that doctrine was an unfamiliar category of thinking and we could be inundated with programmatic spin losing the flavor of enduring principles."[23]

After numerous review boards with active and retired admirals and generals, *Naval Warfare:* Naval Doctrine Publication 1 (NDP-1) was released in March 1994, a month before Kelso retired and nine months before "Forward . . . From the Sea" was released.[24] NDP-1 was a seventy-page booklet that was filled with historical vignettes that amplified themes from " . . . From the Sea," fused the two services' doctrinal approaches, and explained the principles of war from a naval perspective. Included in this explanation was the difference between attritional warfare (which was about destroying the enemy's forces) and maneuver warfare (which was conceived as the sort of artful and indirect approach to combat necessitated when a smaller force needed to use speed and surprise to attack the larger forces of an opponent or its centers of gravity). In the 1970s both the Marine Corps and the Army had embraced maneuver warfare. NDP-1 stated that naval forces prefer maneuver warfare to attritional.[25] The command's deputy commander, a Marine colonel, was an expert in Marine Corps doctrine and helped the Navy representatives to accept the idea of maneuver warfare before anyone at the Naval Doctrine Command really understood what it was.[26] While naval warfare involves maneuvering on, under, and above the sea, "naval battle," as Wayne P. Hughes Jr. noted, "is attrition centered. Victory by maneuver warfare may work on land but it does not at sea."[27]

In NDP-1 doctrine was defined as the bridge between strategy and the tactics, techniques, and procedures of naval operations.[28] It was authoritative, signed by both Kelso and the commandant, General Mundy, and was intended to be the agreed-on enduring principles representing the two services' approach to warfighting. The unspoken agreement in Naval Doctrine Command was that NDP-1 was to be a basic, uncontroversial document. Fundamental differences between the Navy and Marine Corps would be resolved in *Naval Operations: Naval Doctrine Publication 3* (NDP-3).[29]

Overall, NDP-1 received generally supportive reviews, mainly because the Navy demonstrated it could write doctrine. NDP-1 did what it had to do: set the stage for NDP-2 through NDP-6 and sit cleanly on the shelf next to Joint Publication 1 with its counterpart publications from Army, Air Force, and even the Marine Corps.[30] (The NDPs were purposively sized to match that of the joint doctrine publications.[31]) The Naval War College modestly endorsed it, mainly because it was drafted without its formal participation. As Zalaskus noted, the decision to draft NDP-1 in house contributed to its tepid reception by the Naval War College, which was home to scholars who were experts in Navy doctrine and its history.[32] The Naval War College had been brought in late in the process, perhaps too late for Zalaskus, who noted that the command's perspective worked to prevent engaging academia earlier and to a greater degree.[33] As expected, its impact on fleet day-to-day operations was minimal as it captured at a high level what the fleet was already doing. NDP-1 was surprisingly popular among the other U.S. military services and their war colleges as well as among other navies, and remains so.[34] To them, NDP-1 had the Navy's imprimatur, but to the fleet it was neither significant nor important.

The crown jewel of the Navy's doctrinal efforts was supposed to be *Naval Operations:* NDP-3, but early drafts became mired in a host of differences between Naval Doctrine Command and the Marine Corps Combat Development Command (which is in Quantico, Virginia), where the Marine Corps' doctrine is developed. One difference involved the command structure for the naval expeditionary force, the basic unit of littoral warfare whose central elements were a carrier battle group (commanded by an admiral) and a Marine Air-Ground Task Force embarked on amphibious ships (commanded by a Marine general).[35] Determining which of these two would have precedence in given circumstances proved to be a difficult problem.[36]

Another difference involved a coordinated versus an integrated view of jointness. The Naval Doctrine Command, backed by OPNAV, hewed to the former, while the Marines, broadly speaking, favored the latter. There was also reluctance on the part of the Marine Corps to diminish the highly regarded authority of its own doctrine command, compounded by a reluctance on the part of the Navy to embrace a dominant doctrinal approach tied to warfare on land.[37] As CNO Boorda noted when NDP-3 was being developed, "Some have argued that we only need capabilities for one discrete mission or another. Operational maneuver from the sea is an example. While I firmly support this [Marine Corps] concept and our current budget decisions reflect that position, it is only one of several warfighting capabilities naval forces must possess."[38] Boorda was voicing what many Navy officers had been thinking. Namely, that with " . . . From the Sea," the Navy had allowed the Marine Corps to shape a prohibitively narrow vision of its usefulness.

From 1995 to 1997 NDP-3 would go through forty iterations. All were rejected, most of them by the Marine Corps Combat Development Command's commanding general, Lt. Gen. Paul K. Van Riper, a sharp-tongued critic of the reductionist thinking on which the revolution in military affairs was based. Van Riper undoubtedly saw the Navy's positions in NDP-3 as arguments for particular weapons systems. In the end, NDP-3 was never published, which undermined the other five NDPs, the Naval Doctrine Command's stature, and the expectation that the Navy could develop doctrine to explain its warfighting approach. The failure sent Marine and Navy leaders searching for other ways to realize " . . . From the Sea" and their strategic partnership.

The Naval Operational Concept

In the summer of 1995, the new commandant of the Marine Corps, Gen. Charles C. Krulak (1995–99), was pushing Boorda to codevelop another document.[39] Krulak, who had headed the Marine Corps Combat Development Command between the release of " . . . From the Sea" and "Forward . . . From the Sea," was frustrated by the lack of doctrinal progress.[40] Krulak wanted an overarching conceptual framework, one that was not tied to resources, but preferably one that could get the Navy on board with the Marines' principal operational concept, which was called "Operational Maneuver from the Sea."[41] Krulak did not want another document like "Forward . . . From the Sea." Dalton and Boorda had already signed the latter and saw no need for another.[42] Instead, it was to be a naval operational concept, which would fuse the inchoate ideas in " . . . From the Sea" with the more concrete ideas in "Operational Maneuver from the Sea."[43] (Krulak and the Marine Corps Combat Development Command saw "Forward . . . From the Sea" as a movement away from expeditionary warfare and largely ignored it.) To the Marine Corps, an operational concept was an instrument to flesh out and organize promising ideas. Generally speaking, the Navy lacked an institutional equivalent.

The head of OPNAV's N513, Cdr. Joseph F. Bouchard, was already working on an operational concept of sorts.[44] He and several other surface officers in N3/N5 thought the post–Cold War era would generate strong demand for the Marine Corps' capabilities. Like Bouchard, who held a doctorate from Stanford University, they believed that Navy doctrine, which they saw as little more than explanations of how to employ weapons systems, was in no shape to influence joint doctrine or serve as a basis for Navy–Marine Corps integration. They saw the tenets of the Marines' maneuver warfare doctrine as compatible with classic Navy thinking, given its emphasis on initiative and delegation of authority. To redress the Navy's doctrinal deficiencies and otherwise jumpstart the stalled process, they sought a Navy–Marine Corps document that fused Marine doctrine with Navy thinking and embedded Navy doctrine in the context of emerging joint doctrine. In essence, they saw a naval operational concept as a new integrative instrument that had not previously been required, one by means of which the Navy could emerge as the leader in innovating and expanding joint doctrine.

Bouchard briefed OPNAV's three-star admirals, who did not endorse sending the proposal to Boorda.[45] Sitting in the back, however, was the head of OPNAV's N85 Expeditionary Warfare Directorate, Maj. Gen. James L. Jones,

USMC (commandant, 1999–2003), who convinced them otherwise. Krulak, ever the driving force in Marine doctrinal innovation, secured Boorda's promise to proceed with the project, which was launched in October 1995 and co-chaired by Bouchard.[46] The sixteen-person group consisted of representatives from N513, N8, Naval Doctrine Command, Headquarters Marine Corps, and Marine Corps Combat Development Command.[47]

The Naval Operational Concept was to be a broadly focused document that bridged the strategic concepts found in " . . . From the Sea" and "Forward . . . From the Sea" with the tactics, techniques, and procedures of the Navy's and the Marine Corps' doctrinal publications.[48] It would cover the spectrum of conflict and the continuum of response from presence to crisis response to warfighting. As the draft report of the project concept noted, it not only was to "serve as a catalyst for the development of doctrine, operational organizations, training and education, equipment and the supporting establishment" but also would "drive . . . the identification of capabilities."[49]

The Naval Operational Concept was an ambitious project, one beset with obstacles. For one, the Marine Corps had three operational concepts: (1) "Operational Maneuver from the Sea," (2) a concept for employing its nonamphibious land-based air wings and brigades, and (3) a concept for its maritime prepositioning force, which was a group of specially designed ships stationed worldwide that contained tanks, ammunition, and stores for instant deployment. The group had initially focused on "Operational Maneuver from the Sea" but was told by Headquarters Marine Corps, particularly its N8 equivalent, that it needed to encompass all three to justify a larger force structure for the Marine Corps.[50]

For its part, the Naval Doctrine Command saw the project as a move by OPNAV to usurp its authority.[51] The project was encroaching on its turf, but only because NDP-3 had become hopelessly mired in disagreement. As usual, those in N8 viewed the project as a ploy by the Marine Corps to lay claim to a greater share of the Navy Department's shrinking budget. N8's leaders wanted the group to encompass only amphibious warfare and "Operational Maneuver from the Sea," largely because they were struggling to fund the new F/A-18 E/F Super Hornet long-range attack and fighter jet, the new *Virginia*-class attack submarine, and operations in the Persian Gulf, Bosnia, and off of North Korea.

OPNAV's Air Warfare Division (N88) and naval aviators in general opposed the project as well.[52] They were pushing the Navy to adapt a carrier-strike warfare-centered interpretation of " . . . From the Sea" and "Forward . . . From the Sea," which they saw was more in line with emerging realities and the new direction of foreign and defense policy than large-scale interventions in the littoral. Moreover, such a move supported the F/A-18 E/F Super Hornet, the Navy's top budget priority, whereas Bouchard was, in essence, arguing for small, fast, and expendable ships designed for littoral operations. Not surprisingly, Bouchard became none too popular in N8 or the Naval Doctrine Command. His career took a large hit when Krulak, in a lengthy email to generals and admirals that presented his views on doctrine, praised Bouchard as the "Billy Mitchell of the Navy." This was a reference to the American airpower advocate of the 1920s who, as a general in the Army's air arm, was court-martialed for accusing Army and Navy leaders of treason for ignoring the virtues of airpower. Not surprisingly, the project foundered by spring of 1996.

"2020 Vision"

There was another controversial project under way, one whose fate would be similar. This was a white paper, "2020 Vision," that was being developed in the CNO's Executive Panel (N00K) by Capt. Ed Smith, who had participated in the Naval Force Capabilities Planning Effort. "2020 Vision" would present a view of what the fleet should look like in 2020. It was to be the first of two documents that established the Navy's priorities for strategy, doctrine, and future programs.[53] In March 1996 Boorda testified that he would sign out "2020 Vision" in the spring of 1996 and the companion "Navy Long Range Planning Objectives" later that summer. He noted that both would be updated every two years to ensure the Navy was adapting to changes in defense policy, technology, and operational concepts.

"2020 Vision" reflected the beliefs of those admirals that had shaped " . . . From the Sea." They held that U.S. naval power projection was decisive, which was owed to the fleet's mobility, flexibility, and revolutionary precision-strike and information technologies. To them, " . . . From the Sea" was about standoff precision strike warfare as a freestanding strategic expedient as much as it was about supporting naval forces on shore. "2020 Vision" expanded on that idea. It was more regional than littoral, more joint than naval. But it went one step farther by emphasizing the decisiveness of Navy strike warfare.[54] It argued that a massed engagement of sea-launched precision munitions, supported by advanced surveillance and communication technologies that identified political and military centers of gravity, could take down an enemy's political or military infrastructure in a matter of hours.

The centerpiece of "2020 Vision" was the arsenal ship, which, according to one reporter who had access to the draft, was not specifically mentioned in the seventeen-page paper.[55] This was essentially an 825-foot floating missile battery that contained five hundred vertical tubes designed to carry thousands of missiles. It could be filled with fifteen types of missiles, many of which could be controlled remotely by any of the services for use against targets on land, at sea, and in the air, including theater ballistic missiles. The ship was designed to be stationed overseas near hot spots and could be moved to signal U.S. resolve. It would have a double hull for protection against torpedoes, mines, and cruise missiles and would ride low in the water to lessen the chances of being detected by radar and hit by sea-skimming missiles. One or two of these ships could slow an enemy's invasion force or other movements until other U.S. forces arrived. Boorda called it the "modern equivalent to the battleship" and said that it was among the Navy's highest priority programs.[56]

Much of the ship's rationale revolved around cost. The 1,700 crewmembers on the recently decommissioned USS *Missouri* cost $67 million annually in pay and benefits, for example. The thirty-odd sailors on an arsenal ship would cost $1.4 million annually, while placing far fewer lives at risk.[57] An arsenal ship would cost $750 million to design and construct, compared to a carrier's $4.5 billion, and would be far less expensive to operate and maintain.[58] According to the same reporter, the draft stated, "Replacing a whole platform every time a weapon system becomes obsolete is impractical and unaffordable."[59] Six arsenal ships were planned. They were to be stationed near Korea, in the Mediterranean, and in the Persian Gulf.[60]

Two arsenal ships, supplemented by a carrier and a few surface combatants armed with cruise missiles, could deliver more firepower and with less warning than United States–based Air Force bombers, the proponents of the arsenal ship argued, and would therefore be a greater deterrent. They could maneuver away from reprisal attacks as long as the Navy held local sea and air control, which of course called for a balanced fleet. The ship's kinetic potential was thought to improve the quality of the fleet's presence operations, crisis response, and deterrence. In addition, by providing a mobile sea-based defense against theater ballistic missiles, task forces incorporating arsenal ships might gain the U.S. government more cooperation from potential coalition partners.[61]

The arsenal ship had many supporters. "This is the first totally new warship concept by the Navy since the 1950s, when it developed the fleet ballistic missile submarine," said Norman Polmar. "It's an opportunity for Navy admirals to show they're not fighting the [World War II] battle of Midway, but taking advantage of the newest technologies."[62] But the ship had as many detractors. Critics called it a sitting duck, a target too lucrative for the enemy to pass up. They noted that Tomahawk cruise missiles cost $1.3 million apiece, so loading up the ship would be extremely expensive, and losing one prohibitively so. The cost of munitions launched by one arsenal ship in a month-long campaign was estimated to be $1 billion a day.[63] Since the project was still experimental, no one knew which shipyard would get the contract. Consequently, members of Congress were hesitant to support it, particularly since doing so might put at risk ongoing long-term contracts for carriers and submarines.[64] The project threatened the Air Force's long-term recapitalization plans for its older B-52 and B-1 bombers. As Andrew Krepinevich noted, "The Air Force could feel itself crowded out by the arsenal ship."[65] The submariners thought the idea would be better realized by outfitting a retired *Ohio*-class SSBN to carry 150 cruise missiles. (This is an idea that did materialize in the form of 4 such submarines.) Some surface officers thought the project would be funded at the expense of other surface combatant programs.[66]

Naval aviators were especially hostile to the project.[67] "The arsenal ship is the same challenge to aircraft carriers as the first carrier was in the 1920s to battleships," noted Krepinevich. "It's not going to make the carrier extinct overnight, but it will make it a less important part of the battle fleet."[68] Aviators thought the arsenal ship was prohibitively expensive, not sophisticated enough to defend itself without considerable support, and deficient in capabilities beyond kinetic response. In short, it was not versatile enough for the range of missions, particularly those demanded by the CINCs.

Johnson Sets a Low Profile

It was neither intramural sniping nor interservice rivalry that dispatched the arsenal ship, however, but the suicide of Admiral Boorda, who took his own life in May 1996 in the face of public controversy over his right to wear two medals dating from his service in Vietnam. This was the last straw, perhaps, for the man who had been obliged to sweep up after the humiliations of Tailhook and the sexual harassment and cheating scandals of the Naval Academy. Boorda's successor was the vice CNO, Adm. Jay L. Johnson (1996–2000). At age fifty, he was the second-youngest CNO after Zumwalt and the first aviator since Hayward. A 1968 Naval Academy graduate, Johnson was a fighter pilot with two combat tours in Vietnam. He had been a member of the Strategic Studies Group and had attended the Armed Forces Staff College. Like Boorda, Johnson had a background in manpower, having served two tours in the Bureau of Personnel. Still, Johnson had relatively little experience in the Pentagon and was comparatively junior compared to most CNOs. His selection owed as much to the fact that he was the vice CNO, whose job entailed understanding and defending Navy programs, as it did to his brilliance, however understated it was. He had, after all, earned three of his four stars in the previous two years.

Johnson sought a low profile for himself and the Navy and was generally skeptical about the value of top-down statements of strategic vision.[69] He was less concerned about the direction of Navy strategy, which he regarded as well established, than he was about funding a new long-range heavy attack bomber.[70] Shortly before the Gulf War, Secretary of Defense Cheney cancelled the Navy's stealthy A-12 carrier attack jet program. It was $1 billion over budget and the aircraft was nowhere near ready to fly.[71] It was to replace the Vietnam-era A-6E Intruder, which was too slow to evade modern surface-to-air missile systems. However, the Navy's aircraft procurement funds had been halved since the end of the Cold War. Additionally, the case for the A-12 was undermined by the Navy's own Tomahawk cruise missile. As Barry Posen noted, "The problem the Navy created for itself, is that (it) proved that many of the targets you would customarily have allocated to a deep-attack aircraft can be successfully engaged by a Tomahawk, which can be widely distributed across the fleet. . . . [All this] undercut[s] the argument that you need large-deck carriers."[72]

Absent the A-12, the future of the Navy's ability to deliver a punch with a manned aircraft was pinned chiefly on the F/A-18E/F Super Hornet, which, in Johnson's words, represented the "cornerstone of the future of naval aviation."[73] The Super Hornet was a larger, longer-range version of the F/A-18C Hornet. The Super Hornet was forced to compete for budget space with two high-profile programs: the Air Force's revolutionary F-22 and the Joint Strike Fighter (F-35), the latter of which was to be produced for the Air Force, the Marine Corps, the Navy, and the British Royal Air Force, among others. Unlike these two, the Super Hornet was neither revolutionary nor stealthy.[74] It was a basic multipurpose attack and fighter jet whose chief virtue lay in the fact that it would cost the Navy a half to a third as much as an aircraft designed and built from scratch.[75]

The Navy had no choice. The all-weather long-range heavy attack mission lay at the heart of the carrier's power-projecting capabilities, which in turn was at the heart of the Navy's strategic vision. As former Secretary of the Navy Lehman noted after the A-12 was cancelled, "Carriers are to be cut to 12 from 15—but without a replacement for the A-6Es, there isn't much point in having even 12."[76] For Johnson, naval strategy necessarily boiled down to securing funding for the Super Hornet because without it the Navy could not project power in a manner that had been laid out in " . . . From the Sea."[77]

Conclusion

Encouraged by the ad hoc pragmatism that characterized Clinton's foreign policy, the U.S. defense establishment was not thinking about grand strategy. The Pentagon's leaders were preoccupied with more pressing concerns. Steeped in a milieu of system analysis, programmatics, and congressional interests, these industrial-managerial technocrats saw their problems in terms of how best to optimize the military's warfighting ability in light of technological opportunities, Goldwater-Nichols, and a fiscally restrained environment. Their focus was on how to make decisions more efficient and consensual, which is not the same as making effective decisions. As Colin Gray noted, "It can be a revelation that armed forces have been known to be so self-absorbed in the complex and demanding task of managing themselves that they forget what they are for."[78] In these respects the outlook of the Navy's leadership, as with those of its sister services, followed that of OSD and the Joint Staff.

To oppose the big ideas of jointness and the revolution in military affairs was becoming more difficult and politically risky, particularly after the Gulf War and the events in Bosnia. These successes made it easier for defense officials to dismiss well-argued skepticism as mere self-serving arguments of dinosaurs who refused to adapt.[79] Neither jointness nor the revolution in military affairs had much to do with strategy, however, except perhaps in the negative sense that they encouraged the assumption that tactical results would speak for themselves. The fixation on optimizing the military to realize decisive victory through advanced technology obfuscated the difference between warfare (i.e., the act of waging war) and war (i.e., the use of warfare for political purpose). Both jointness and the revolution in military affairs, in any case, were about warfighting of a rather peculiar kind, one that conceived the enemy as an array of targets, whose efficient destruction was the overarching purpose of military force.

In some respects, however, the direction of foreign and defense policy that emerged during Clinton's last years was aligned with at least some strands of Navy thinking. In practice, the Clinton foreign policy was about forward presence, crisis management, and airpower-intensive, risk-averse power projection. In such circumstances, the Tomahawk cruise missile was proving invaluable as a means of coercive diplomacy, which was rooted in its ability to limit both collateral damage and the chances that U.S. or NATO aircrews would be captured. It could be launched from a variety of ships and submarines that were more or less continuously on station overseas. Overall, the Navy's forward-deployed structure, flexible fleet, and expeditionary experiences were demonstrating the service's worth in the eyes of the CINCs. The direction of defense planning, which was based on precision airpower and power projection in general, was also well aligned with the Navy's strategic vision of carrier- and Tomahawk-led power projection.

"2020 Vision" advanced the notion that the Navy—and not the Air Force—should be the primary enabler of decisive strike warfare. It promised a fleet structured around a dominant, specialized mission. This was an attractive idea in budgetary terms, perhaps, but one sharply at odds with the outlook of the strategists in the N513, whose Naval Operational Concept continued to emphasize a carrier-led fleet in which balance was associated with flexibility across a wide range of kinetic and nonkinetic missions. This potentially crippling divergence was resolved by default. Johnson never signed out "2020 Vision" and let the arsenal ship project die from lack of support. In the end, no tough decisions were called for, and none was made. Given the generally supportive direction of foreign and defense policy, there was nothing to motivate a need for an alternative strategic approach, one that sought to advance a systemic grand strategy.

Throughout this period, the best strategic minds in the Navy were concerned chiefly with how to elevate the Navy's partnership with the Marine Corps beyond rhetoric, and how to advance the Navy's relevance in the joint doctrine arena. Writing Navy doctrine was itself a daunting problem. The Navy had little interest or institutionalized capacity to do such a thing during the Cold War (other than that needed to operate with the navies of NATO allies). Jointness made writing naval doctrine an imperative, and with it, the need to find a mechanism to bridge the conceptual gulf between the Navy and the Marine Corps.

Conceptually and bureaucratically, the Naval Operational Concept, which was cancelled shortly after Boorda's death, was a bridge too far.[80] All bets were off when capability requirements were on the table. "I take nothing away from the Marine Corps," noted a senior admiral. "They're awesome. I love 'em. But they're also very good and very aggressive and relentless in their pursuit of things for the Marine Corps. What the hell's wrong with that? Nothing! But when you're both vying for the same resources, it's tough. It's hardball." As one senior Marine stated, "The relationship between the Navy and the Marine Corps, inside the Beltway, is tied directly to resources. When resources are tight, I don't care whether the CNO and the commandant are in love with each other, it is not going to be pretty."[81]

The Navy's interest in doctrine faded after Kelso's departure. In terms of institutional importance, prominence, and expertise, the Naval Doctrine Command never measured up to its much larger Army and Marine Corps counterparts—nor could it. Unlike the Naval Doctrine Command, these counterparts were established in the early twentieth century, led by a four-star and a three-star, respectively, and staffed by upwardly mobile officers. In 1998 the Naval Doctrine Command was moved from Norfolk to the Naval War College in Newport, Rhode Island, and renamed the Navy Warfare Development Command; it was destined never to be commanded by a Marine, leaving unfilled a promise made in " . . . From the Sea." In 2009 it found its way back to Norfolk and was placed under U.S. Fleet Forces Command. To this day, *Naval Operations: NDP-3* has not been released.

There was a revolution of a sort in Navy doctrine during the 1990s, however. It was not about the Navy–Marine Corps team, nor did it require much cogitation. It was about naval aviation's de facto adoption of the Air Force's operational doctrine, a process that unfolded organically in the course of integrated air campaigns like Southern Watch (enforcement of no-fly zones in Iraq) and Deliberate Force. This practical success further reinforced the big ideas of jointness and the revolution in military affairs, all of which shifted the Navy's operational outlook—not toward global and systemic requirements, however, but toward the problems of warfighting on land.

Chapter *7*

Anytime, Anywhere, 1996–97

Joint Vision 2010: The Military's New Template

I n July 1996 General Shalikashvili released his vision. Entitled *Joint Vision 2010*, it was one of the most influential and emblematic documents of the post–Cold War era.[1] It was a glossy, purple-jacketed publication filled with thirty-four pages of photographs, schematic drawings, and double-spaced paragraphs that defined the operational concepts and capabilities the services needed to support the chairman's warfighting requirements.[2] Like Admiral Owens' Joint Resource Oversight Council, the purpose of *Joint Vision 2010* was to influence the services' resource decisions.[3]

Joint Vision 2010 represented a fundamental shift: with it, the chairman had gone from providing strategic guidance and submitting to the secretary of defense alternative recommendations for the services' program choices and budget proposals to governing their visions and resource decisions. "*Joint Vision 2010* had a profound influence on the Services' ability to identify mid- to long-term requirements," as a RAND study noted. "The Joint Staff has encouraged the Services to continue their own institutional vision work and strategic planning activities," it continued, "but these activities must be responsive to [*Joint Vision 2010*] and the ["Joint Vision Implementation Plan"]. . . . [Even though] there is no formal legislation or DoD regulation that requires the Services to support or respond to [them]."[4] Rooted in the Cold War, the trends of centralized decision making and, as will be seen, prescribed patterns of military thought were now being fully realized in the post–Cold War era.

The dominant issues in *Joint Vision 2010* were not strategic, but operational. As Shalikashvili noted on its signature page, *Joint Vision 2010* "provides an operationally based template for the evolution of the Armed Forces. . . . It *must* become a benchmark for Service and Unified Command visions."[5] *Joint Vision 2010* had four organizing principles: (1) dominant maneuver; (2) precision engagement; (3) full dimensional protection; and (4) focused logistics. *Joint Vision 2010* declared that the military's primary task was "to deter conflict—but, should deterrence fail, to fight and win our nation's wars," and that "power projection, enabled by overseas presence, will likely remain the fundamental strategic concept of our future force."[6]

Joint Vision 2010 sought to increase warfighting effectiveness by finding efficiencies: "To retain our effectiveness with less redundancy, we will need to wring every ounce of capability from every available source. That outcome can only be accomplished through a more seamless integration of Service capabilities."[7] If there had ever been any question that jointness was ultimately about economy of force, Shalikashvili had answered it.[8]

Joint Vision 2010 was about realizing the revolution in military affairs. The vision's primary theme was the promises of advanced technology. In strident language, it noted that new information technologies would link what it called all-source intelligence (those sources being satellites, radar, or sonar, for example), sensors, and platforms to command and control organizations in ways that would improve "the ability to see, prioritize, assign, and assess information . . . [and] collect, process, and distribute relevant data to thousands of locations."[9] In so doing, the United States "will gain *dominant battlespace awareness*, an interactive 'picture' which will yield much more accurate assessments of friendly and enemy operations." There was no doubt, however, about which technology was the most important: "Long-range precision capability, combined with a wide range of delivery systems, is emerging as a key factor in future warfare." *Joint Vision 2010* concluded, "The combination of these technology trends will provide an order of magnitude improvement in lethality. Commanders will be able to attack targets successfully with fewer platforms and less ordnance while achieving objectives more rapidly and with reduced risk."

For all intents and purposes, *Joint Vision 2010* was a theory of strategic airpower rendered more lethal and efficient by new information technologies. As Fred Kagan noted, *Joint Vision 2010* was essentially a watered down version of, in his words, the Air Force's "nearly airpower-pure doctrines" of Dominant Battlespace

Knowledge and Shock and Awe.[10] Both doctrines saw war as an exercise in determining, identifying, and destroying targets, with the former attriting enemy forces
in the field and the latter destroying, isolating, manipulating, and otherwise disorienting the enemy's leadership. Jointness came to be understood as involving
little more than the integration of the services' informational and kinetic technologies to deliver an efficient, swift, and unambiguous victory over a generic and
otherwise inert foe in support of (if not the more preferable) tactical forces on
the ground.

Johnson Tasks the "The Navy Operational Concept"

Joint Vision 2010 did not obviate the need for the Navy to develop a major doctrinal statement of its own. If anything, it made it more imperative. More than
ever, joint visions and doctrine were governing the services' decisions, while the
services' avenues to influence U.S. strategy and defense policy had narrowed.
Joint doctrine was proving to be a battleground for the services to push weapons
and concepts that served their respective interests. This placed at an advantage
those U.S. military services that were already organized around doctrine, namely
the Army and the Marine Corps, as well as those that were already adept at developing innovative concepts, namely the Marine Corps and the Air Force. The Navy
had yet to find anything to influence that process, which worried admirals like
CNO Johnson, who remembered all too clearly how the Navy had been marginalized in the Gulf War because it was not on board with what was then considered joint doctrine.

Yet many admirals outside the Pentagon could not understand the importance of joint doctrine or the need to correct the service's dismissive attitude
toward doctrine in general.[11] The CNO wanted to elevate the importance of doctrine, invigorate doctrinal thinking, and end criticism from the Marine Corps
and others that the Navy did not have an operational concept. The CNO did not
want to burn bridges to the Marine Corps, but he wanted a Navy answer to "Operational Maneuver from the Sea" that affirmed the Navy's value not just in the
prosecution of regional conflict or amphibious operations, but across the board.

Commander Bouchard, the chief of N513, was tasked to draft a "Navy
Operational Concept," as distinct from a naval (i.e., Navy and Marine Corps)
operational concept.[12] The CNO told Bouchard to work with Vice Adm. Art
Cebrowski, OPNAV's director of Space, Information Warfare, and Command and
Control (N6), to incorporate Cebrowski's innovative ideas. These ideas would

later crystallize into what would be known as network-centric warfare, which would come to dominate American strategic thinking in the post–Cold War era. Johnson, who was neither a visionary nor an innovator, knew Cebrowski well and believed that the Navy had to harness Cebrowski's visionary concepts.

Cebrowski believed that the world wars' industrialized violence was too inherently indiscriminate to address contemporary strategic requirements, and, specifically, that its callousness toward civilian casualties was immoral.[13] To Cebrowski, the technologies of the so-called Information Age offered a more discrete and efficient use of violence. Owens and Cebrowski had shaped *Joint Vision 2010*, this at a time when Cebrowski was serving as the Joint Staff's director of Command, Control, Communications, and Computers (J6), a position he held before moving to OPNAV as the director of N6.[14]

Cebrowski was among a small number of influential and visionary admirals who came to the fore in the 1990s. They were the post–Cold War equivalents of those who had led the Navy in the 1950s, none more so than CNO Arleigh Burke. Over their careers, Adm. Archie R. Clemins, Vice Adm. Art Cebrowski, Vice Adm. Jerry O. Tuttle, and Rear Adm. Wayne E. Meyer, and even Adm. Bill Owens to a degree, had immersed themselves in the use of computers and information technologies to solve operational problems. They were well suited to the critical task of overhauling the Navy's command, control, communications, and intelligence systems, the result of which vastly increased capabilities in surveillance, target acquisition, and precision-guided munitions, among others.

"The Navy Operational Concept" was drafted primarily by Bouchard and Cebrowski.[15] As Bouchard admitted, they were an odd pair. Cebrowski was a cerebral technologist who sought to apply advanced commercial computer and network technologies to the problem of organizing naval and joint forces to defeat a generic enemy on shore. Bouchard was a self-styled maneuverist, one of a group of mostly surface officers in OPNAV's N51 who saw naval maneuver warfare as an attractive organizing principle that was fully consonant with the Navy's traditional preference for decentralized command structures, a minimum of doctrine, and empowerment of on-scene commanders to seize the initiative. Bouchard also believed that maneuver warfare was consonant with joint doctrine, which Navy strategists saw as following AirLand Battle's construct of integrating precision interdiction strike warfare and close air support with maneuvering armored forces.

Bouchard and Cebrowski agreed that network-centric warfare could take the theory of maneuver warfare to the next level of sophistication, which would provide the Navy with an opportunity to drive joint doctrine instead of reacting to it. Throughout late 1996 Bouchard spent many hours after work in Cebrowski's office trying to envision an approach to naval maneuver warfare that embraced Cebrowski's somewhat enigmatic ideas about the role of information in a way that would be comprehensible to the average fleet officer.

"The Navy Operational Concept"

"The Navy Operational Concept" was completed in January 1997. It was not organized around *Joint Vision 2010,* which came out six months earlier, but rather around the more accommodating *National Military Strategy* of 1995.[16] It viewed the military's purpose not in terms of jointness, technology, or the battlefield, but in terms of supporting its three pillars of peacetime engagement, deterrence, and conflict prevention, and fighting and winning the nation's wars, all of which highlighted the need for forward deployment and the fleet's full-spectrum capabilities. "The primary purpose of forward-deployed naval forces," noted "The Navy Operational Concept," "is to project American power from the sea to influence events ashore in the littoral regions of the world across the operational spectrum of peace, crisis and war."[17]

U.S. naval forces provided on-scene capabilities that contributed to peacetime engagement, deterrence, and conflict prevention, and fighting and winning, and could do so without violating any nation's sovereignty, the result of being able to operate in international waters.[18] As the document noted, peacetime engagement produced the "sense of security" needed to enlarge the number of free-market democracies, which was important because democracies were presumed to be less likely to threaten U.S. interests and more willing to cooperate.[19]

Deployed naval forces contributed to deterrence and conflict prevention because they were always at the highest readiness level and possessed combat-credible capabilities that could transition rapidly from peace to crisis to war. The broad range of options that naval forces presented would leave a potential aggressor uncertain as to what course of action U.S. leaders would take.[20] Naval forces could react to ambiguous warning signs that would not, in themselves, justify costly reactive deployments by United States–based ground and air forces, making naval forces "a potent and cost-effective alternative to power projection from the continental United States."[21]

"The Navy Operational Concept" noted that the United States usually enters a conflict only in response to naked aggression against U.S. interests or allies. As a result, U.S. and allied forces find themselves on the defensive until reinforcements arrive, disembark, and deploy into the field. Until then, naval forces help to fight and win. "Our ability to deliver a wide range of naval firepower and generate very high aircraft sortie rates can have major impact on the course and outcome of a conflict, especially during this critical early period of a joint campaign, when continental U.S.-based forces are just starting to arrive in theater."[22] Naval forces could also leverage "our robust command and control systems and the reach of our sensors and weapons to concentrate combat power from dispersed, net-worked forces and project power far inland."[23]

In limited contingencies, U.S. naval forces could by themselves exert a "deci-sive impact."[24] In larger conflicts, they were viewed as an integral element of joint operations; this was a modest retreat from the claims in " . . . From the Sea" and "2020 Vision" that naval forces could be decisive in larger and more-protracted conflicts.[25] The Navy had thus finally come around to an integrated understanding of jointness, thanks largely to Cebrowski's ideas about network-ing and the Navy's desire for joint task force commanders to use its fleet flagships and carriers as fully equipped command centers.

The fight and win section is where Bouchard attempted to reconcile maneu-ver and network-centric warfare. He argued that naval operational maneuver and speed of command could be combined with decisive effect. He uses the term "oper-ational maneuver" to mean leveraging the right of navies to operate unimpeded in international waters, a right that, in the American case, was enhanced by the improbability that an enemy navy might wish to contest the issue. Naval forces can, by nature, concentrate and disperse rapidly; they can move constantly and change capabilities with the additions of different kinds of ships. They can appear to be a distant presence, yet strike suddenly with either precision naval fires (i.e., bombs, missiles, or gunfire) or by landing Marines ashore. As the document noted, naval forces exemplified "the ability to rapidly collect information, assess the situation, develop a course of action, and immediately execute with over-whelming effect"; the speed of command would resemble the operation of the contemporary high-tech marketplace, where "disproportionately larger returns for relatively modest, but precisely placed, initial investments" could be achieved. The aim overall was to "lock out enemy solutions, while locking in our success."[26]

The Navy's three- and four-star admirals thought "The Navy Operational Concept" did not sufficiently emphasize the time-honored war-fighting themes and operational virtues that were used to justify Navy programs; they did not disagree with its ideas on maneuver or network-centric warfare, but they did not see how those ideas could help defend the Navy's budget.[27] Led by N8, OPNAV was tied up attempting to shape the direction of the *Quadrennial Defense Review* (QDR) and readying arguments for its release in the spring of 1997. The congressionally mandated QDR and *Joint Vision 2010* were both all too clearly an extension of the Air Force's recently revitalized conception of strategic airpower. As the Air Force claimed, its idea of strategic airpower had been rendered more effective and precise by the same technologies the Navy was claiming as its own. The unabashed embracing of long-range strike warfare as the essence of jointness was such that many feared that the defense budget's postwar apportionment—24 percent for the Army, 29 percent for the Air Force, and 32 percent for both the Navy and Marine Corps—would be shifted in favor of the Air Force.[28]

The budgetary battles were permeating everything in OPNAV.[29] Even though the purpose of "The Navy Operational Concept" had nothing to do with programs, it was assumed that anything that came out of OPNAV was related to the battle of the budget, and therefore had to be bottom-lined by N8. This assumption had always reinforced service parochialism in the Navy's strategic statements and stifled creative and independent thinking by the Navy's strategists in N51.

These considerations led to the decision not to publish "The Navy Operational Concept."[30] Instead, it was emailed to the Navy's admirals and then posted on the Internet in January 1997. This approach reflected Johnson's skepticism about strategic statements in general, as well as his desire to keep a low profile. He also wanted to avoid the impression that it was replacing "Forward . . . From the Sea" because Secretary Dalton did not want another vision during his tenure. Only later that year, in May, was the decision made to publish it in a periodical, and then not in *Proceedings*, the Navy's professional journal, but in *Sea Power*, the magazine of the Navy League, a civilian not-for-profit organization established to educate Americans on the importance of sea power.

Despite being one of the Navy's most innovative postwar documents, "The Navy Operational Concept" was all but ignored in the Navy. It failed to invigorate doctrinal thinking, at least partly because of the half-hearted way in which it was promulgated. Over time, however, its influence grew, chiefly as a launching pad for further work on network-centric warfare. Because it promised to increase performance and cost efficiencies by means of precision strike warfare, network-centric warfare became increasingly synonymous with jointness in the next decade, and would become the centerpiece of the Pentagon's efforts to transform the military.

"Anytime, Anywhere"

"The Navy Operational Concept" had not been conceived as the Navy's way of acknowledging to *Joint Vision 2010,* and the pianissimo way in which it had been sent out into the world ensured that it would not be perceived as satisfying that obvious need. While the Army and the Air Force had produced "Army Vision 2010" and "Global Engagement: A Vision of the 21st Century Air Force," respectively, the Navy's vision remained "Forward . . . From the Sea," published in 1994.[31] Nor had the Navy responded to three national-level strategic documents, all of which came out in May 1997: the QDR; Shalikashvili's new *National Military Strategy: Shape, Respond, Prepare Now*; and the Clinton administration's *National Security Strategy for A New Century.*[32]

Meanwhile, the number of ships in fleet continued to decrease. It went from the Base Force's 451 ships (later 416) to the 346 of the "Bottom-Up Review," and then to the 1997 QDR's 305 (later 310). By the summer of 1997 the fleet numbered 354 ships, with the construction of four in fiscal year 1997 and five authorized for the year after.[33] As Vice CNO Donald L. Pilling noted, "If we can buy eight to ten ships a year, that will keep us about three hundred ships. That's sort of where our redline is."[34] However, Johnson's low-key lobbying of Congress was successful in terms of support for the F/A-18E/F Super Hornet and twelve carriers.

To many in OPNAV, however, the Navy's silence in the marketplace of ideas was deafening. The lack of a CNO-signed vision, for example, was causing the Navy's warfare communities to advance their own self-serving visions. To many in Washington, it appeared the Navy was unable or unwilling to defend itself from the Air Force's attack on the alleged inadequacies of the Super Hornet, and, in a larger sense, the attack on the Navy's relevance. As one reporter noted, "Though Johnson's understated style has ruffled no feathers, it had some Navy boosters on Capitol Hill privately worried this spring that he and the service would be outmaneuvered in the Pentagon's deliberations over the *Quadrennial Defense Review.*"[35]

By the late summer of 1997, several high-ranking admirals in OPNAV had convinced Johnson to promulgate a vision, whose development would be overseen by an ad hoc brain trust called the CNO Strategic Planning Group.[36] The group consisted of the vice CNO, Pilling; Vice Adm. Art Cebrowski (N6); Vice Adm. James O. Ellis (N3/N5); Vice Adm. Conrad C. Lautenbacher (N8), Rear Adm. Kendall Pease (Chief of Naval Information, i.e., the Navy Department's chief public affairs official), and Capt. R. Robinson "Robby" Harris, the director of N00K. Johnson was willing to give the vision a shot, but wanted it in the form of a *Proceedings* article, which was drafted by Capt. Ed Smith, a member of Harris' staff.

The article came out in the November 1997 issue.[37] At less than three pages, "Anytime, Anywhere: A Navy for the 21st Century" was considerably shorter than other CNO articles. "Anytime, Anywhere" was not well related to "The Navy Operational Concept," which had been developed in N51.[38] While the latter was meant to catalyze American naval doctrine and vault the Navy into a leading role in joint doctrine, "Anytime, Anywhere" was simply how CNO Johnson saw the Navy's role in U.S. security. His was a narrow, operationally oriented interpretation of the Navy's purpose, which accorded with his overall focus on operational primacy.[39] The Navy's purpose "is to influence, directly and decisively, events ashore from the sea—anytime, anywhere," noted the CNO. "That straightforward statement is the core of my vision. . . . It describes who we are and what we do." The article claimed that the Navy was redefining American sea power to shape the strategic environment and deter conflict, stop the actions of an aggressor, or enable the entry of heavier joint forces. In a bit of hyperbole, it noted that the task to reorient American naval power to influence events on shore was greater "than any other navy has ever undertaken."[40]

"Anytime, Anywhere" focused on warfighting. A "military force that cannot win is worthless, in war and peace," it noted.[41] It argued for the decisiveness of naval power, which had been somewhat muted in "The Navy Operational Concept." Presence was not related to anything but preventing crisis and conflict. The terms "democracy," "free trade," and "globalization" were not to be found in the article. Forward naval forces were conceived as a force-in-being, a part of the region's local security calculus that aggressor states could not ignore.

The article offered a generalized tribute to Cebrowski's ideas. "We stand on the threshold of a new century, in an era of almost dizzying technological change," it noted. "Change is our ally. It presents an unprecedented opportunity to transform the face of warfare, to give a new dimension to sea power, and to expand enormously the contribution [of] the U.S. Navy." Using the language of *Joint Vision 2010* and the Air Force's Shock and Awe, it noted, "We will possess the means to disorient and shock an enemy sufficiently to break his resistance."[42]

The article did not address the Marines' role, a reflection of the growing separation with the Marine Corps, which had moved on to another operational concept.[43] This was the Three Block War, which did not rely much on the Navy. In the 1990s the Marines were responding to lower-intensity crises on the order of once every five weeks, which was three times the incidence of the late Cold War. These crises were increasingly complex and chaotic, characterized by lack of local governance, proliferation of small arms, and decentralized actions by nonstate actors. The commandant, General Krulak, believed these crises might well require Marines to conduct at the same time full-scale combat operations on one city block, peacekeeping operations among ethnic groups in an adjacent block, and humanitarian assistance on the next block—hence the name Three Block War.

"Anytime, Anywhere" simply described what the Navy did. It was organized around Vice Adm. Stansfield Turner's four essential missions, which he had defined in 1974: (1) power projection; (2) presence; (3) strategic deterrence (both nuclear and conventional); and (4) sea control.[44] Few of the Navy's postwar strategic documents highlighted the need for sea control more emphatically, a trend that was to continue, due in part to the need to support the new *Virginia*-class fast attack submarine, the replacement for the Cold War's *Los Angeles* class. Sea control now included area control in the littoral, the achievement of which was, according to the document, the Navy's greatest challenge. "If we cannot command the seas and the airspace above them," the article noted, "we cannot project power to command or influence events ashore; we cannot deter; we cannot shape the security environment. That is a consequence of our geography; it will not change in the 21st century."[45]

The article also expressed reservations about the direction of U.S. strategy, calculated to blunt the Air Force's extravagant claims about the decisiveness of strategic airpower. "There is no simple, absolute technological answer to all our warfare problems," it noted. "We cannot assume that our future conflicts will be swift and bloodless. We still will face many contingencies in which more traditional combat capabilities on land and at sea will be needed and may be our only option."[46] In a decade that was all about the salutary promises of technology, this was one of the few occasions between 1989 and 2007 when the Navy bluntly pushed against the assumption that technology was the answer to the nation's strategic questions.

In the fleet, "Anytime, Anywhere" was more popular than anything since " . . . From the Sea." It was short and easy to read. In a time of institutional self-doubt, its title reinforced how the Navy saw its purpose. However, it had little impact elsewhere. Like "The Navy Operational Concept," it lacked CNO ownership and follow-up.[47] It was highly parochial, perhaps too out of step with U.S.

strategy. Arguments about the decisiveness of naval forces simply were not being borne out. The scenarios envisioned in " . . . From the Sea," which highlighted the need for Navy–Marine Corps integration in the littoral, were not panning out either, to the point where it was becoming obvious that the two services were going their separate ways.

Conclusion

As manifested in *Joint Vision 2010,* the U.S. military adapted a simple and compelling formula for how to wage war in a quick, efficient, and decisive manner by employing state-of-the-art technology. After the Cold War, the American defense establishment behaved much as it did after World War II. The focus was on how, not why, the military fought. Strategy was made inferentially, as a derivative of technological progress and the salutary capabilities it promised.

The preoccupation on how to precisely destroy targets relieved the military from the more difficult task of relating the results of such destruction to political goals, which were assumed to materialize at some point, mostly beyond the pale of the military's interest. As Colin Gray reflected, "The true parent of American thinking on national security is Jomini, not Clausewitz."[48] Mahan's battleships, the strategic bomber, the nuclear bomb, and now the information-led revolution in military affairs were compelling, in part, because they conformed to American cultural assumptions and preferences, an unavoidable and necessary connection in a democracy like the United States, however suboptimal the strategic implications of such concepts may be in theoretical terms.

Nevertheless, it is hard to argue that "The Navy Operational Concept" was not suited to its moment. It emphasized the Navy's unique capabilities across the board, with particular emphasis on the value of forward deployment in relation to conventional deterrence and crisis response. These virtues would have been less in demand had not the Clinton administration's foreign policy been so broad, and had it not focused on regional stability and democratization. In this sense, Clinton's foreign policy was far more accommodating toward U.S. naval interests than that of his predecessor or his successor. America's engagement with the world in the 1990s placed a premium on how the military was adapting to expeditionary missions across the spectrum, and this advantaged the Navy and the Marine Corps, which were already organized for such tasks and had experience in carrying them out.

Yet justifying the Navy solely in relation to abstract notions of its operational uniqueness and its capacity for aiding the spread of democratic and free-market ideals was risky. Despite how the military was actually being used, such a course went against the grain of American post–Cold War thinking, which continued to see anything other than major war as a lesser-included case for purposes of planning and budgeting. Throughout the 1990s CNOs testified to Congress about the virtues of presence and how the Navy promoted stability. But Congress simply was not interested. It was not opposed to such missions, but it could not fathom how they related to Congress' job of supplying the means of warfare. Not the least reason why all the U.S. military services continued to emphasize the procurement of advanced weapons systems long after it had become apparent that America's most likely adversaries were not going to possess them, was that such weaponry was the easiest thing to sell to Congress.

It comes as no surprise, then, that the Navy's most innovative concepts of the post–Cold War era involved the application of technology to traditional operations. The visionaries that emerged from the ranks of the Navy were well equipped to realize advancements in computer-based information and precision strike munitions that were developed in the 1970s and 1980s. These admirals integrated the Navy within the new framework of joint operations by solving practical problems. They allowed the Navy to demonstrate its usefulness to the CINCs, specifically by showing that naval strike warfare was just as sophisticated as the Air Force's, and incorporated important advantages in the areas of speed, sustainability, and flexibility that made naval forces an attractive option.

To Navy leaders, the service's greatest challenge in the 1990s was not strategic in nature. They did not have to find a way out of a conceptual cul-de-sac, as had their predecessors in the late 1970s, a dilemma that demanded the wholesale improvement of the Navy's strategic thinking. While Navy leaders struggled initially to demonstrate the fleet's capabilities across the spectrum, their greatest challenge was to redress the political vulnerability that came after the Gulf War. As Owens noted in 1995, "The issue facing the nation's naval forces is not whether strategic-bombardment theory is absolutely correct; it is how best to contribute to successful strategic-bombardment campaigns."[49] The Navy was able to overcome such challenges in about six years, mainly by harnessing network-centric ideas and technologies and applying them to the problems of precision strike warfare waged from the sea, all of which did little to shift the institution's outlook away from the problems of warfighting on land and toward a greater understanding of U.S. grand strategic requirements.

The Navy Strategic Planning Guidance, 1998–2000

Chapter 8

Clinton's Dilemmas

By the start of 1998 it was clear that the Clinton administration's flexible approach to foreign policy was not faring any better than its failed interventionist approach. American intelligence agencies identified no fewer than fifteen priorities, which essentially meant there were no priorities and nothing on which to create a consensus about U.S. interests.[1] No bumper sticker had emerged to replace enlargement or containment, making it difficult for the administration to find domestic support for its many diplomatic initiatives and military operations overseas. The multilateralism that emerged from the Gulf War coalition had worn away, particularly with respect to Iraq. International support for American-led actions declined. "The president had no overall strategy to guide his expenditure of time, energy, and resources," noted Hal Brands, "and the direction of U.S. policy ended up reflecting the president's personal inclinations rather than a systematic assessment of means and ends."[2]

The administration's refusal to increase the budget or reduce overseas commitments was straining the military.[3] It was stretched thin in operations to contain Iraq and keep the peace in the Balkans. The Army had had twenty-nine overseas deployments since 1989, compared with ten over the previous four decades.[4] In the Navy 18,000 operational billets remained unfilled.[5] Morale and readiness plummeted.[6] While it did not unduly change the services' budget apportionment, as some had feared, the 1997 QDR only exacerbated the problem.[7]

Given a limited budget, it had considered three options: (1) focus on current threats and ignore future ones, (2) focus on future threats at the expense of present threats, and (3) focus on realizing a revolution in military affairs. This third option was the one that the Pentagon's leaders selected, despite the fact that those weapons systems would not be fielded for a decade or more. The choice short-changed parts, training, and retention bonuses.[8]

The Navy's low readiness, morale, and retention were undermining confidence in its leaders: as one reporter noted, Secretary Dalton and CNO Johnson had "been too supportive of the administration's policies of curbing budgets and cutting units while committing forces to an increasing number of humanitarian and crisis-response missions."[9] The administration responded by sending a budget to Congress calling for the first increase in the defense budget in fifteen years, which the president signed into law in October 1999.[10]

Enter Danzig

It was in this unpromising context that Richard Danzig was sworn in as Secretary of the Navy in November 1998. Despite being in a lame-duck administration, Danzig was the most activist secretary since John Lehman, which invariably led to tensions with the CNO and commandant. Danzig had a doctorate in history from Oxford and a law degree from Yale, and had been a law professor at Stanford and Harvard. He had been the deputy assistant secretary of defense for Manpower, Reserve Affairs and Logistics in the Carter administration, and the Undersecretary of the Navy from November 1993 to 1997. He had an intimidating intellect, even to the likes of Admiral Johnson and General Krulak. Like Lehman, Danzig was an energetic advocate of the Navy and sought to rebuild the service. Unlike Lehman, Danzig was not a divisive figure in Congress. He was one of the few Clinton appointees in the Pentagon that had the support of both parties, which, given a highly partisan Congress, was a requirement to push through his many initiatives. He gained the reputation on Capitol Hill as an effective and innovative administrator and as a figure savvy enough to change what many saw as a hidebound and scandal-ridden service.

Danzig was well aware of the Navy's and Marine Corps' strong institutional tendencies. He believed the military needed strong civilian leaders to keep it energized and, in his words, continually "rethinking itself."[11] In meetings with admirals in OPNAV, Danzig probed those tendencies and questioned assumptions and unassailable beliefs. In a meeting with the director of Surface Warfare (N86),

Rear Adm. Michael G. Mullen (CNO, 2005–7 and chairman of the Joint Chiefs of Staff, 2007–11), for example, Danzig dissected Mullen's brief, which, among others, tried to explain the need for American sea power:

> You begin by saying we're a maritime nation. . . . My problem with it is I'm not sure how evocative it is for most people to call us a maritime nation when we're 800 billion other things. A cybernation, a financial nation, and so on. It doesn't make the case for sea power for me to begin with that true-but-not-evocative proposition. And then you continue on to say that "Forward presence is our job one." But what you're citing for this is the CNO's comments, and so it's self-referencing. If it's designed for an external audience, it doesn't persuade me that forward presence is all that important just 'cause, to us, it seems important. . . . So why do you need to be present?[12]

These were not the kinds of questions that admirals were used to hearing from a Secretary of the Navy or from anyone else of consequence.

To many in the service, Danzig was rethinking the Navy too much, trying to accomplish too much in his two years in office.[13] As CNO Johnson noted, "With an organization this big, and with as many moving parts as it has, change can be very useful. But you have to be very careful how you put it into the system. . . . Putting five degrees of rudder on this machine takes a long time." There was an ever-present anxiety in OPNAV that Danzig would do something radical. Unlike his predecessor, John Dalton, who signed documents like "Forward . . . From the Sea" with little reservation, Danzig had the intellectual firepower and political backing to develop a new strategic approach by himself, whose direction seemed impossible to anticipate. Some feared that he would abandon the Navy's commitment to forward deployment, others that he would elevate the Marines' comparative stature because, as undersecretary, he had shifted $600 million from the Navy to the Marines' side of the budget.[14] From the perspectives of the Navy's and Marine Corps' leaders, there would be little time for Danzig to put the genie back in the bottle if his approach went south.

"A Maritime Strategy for the 21st Century"

When Danzig arrived, N513 had been working on a concept called 4 x 4. The concept, so called because it had four strategic concepts and four tactical concepts, was shelved after the arrival in the fall of 1998 of the new deputy CNO for Operations, Plans and Policies (N3/N5), Vice Adm. Thomas B. Fargo. Capt. Sam Tangredi started work on a new project, under the direction of Rear Adm. Joe Sestak, the head of N51. According to some, the project was a top priority of Danzig, who wanted a new strategic statement in place before the services began organizing in early 2000 for the 2001 QDR. In June 1999 one reporter noted that the secretary, CNO, and commandant would sign out a new strategy statement within months.[15] As will be seen, "A Maritime Strategy for the 21st Century," as Sestak's concept was titled, was never released.[16] The document was remarkable in the sense that it introduced the topics of globalization and anti-access.

The authors stated that "A Maritime Strategy" was a logical continuation of " . . . From the Sea" and "Forward . . . From the Sea." In the lengthy, fourteen-page document, they stated that the U.S. naval services still needed to focus on influencing events on shore, primarily because of two factors: first, the continued absence of a global adversary, and second, the inexorable process of globalization. The document defined globalization as "the accelerating process of economic, technological, cultural, and political integration throughout the world."[17] It noted that aggressors would avoid a conventional war with the United States, and instead apply asymmetric means such as terrorism, nuclear-biological-chemical threats, information warfare, or environmental sabotage. If the aggressors chose asymmetric approaches, it argued that forward-deployed naval forces' ability to deter and respond to conventional and asymmetric attacks were broader and more responsive than United States–based Army and Air Force units.

Globalization meant the United States would increasingly be affected by events overseas. According to the document, "Global economic interdependence has implied an expanding network of interests and trade that constitute a vital element of U.S. national strength. However, this factor also portends a set of interlocking dependencies that make a global economy like the United States vulnerable to crisis and conflict overseas."[18] Relating globalization to the Navy, the authors asserted that "economic interdependence has reinforced the long-standing, traditional role of U.S. naval forces to ensure high seas mobility and access to resources and markets, in peacetime as well as war."[19] Forward presence, conventional deterrence, and regional crisis management were thus no longer merely operational concepts, points on a spectrum of conflict, but were directly linked, for the first time, to the health of the American and global economy.

"A Maritime Strategy" was organized around the ends-ways-means paradigm. The ends were regional stability, deterrence of aggression, timely initial crisis response, and the readiness to fight and win wars. These were hardly revolutionary in systemic terms, and kept with the general operational focus.[20] The means were labeled Forward Presence and Knowledge Superiority. In short, informational technologies increased the importance of forward presence in general.[21] Together, informational technologies and forward presence gave joint and allied/coalition forces "an unprecedented awareness and understanding of the battlespace." Achieving Knowledge Superiority, which "places a priority on sensors over weapons and network over platform," means the enemy's anti-access strategies and weapons could not frustrate U.S. actions. With "credible combat capabilities," Knowledge Superiority increased the deterrent value of U.S. naval forces.

Like the means, the ways represented an attempt to integrate the ideas of *Joint Vision 2010* and Cebrowski not in terms of systemic goals, but in terms of the battlefield. The ways were Battlespace Control, Battlespace Attack, and Battlespace Sustainment.[22] Battlespace Control was about projecting offensive power and defensive control over the battlespace; defensive control included theater ballistic missile, cruise missile and air defense, and layered under-sea defenses against submarines and mines. Battlespace Control reflected the emphasis on local sea control, which supported the need for the *Virginia*-class attack submarine. The new submarine was designed to operate not only in the open ocean but in the shallower waters of the littorals against the much quieter Russian-made diesel *Kilo*-class submarine that Iran possessed, for example. Battlespace Attack was about using massed precision naval fires or Marines to neutralize the enemy's anti-access weapons and command networks and to attack its warfighting capability either as a stand-alone force or as part of a joint team. Battlespace Sustainment discussed how a mobile and tailored sea-based logistics system could support widely dispersed, fast-moving, and networked naval maneuver operations, as envisioned in the Marines' "Operational Maneuver from the Sea."

"A Maritime Strategy" offered an interesting argument. In light of revolutionary technological change, it was demanding that the U.S. military reconsider the traditionally understood boundaries of naval influence. It noted, for example, that in the nineteenth century the limits of naval battlespace were determined by the limited range of ship- and shore-based guns. Now, advanced technology was expanding the physical and informational battlespace and was increasing the reach and decisiveness of U.S. naval forces. "A Maritime Strategy" was a logical continuation of " . . . From the Sea" and "Forward . . . From the Sea" in the sense that it leveraged the promise of technology to argue that U.S. naval forces were even more decisive and their influence was even more global than what was asserted in those two documents.

"A Maritime Strategy" also offered a narrow and familiar understanding of what a maritime strategy was. Now, having achieved command of the seas, "the Navy and Marine Corps . . . [can] turn their attention to the ultimate objective of *maritime* strategy that will be a critical element of America's national security and military strategies in the decades to come," as the document noted. This objective was "*to influence directly and decisively events ashore by continuing to operate in forward regions and to take full advantage of revolutionary capabilities of information systems for knowledge-superiority operations.*"[23] The objective of any maritime strategy is to influence events on shore. Humans live on land and not on water. But "A Maritime Strategy" was also a logical continuation of the 1980s' Maritime Strategy: neither could escape the verities of American thinking, to which warfighting was central and the system and its importance were largely ancillary. The Navy did not understand the term "maritime strategy" in classical systemic terms, but in comparative terms. In this context, the word "maritime" simply referred to the domain that the Navy operated in and from, which was the maritime domain—as opposed to the Air Force's air domain and the Army's land domain. With its maritime domain–based strategy, the Navy was offering U.S. defense leaders a choice between what U.S. naval forces could provide and other operational-level approaches that the Air Force (e.g., Shock and Awe) and Army were advancing.

Naval experts questioned "A Maritime Strategy," whose drafts were floating around the Pentagon in the summer of 1999.[24] Not surprisingly, given the nature of American naval thinking, most saw nothing fundamentally new or different about it, this despite its appreciation of globalization and its implications to U.S. security. "As a statement of where the Navy is going for the future, I think there needs to be something more in here," noted Ronald O'Rourke.[25] He was implying that the paper did not address force structure. At least in Washington, the use of the term "strategy" in the title of a strategic statement means it is not just a vision or a concept or a white paper, the last of which introduces a new idea. Instead, it means the statement squarely addresses means-ways-ends thinking primarily—if not exclusively—in terms of a particular force structure, which O'Rourke believed was wanting in this case, and indeed it was.

The Marines did not like it either, and reportedly balked at endorsing it.[26] They never shied from relating naval forces, diplomacy, and crisis response. But

like "Forward . . . From the Sea," global thinking on the part of the Navy did
not enthrall the Marines. They wanted the focus on warfighting and expeditionary
operations, the core of their institutional ethos. As Krulak noted, "Our identity
is tied to that ethos. There are unintended consequences [to changing it]. You
think in the short term you're achieving a certain goal, but in reality, the unintended consequence is something bad for the Navy or the Marine Corps."[27]

"A Maritime Strategy" was never signed. The reasons are murky.[28] There is
some evidence that Sestak did not want the Marine Corps to review it, so that
when the Marines obtained a draft of "A Maritime Strategy," they quietly killed
the project near the end of 1999. Other sources indicate that the document went
through several Navy–Marine Corps revisions before being signed by Johnson
and Krulak. But when Danzig attempted to rewrite it himself, the two chiefs
balked and rescinded it. Despite the pushing by the most aggressive of the Navy
postwar strategists (Sestak) and the pulling by the most activist of Navy secretaries (Danzig), "A Maritime Strategy" was not published.

Sestak's Goals

The start of 2000 found Rear Admiral Sestak still searching for a vehicle to promote the ideas in "A Maritime Strategy" as a way to guide OPNAV's preparations
for the 2001 QDR.[29] To shape the direction of the QDR during its yearlong
development process to one more amenable to Navy interests, OPNAV's leaders,
like those of the other services' headquarters staffs in the Pentagon, tasked the staff
to assess the leanings of the presidential candidates, the trends in the domestic
political and strategic environments, and the Navy's priorities as well as those of
the other U.S. military services. Those tasks required organizing research teams
and determining themes and messages for Navy leaders' testimony and speeches.
Those tasks included writing white papers that asserted the Navy's comparative
importance, which were widely delivered. To defend the Navy's capability needs
and programs, a slew of analytic studies were prepared and provided to the team
that was writing the QDR. In contrast, OPNAV's preparation for the 1997 QDR
had been far less organized. OPNAV's leaders did not accord it much priority and
saw no need to tell a new story. Despite their passive approach, the 1997 QDR
was, fortunately for the Navy, generally supportive of its contribution to U.S. security. Judging by their preparations to the 2001 QDR, Navy leaders like Sestak
learned from that experience.

Sestak saw an opportunity to leverage his position as the head of OPNAV's
QDR team to institutionalize a new decision-making process in OPNAV. In

short, he wanted strategy to shape programmatic decisions instead of the other way around. From his perspective, programmatic decisions were being made in a vacuum of strategic thinking. In essence, there was no strategic planning going on in OPNAV, only strategic programming. As far as OPNAV was concerned, the Planning, Programming, and Budgeting System (or PPBS) was really pPBS. OPNAV lacked a comprehensive process that represented the planning phase. Sestak wanted such a process, and wanted it fully integrated with OPNAV's programming and budgeting processes. OPNAV's programming process was based, largely, on the CINCs' warfighting requirements, which were derived from their campaign plans for major combat operations. Strategic planning, in contrast, meant examining the long-term trends in the strategic, technological, political, and fiscal environments, and issuing guidance to shape resource decisions, which included milestones and feedback mechanisms to ensure those decisions actually followed the strategic guidance.

Two years earlier, Cdr. Joe Bouchard had tried unsuccessfully to do the same thing.[30] His idea for a strategic planning process was based on a two-year cycle that was synchronized with the OSD's budget process, which, in turn, was synchronized with Congress' two-year budget cycle. The product of his planning process would organize and guide the decisions of OPNAV, the fleet, and the rest of the Navy in much the same way the Maritime Strategy had aligned the Navy's activities in the 1980s. Bouchard pitched the idea to OPNAV's senior admirals, but the three-star deputy CNOs did not see a need for it, in part because it appeared to grant N3/N5 more authority over a process that had heretofore been dominated by N8, Manpower and Personnel (N1), and (more recently) the renamed Space and Electronic Warfare (N6). The barons, the two-star admirals that represented the warfare communities, did not like it either. The interactive, consensus-building process institutionalized by CNO Kelso and Vice Admiral Owens had broken down. It needed a personality like Owens to run it and bring consensus and a sense of teamwork among the ten or so junior admirals involved.[31] Absent such compelling leadership, the barons enjoyed a measure of freedom and did not want to be constrained by an authoritative top-down document. There was one part of OPNAV that was receptive: this was N81, which, because of its expert analysis role, had grown in importance. As Peter Swartz noted, N81 overshadowed the "collective role of [the] flags."[32] Like OP-07 before it, N81 was becoming the integrator of requirements and the arbitrator of priorities within OPNAV. Consequently, as Bouchard would have it, N81 and N51 would work together to draft the strategic planning guide.

In August 1999, two years after Bouchard had transferred from OPNAV to the National Security Council, OPNAV released something like what he had proposed. It was called the "Navy Strategic Planning Guidance: Long Range Planning Objectives."[33] Unlike Sestak's ambitious and higher priority "A Maritime Strategy," which would be snuffed out by the end of the year, the classified, fifty-five-page "Navy Strategic Planning Guidance" was an internal staffing document. Its intent was to guide OPNAV's development of the Navy's proposed budget for fiscal year 2002. No doubt, Sestak thought the document, which had been on the periphery of his attentions, lacked sufficient substance to link strategy and resources. But, having lost "A Maritime Strategy," he was not in a position to quibble. Besides, all things considered, it was an ideal vehicle to accomplish his many goals. It could promote the ideas from "A Maritime Strategy" without the need for Danzig's signature. It could organize OPNAV's efforts to prepare for the QDR, and, for the first time in the post–Cold War era, it could help institutionalize a strategy-based approach in OPNAV.

The "Navy Strategic Planning Guidance"

In the spring of 2000, Sestak overhauled the "Navy Strategic Planning Guidance" and had CNO Johnson sign it in April 2000. Compared to the August 1999 version, the document, at ninety pages, had nearly doubled in length and was now unclassified. The first of four sections, "The Strategic Environment," described the strategic context. Like "A Maritime Strategy," it discussed globalization and the rise of regional actors and their anti-access weapons and area-denial strategies. "Our potential adversaries," it noted, "will continue to pursue area denial strategies over the next 15 to 20 years."[34] Included in the first section were two summaries prepared by the Office of Naval Intelligence. The first, entitled "Potential Adversary Capabilities," discussed trends in theater ballistic missiles, submarines, mines, and antiship cruise missiles. The second, "Probable Other Areas of Concern," discussed asymmetric warfare as waged by state and non-state actors, including terrorist attacks on the homeland.[35]

The document stated that the next global threat would not appear before 2020. Consequently, "We must continue to be prepared to fight and win at the high end of military conflict, while maintaining a clear focus on the day to day shaping responsibility through the forward presence and engagement activities." Under such conditions, the point of a fleet built for high-end conflict was chiefly to deter regional powers from attempting to turn into peer competitors, a role in which China was already being cast. As the document noted, "The Navy must maintain the capability to dominate the maritime environment to dissuade global naval ambitions by a future regional power."[36]

The second section, termed "The Maritime Concept," was a recapitulation of "A Maritime Strategy." It stated, "The maritime concept clearly articulates our overarching strategic imperative as Maritime Power Projection," and "the paramount objective of the Navy and Marine Corps will remain the global projection of American power and influence—*anytime, anywhere*."[37] The document used the same means-ends-ways construct used in Sestak's earlier "A Maritime Strategy." It noted that the Navy would be guided by two complementary capstone operational concepts. "Naval Operations in the Information Age" was about how the Navy would transition from platform-centric to network-centric warfare, while "Operational Maneuver from the Sea" dealt with the conduct of naval operations in the littoral.[38] Also discussed was the need to protect the twenty large hub ports of the world against conventional and asymmetric attacks, and how the Navy should work with civil authorities in response to terrorist attacks and natural disasters at home.

The third section, "The Process," explained the planning process that Sestak wished to institutionalize. It entailed developing and refining a strategic concept, operationalizing the concept into warfighting concepts and capabilities, establishing a set of prioritized strategic planning objectives to realize the operational concepts, and assessing how those capability requirements would be translated into program recommendations.[39]

With his focus on capability requirements, Sestak was accounting for a change in how OPNAV now determined its programmatic priorities. Owens' Joint Mission Area assessment system, which saw the shift from basing priorities on naval warfare areas to joint warfare areas, had been replaced with the Integrated Warfare Architectures assessment process, which was based on what capabilities were required. These were still shaped by the needs of the CINCs and their respective naval operational commanders, but now, as the "Navy Strategic Planning Guidance" noted, the "primary focus [was] . . . on warfighting *capabilities* as opposed to the traditional focus on platforms and systems."[40] Instead of seven Joint Mission Areas (joint strike, joint littoral warfare, joint surveillance, joint space and electronic warfare/intelligence, strategic deterrence, strategic sealift/protection, and presence), the new process, which was led by N81, was oriented around five warfare and seven support assessment areas. The warfare areas were information superiority and sensors, sea dominance, air dominance, power projection, and deterrence. The support areas were sustainment, infrastructure, manpower and personnel, readiness, training/education, technology, and force structure.[41] In short, because of advancing technology OPNAV saw the need for a new staff methodology to ensure the fleet was integrated along capability versus platform lines.

The third section also laid out OPNAV's preparations for the QDR. It named the research teams and provided a milestone roadmap that included roundtable discussions, war games, and workshops. More important it identified the three themes or talking points for the QDR, which were rooted in "From the Sea," "Forward . . . From the Sea," Cebrowski's ideas, and the U.S. military's emphasis on advanced technology:

> The Navy's *enduring contribution* is combat-credible forward presence, providing our Nation with the means for both continuous shaping and timely crisis response. The other Services are transforming to become *expeditionary*— which we already are.
>
> The Navy's *transformation* is into a knowledge-superior force, enabling it to dictate the operational tempo across sea, air, land, space, and cyberspace— an *expanded battlespace*.
>
> Technology is driving [the] Navy into *new mission areas*—such as theater ballistic missile defense and deep land attack—and these, in turn, drive requirements for both new capabilities and additional capacity.[42]

With its third theme, the Navy was leveraging the promise of technology to argue for budgetary support for those capabilities that expanded its physical and informational battlespace, and with it the reach and decisiveness of U.S. naval forces.

Finally, the fourth section, "Long Range Planning Objectives," spoke to the need to align the Navy's many activities around the document's maritime concept. "We must look at every program, platform, organization, concept and technology," it noted, "to systematically judge whether it supports the maritime concept and provides positive progress along the path toward a Navy that is fully 'knowledge-centric,' present forward and combat-credible."[43]

The document then addressed the ways and means in terms of associated operational concepts and the capabilities needed to realize them. It assessed required capabilities in terms of five levels of risk, the highest of which was severe. Thirty-five capabilities were deemed severe. The top ten led off with contemporary issues (recruiting, retaining personnel, and measuring readiness), and continued with enduring issues (maintaining and deploying carrier and amphibious battle groups and maintaining survivability as a design characteristic of all platforms). Rounding out the top ten were high-tech capability requirements needed to integrate the fleet, particularly for anti-access operations; directing naval, joint, and combined task force operations afloat; linking shooters, sensors, and command nodes; establishing a common data link system for the fleet; producing a single integrated air picture that fused sensor and intelligence inputs; and conducting covert surveillance in the littoral battle space, which was accomplished primarily by fast attack submarines.[44]

In the end, however, the "Navy Strategic Planning Guidance" never had a chance to influence anything. Sestak had found a vehicle to carry his ideas, but it had not been marketed for a wider audience as "Forward . . . From the Sea" had been, nor could it have been, since that would have required Danzig's signature. Most of the admirals that either developed or supported it detached shortly after its release. Vice Adm. Robert J. Natter, who had replaced Fargo as N3/N5, transferred in June 2000. CNO Johnson retired in July, four months after signing the "Navy Strategic Planning Guidance."

Sestak himself transferred in October 2000 to the newly created QDR division in N8. Despite his occupying this seemingly key post, his ideas did not influence programmatic decisions, in part, perhaps, because they were perceived as too closely tied to his personal initiatives.[45] OPNAV's new leaders were either unsure of Sestak's ideas, not having been a part of their development, or had entirely different ideas. As with many of the Navy's strategic statements, the "Navy Strategic Planning Guidance" was hamstrung by the lack of a long-term follow-up plan, which might tread on the command prerogatives of the next CNO, whose appointment, in the nature of things, was never more than a few years away.[46] Yet, as with many statements that were institutionally abandoned or marginalized, its ideas percolated through the bureaucracy and the ranks of the Navy's strategists, and, to a lesser extent, the Navy's leaders, and would eventually emerge in a more crystallized form in the next set of strategic statements.

Clark: CNO as CEO

In July 2000 Adm. Vernon E. Clark (2000–2005) took the reins from CNO Johnson, who had led the Navy out of the traumatic years that followed Tailhook and secured the F/A-18 Super Hornet. Clark would serve five years in office, the second-longest tenure after that of CNO Burke. Clark was a surface officer who had entered the Navy in 1968. He was neither a graduate of the Naval Academy nor a graduate of the Naval War College, but had a master's degree in business administration, which was a first for a CNO. He had three programming tours under his belt, two of them in OPNAV and one as U.S. Transportation Command's director of Financial Management and Analysis (J8). During the Gulf War, he had been the director of J3 on the Joint Staff, and later was the director of the Joint Staff, the most important three-star position in the military.

The choice of Clark reflected the prevailing trend within the Department of Defense toward jointness and corporateness. As Pentagon spokesperson Kenneth Bacon noted, Secretary of Defense William S. Cohen had selected Clark because in his words "he had displayed a commitment to operating in an integrated way with other services" and could "bring innovative solutions" to the Navy's problems.[47] Clark often cited his joint and business experiences as influencing his decisions.[48]

From Clark's perspective, the Navy had no business advancing a strategy. That responsibility lay with OSD and the Joint Staff. A service-specific strategy was inherently self-serving and went against the grain of jointness. Having served as the Joint Staff's director, Clark was comfortable with how the process of strategy formulation worked, and was confident that those in OSD and the Joint Staff would make the right calls. Moreover, he was confident of his ability to redress such problems if they did not.[49]

To Clark, the Navy's strategy was its budget submission, and, like Johnson, he was skeptical of any kind of glossy strategic statement.[50] "I didn't come into the job with the idea of publishing another 'vision' document," Clark noted.[51] From his view, the CNO was the chief executive officer of an industrial corporation whose purpose was to provide his "customers," as Clark phrased it, who were the secretary of defense and the CINCs, with the right capabilities at a low cost. "We must extract the maximum advantage from the resources provided us and demand a high rate of return on our investments," he noted.[52]

In his first two years, Clark focused on his top five priorities: manpower, current readiness, future readiness, quality of service, and organizational alignment.[53] "Alignment" was Clark's word for reorganization, which he pursued with determination. For example, to consolidate the fleet's readiness requirements and assessments in one office, Clark moved the responsibilities for fleet readiness from N3/N5 to Logistics (N4), now titled Fleet Readiness and Logistics. More important, Clark reestablished Warfare Requirements and Programs (N7), which CNO Kelso had abolished earlier in the decade after transferring its responsibilities to N8, which, since then, had grown too powerful. Clark, like CNO Trost, saw merit in a balanced (if not competitive) power structure in OPNAV, whose primary elements were the so-called honest brokers of N8, the current readiness advocates of N4, and the future requirements experts in N7.[54] In October 2000 Clark transferred responsibility for the QDR preparation from N3/N5 by forming the QDR division in N8. In 2001 he elevated the billet of the director of the Navy Staff (i.e., OPNAV) from a one-star to a three-star position to match the Joint Staff's. This was just the start. Over the next five years, his reorganizational changes were "numerous, continuous and affected almost every office in OPNAV," Peter Swartz noted. "Taken as a whole, they changed OPNAV almost as much as the revolutionary changes of Admirals Zumwalt and Kelso."[55]

Conclusion

President Clinton never was able to develop a convincing strategic framework for the post–Cold War era. He expanded the bounds of U.S. foreign and economic policy and broadened the government's focus beyond traditional threats. He raised economic policy on par with foreign policy. He focused on global trade agreements and currency stabilization, and addressed financial crisis such as the one in East Asia in the summer of 1997, whose devastating effects radiated through the U.S. economy and caused a global economic crises that he labeled as the worst in half a century.[56] Despite his lack of strategic imagination and a society that was largely indifferent to the United States' preeminent role as manager of the international system, in all these respects Clinton created conditions in which it became reasonable to raise the question how military force could be configured and employed to expand free markets and democracies, and be used to advance and protect the international system. But he was unable to supply a firm and consistent answer.

Characteristically, neither Congress nor the Pentagon was much help. They were consumed with solving second- and third-order problems, which centered on determining the right weapons given a reduced allowance. As Robert Art noted, Congress for the most part examines "the details of defense spending, but rarely [looks] at the big picture."[57] The regional CINCs, which were those that dealt most directly with applying military power in the service of Clinton's economic and political goals, did not have backgrounds in international finance, banking, and law, for example. The Cold War experiences of the regional CINCs, who were, in effect, the U.S. empire's viceroys and proconsuls (much to the annoyance of U.S. diplomats), left them ill-prepared to understand how to relate progressive liberal policies to U.S. military power in order to serve the U.S. system in an era of globalization. As Clinton had remarked, "We're fighting a rear-guard action between the forces of integration and disintegration."[58] This was not a war his military leaders were equipped to wage, but one that they continually found themselves engaged in throughout the post–Cold War era.

The problems associated with affording both the high pace of overseas operations and the programs to bring about the revolution in military affairs given reduced budgets structured the behavior of the services' leaders. On one hand, the prospect that the fiscal climate would get worse drove them to fund the top of their (traditionally conceived) wish lists. On the other, they were obliged to compete for new missions and to demonstrate their capacity to address new threats or risk a reduction in their respective budget share. To make up shortfalls, Navy leaders, none more so than Clark, were consumed with bringing about a revolution in business affairs. Congress encouraged such an outlook by allowing the services to plow back into weapons systems funds that came from realizing cost efficiencies. These were found, for example, by modernizing the management of personnel, optimizing the time in which parts were repaired, buying commercial off-the-shelf technology, cutting manpower, and reducing training hours. Increasingly, to Navy leaders, the service's most pressing problem—apart from rationalizing itself—was how to afford itself.

It was in this difficult context that the Navy's strategists found themselves. The focus of OPNAV narrowed to a greater degree on meeting the CNO's Title 10 responsibilities of equipping, organizing, and training the fleet, which was manifested in the increased emphasis placed on assembling the Navy's POM and lobbying Congress, OSD, and the Joint Staff on its behalf. More and more, the strategists found their purpose to be limited to advocating. For any strategic statement to see the light of day, as Bouchard noted, it had to support the Navy's current programming and budget message and justify its current programs.[59]

Despite the fact that Clinton had elevated economic policy and trade to matters of strategic importance and established perhaps the richest conditions in the post–Cold War era for the Navy to at least contemplate implanting a systemically oriented maritime strategy, Navy leaders neither demanded nor expected that the Navy's strategists think creatively about what was happening in the broader world. While scholars were examining how the economic, political, social, and technological dimensions of globalization and the trends in international finance and trade were leading to a profound shift from a state-centric to a market-dominated international economy and a reconfiguration of political power, Navy leaders focused even more on internal processes and how to enable the decisiveness of U.S. naval forces. Given their backgrounds and the means-centric nature of OPNAV, innovative strategic ideas were neither encouraged nor welcomed. The process of vetting strategic statements, which was a process designed to identify and codify consensus among the Navy's senior admirals, worked only to marginalize such ideas. The Navy strategists were left with few avenues to advance them, which explains why they sought to establish a respectable planning process.

These bureaucratic obstacles were compounded by the fact that arguments about the importance of the Navy for international trade and globalization invariably fell on deaf ears in Congress and among senior defense officials. For the first time in the post–Cold War era, the Navy had related its purpose to globalization, systemic stability, and the health of the U.S. and global economies. One should not, however, make too much of this. No doubt, Navy strategists wrestled with understanding globalization, but in general the administration's appreciation of globalization was leveraged more to suit the Navy's own ends. Within OPNAV, strategy had more to do with its relationship to the other U.S. military services than to the larger world. Relating U.S. naval purpose more deeply in terms of globalization, international trade, and the health of the U.S. economy was clearly too risky in such a context. The steady trade winds of American strategy and defense policy were all about warfighting and airpower, before which the Navy remained content to sail. Consequently, the Navy's "overarching strategic imperative," as the "Navy Strategic Planning Guidance" had noted, remained power projection—and the winds of war over the coming years would only sustain it.[60]

Chapter 9

Sea Power 21, 2000–2004

Bush and the Reprisal of the U.S. Cold War Approach

In January 2001 George W. Bush (2001–7) assumed the presidency after a close and bitterly contested election. He had little prior foreign policy experience and had to rely on his experienced national security team. The team included two former secretaries of defense (Vice President Cheney and Secretary of Defense Donald H. Rumsfeld), a former chairman of the Joint Chiefs of Staff (Secretary of State Powell), a former undersecretary of defense for policy (Deputy Secretary of Defense Wolfowitz) and a former assistant secretary of defense (Deputy Secretary of State Richard L. Armitage). Having spent their formative years in the Pentagon during the Cold War, they saw military power as the driving force of U.S. foreign policy. Unlike President Clinton, they did not see globalization as central to America's core interests or a catalyst for new threats. Republicans in general had shown little interest in understanding "globaloney," as some had called it.[1] The team thought U.S. foreign policy should not be based on economic relationships, but on great power politics backed up by a dominant military. As Bush noted, the military's purpose was not to engage in "vague, aimless and endless deployments," but to "deter wars—and win wars when deterrence fails."[2]

To reassure a traumatized America, gain societal and international consensus, and organize the government in the wake of 9/11, President Bush used the rhetoric of the Cold War and reprised America's Cold War approach, with its Manichean and threat-oriented outlook.[3] He replaced the implacable Soviet threat with the implacable threat from international terrorism. Before a joint session of Congress on September 20, 2001, Bush declared the nation was at war with the "enemies of freedom" who threatened not just lives and property but also the American way of life and the values on which the Republic was founded. "We have found our mission and our moment," he noted. "The advance of human freedom . . . now depends on us." He reduced complex issues into simple declarations and divided the world into two irreconcilable camps, declaring, "Every nation . . . now has a decision to make. Either you are with us, or you are with the terrorists."[4] Bush wanted to strike back at al-Qaeda immediately, telling the military, "Be ready. . . . The hour is coming when America will act."[5]

The Transformation Bug

Bush was a true believer in the revolution in military affairs, if only as a convert brought to it by his team of experts. His administration's outlook was shaped by the general trends in post–Cold War defense policy, which, as Fred Kagan noted, saw war as "fundamentally a targeting drill and the only systems in the future that would matter would be those that improved America's ability to put metal precisely on target."[6] The term used to convey Bush's defense policy goals was "transformation," a loosely defined concept that organized his ambitious defense reform plan, which was centered on network-centric warfare. "Transformation," as the 2001 QDR stated, "results from the exploitation of new approaches to operational concepts and capabilities, the use of old and new technologies, and new forms of organization that more effectively anticipate new or still emerging strategic and operational challenges and opportunities and that render previous methods of conducting war obsolete or subordinate."[7] Bush noted that he wanted a "force that is defined less by size and more by mobility and swiftness, one that is easier to deploy and sustain, one that relies more heavily on stealth, precision weaponry, and information technologies."[8] Such a force would deter the rise of great powers and the aggressions of state actors and international terrorists. "The best way to keep the peace," he noted, "is to redefine war on our terms."[9]

However, because of his $1.35 trillion tax cut and modest defense budget, Bush's reform plans ebbed once in office. Transformation would have to come at the expense of operating budgets, manpower, and weapons programs, a move that Congress and the services planned to resist.[10] As Loren Thompson noted, the services' attitude was, " 'Look, I'm already overextended. Why do you need this money for something that hasn't materialized?' "[11] Amid the lack of political or public support for fundamental change, Rumsfeld's attempts to bring change had, in Cheney's words, provoked "a great deal of resistance on the Hill and I guess in the [Pentagon] as well. . . . It is going to be tough, and he's going to have to break some china. But he's just the guy to do it."[12] Rumsfeld irked Congress when he missed the spring deadline for the release of the 2001 QDR, which would be based on Bush's vision. Congress complained that both it and the military were being excluded from the process.

Rumsfeld believed civilian control over the military had been undermined under Clinton. To implement change, that situation needed to be reversed. Rumsfeld was not about to let the chairman wield the power that Powell once held. Rumsfeld and his senior appointees in OSD brusquely reasserted control, alienating the uniformed leadership in the process. "I think we'll recover," noted a Rumsfeld appointee, but conceded, "we've dug a steep hole to climb out of."[13] By September 2001 Rumsfeld's reforms had stalled amid bureaucratic infighting, and, in Washington, the general consensus was that it would ultimately fail and Rumsfeld would be the first cabinet member forced to resign.[14]

In short order, however, 9/11 and the opening front of what the Bush administration called "the global war on terror" in Afghanistan seemingly vindicated the need for transformation.[15] Operation Enduring Freedom, which began on October 7, 2001, sought to topple the Taliban regime, capture Osama bin Laden, destroy al-Qaeda, and establish a new government in Afghanistan. There was neither the patience on Bush's part nor the infrastructure in the region to amass a Gulf War–like invasion, which the Central Intelligence Agency warned would only rally Afghanis and radical Islamists to the Taliban.[16] Consequently, Rumsfeld had to employ an unconventional CIA plan that used proxy tribal armies, U.S. Special Operations Forces, and U.S. airpower. Many predicted U.S. forces would get bogged down and beaten by the same battle-hardened warriors that had defeated the Soviet invasion force in the 1980s.[17] Within two months, however, all the cities in Afghanistan had been taken, the Taliban had been deposed, and al-Qaeda had been dispersed.

Bush declared that Afghanistan was "a proving ground for this new approach."[18] The Department of Defense's director of Force Transformation, the recently retired Art Cebrowski, agreed. "The need for transformation, I think, has been well established as compelling, and certainly after 9/11 it should be self-evident."[19] "This war is kind of a wake-up call for transformation," added Andrew Krepinevich. It is "Exhibit A in the list of evidence that warfare is changing."[20] Loren

Thompson noted, "Much of the resistance to transformation was based on the fact that new threats were nebulous. Now they're not, so it's going to be harder to resist changes in strategy and programs."[21] The transformation craze swept through the defense establishment. It became the blueprint, the prescribed big idea, and the rubric by which the services were measured even as they struggled to demonstrate that they were in fact transforming.

Operation Enduring Freedom and the Carrier's Vindication

Enduring Freedom validated the Navy's post–Cold War emphasis on precision strike and information technologies, and the need for carriers in a way not seen since the Korean War. Five days after 9/11, two carriers were in the North Arabian Sea ready to launch strikes into Afghanistan. Two more arrived around the campaign's start, one of which deployed not with its air wing, but with U.S. Special Operations Forces, which used the carrier as a forward operating base for their helicopters. Unlike in Desert Storm, there were no suitable air bases close enough to support significant numbers of land-based tactical aircraft.

By necessity, the carriers became the primary strike element. Carrier aircraft, supported by Air Force tankers, flew 10-hour missions to strike targets 400 to 750 miles away. By the end of December 2001 carrier strike aircraft had flown 75 percent of the total number of U.S. strike sorties.[22] Expensive standoff weapons like the Tomahawk were not needed after Afghani air defense systems were destroyed on the war's second night.[23] Compared to the Gulf War and events in Bosnia, this war's targets were more mobile, and their destruction more time-critical. Close air support of ground forces amounted to two-thirds of the carriers' strike sorties. The remainder consisted of interdiction strikes and included time-critical targets like high-priority al-Qaeda or Taliban leaders who had to be identified, tracked, and struck before they moved underground or into areas where collateral damage was possible in the event of a strike.[24] Consequently, the joint air commander lacked for more fast and responsive strike fighters.[25] By the end of October 2001 almost all targets engaged were time-critical. Eighty percent of carrier-based strike missions dropped ordnance on targets that were unknown to the aircrews before they launched.[26] Such an environment was ill-suited to the Air Force's centralized planning and command structure, based as it was on set-piece battles and sequential campaigns. The war was a showcase for the adaptability of the Navy and naval aviation's increased precision and lethality. Of the naval munitions expended, 93 percent were precision-guided (i.e., either satellite-aided or laser-guided). Of the naval sorties that expended ordnance, 84 percent hit at least one target.[27]

The war also demonstrated that carriers could form the backbone of a major joint air campaign. The Navy's carriers had expanded the physical and informational battlespace and upheld the decisiveness of precision strike and network-centric warfare at a time when the White House had embraced these concepts as the locus of U.S. defense policy. By integrating naval aviation within the framework of joint operations, the Navy demonstrated that carrier strike warfare was just as sophisticated as the Air Force's, yet had unique advantages in speed, sustainability, and flexibility. As in the Korean War, the Navy's performance provided a concrete reminder of the need for its capabilities in a way that strategic statements or doctrine could not. "This is not about a point paper in the Pentagon," noted the commander of U.S. Naval Air Forces Pacific, Vice Adm. John B. "Black" Nathman. "There were real effects."[28]

Clark and the Restructuring of the Navy's Strategy-Making Process

In 2001 CNO Clark reorganized OPNAV's strategy-making structure to a degree not seen since the late 1970s, placing most of it directly under his control. As he had done on OPNAV's resource side, Clark established new offices with overlapping responsibilities. After 9/11, Clark changed the QDR cell into the Navy Operations Group, which was expanded under Rear Adm. Joe Sestak and renamed Deep Blue in early 2002. Its director, Rear Adm. Jim Stavridis, reported directly to Clark. Deep Blue's initial purpose was to develop innovative concepts to support combat operations associated with the global war on terror.[29] Over time, however, it became a multimission think tank staffed by promising officers. Like OP-603 in the 1980s, Deep Blue became the locus of Navy thinking. The only difference, and it was a revealing one, was that Deep Blue was more operationally oriented than OP-603 had been.

Clark also established the Strategic Actions Group (N00Z), whose director, Capt. Frank C. Pandolfe, also reported directly to him. Like Stavridis, Pandolfe had a doctorate from Tufts University and was a member of the Navy's strategy community. Pandolfe had served in N513 in 1996 under Commander Bouchard before taking over in 1997. His group took over many of the duties of the CNO's N00K such as writing policy papers and preparing the CNO for congressional testimony.

Clark now had five offices—Deep Blue, N00Z, N00K, N81 (now headed by Rear Admiral Sestak), and N513—working on five overlapping strategic projects during 2002 and 2003, numbers unprecedented in the post–Cold War era. Remarkably, all these offices were led by senior members of the Navy's strategy community. Their projects were not well coordinated. Capt. C. Will Dossel, the deputy N51, noted that rampant confusion reigned about which office was supposed to be doing what.[30]

Navy Strategic Thinking Atrophies

Because of his focus on resource and operational problem-solving, and his belief that strategy was the responsibility of OSD and the Joint Staff, Clark allowed the Navy's capability for strategic thinking to atrophy to a level not seen since the early 1970s. That belief was reinforced during the Rumsfeld years, a period when OSD aggressively reasserted civilian control over the Joint Staff and the services, the latter of which, for all practical purposes, were prohibited from doing strategy.[31] They could do doctrine and visions (although Rumsfeld put a stop to the services' glossy self-serving pamphlets), and were encouraged to think globally, but they could not do strategy.[32] The Pentagon's civilian leaders and their staffs viewed the services developing a strategy on their own as gross insubordination.

In OPNAV, N3/N5 became known as Big 3/little 5, meaning senior leaders focused on current operations and ignored broad strategy.[33] Despite intense lobbying efforts by the leaders of N51, Navy leaders were not interested in a big-picture strategy.[34] The billet for the deputy CNO for N3/N5 was gapped for most of 2002. When Vice Adm. Kevin P. Green arrived in October 2002, he reportedly told Clark that the Navy did not have a strategy, that it needed one, and that he was going to write it. In a revealing statement, Clark replied that the Navy had a strategy, and it was called the POM (i.e., the Navy's Program Objective Memorandum).[35] Like most N3/N5s, the CNO had appointed Green to perform what the CNO saw as the task at hand; this was not strategy, at least according to Clark, but operations, which in this case were those associated with Enduring Freedom and, more important, those operations already being prepared for the invasion of Iraq, which was scheduled to commence in early 2003.

To OPNAV's leaders and the Bureau of Personnel, managing the Navy's strategy community was no longer a priority.[36] Increasingly, those that were assigned to N51, particularly the one-star admirals that headed it, were relatively more junior.

As a result of Goldwater-Nichols, the Navy was sending its best, most promising officers not to N3/N5, as had been the case in the Cold War, but to OSD and the Joint Staff. The newcomers lacked the education and experience in strategy billets of those that came before, and had little awareness of the ideas that had animated the Navy's previous strategic documents.

Between 1970 and 1997 the head of N51 had almost always been a strategy-minded two-star admiral, whose advancement was already ensured just by being in the billet. In 1997 the billet was downgraded to a one-star position. As a result, most were now serving in their first assignment as an admiral. No longer ensured of advancement, they felt the need to prove their worth, particularly against those one-star admirals in N8 (particularly N81) who were in traditionally more upwardly mobile billets. At stake was, of course, advancement. Less than half of the eligible one-star admirals in OPNAV were selected for carrier battle group command, the next rung for surface officers and aviators. The most effective way to break out against their peers, it was thought, was to respond to the day-to-day priorities of the CNO and N3/N5, priorities that rarely concerned themselves with strategy, broadly speaking.

Fewer of those that led N51 and N3/N5 came from the Navy's strategy community. The nonmembers felt little responsibility for its health. Having reached its heyday in the 1980s with the Maritime Strategy, the community was no longer held in high regard. Its band-of-brothers mentality was a thing of the past. The locus of the community—N513—languished and became a quiet place to work. It became a rump office as its officers were farmed out around OPNAV, particularly to N81, for various manpower-deficient projects.[37] After four of the ten members of N513, including its chief, Capt. Robert E. Dolan, had been killed when American Airlines Flight 77 hit the Pentagon, OPNAV's leaders had made little effort to rebuild the branch.[38]

Support for programs to educate Navy officers as strategists declined. One of the Navy's two pipelines for educating its strategists was shut down: this was the Naval Postgraduate School's two-year strategic planning master's degree program. The curriculum, which was established in 1982, was terminated shortly before 9/11 on the grounds of cost efficiencies. The school's superintendent argued that the curriculum had too few Navy students and was redundant given the Naval War College's nine-month-long master's degree in national security and strategic studies, which, in contrast, did not require a thesis.[39] The Navy had graduated far more officers per dollar spent from the Naval Postgraduate School pipeline than the other one, which was the civilian master's degree program in political science and international relations. Set at institutions like Tufts and Harvard, this program had produced most, if not all, of the community's doctorates. Now, however, for the first time since the 1970s, the branch lacked an officer with a doctorate.

There were other signs that the Navy's ability to think strategically was deteriorating. The Bureau of Personnel no longer sent N51 alumni to the Naval Postgraduate School to teach maritime strategy or to fill the strategic planning chair, a chair that was eventually axed. The once influential Navy Strategy Discussion Group, which was made up of active duty and retired officers from the Navy's strategy community, and naval scholars and analysts, and that had been run by David Rosenberg (a naval historian and Navy reserve intelligence officer, with a doctorate), ended in 2005 after thirteen years.[40] The Naval War College–based Strategic Studies Group, the one-year think tank for upwardly mobile Navy captains and Marine colonels that had started in the early 1980s and had been influential in the Maritime Strategy's development, still followed CNO Boorda's mandate to focus not on strategy, as it had done in the 1980s, but on talismanic technologies and associated concepts.

In short, despite leaning heavily on the senior members of the Navy's strategy community, Clark—the longest-serving CNO of the post–Cold War era— was largely indifferent to its health. He did not believe the Navy had any business doing strategy, hence felt no responsibility to ensuring the institution had an independent capability to think strategically.

The Global Concept of Operations

As a result of the Bush administration's new force planning construct, which was outlined in the 2001 QDR, N81 started work on an operational concept called the Global Concept of Operations. The 1-4-2-1 construct, as it was known, meant, in order, (1) defending the homeland (a unique and singular task); (2) maintaining regionally tailored forces forward-deployed in four regions (Europe, Northeast Asia, the East Asian littoral, and the Middle East/Southwest Asia); (3) swiftly defeating attacks in any two of the four regions more or less simultaneously; and (4) being able to win decisively in one of those two regions.[41]

However, the fleet did not have enough ships and forward-based infrastructure to support four regions. During the Cold War, to keep more ships forward deployed longer, the Navy established two operating hubs; one was in the Mediterranean and another was in the Western Pacific. In 1979 the Navy established a third in the Middle East and the Indian Ocean following the Soviet invasion of Afghanistan and the fall of the shah of Iran. In the early 1990s the Pentagon established the policy for global naval force presence to distribute the U.S. naval assets needed to meet the regional CINCs' presence requirements. During the 1990s those requirements increased to the point where it became impossible to have a carrier battle group present 100 percent of the time in each of the hubs. The two-week gaps between the departure of one carrier battle group and the arrival of the next were being filled by an amphibious ready group combined with a Tomahawk-equipped surface action group. Now down to 313 ships, however, the Navy was hard pressed to cover even three regions.

To address these problems, N81 developed a plan to maximize the fleet's combat flexibility by reorganizing the fleet. The fleet was based on twelve carrier battle groups, seven Tomahawk-equipped surface actions groups (about three ships each), and twelve amphibious ready groups. Only the first two (i.e., carrier battle groups and Tomahawk-equipped surface actions groups) had the long-range striking power deemed necessary to deter aggression, however. The plan expanded the number beyond nineteen by moving Tomahawk-equipped cruisers and destroyers out of the carrier groups as the carrier's precision strike capabilities had proven so lethal in Enduring Freedom. These cruisers and destroyers were dispersed among the twelve amphibious ready groups (thereby making them into expeditionary strike groups) and made two more surface action groups, which yielded thirty-three strike groups. To that total, N81 added four *Ohio*-class ballistic missile submarines that had been permanently reconfigured to carry 154 Tomahawks each to give the Navy thirty-seven strike groups.

The Global Concept of Operations, which was intended for joint and naval operational planners, proved highly influential inside the Navy and the Pentagon. Vice Admiral Mullen, deputy CNO for N8, used the concept in the spring and summer of 2002 to justify to Congress and to OSD a shipbuilding program that supported a 375-ship fleet. Reportedly, OSD policymakers were impressed with the concept, even calling it transformational.[42] But neither the operational side of N3/N5 nor the CINCs (which, following an order by Rumsfeld in October 2002, were now known as combatant commanders) were happy with the assertion that an expeditionary strike group could somehow substitute for a carrier battle group (now renamed carrier strike group).

"Sea Power 21"

In early 2002 Captain Pandolfe started work on "Sea Power 21."[43] Of all the Navy's postwar strategic statements, few sought to solve a greater range of problems. It was a complex, sprawling, and multifaceted beast that sought to demonstrate the Navy was transforming, to develop a new strategic approach based on the 1-4-2-1 construct, and to assert that the Navy was a fully integrated joint player, and not just an enabling force. Indirectly, it sought to justify Clark's goal of a 375-ship fleet; establish a new cross-functional analysis approach for OPNAV (which had replaced the Integrated Warfare Architectures assessment process); codify, explain, and promote Clark's resource-related initiatives; and align his new structure. Since he reported directly to the CNO, Pandolfe was able to avoid the entangling agendas of OPNAV's three-star and the Navy's four-star admirals, which allowed for a more coherent document, one true to the views of Clark.

In June 2002 the CNO introduced "Sea Power 21" in a speech at the Naval War College. Having achieved success in the first two of his top five priorities—manpower and current readiness—he noted it was time to turn to the next one, future readiness, which was what "Sea Power 21" was, at least to him, all about. He said that future readiness meant transformation, noting, "'Sea Power 21' is the most complete, and recent, depiction of the Navy's transformation vision."[44] "Sea Power 21" was the basis for the Navy's transformational roadmap, which Rumsfeld had asked the services to submit by June 2002.[45] In the speech, Clark sketched out a strategic environment where a broad range of regional powers and widely dispersed and well-funded international terrorist and criminal organizations threatened U.S. interests with frequent and often unforeseen crises. He explained how the primary concepts of "Sea Power 21"—Sea Strike, Sea Shield, and Sea Basing—were tied together by the network-centric concept of ForceNet, and supported by three implementing initiatives: Sea Trial, Sea Warrior, and Sea Enterprise.

In the October 2002 issue of *Proceedings*, Clark laid out "Sea Power 21" in detail. In now familiar language, its opening paragraph summed up the strategic approach of "Sea Power 21": "The 21st century sets the stage for tremendous increases in naval precision, reach, and connectivity, ushering in a new era of joint operational effectiveness," it noted. "Innovative concepts and technologies will integrate sea, land, air, space, and cyberspace to a greater extent than ever before. In this unified battlespace, the sea will provide a vast maneuver area from which to project direct and decisive power around the globe."[46] The article highlighted the unified battlespace concept that had been sketched out by Bill Owens, theorized by Art Cebrowski, and articulated in Joe Sestak's "A Maritime Strategy for the 21st Century." As evinced in Enduring Freedom, the Navy was emphatically portrayed as more than an enabling force; the full title of "Sea Power 21" was "Sea Power 21: Projecting Decisive Joint Capabilities." Pandolfe had seen first-hand the harmful effects of the de-emphasis of "Forward . . . From the Sea" on decisive naval power and an emphasis on the enabling role of the Navy and the Marine Corps.[47]

Reflecting Bouchard's ideas, the inherent advantages of sea-based forces were also noted. Highly mobile, self-defending, and self-sustaining naval forces used the seas as a vast maneuver area to broaden the range of possibilities the enemy had to prepare for. "Sea Power 21" also emphasized that sea control was required to unify the battlespace. Clark asserted that U.S. naval forces gave the United States, in his words, "unique" and "powerful" "asymmetric strengths" that were difficult for regional and transnational adversaries to counter.[48]

Sea Strike was essentially the same as Sestak's Battlespace Attack: it was about projecting precise and persistent offensive firepower. Sea Shield encompassed Sestak's Battlespace Control, which emphasized layered defenses to ensure sea control and area control. Sea Shield also added the ability to project defensive power deep overland with theater ballistic missile defense and addressed the growing concern among Navy leaders about the proliferation of advanced anti-access technologies among regional powers that could deny the ability of U.S. naval forces to project power. It also incorporated Sestak's Forward Presence and expanded Sea Shield beyond Battlespace Control to include defense of the homeland, even from ballistic missiles. Sea Shield sought to integrate forward-deployed naval forces with new post-9/11 civil and military agencies to "extend the security of the United States far seaward, taking advantage of the time and space afforded by naval forces to shield our nation from impending threats."[49] As in the Cold War, the Navy saw its role in terms of forward defense, which of course required forward deployment.

Sea Basing was about putting more capabilities at sea to support joint and coalition operations, which included "offensive and defensive firepower, maneuver forces, command and control, and logistics."[50] It reflected Bouchard's thinking about the advantages of operating at sea and Sestak's Battlespace Sustainment as well as Owens' ideas about a mobile sea base, which was a floating airstrip for land-based aircraft that could house thousands of Marines and soldiers. "As enemy access to weapons of mass destruction grows, and the availability of overseas bases declines," it noted, "it is compelling both militarily and politically to reduce the vulnerability of U.S. forces through expanded use of secure, mobile, networked sea bases."[51] ForceNet was the glue that bound Sea Strike, Sea Shield, and Sea Basing together and reflected Sestak's Knowledge Superiority.

In short, "Sea Power 21" was a logical continuation of " . . . From the Sea" in the sense that it also leveraged the promise of revolutionary technology to argue that U.S. naval forces were even more decisive and their reach was even more global. "Sea Power 21" was about dominating the battlefield by means of high-end weapons systems that were designed for fighting regional powers. It emphasized stand-off precision strike warfare as a freestanding strategic expedient, supplemented and supported by communication and surveillance technologies. It did not address globalization, international trade, or the global economy, nor presence missions in support of political and economic objectives. It portrayed the Navy's primary purpose in terms of major conflict and downplayed the Navy's role on either side of major conflict. After its overwhelming success in Enduring Freedom—which, compared to Operation Desert Storm in 1991, did not see a large-scale deployment of the Army or the Air Force—the Navy was not about to yield the field of major conflict. Power projection reigned supreme at the center of the Navy's strategic vision. Transformation was suiting the Navy just fine.

"Sea Power 21" was more influential over a longer period than any statement other than " . . . From the Sea," of which it was, in any case, an echo and elaboration. Unusual for a Navy strategic statement, it was well-timed, coming after new defense policies and success in combat that vindicated those policies. It had a simple construct, which was repeated relentlessly in articles, congressional testimony, and speeches by Navy leaders. Also unusual, it had the interest and steady backing of the CNO and benefited from an organized and sustained rollout campaign involving high-ranking admirals to demonstrate consensus.[52]

"Sea Power 21" was not influential outside the Navy, however. It said all the right things about jointness, but in tone and substance it was overtly parochial. Although touted as a new operational construct, many did not see anything new or innovative in it. It synthesized and repackaged ideas from Owens, Cebrowski, Bouchard, and Pandolfe himself, when he had worked in N513. There was little about it that was thought to be transformational, a concept whose meaning was never easy to pin down anyway. Weapons systems already in the pipeline were touted as transformational. No major programs were cancelled to free up funds for new initiatives. The Navy wanted to modernize incrementally, not skip a technological generation.[52] Its transformation efforts rested on network-centric warfare, which was already becoming a familiar idea to the rest of the defense establishment. Yet even if Clark wanted to radically transform the fleet, its basic structure could not be changed in less than a decade. The only way to do so was by using advanced technology. With a fleet that cannot be radically changed and whose precepts such as sea control and forward presence are enduring, one should not be too dismissive of efforts to repackage ideas, particularly given Washington's constant demand for change.

"Sea Power 21" did not resonate in the fleet either. It was laden with buzz-words, whose meanings are less self-evident the farther one is outside the Beltway. Few saw it as new or innovative.[54] Its four-element construct was simple, but abstract. Sea Strike was understandable, but Sea Shield and Sea Basing were not. Sea Shield was defensive-minded, and smacked of seeking political support for more ships with ballistic missile defense capabilities. As for Sea Basing, it was hard to see it as a mission; it was just something that happened when a group of ships gathered for a task. While they may be important, concepts like Sea Enterprise, Sea Warrior, and Sea Trial were not about operations, which was the fleet's bailiwick, but rather were about the concerns of shore-based admirals.

"Sea Power 21" suffered from internal tensions. Pandolfe was hard pressed to organize Clark's far-ranging initiatives around a conceptual framework that made clear his managerial-oriented priorities in a way that also defined the Navy's purpose as strike-oriented power projection. To Clark, the purpose of "Sea Power 21" was not strategic in nature, but managerial. His focus, after all, was on how to improve the fleet's readiness and find the cost efficiencies required to fund the fleet's expansion. To him, "Sea Power 21" was more about explaining his intrusive, resource-related initiatives to the fleet (as well as to OSD and Congress) and establishing a well-understood and institutionally acceptable framework to align the Navy's expanded resource and administrative activities than it was about promoting a new strategic approach. In these regards, "Sea Power 21" was successful.

But the CNO's initiatives were only loosely connected with the strategic approach of "Sea Power 21," which gave the document its Janus-faced look. The audience for the managerial face was internal, and the focus was on programmatics, the budget, and cost-efficiencies. At the same time, "Sea Power 21" asserted the comparative importance of the Navy, which meant the audience for the strategic approach face was external and the focus was on operations. Pandolfe's desire for a vision that could elevate its central ideas without the restraints of resource issues was frustrated first by Clark's focus on management and second by the increasing use of "Sea Power 21" by elements in OPNAV to rationalize a litany of new weapons programs, which opened the Navy up to accusations that the document was little more than a justification for a 375-ship navy.[55]

The Rise of the Enterprise

Shortly after 9/11, CNO Clark had established the U.S. Fleet Forces Command and elevated its stature. The command was the Navy component command of U.S. Joint Forces Command, which was a functional combatant command responsible for training the military that Rumsfeld made into his agent of transformative change. Located in Norfolk, Virginia, U.S. Fleet Forces Command was headed by a four-star admiral, who was, in effect, the CNO's chief right-hand person and his executive agent in ensuring the fleet was organized, trained, equipped, and ready to be assigned to the geographic combatant commanders. U.S. Fleet Forces Command was responsible for integrating the fleet's warfighting capabilities requirements, developing joint and operational concepts, determining the fleet's deployment schedules, and dictating how and at what cost the fleet would train.

Clark handed to U.S. Fleet Forces Command responsibilities that had belonged to OPNAV. In particular, those of the barons—the one-star admirals who were the community representatives in OPNAV—were in effect shifted to the warfare communities' three-star shore-establishment type commands (like U.S. Naval Air Forces Pacific), whose primary responsibility was to support the fleet and who reported directly to U.S. Fleet Forces Command.

U.S. Fleet Forces Command led "the Enterprise," which became a profound term, like "the fleet" and "operations," and whose saliency was assumed to be self-evident. "Involving Navy headquarters, the systems commands, and every commander throughout the Navy," the vice CNO, Admiral Mullen, noted, the Enterprise "seeks to improve organizational alignment, refine requirements, and reinvest the savings to help us recapitalize and transform the force." He continued, "It provides a means to scrutinize the Navy's spending practices from the top line all the way to the bottom dollar. . . . It . . . is about delivering the right force, with the right readiness, at the right cost."[56] According to CNO Clark, the Enterprise was to draw "on lessons from the business revolution" to "reduce overhead, streamline processes, substitute technology for manpower, and create incentives for positive change."[57] It sought to deliver greater process efficiencies, divest noncore functions, streamline organizations, and enhance the investment in warfighting effectiveness. In short, to Navy leaders the service's most pressing problem was not rationalizing itself, but affording itself.

Enterprise mania swept through the Navy. Terms like "Six Sigma," "lean manning," and "cost-wise readiness" entered the fleet's lexicon.[58] The CNO's recommended reading list was not filled with naval classics, as generally had been the case, but rather with books on management and corporate leadership. In time, the Enterprise became a crusade, the cost-efficiency metrics of which permeated almost every activity of operational units, even those in combat.[59]

Clark's initiatives were his crowning achievement, and his legacy. They impressed Congress and provided a model for the other U.S. military services, which were far behind in such thinking, and can be counted among the Navy's most notable successes in the post–Cold War era. But it was a managerial success, not a strategic one.

"Naval Power 21 . . . A Naval Vision"

The third of five strategic documents developed during this period was signed by Secretary of the Navy Gordon R. England (2003–6), CNO Clark, and the commandant, Gen. James Jones, in October 2002. "Naval Power 21 . . . A Naval Vision" was the first Navy–Marine Corps statement since 1994's "Forward . . . From the Sea."[60] "Naval Power 21" was an attempt by England to provide an overarching document that summarized and encompassed both "Sea Power 21" and the Marines' "Marine Corps Strategy 21," which was based on its Expeditionary Maneuver Warfare document of 2001.[61] England wanted to endorse both visions, support Clark's goal of a larger fleet with more deep strike capabilities, and otherwise bring the two services closer.[62] The relationship was improving in any case, as it usually did when budgets were larger.

"Naval Power 21" was a straightforward document developed for England by Rear Admiral Stavridis in Deep Blue, as supported by Dossel in N513. It envisioned naval power as resting on three pillars: (1) ensuring access for "military operations, diplomatic interaction, and humanitarian relief efforts," (2) fighting and winning wars by "projecting power to influence events at sea and ashore both at home and overseas," and (3) *"continually transforming to improve . . .* [which] is at the heart of America's competitive advantage and a foundation of our strength."[63] It stated that its purpose was to define how U.S. naval forces "will be equipped, trained, educated, organized, and employed both today and in the future."[64] The document, which was published on the Internet, had little influence or follow-up by England and was remarkable only to the extent that all three leaders signed it, and that it called for a renewed attempt at a naval operational concept. A project was already under way to renew such a concept, but it was foundering badly, the victim of irreconcilable differences between the Navy and the Marine Corps.

The "Naval Operating Concept for Joint Operations"

The development of a naval operational concept, the first since the failed attempt in 1996, had started in early 2002 under the direction of Will Dossel in N513. Ostensibly, its aim, like that of the earlier effort, was to articulate how the Navy–Marine Corps team would contribute to the joint force, a problem that was now reinterpreted in terms of the 1-4-2-1 construct and new operational concepts like Sea Basing, in which the Marine Corps had a major stake.[65] The Marines wanted the Navy to endorse their Maritime Prepositioning Force (Future) concept, which the Marine Corps saw as the cornerstone for Sea Basing.[66] To the Navy, the concept was less of a sea base than it was a way to move and quickly assemble a brigade of 14,500 Marines for combat.[67] The Navy wanted to broaden the definition of Sea Basing in general beyond the battlefield to encompass a wider range of missions, such as deterring regional aggressors and protecting allies and friends.

As usual, the Marines sought to distill big-picture statements like " . . . From the Sea" and "Sea Power 21" down to the tactical level. They sought an a priori understanding of how the two services would fight together, which would yield greater clarity on command relationships and doctrine, which, in turn, shaped decisions on weapons systems, for example. As usual, the Navy resisted attempts at drilling down to the tactical level. Particularly since airpower was proving so decisive, the Navy did not want to be unduly bound to concepts and programs that focused on the battlefield, which might narrow the fleet's capabilities. Not surprisingly, the effort to develop a naval operational concept was ended in the spring of 2002, namely because Navy and Marine Corps three-stars could not come to an agreement on the document.[68]

In the fall of that year, however, the effort was resurrected. The Naval Warfare Development Command took the lead for the Navy. The new head of N51, Rear Adm. Eric T. Olsen, who was a Navy SEAL (and commander of U.S. Special

Forces Command, 2007–11), led discussions with the Marines, while Dossel nego-
tiated with them in the final stages. Clark and the commandant, Gen. Michael
W. Hagee (2003–6), signed the twenty-three-page document, renamed "Naval
Operating Concept for Joint Operations," which was published on the Internet
in April 2003. They noted that it was "an initial effort of an iterative process to
describe how the Navy and Marine Corps will train, organize, deploy, employ,
and sustain a more capable and ready force, now through 2002, as part of the
Joint Force."[69]

The document was a work of consensus, more abstract and far-sighted than
its failed predecessors. It fleshed out the four elements of the Sea Strike–Sea
Shield–Sea Basing–ForceNet construct and discussed the rationale behind the
Global Concept of Operations. It also examined Army, Air Force, and joint
operational concepts in detail and sought to link those concepts with Navy and
Marine Corps visions and concepts. It called for more Navy–Marine Corps integration in education, training, experimentation, and research and development,
and for an update to *Naval Warfare*: NDP-1, which had been signed in 1994.

In tone and substance, the difference between the "Naval Operating Concept
for Joint Operations" (which came out in April 2003) and "Sea Power 21" (which
was released in June 2002) was great. The Marines' influence was evident, if
not preeminent. The "Naval Operating Concept for Joint Operations" had the
markings of the Marines' more measured and more grounded Clausewitzian style
of strategic thinking, which meant there was little euphoria about the salutary benefits of technology or the promise of decisive victory. It discussed the unique ability of naval forces to operate across the spectrum of warfare. With less Beltway
jargon, it laid out why naval forces were relevant and how they contributed to
American post-9/11 security. It asserted the importance of naval power projection,
declaring, "The Navy and Marine Corps must continue to operate effectively as
a forward-postured, immediately employable force."[70]

The "Naval Operating Concept for Joint Operations" painted a picture of a
strategic environment that demanded a contingent approach and a generic force
that was flexible, mobile, and adaptable. That was the same picture the Navy had
been painting all through the Cold War, and the kind of approach and force
structure the rest of the military had been moving toward since 1989, a state of
affairs the Navy seemed unable to point out. With the "Naval Operating Concept
for Joint Operations," the naval services were nonetheless implying that joint

doctrine—colored as it was by the Army's and Air Force's way of fighting—needed to adopt the naval services' way of thinking instead of the other way around.

Even so, the "Naval Operating Concept for Joint Operations" did not stray outside the lines of the Bush administration's strategy and defense policy. The two services made their case on warfighting, deterring wars, and managing crises. The terms "democracy," "free trade," and "globalization" did not make appearances. There was not any repackaging of Sestak's expansive explanation of American sea power, which had related naval purpose in terms of forward presence, regional stability, and the health of the American and global economies.

The "Naval Operating Concept for Joint Operations" had more influence in the Marine Corps than in the Navy. Clark did not provide much follow-through, as he had for "Sea Power 21." The Navy generated little publicity for it, and in general the concept was swamped by the continuous fanfare about "Sea Power 21." Institutionally, as Peter Swartz noted, there remained "little [Navy] interest in formal long-range concept development in general, and in conformance to joint concept development processes and definitions in particular."[71] There was little indication it had much influence on joint doctrine, whose relevance and direction would be cast into doubt within the year as the insurgency in Iraq began to expose the limitations of the American approach to war.

The Fleet Response Plan

The signature page of the "Naval Operating Concept for Joint Operations" contained a peculiar word, one that has not been seen in a Navy strategic statement since "The Way Ahead" in 1991. That word was "surge," a dirty word in the Navy. Surging (i.e., deploying the fleet from its homeports only when needed) contradicted the need for forward deployment and portrayed the Navy's identity as a garrison service. But the summer of 2002 saw a change in national defense policy that caused the Navy to embrace the concept nonetheless. As the 2002 *National Security Strategy* noted, "A military structured to deter massive Cold War-era armies must be transformed to focus more on how an adversary might fight rather than where and when a war might occur."[72] It noted that the military had to scramble because Afghanistan had been low on the list of planning contingencies. And it stated that the services should be prepared for more of these surged deployments.[73] The military had to prepare for a greater diversity of threats and a much broader set of measures to address them. Added to the 1-4-2-1 construct was the

10-30-30 concept: the military should plan to deploy to seize the initiative within ten days of the start of a war, defeat an enemy within thirty days, and be prepared within another thirty days to shift to another area.[74]

The policy deemphasized the need for forward presence and exposed the Navy's inability to surge its carrier strike groups when required. The change threatened to undermine the Navy's rationale for a fleet structure that was based on the geographic combatant commanders' forward presence requirements.[75] During the intervening years, the Navy had no reason to change its heel-to-toe deployment rotation cycle model or dispense with its three-hub architecture, both of which the Navy had developed during the Cold War, and merely adjusted them to address regional threats afterwards. In the post-9/11 world, however, ubiquitous presence did not make sense to the Bush administration, which was more concerned with how the adversary would fight than with where. The sizeable U.S. naval forces deployed in the Persian Gulf and western Indian Ocean had not deterred al-Qaeda, nor was it clear why they should have. Adhering to combat-credible forward presence might spell disaster for the Navy's force structure.

Starting in the summer of 2002, less than a year before the invasion of Iraq in March 2003, the Navy came under increasing fire from the Bush administration for its inability to have more carriers available to surge. After Enduring Freedom, few doubted that the Navy's primary mission was carrier strike warfare. The flip side of the carrier's success was OSD's intense scrutiny of how the Navy employed its carriers, specifically its ability to surge the carrier strike groups, and its annoyance with what it perceived to be a lack of urgency on the part of the Navy to make more available.

The Navy employed a three-stage, eighteen-month process during which carrier strike groups were either working up for deployment, on deployment, or standing down after deployment. Broadly speaking, at any given moment one of the Navy's twelve carriers was in long-term overhaul, one was permanently forward deployed (based in Japan), two were on deployment, two were in the final stages of work-ups, and the rest were in various stages of standing down or just starting work-ups. As Undersecretary of Defense for Personnel and Readiness David Chu noted, "I have four to eight carriers that I can't send anyplace . . . because they're being overhauled, retrained, etc. . . . . There is in the Navy and the Marine Corps a substantial portion of structure that is unavailable to the president on short notice, short of heroic measures."[76] In short, due to OSD's policies, the term "forward deployment" became a dirty one in the Pentagon during these years.

The fall of 2002 thus found Rear Adm. W. Douglas Crowder, the head of Deep Blue (who was another member of the strategy community), working to increase the availability of carrier strike groups. Taking advantage of the fleet's much improved readiness, which would not have been possible without CNO Clark's single-minded focus on materiel and manpower readiness, Crowder developed a plan such that six carrier strike groups would be deployable within thirty days and two strike groups would be deployable within three months. After deployment, ships and squadrons would be quickly reconstituted and available for redeployment. The old three-stage process of tiered readiness was replaced with one of near-constant readiness; the new process required a massive overhaul of resourcing, training, and manning procedures and practices, which again would not have been possible without Clark's new business practices.[77]

With the vastly improved readiness, the Navy was able to employ six carriers in support of Operation Iraqi Freedom and had eight available for the start of hostilities in mid-March 2003.[78] At that time, the Navy had seven of the twelve carrier strike groups, ten of twelve amphibious groups, and thirty-three of fifty-four attack submarines deployed, which represented about 70 percent of the fleet.[79]

Two months after the start of Iraqi Freedom, Adm. Robert Natter, the head of U.S. Fleet Forces Command, released the Fleet Response Plan. It proved highly influential throughout the Navy and did much to support the need for a twelve-carrier fleet. It was also a big hit with Secretary Rumsfeld, who called it "transformational."[80] Developed in part by Captain Bouchard, who was now in Deep Blue, the two initiatives adjusted the schedules of deployed naval forces and aligned their activities in accordance with OSD's new guidance on security cooperation with other nations. After 9/11, OSD policymakers had overhauled how the Department of Defense interacted with foreign defense establishments. OSD defined security cooperation as "those activities conducted with allies and friends . . . [meant] to build relationships that promote specified U.S. interests; build allied and friendly capabilities for self-defense and coalition operations; [and] provide U.S. forces with peacetime and contingency access."[81] The security cooperation guidance informed the regional combatant commanders' respective theater security cooperation plans, both of which were detailed, metric-based engagement activity plans (i.e., joint exercises, United States–funded training and education, high-level talks, and port calls) and assessment tools designed for specific states and regions. The themes of the security cooperation guidance were

"combating terrorism; influencing strategic directions of key powers; transforming the U.S.–Russian relationship; cooperating with parties to regional disputes;
supporting realignment of U.S. global posture [i.e., the military's overseas infra-
structure]; and strengthening alliances for the future."[82]

Within the year, however, the Navy began to backpedal on surging, claiming that while the intent of the Fleet Response Plan was to make more ships
available for crises, routine deployments were going to continue. The Navy was
now on a balancing wire. It had to demonstrate it could surge, but still had to
assert the need for continuous forward presence, particularly given the importance of OSD's security cooperation guidance and the geographic combatant
commanders' associated presence requirements, which went a long way in justifying the fleet's size. Vice Adm. Charles W. Moore Jr., deputy CNO for N4,
noted in February 2004 that a more surge-capable Navy did not mean that fewer
ships would be on deployment.[83] "I don't like to look at presence on one hand,
and call it mutually exclusive with the Fleet Response Plan on the other," echoed
Clark in March 2004. "I'm trying to . . . communicate to Unified Commanders
[i.e., the combatant commanders] that look, if you are going to have the value of
naval forces in your AOR [Area of Responsibility], make it count."[84] By the end
of 2004 there was a clear shift in emphasis away from using surge capacity as a
metric and back to routine forward deployments with a more focused approach
on presence. It was, at this point, becoming apparent to all in the U.S. military that
the future would not be filled with preemptive high-tech wars against the likes of
North Korea or Iran. Instead, it would be filled with a military that appeared likely
to be mired in a land war in Iraq for a long time.

Conclusion

The years between 9/11 and late 2004 were arguably the period when prospects
for the development of a maritime strategy were at their lowest. The Bush administration's reprisal of the United States' Cold War strategic outlook provided the
basis for a new societal consensus oriented around a new global threat: terrorism.
And while it was apparent that international terrorist organizations like al-Qaeda
lacked the capacity to destroy the United States in a day, some said it threatened
America's way of life and its values, just as the Soviets had done. The decision
to rationalize al-Qaeda in such terms is a reflection, perhaps, of the Cold War
administrations' politics of insecurity theme, which might be necessary to ensure

support from a democratic society. The global war on terror allowed substantial portions of the government to be reorganized to wage a new kind of war. As during the Cold War, it was now difficult to define U.S. interests apart from the threat, now recast into a familiar shape. As Vice President Cheney and Secretary of State Powell noted, it was far easier to attack states that sponsored terrorism than it was to attack terrorists, so the administration made no distinction between the two.[85] The mismatch between the nature of the threat and the tools at the government's disposal channeled the conduct of the war on terrorism toward interstate war. There was little reason to relate the purpose of the U.S. military to American interests in an increasingly interdependent, globalizing world beyond what was required to wage that war.

Few in the Pentagon or Congress actually imagined how the global war on terror might be won. Instead, they continued to focus on improving how the military fought. That focus was reinforced by the initial success of Enduring Freedom, which was supposed to have vindicated transformation, despite the fact that the nebulous political goals of the campaign had not been achieved, and that there was little novel about the opening stages of the conflict other than the fact that the airpower was supplied by one nation and the ground forces by another.[86] The tactical advances demonstrated in Afghanistan and during the invasion of Iraq were the result of evolutionary changes that had been under way since the 1970s. Neither Enduring Freedom nor Iraqi Freedom was transformational, a concept that had little meaning other than as a way to discredit those who dared to oppose Rumsfeld's policies. As Kagan noted, "It was easy enough to argue that anyone who opposed transformation also opposed innovation and was simply defending some self-serving bureaucratic objective . . . and that anyone who opposed NCW [Network-Centric Warfare] had not adjusted to the new realities after 9/11."[87]

Few in the Pentagon or Congress stopped to contemplate the apparent mismatch between a high-tech conventional military and an unconventional, amorphous adversary in al-Qaeda living off the heat generated by deeply rooted social and cultural resentments. The revolution in military affairs—and, by association, transformation and network-centric warfare—were ultimately solutions in search of a problem.[88] To quote Kagan, "The history of U.S. military transformation efforts since the end of the Cold War has been the story of a continuous movement away from the political objectives of war toward a focus on killing and destroying things."[89]

That movement had been fine with the Navy's post–Cold War leaders. They believed that their responsibility was confined primarily to readiness and resource management. That focus, which was reinforced by the Navy's profoundly operational outlook, was for the most part vindicated in the opening stages of Enduring Freedom and the invasion of Iraq. The immediate goal was to attend to the fleet's health, without which political goals could not be achieved.

By most standards, CNO Clark was the most successful of the post–Cold War CNOs. He did his job and did it well. But like the other CNOs, he did not believe he was responsible for anything other than equipping, training, and organizing the Navy. Strategy—as well as understanding the implications of a globalizing world—was someone else's job. CNO Clark was a sublime manifestation of the limitations (and strengths) of U.S. strategic thinking and the Navy's institutional thinking. He regarded good management as a substitute for good strategy, and sincerely believed the Navy had no business doing strategy. All this goes some way to explain why he was rather indifferent to his responsibilities to represent the maritime dimensions of American strategy, which required ensuring that the institution had a capability for strategic thinking.

The Navy's other post–Cold War innovators, like Bill Owens and Art Cebrowski, did not focus on strategy either. They found their substitute in advanced technological solutions to operational problems. The Navy's post–Cold War intellectual luminaries, namely technocratic visionaries like Owens, did much to encourage the "comfortable and placid acceptance of a single idea, a single and exclusively dominant military pattern of thought" as Wylie had warned against, because subscribing to a narrow and prescribed vision served the Navy's institutional interests.[90]

Like " . . . From the Sea," "Sea Power 21" was a kinetically oriented approach that saw the Navy's primary purpose as projecting power in support of major combat operations. It also hewed to the Bush administration's technocratic and transformational defense priorities, which ensured that, in practice, some services—namely the Air Force and the Navy—were more equal than others. As in Korea and Vietnam, carriers had proven once again that they possessed unique advantages in speed, sustainability, and flexibility with aircraft and systems every bit as sophisticated as the Air Force's.

On the whole, then, the post-9/11 world seemed to be one well suited to reinforce the Navy's long-standing preferences for a fleet organized around carriers and oriented toward power projection and the prosecution of interstate war. That shining moment did not last, however. As the quagmire in Iraq deepened, all the familiar certainties and Cold War shibboleths that the global war on terror had seemed, however improbably, to have revived, would once again be cast into doubt.

Chapter 10

The 3/1 Strategy, 2005

Operation Iraqi Freedom and the Vindication of Transformation

September 11 provided the Bush administration with what it saw as an opportunity to serve U.S. long-term interests by installing a democracy in Iraq. President Bush and national security adviser Condoleezza Rice saw in the immediate post-9/11 period an era of opportunity not unlike the years just after World War II. That had been a time when the United States installed the political, economic, and security mechanisms of its international economic and political system, which eventually produced free-market democracies like West Germany and Japan. As Rice noted, "Our goal today, then, is not just a favorable balance of power [in the Middle East], but what President Bush has called a balance of power that favors freedom."[1] By installing a democracy in Iraq, Bush sought an enduring solution to the chronic instability and social disillusionment in the Middle East, the social and political deficiencies of which had, in the view of his advisers, led to Islamic terrorism and threatened the flow of petroleum, the wellspring of the international economy.

From the start, Secretary of Defense Rumsfeld sought to apply the lessons of Enduring Freedom to Iraq. "I'm not sure [400,000 troops are] needed given what we've learned coming out of Afghanistan," he noted to Gen. Tommy R. Franks, USA, the head of U.S. Central Command.[2] The invasion plan thus relied on precision strike, information dominance, U.S. Special Operations Forces, and a small maneuver force of 145,000 troops. The success of the invasion, which started on March 20, 2003, was seen as vindicating the administration's transformation efforts, particularly the need for a leaner and more mobile Army. The invasion force of one Marine, one British, and two Army divisions sliced through Iraq and deposed Saddam Hussein in three weeks. The United States suffered only 138 fatalities, fewer than those suffered by Operation Desert Storm's eleven-division coalition force twelve years earlier.

Similar to the invasion of Afghanistan, the invasion of Iraq highlighted the Navy's proficiency in strike-oriented power projection.[3] The Navy launched over 800 Tomahawk cruise missiles, while its F/A-18 Hornets served as the campaign's workhorses and its E-2C Hawkeye command and control aircraft unsnarled problems on the fly in the fast-paced drive to Baghdad. The campaign, which saw the successful debut of the new F/A-18 Super Hornet as well as unprecedented service integration, appeared once more to have demonstrated the lethality of airpower and validated the direction of U.S. naval strategy in the post–Cold War era. At this point, few had reason to question "Sea Power 21," which had been released a year earlier.

Iraq: Exposing the Assumptions of American Strategic Thinking

Iraq began to unravel soon after, however. Insurgent attacks mounted as lawlessness increased. Commanders on the ground were clamoring for more troops and guidance on how to reconstruct the instruments of governance and social services. After replacing Franks in July 2003, Gen. John P. Abizaid, USA, bluntly contradicted the administration when he declared that U.S. forces were confronting a campaign of guerilla insurgency. In the summer of 2004 a new team of Army and State Department leaders implemented a campaign plan based on classic counterinsurgency doctrine, which had been shelved after the disillusionment of Vietnam, but which was now dusted off and brought forward with much fanfare. But one thing was clear: the United States was mired in a long war, one it was uncomfortable waging.

The war mercilessly exposed the limitations of the Americans' reductionist, strike-oriented way of war. The promises of a revolution in military affairs based on the more precise violence of a new generation of weapons were proving empty. The realizations that U.S. information dominance and precision strike warfare were insufficient to subdue a patient and adaptive adversary came, however improbably, as a surprise. The real battlefield, it turned out, was, as always, psychological, and it could not be rendered transparent by technology. With the focus on "killing and destroying things," as Fred Kagan noted, the military had lost sight of the larger purpose of war.[4]

Bush's New Strategic Approach

In Washington the shock that the United States might lose the war in Iraq brought about a sobering reappraisal of U.S. strategy. In March 2004, a year after the invasion, OSD released a classified document that signaled a fundamental shift in the Bush administration's strategic approach.[5] Based on undisclosed sources, a reporter noted that the Strategic Planning Guidance (formerly known as the Defense Planning Guidance) sought to increase the capabilities needed to address the challenges of the global war on terrorism, which would come at the expense of high-end, revolutionary technologies. Specifically, Rumsfeld was directing the services to shift their focus from traditional challenges, where the likelihood of conflict and U.S. vulnerability was low, to irregular challenges posed by the adoption of unconventional methods by nonstate and state actors, catastrophic challenges posed by the threat of weapons of mass destruction, and disruptive challenges by competitors using breakthrough technologies in biotechnology, cyber operations, space, or directed-energy weapons, for example, which could negate U.S. advantages in operational domains.

In other words, the air had officially come out of transformation. Its talismanic weapons were too expensive and would not be fielded for years. They were deemed irrelevant to the task at hand, which was to wage campaigns of counterinsurgency and pacification simultaneously in Iraq and Afghanistan. Nevertheless, despite having shifted the lines of strategic argument, the Pentagon's new guidance was vague in matters of detail. In particular, it left much to be desired about how the services were to reallocate resources from established programs to new ones whose detailed requirements were as yet undefined.

Released in March 2005 by the Pentagon, the unclassified *National Defense Strategy* built on the Strategic Planning Guidance and made clear its underlying strategic assumptions.[6] The document held foremost that the United States was the guardian of the international system. It argued for a systemic and collective understanding of America's security, and that of its allies and partners. It was, at that point, the most systemically oriented strategic statement to come out of the Pentagon since the end of the Cold War.

The administration believed that U.S. dominance in high-intensity warfare had forced its enemies to adopt more irregular means to achieve their political goals. It also believed globalization was a catalyst for new threats. "While the security threats of the 20th century arose from powerful states that embarked on aggressive courses," the *National Defense Strategy* declared, "the key dimensions of the 21st century—globalization and the potential proliferation of weapons of mass destruction—mean great dangers may arise in and emanate from relatively weak states and ungoverned areas."[7] The administration had come a long way from the Republicans' "globaloney" days.[8]

The *National Defense Strategy*'s assumptions were organized around a strengths–vulnerabilities–opportunities construct. American strengths included a network of alliances and partnerships, the lack of a peer competitor, a military with unmatched traditional capabilities, and other elements of national power such as political, economic, technological, and cultural assets.[9] Vulnerabilities included the lack of capacity to address global security challenges, the lack of capacity or fortitude among U.S. allies and partners, institutional inertia and resistance to change that inhibited military transformation, and a leading position in international affairs that was liable to breed resentment and resistance.[10] Opportunities included the capacity to influence international events to bring about a new and peaceful state system, the possibility of deepening security relationships with key partners that shared America's interest in systemic stability, more international partners seeking integration into the United States–led system, and the likelihood that "problem states" would be increasingly "vulnerable to the forces of positive political and economic change."[11]

The *National Defense Strategy* had four objectives: (1) prevent attacks on the homeland by dissuading, deterring, and defeating enemies by engaging them ("when possible") "early" and at a "safe" distance; (2) secure "strategic access" to key regions, lines of communication, and the global commons, and otherwise retain global freedom of action, all in order to protect the "*integrity of the international economic system*"; (3) strengthen and expand alliances and partnerships with like-minded states and improve their ability to defend themselves, which, as the *National Defense Strategy* noted, was necessary since "a secure international system requires collective action"; and (4) "establish favorable security conditions" by countering acts against U.S. partners and interests. "Where dangerous political instability, aggression, or extremism threatens fundamental security interests," it noted, "the United States will act with others to strengthen peace." It continued,

"We will create conditions conducive to a favorable *international system* by honoring our security commitments and working with others to bring about a common appreciation of threats."[12]

In light of the Pentagon's new systemically and cooperative-oriented strategic approach, the *National Defense Strategy* presented the Navy with an opportunity to assert its relevance. The document promised to elevate the Navy's standing and the virtues of a forward-deployed Navy, with its ability to address threats far from the homeland, ensure access to petroleum, and maintain global freedom of action. The fact that the new vulnerabilities were recognized as potentially arising almost anywhere highlighted the Navy's global mobility and ability to deter conflict, manage crises, and sustain the international system. It was, to all appearances, an opportunity to assert that if the United States was the guardian of the international system, the Navy was its most important instrument. Navy leaders were not paying attention, however. Instead, they were preoccupied with an institutional crisis the likes of which had not been seen since the dark days of the 1970s.

An Institution in Crisis: The Navy in Heavy Seas

That crisis arose chiefly from the fact that by the end of 2004 the United States was engaged in what appeared to be two long-term ground wars, whose implacable requirements had elevated the importance of the Army and the Marine Corps, and called the importance of the Navy into question. Unlike Vietnam, where its carriers played a visible role, the Navy had not found a similar institutional handhold. In a bewildering reversal of fortunes, the Navy and the Air Force, once the darlings of the Bush administration's transformation policies, found themselves on the margins. The nature of the U.S. operations in Iraq and Afghanistan were rapidly depreciating the Navy's hard-won and much-celebrated proficiency in strike warfare.

The Navy also faced a monumental budget and shipbuilding crisis. To help pay for the wars in Iraq and Afghanistan, the Bush administration had transferred $9 billion over five years from the Navy's shipbuilding programs.[13] Meanwhile, many of the ships and aircraft that had entered the inventory in the 1970s and 1980s were being retired in advance because their maintenance was prohibitively expensive. But the Navy could only fund four ships for the fiscal year 2006 budget, five for 2007, and what would be three for 2008.[14] Of the four ships funded for 2006, only one was a submarine, this in a year when the Chinese built eleven.[15] Funding even one of these $2.5 billion *Virginia*-class submarines was a tall order.[16] Since Congress insisted that ships be completely financed before construction starts, the Navy could afford little else in those budget years that funded a submarine or a carrier.[17]

Shipbuilding had not been among CNO Clark's top five priorities. In terms of the normal budgetary trade-offs between capability, capacity (i.e., numbers), and readiness, he focused on the latter, both current and future. During his tenure, the fleet had shrunk from 318 to 282 ships, the lowest number since before World War I.[18] (The Navy had about 566 ships when the Berlin Wall fell in late 1989.[19]) "Where would we be today if five years ago I made shipbuilding my No. 1 priority? Where would we be?" Clark asked before his retirement in July 2005. "We wouldn't have been ready [for Enduring Freedom and Iraqi Freedom]."[20] And, indeed, it is difficult to argue that ships should be built if there is not a budget to maintain them in a state of combat readiness.

Clark had intended to use the funds recouped from cost efficiencies and manpower cuts to help pay for weapons systems.[21] With more than 60 percent of the Navy's $125 billion annual budget going to payroll costs, Clark had already cut 20,000 sailors since 2001 and planned to cut another 60,000 over the next seven years. For each 10,000 cut, the Navy freed up $1.2 billion to fund ships and aircraft. As Vice Adm. Lewis W. Crenshaw Jr., deputy CNO for Resources, Warfare Requirements, and Assessments (N8), noted, "The key to buying things in the future is controlling people costs."[22]

Nevertheless, the savings from manpower cuts paled alongside the costs of the next-generation warships. The price tag for the first of thirty DD(X) destroyers was $3.3 billion, and that of the nineteen CG(X) defense cruisers even more.[23] DD(X) "is a revolutionary platform," noted Clark, "[and] it is going to change the way we do everything."[24] Clark poured vast amounts of research and development funds into these stealthy ships, which were not the floating versions of the F/A-18 Super Hornet, an aircraft that was neither revolutionary nor stealthy, but merely affordable.

Clark was not able to reinvest his savings, however. Instead, it went to fund Army and Marine Corps operations in Iraq, a decision that disgusted Navy leaders. Unlike the Navy, the Army had done little to find cost efficiencies even before 9/11. Rumsfeld had lauded Navy Secretary England's and Clark's managerial skills and their success in transforming the Navy more than any other service.[25] Nevertheless, the force of events worked against the Navy. Clark summed up the Navy's problems in testimony in early 2005: "Rising operational and overhead costs are competing with my Navy's ability to transform. . . . We are absorbing costs of the war that are not funded. . . . Competing costs are slowing the pace and reducing the scale of [our] . . . important programs." He continued, "Shipbuilding and aircraft procurement costs are escalating at an alarming rate and eroding our buying power. . . . And finally, personnel costs continue to rise, especially regarding health care."[26] Given such intractable problems, one can understand Clark's focus on the bottom line. He would need a 20 percent increase in the shipbuilding budget to rebuild the fleet, money he simply did not have.[27]

Money, moreover, was itself no more than a stand-in and symbol for the main issue. "The real challenge to the future of the Navy is relevance," declared a former House Armed Services Committee staffer, who noted that lawmakers questioned the need for a Navy when United States–based bombers could strike targets around the world in hours.[28] When asked in May 2001 which service was the most important to U.S. security, 42 percent of those polled chose the Air Force, 18 percent the Army, 15 percent the Navy, and 14 percent the Marine Corps. When asked the same question three years later, a year into the war in Iraq, the Army, Marine Corps, and the Air Force were tied at around 24 percent. The Navy and the Coast Guard came in a distant 9 and 4 percent, respectively.[29]

On top of all that, the Navy's benefactors in Congress were not happy with Clark.[30] They were annoyed with his unwillingness to confront the shipbuilding crisis and declare emphatically how many ships were required; this figure ranged from 225 to 375. In the summer of 2004, when the search began for the next CNO, it was clear that the Navy's greatest challenge was the shipbuilding crisis. Since CNOs are selected for the skills they bring to bear on the problem at hand, the search inevitably narrowed to those who had a programmatic background, a superb reputation in Congress, and the political skills to leverage scarce funds. As one reporter noted, "The service will need a sustained lobbying effort to convince Congress and voters that ships are a good investment—a major challenge in an era where the Navy has taken a back page in the public mind to the Army and Marines."[31]

Clark and the Garrisoning of the Fleet

The CNO and Vice Admiral Moore, the deputy CNO for N4, desperately searched for cost efficiencies. "We're not a business," noted Moore, "but we ought to run war like a business," which, in essence, was Clark's mantra.[32] In terms of the fleet, they embraced the concept of supply and demand, surging forces in response to wartime requirements but otherwise keeping them close to home in order to stretch available readiness dollars. The massed deployment of ships for the invasion of Iraq had upset the fleet's routine deployment schedule and created a potential window of vulnerability that an adversary might exploit. As one reporter noted, "With nearly a third of the fleet deployed or returning from wartime service, it may take up to six months before the Navy could deploy a similar force to handle another large-scale contingency, such as operations against a hostile North Korea."[33]

But that contingency never materialized. The summers of 2003 and 2004 came and went. Ships returned, but were not redeployed.[34] Having improved the fleet's readiness and institutionalized the Fleet Response Plan, Clark grew content to rest on the fleet's ability to surge for major conflict and recoup the operating costs. Clark began to portray the Navy as a rapid-reaction force to be sent out for emergencies. The average number of ships deployed began to plummet. In time the Navy would have fewer ships deployed than before 9/11. Clark was garrisoning the fleet, namely because it made good business sense to do so.

Morgan and the Lack of Strategic Perspective

In the summer of 2004 the first of two figures responsible for the Navy's turn to a maritime-systemic strategic approach appeared on the scene. This was Vice Adm. John G. Morgan Jr., who took over N3/N5 in August 2004. His appointment to the traditionally upwardly mobile position was rather implausible. While all but one of his eight post–Cold War predecessors had been promoted to a fourth star, Morgan knew coming in that he would not be promoted.[35] Unlike many of his predecessors, he had not been a fleet commander. His previous job was senior military assistant for Secretary of the Navy England. Although he had commanded a carrier strike group, his peers did not consider him to be operator (unlike his predecessor, Vice Admiral Green). In Navy circles, Morgan was known as an antisubmarine warfare expert, having established the Antisubmarine Warfare Division (N84) in OPNAV in the late 1990s after the Navy realized its capabilities in that warfare area had atrophied.[36] All this meant that Morgan did not have the same level of legitimacy in the eyes of the Navy's three- and four-star admirals as did his predecessors.

Outside the confines of the Navy, however, Morgan had a reputation as an insightful and creative strategic thinker. While serving under England, one of the most respected free-thinkers in government, Morgan had spearheaded several projects that highlighted the need for new thinking, including the well-received edited work *Rethinking the Principles of War*.[37] Morgan also had a bachelor's degree in economics, which enabled him to perceive relationships in geoeconomic terms. His stint as N3/N5 would last an unprecedented four years; these years were the most creative period of U.S. naval strategic thinking in the post–Cold War era.

Morgan had definite plans on what direction to take U.S. naval strategy. From his perspective, however, the Navy was not in any condition intellectually to come about. He believed that since the end of the Cold War, the world had changed fundamentally, while the Navy's ability to understand those changes and relate them to its own utility had atrophied beyond use.[38] According to Morgan, the Navy lacked what he called a macro perspective, which left it ignorant—if not confused—about the strategic environment and its purpose within it. In OPNAV, and in particularly in N3/N5, he found no evidence of strategic thinking. He declared that the Navy needed someone or some organization to step back and provide a broader perspective on the strategic environment and the Navy's role within it.

According to Morgan, achieving the level of consensus needed to change the Navy's long-accustomed course required a pedagogic campaign. He wanted to spark a strategic dialogue in OPNAV, a dialogue that he could shape and manage.[39] He wanted to put N3/N5 back on the map and to put the first P back into the now renamed Planning, Programming, Budgeting, and Execution process.[40] To make N3/N5 an agent of change, he overhauled N5 and cut excess billets and established new office codes, which meant, for example, that the Strategy and Concepts Branch went from N513 to N5SC (Strategy and Concepts).[41] N3/N5 became Information, Plans, and Strategy. All of this was done despite the absence of a clear demand signal from Clark.

Even though the war in Iraq was undermining "Sea Power 21," Clark had no intention of replacing it. He gave no orders to Morgan, but gave him considerable latitude, perhaps because of Morgan's prior association with England, for whom Clark had immense respect.[42] Clark was not about to show discourtesy to England by reining in Morgan and quashing any of his initiatives, which probably would not have amounted to much anyway. New CNOs tend to clear the slate and lay down a new set of priorities, which is what Clark had done. With less than a year before retirement, Clark was not looking to saddle his successor with a legacy of initiatives.

All of this meant that Morgan had a clear road to pursue his agenda for change, which presented an opportunity to shape the thinking of the next CNO, who almost certainly would have a narrow, programmatically oriented view of the world. He was emboldened by the knowledge that a fourth star was not in the offing, a fact he shared with his officers to emphasize that his disruptive actions were not careerist in nature.[43]

From day one, Morgan told his officers he wanted a maritime strategy as classically understood.[44] He felt no need to reiterate the Navy's operational virtues to win over those who controlled the purse strings. Where others saw an intersection of trends that was undermining the Navy's relevance, Morgan saw a different set.[45] In general, Morgan believed that globalization, the threats from international terrorists, and the wars in Iraq and Afghanistan had elevated the significance of the international system. Globalization also had elevated the need to sustain its orderly functioning against a range of threats like al-Qaeda, threats whose shared characteristic was engrained hostility to—and alienation from—the system itself. Morgan thought globalization had shifted the security calculus toward a greater emphasis on economics, which was the central element around which any maritime (as distinct from naval) strategy was organized, regardless of whether it was exercised in war or peace. Morgan knew that a globalization-centered strategic approach would essentially be a repudiation of the Bush administration's preemptive go-it-alone policy. But with globalization, American economic and political interests were increasingly linked to those of other nations. In such an era, trade, commerce, and the accumulation and distribution of wealth among allies became critically important. Consequently, the ability to protect and sustain the international system—the wellspring from which the United States and its allies and trading partners prospered—became critically important as well.

According to Morgan, it was not just about globalization writ large, but also about the kinds of threats that were emerging from globalization that necessitated a shift from a threat-centric to a systemic approach. International terrorist organizations like al-Qaeda did not pose a direct existential threat to the United States the way the Soviet Union had. However, al-Qaeda's desire to destroy the system and its ability to operate in close proximity to the world's supply of petroleum and to the maritime choke points through which it flowed, along with most of global trade, made it a conceptual if not indirect existential threat. The first step in developing a genuinely strategic response (as opposed to merely responding reactively in the wake of attacks) was for the Navy to rethink its required capabilities.

Like many Navy strategists before him, Morgan wanted strategy to shape pro-grammatic decisions instead of the other way around. As he was fond of saying, every one of the Navy's POMs was, in fact, a strategy. The question was whether the strategy reflected an explicit conceptual framework or the budgetary horse-trading that was the inevitable result of treating war as if it were a business. The POM-as-strategy approach that Clark espoused did little to advance the Navy's case in the greater marketplace of ideas, nor did it provide a conceptual frame-work for the fleet. Every one of the Navy's POMs may be a strategy, but a POM does not speak for itself.

Morgan was worried about the perception among OSD's policy leaders that the Navy was reluctant to engage in the global war on terror. The Pentagon was a place where being perceived as relevant was as important as actually being relevant. Clark, despite his joint background, started stiff-arming requests to send Navy forces and personnel overseas to support the United States' global counterterrorism efforts. Morgan's first problem was thus to overcome Clark's reluctance to get the Navy more involved.

Morgan believed that while al-Qaeda constituted the immediate threat to U.S. security, the costs of the wars in Iraq and Afghanistan represented the long-term threat. Like the Vietnam War, America's protracted and inconclusive engagements overseas in the twenty-first century were proving costly to its political and economic power. The staggering debts incurred to pay for the campaigns threatened the United States' long-term ability to fund a military to protect the homeland and the stability of the system, and sustain the system's motor, which was the U.S. econ-omy. Morgan understood that Americans were war weary, and when the wars were wrapped up, they would have no stomach for overseas adventures or horta-tory threat-centric approaches of the sort Bush had advanced after 9/11 to secure public opinion. As Morgan noted, the opposite of a threat-centric approach was a systemically oriented one that sought to prevent war. And the challenge of China, he argued, was far more complex than that of a mere threat.

For Morgan, the fact that the Navy had only a modest share in the fighting in Afghanistan and Iraq represented an opportunity to shift the terms of debate about U.S. strategy. One more in a litany of proclamations about the decisiveness of U.S. naval forces would only confirm perceptions in OSD (and Congress) that the Navy was hidebound and unable to grasp the requirements of the new U.S. strategic approach. A maritime strategy would put the efforts of the Marine

Corps and the Army into a wider perspective in a way that did not impugn their efforts, nor seek to claim undue credit for them. Politically, it was a way to assert the Navy's relevance without explicitly calling those wars and their costs into question. Morgan knew that the world was heading in a direction defined by globalization and wanted to fit the Navy into a world that had been evolving as such since before 1989. He wanted a strategy that would place the Navy in an advantageous position in advance of the inevitable moment when the wars ended and the national debate about how to recapitalize the military and what the new U.S. strategic approach should be would be taken up in earnest. He was, he said, "shooting ahead of the duck."

One thing kept Morgan awake at night, however. Everything depended on forward deployment: the rationale for a maritime strategy, the recognition that the Navy had a special relationship with the international system and played a key role in its maintenance, the ability of the Navy to use its unique cross-spectrum capabilities and demonstrate its systemic effects, the size of the fleet, and the Navy's day-to-day relevance. Morgan believed Clark's move to garrison the fleet was a "strategic mistake." A garrisoned fleet could not manage crises, provide systemic stability, and otherwise deter expensive, large-scale conflicts. Only when the fleet was built to handle just about any contingency—including those associated with the post-9/11 strategic environment—and also was forward deployed could the benefits of American sea power be fully realized and rationalized.

Garrisoning the fleet invited criticism that the Navy was not getting it, specifically that its leaders were more concerned about the fleet's readiness and its fiscal health than about supporting the new kind of fight in which the nation found itself. Knowing that prohibitively high debts and expensive land campaigns had brought about the decline of the Spanish, French, and British navies in the seventeenth, eighteenth, and twentieth centuries, respectively, Morgan was not about to let the Navy and the United States launch themselves down the same unrecoverable glide slope.

Morgan Starts a Dialogue

Once in office, Morgan focused on strategy, not operations. The role of OPNAV's operations officer was one that many of his predecessors had naturally assumed. Morgan handed the day-to-day operational responsibilities to his two-star deputy and turned to the task of sparking a dialogue in OPNAV about a new strategic initiative, one that was conceived along new and less parochially operational lines.[46]

To head N51, Morgan brought in Rear Adm. Charles W. Martoglio.[47] They were a formidable team. Martoglio, who was also a surface officer, was not only a superb strategic thinker and administrator but also a savvy bureaucrat. He had gained invaluable knowledge of backroom Navy politics while serving as the executive assistant to the vice CNO as well as to the commander of U.S. Fleet Forces Command. He knew how to peddle potentially controversial initiatives to the deputy CNOs, many of whom were the caretakers of embedded billion-dollar programs, and who therefore jealously guarded their turf.

In November 2004 Morgan and Martoglio were ready to present the outlines of their initiative. Their concept was based on a Venn diagram that they had drawn up, which was known as the Bear Paw because it resembled a bear's paw print.[48] (See figure 10.1.) Martoglio showed the diagram to CNO Clark, who liked it and who immediately showed it to Secretary England.[49] Clark wanted to use it for his upcoming congressional testimony to explain how the Navy was contributing to the war on terrorism.[50] For Clark the Bear Paw was an easily grasped concept that could be used to organize his post-9/11 resource initiatives, like the Navy's new riverine force. For Morgan the concept was a way to get Clark to ungarrison the fleet and to support the war on terror to a far greater degree. Given Clark's general approval, Martoglio began presenting the brief to audiences in OPNAV and (possibly unbeknownst to Clark) to think tanks. In January 2005 Clark officially introduced the Bear Paw concept at the annual Surface Navy Association Symposium in Washington, DC. In the spring of 2005, several high-profile workshops were held, the result of a collaborative effort by Morgan and think tanks.

By this time, Morgan had sent the brief to several Navy leaders along with an accompanying paper written by N5SC's Cdr. Paul N. Nagy. He also sent it to Admiral Mullen, the commander of U.S. Naval Forces Europe, since there was widespread expectation that Mullen would be the next CNO.[51] Mullen, a surface officer, had a background that was profoundly programmatic, perhaps more so than any CNO before or since. He had been CNO Johnson's director of N86, where he gained a reputation for being a forceful and skillful advocate of the surface navy; he was not known as a friend of naval aviation. He was Clark's vice CNO and before that Clark's deputy CNO for N8. A 1968 Naval Academy graduate with a master's degree in operations research from the Naval Postgraduate School, Mullen was very much his own man.

As commander of U.S. Naval Forces Europe, Mullen blossomed intellectually.[52] Unlike other Navy component commands, notably U.S. Pacific Fleet,

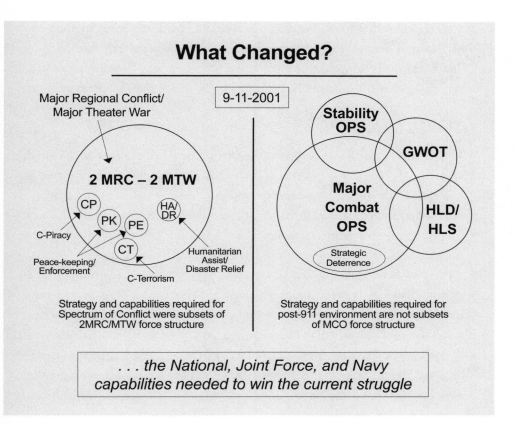

What Changed?

9-11-2001

Major Regional Conflict/
Major Theater War

2 MRC – 2 MTW

CP
PK   PE
CT
HA/DR

C-Piracy

Peace-keeping/
Enforcement

C-Terrorism

Humanitarian
Assist/
Disaster Relief

Stability
OPS

GWOT

Major
Combat
OPS

HLD/
HLS

Strategic
Deterrence

Strategy and capabilities required for
Spectrum of Conflict were subsets of
2MRC/MTW force structure

Strategy and capabilities required for
post-911 environment are not subsets
of MCO force structure

. . . *the National, Joint Force, and Navy
capabilities needed to win the current struggle*

Figure 10.1. The Bear Paw
*Source: "Navy's 3/1 Strategy: The Maritime Contribution to the Joint Force
in a Changing Strategic Landscape," draft paper, version April 12, 2005, 4.*

U.S. Naval Forces Europe had no ships assigned to it (other than the flagship). Because he had no ships to command, Mullen had to find more-nuanced ways to advance U.S. policy. He grew to appreciate so-called soft power, particularly through personal relationships.[53] He worked closely with officials from other nations, U.S. federal agencies, and international organizations. "We do very little anymore as a solitary service at sea," Mullen stated. "If the war on terror has taught us nothing else, it is that the future of national and international security lies in mutual cooperation, jointness and interoperability. Nobody goes it alone."[54]

Mullen's experiences profoundly reshaped how he thought about the world in a way that dovetailed with Morgan's maritime-based approach. Given his background, few in the Navy could have expected that Mullen would undergo such a transcendent conversion to a maritime orientation, particularly so late in his career. Mullen read the paper that Morgan had sent him and reportedly told Morgan that it was the best intellectual piece to have come out of N3/N5 in years.[55] By that time, Morgan's initiative had acquired a new name, the "3/1 Strategy."

The "3/1 Strategy"

The "3/1 Strategy" held that the security environment had changed on 9/11 and again as a result of U.S. operations in Iraq and Afghanistan, which was an oblique reference to the mounting economic and political costs of the United States' increasingly unpopular war in Iraq.[56] The new environment meant the military had to prepare for contingencies that were more diffuse and complex than in the past. It noted, "No other nation state has the military power to directly confront the United States, but a diverse set of increasingly networked adversaries pose a security challenge every bit as threatening as the Soviet Union."[57] Apart from hostile nuclear-armed states, these included international terrorists, advanced weapons proliferators, drug and crime syndicates, and cyber criminals. In contrast to the enemies of yesterday, the enemies of today were networked, dynamic, unpredictable, diverse, fluid, and evolving constantly. They could obtain weapons of mass destruction on the black market and thrived in the murky areas between crime and armed conflict.

The "3/1 Strategy" embraced the Bush administration's argument that the global war on terror would be a long struggle. "One way to think about the [global war on terror] is not as a war," it noted, "but a long-term struggle against a committed ideological opponent, similar to the Cold War against Soviet-inspired Communism."[58] In other words, the conflict could not be waited out by those who might think the Navy did not need to shift its capability portfolio.

The Bear Paw slide captured the basic requirements of the new environment. In addition to the enduring need to be prepared for major combat operations, the "3/1 Strategy" argued for the existence of three new mission sets—global war on terror, Stability Operations, and Homeland Security and Defense—all of which, the strategy noted, required specialized capabilities. The slide portrayed the relationship between the Navy's capabilities and missions before and after 9/11. Before 9/11, the two-regional-war construct drove the military's shape, size, and posture. It noted that the "strategy and capabilities required for the Spectrum of Conflict were subsets of 2 MRC/MTW [Major Regional Conflict/Major Theater

War] force structure." The post-9/11 environment had undermined the two-regional-war construct. Now, the "capabilities required for [the] post-9/11 environment are *not* subsets of MCO [Major Combat Operations] force structure."[59] In short, the Navy could no longer accept the now glaring inefficiencies that came with using high-end platforms for so-called lesser-included missions such as counterterrorism, counterpiracy, peacekeeping, and humanitarian relief. These missions were now critical to winning the war on terror and needed to be addressed directly in their own terms.

The Navy, according to the "3/1 Strategy," needed a strategy that balanced traditional capabilities against those required by the three new missions.[60] It stated that the Navy's core strengths included the ability to aggregate and disaggregate combat power and transition rapidly from missions associated with the war on terror to major combat operations.[61] Although the former dominated the fleet's day-to-day activities, the "3/1 Strategy" noted that the fleet still had to be ready to dominate the high end of the spectrum of warfare.[62] But revealing its true colors, the "3/1 Strategy" noted, "As the Nation's experiences in the [global war on terror] illustrate, there is more to 'warfare' in the new strategic environment than just MCOs [Major Combat Operations]."[63]

The "3/1 Strategy" explained that among the Navy's virtues in the emerging strategic context was the "agility [that] enables it to match a broad range of missions and situations." Another was that, because it can "operate without the political constraints that often hinder land-based forces, the Navy–Marine Corps Team may provide the Joint Force Commander with military options during a crisis not otherwise available." All of this, however, particularly the ability to transition between the new missions and major conflict, could be realized only when it was forward deployed: the "Navy's forward posture is key to its speed of effect and persistent presence."[64]

Foreign governments that feared domestic backlash from too close an association with the United States were, the "3/1 Strategy" noted, more accepting of the presence of U.S. naval forces in the vicinity than Army and Air Forces units, with their large and invasive installations. U.S. naval forces had "persistent presence," had a small footprint on shore, and operated "over the horizon."[65] To help foreign governments provide for their own security, a critical goal of OSD's theater security cooperation plan, U.S. naval forces offered something unique: the ability to train their forces at sea, in the air, and on the ground.

Above all, the "3/1 Strategy" argued for a systemic understanding of the war on terror. It noted that its main theater of operations had an enormous maritime and littoral dimension, stretching from Indonesia to West Africa, from Tanzania in the south to the Black Sea, and including North Africa, the Middle East, and India, Pakistan, and Afghanistan. This area contained six of the world's busiest sea transit choke points (the straits of Malacca, Sunda, Hormuz, Bab el-Mandab, and Gibraltar, and the Suez Canal), and most of the world's petroleum reserves. The collocation of the world's greatest oil reserves with the Islamist insurgency was problematic: "If stability in this region is in the interest of most of the world," it noted, "chaos and anarchy serve the objectives of our terrorist adversaries."[66] Regardless of whether some nations believed the Americans had turned the conflict into a crusade, the war had a systemic dimension that could not be ignored. By shutting down access to petroleum and trade, Islamist terrorists threatened the stability of the international system as a whole, on which the United States and its allies and trading partners relied for their economic prosperity. In a globalizing, more interdependent world where U.S. interests were increasingly linked to those of other nations, the United States needed a strategic approach that placed the security requirements of the United States–led system at its core. For the United States, national and systemic securities were so subtly intertwined as to be indistinguishable in practice. The surest way to defend the vital interests of the United States lay in recognizing the intimacy of that relationship. The military's purpose should accordingly be viewed in relation to systemic requirements.

Within this context, the Navy had a unique role to play in protecting the system and sustaining globalization. According to the "3/1 Strategy," the Navy's role as systemic constable was analogous to that of the British Royal Navy in the eighteenth and nineteenth centuries.[67] The seas are a "vast, ungoverned area . . . [and] imposing order over this lawless domain is a 'public good' or global responsibility that has traditionally been assumed by the world's reigning maritime power." What came next was a surprise: the admittance that "the U.S. Navy cannot accomplish this alone, however. This mission requires the active support and participation of regional nations and their maritime forces." America's own strategic interests thus required the Navy to take a leadership role in developing maritime partnerships to rid the seas of lawlessness and terrorist activities.

The "3/1 Strategy" portrayed the Navy as an instrument that knitted the interests of the United States with its allies and partners, and could do so in a way the other U.S. military services could not. Getting allies and partners to provide their own maritime security served everyone's interests, and it left the shrinking U.S. fleet to operate where it would be most effective. The Navy did not need to be everywhere: it just needed to be where it mattered.

The "3/1 Strategy" framed the Navy's Maritime Domain Awareness initiative as an essential element of the Navy's constabulary role.[68] Its purpose was to generate actionable intelligence on seaborne threats to the United States and its allies and partners. It entailed collecting, fusing, and disseminating information and intelligence supplied by the military, the Coast Guard, the Central Intelligence Agency, and other federal agencies, as well as by allies, coalition partners, and commercial entities. As a means to cohere a maritime-based network of navies, the gathering and sharing of tactical information now had a strategic dimension.

In its discussion of Homeland Defense, the "3/1 Strategy" reiterated the Bush administration's assertion that the U.S. military protected the homeland by conducting offensive operations overseas against terrorist networks, sharing intelligence, and executing maritime defense operations, as well as by supporting civil authorities (when directed).[69] The "3/1 Strategy" echoed the *National Defense Policy*'s call for the military to take an active, layered, and scalable approach to defending the United States and its interests.

This was, evidently, an argument for a forward-deployed fleet. But it also provided a new basis for partnership with the Coast Guard, which was responsible for guarding the maritime approaches to the United States. The Navy, for its part, would keep its forces in readiness to "rapidly augment the Coast Guard" when needed.[70] This represented a modest but palpable strengthening of a relationship that had traditionally been cordial, but distant. The Navy–Coast Guard relationship had always been marked by mutual respect based mainly on the natural bond between sailors. The "3/1 Strategy" now spoke explicitly of "the Navy/Coast Guard Team," comprising the "Sea Services," whose task was to "work together seamlessly to protect the American Homeland."[71] It was a distinctly strong choice of words, given that the sea services had traditionally meant the Navy and the Marine Corps. But with 9/11 the stature of the Coast Guard, which had been shifted from the Department of Transportation to the Department of Homeland Security, had risen with its new counterterrorism role.

The notion of stability operations also loomed large in the document. It noted that stability operations highlighted the Navy's unique ability to protect and stabilize the system by, for example, managing crises and deterring conflict.[72] In general, OSD defined stability operations broadly, as those military operations that maintained or reestablished order, promoted stability, and shaped relations with other nations. In contrast, the Army defined it narrowly as those operations associated with postinvasion stabilization and reconstruction efforts. As evinced in the "3/1 Strategy," the Navy held to a broader understanding as well, namely because such a view highlighted its relevance before and after major conflict. As the "3/1 Strategy" pointed out, "The wide range of operations and missions the Navy has conducted in the Arabian Gulf for over twenty years can also be considered Stability Operations as they promoted stability in an often-troubled region." This assertion also allowed the Navy to highlight its role in conventional deterrence. "Perhaps the most important aspect of Stability Operations for the Navy," it noted, "are those that are intended to deter and/or dissuade regional actors from initiating Major Combat Operations." As the costs of the war in Iraq were skyrocketing, the "3/1 Strategy" pointed out that the costs of a forward-deployed Navy that worked to deter war, high though the costs might be, were nothing compared to the far greater costs in both fiscal and human terms that were incurred when the nation went to war with massed deployment of ground and air forces. "The proactive costs of our Nation's defense," it noted, "are dramatically more affordable than the reactive costs of going to war."

According to the "3/1 Strategy," the Navy's stability operations included sanctions and embargo enforcement, peacekeeping, antipiracy operations, drug enforcement, supporting counterterrorism and counterinsurgency operations, enforcement of maritime agreements, and patrolling oil and gas fields. It noted, "Sometimes known as 'constabulary functions,' these are critical to upholding international law and promoting regional maritime security initiatives."[73] Never before in a Navy strategic statement had the Navy's constabulary role enjoyed such a prominent place alongside its other two roles of warfighting and diplomacy.

The "3/1 Strategy" noted that the Navy was contributing to stability operations on land as well. To free up Marines and soldiers for combat roles, the Navy had deployed seven thousand of its personnel in Iraq and Afghanistan, a number that would grow to ten thousand. Around the world the number of Navy personnel deployed on land was increasing. These included medical and dental officers, linguists, cargo and fuel handlers, port security personnel, maritime security detachments, Seabees, Judge Advocate General Corps officers, and explosive ordnance disposal personnel. And they included SEALs, whose stature as a warfare community, particularly in the public eye, threatened to rival that of the

Navy's air, surface, and subsurface communities due to the wholesale increase in the demand for the unique capabilities of U.S. Special Operations Forces in Iraq and Afghanistan. To many in the Navy, the definition of the fleet was changing. It was encompassing a wide variety of land-based activities and population-centric missions. As the Navy's mission sets broadened to include these land-based activities, the basis of the Navy's knowledge—its operational experiences—was changing and expanding as well.

The "3/1 Strategy" also introduced the Sea Shaping pillar, which reflected the belief of many Navy leaders that the nature of American sea power was changing as well. The tipping point was the Navy's disaster relief efforts off western Indonesia following the earthquake and tsunami in December 2004, which killed nearly 200,000 in Indonesia alone.[74] The Navy had immediately diverted a carrier strike group that was on its way to the Middle East and an expeditionary strike group; these became the nucleus of a massive sea-based relief effort. These efforts dramatically shifted public opinion in Indonesia, the world's largest Muslim country, in favor of the United States and against al-Qaeda.[75]

The strategic effects of the relief efforts came as a surprise to Navy leaders, many of whom now adapted a broader understanding of the Navy's purpose. The new outlook was reinforced in August 2005 when the Navy provided humanitarian assistance after Hurricane Katrina. The economic impact of the closure of the port of New Orleans, the nation's largest and the world's fifth-largest port, also highlighted the need to protect the world's seventeen megaport complexes from terrorist attacks, an inference that further strengthened the conceptual tie between the Navy and the international economy.

The "3/1 Strategy" sought to identify capability gaps.[76] However, it failed to specify what new weapons systems were needed. Only general capabilities were offered. These included naval coastal warfare units, linguists, intelligence officers, medical officers, and security forces, as well as more SEALs and Navy foreign area officers, the latter being officers who had language skills and knowledge of cultural and religious factors, regional politics, and trade issues. The "3/1 Strategy" acknowledged that since the Navy's budget would not increase, any new capabilities would come at the expense of traditional capabilities. "The Navy must accommodate the demand of the new mission sets," it noted, "from within its existing and planned force structure, with the addition of some new, modified, or expanded capabilities that do not currently exist." In other words, Morgan was attempting to rebalance the fleet.

Pushback: Part I

The "3/1 Strategy," of course, proved controversial. Vice Adm. Joe Sestak, the deputy CNO for Warfare Requirements and Programs (N6/N7), did not like it.[77] Neither did Admiral Nathman, the head of U.S. Fleet Forces Command. A fighter pilot, Nathman had been the first commander of U.S. Naval Air Forces (or the Air Boss), a billet established by Clark in 2001. As such, he directed how naval aviation had prepared for Enduring Freedom and was thus well aware of the reasons for carrier aviation's success in Afghanistan and Iraq. Before taking over U.S. Fleet Forces Command, Nathman had been the vice CNO, a job whose chief responsibilities lay in understanding capability requirements and explaining the Navy's weapons system programs. Before that, he had been the deputy CNO for N6/N7, a position that made him OPNAV's advocate for future requirements and fleet readiness. In other words, few other admirals in the Navy had a background that afforded a greater understanding of what the geographic combatant commanders and their respective Navy component commanders were demanding than did he. Neither CNO Clark, Vice Admiral Morgan, nor, for that matter, CNO Mullen, had the benefit of Nathman's more operationally attuned perspective.

The "3/1 Strategy" irritated Nathman to no end.[78] From his perspective, no one in OPNAV seemed to understand that the fleet and its high-end platforms had been adapting, and adapting well, to the post-9/11 challenges, including to the lesser-included missions. He found the silence from OPNAV about the virtues of the Navy's flexible and multimission high-end capabilities to be deafening. Influenced by the subtleties of Washington's shifts in policies, OPNAV was not interested in using such empirical evidence. Instead, the "3/1 Strategy," with its focus on the global war on terror, stability operations, and homeland defense, was pandering to the Bush administration's new concepts while patently ignoring operational realities. In an apparent attempt to help catch the shifting winds of U.S. strategy with its ascendant big ideas about counterinsurgency and counterterrorism, the "3/1 Strategy" advocated shifting the rudder. As a result, the strategy was needlessly distancing the Navy from carrier power projection and naval strike warfare, which endangered such capabilities. In terms of its language alone, Nathman had good reason to be alarmed. One would be hard pressed to find a Navy strategic statement that devalued the carriers and naval strike warfare in general more than did the "3/1 Strategy." In the 10,000-word document, for example, the word "carrier" appeared only five times, all of them as part of the phrase "Carrier Strike Group," which itself was always used with the term "Expeditionary Strike Group."

Nathman believed it was operationally and politically dangerous to downplay the Navy's blue-water capabilities. Morgan was painting a much smaller, more niche-oriented Navy than was required. To Nathman, Morgan was making the term "blue water"—which was already pejorative among the other U.S. military services (signifying a preoccupation on the part of the Navy on high-end power projection and open-ocean sea control despite the lack of a naval threat)—pejorative inside the Navy, too. From Nathman's view, despite the emphasis on irregular warfare that had come to dominate the public discussion of American strategy, such high-end capabilities were still very much in demand from the real arbiters of military capabilities requirements: the geographic combatant commanders.

Nathman's view of the future, once America's current strategic commitments had been unwound, contrasted sharply with Morgan's. The end of the wars in Afghanistan and Iraq would see the start of the budget cuts. The United States was closing many of its overseas bases. Internationally, it was becoming unpopular as more governments were refusing to host U.S. forces on their soil. Americans were war weary and would not support interventions or large defense budgets. China, North Korea, and Iran were acting up. The Chinese were building a technologically advanced anti-access and area-denial navy that would put a premium on the U.S. Navy's blue-water capabilities. Given the looming budget cuts, the Navy simply could not afford to support capabilities that merely demonstrated that the Navy was conforming to guidance. To Nathman, whose way of thinking reflected that of power-projection proponents of the 1970s like CNOs Holloway and Hayward, only a fleet built around the requirements for major combat operations could manage crisis, deter war, and, failing that, prevail in a wider variety of scenarios. No one denied the need to address the emerging missions. But specialized platforms built for niche missions were not versatile enough across the spectrum of warfare. In a period of fiscal restraint and recapitalization, the Navy needed to spend its limited funds on flexible, multipurpose platforms built foremost around the requirements of major combat operations. Rationalizing the fleet in terms of a threat and major combat operations would be more effective in prying funds from Congress than rationalizing the fleet in terms of abstract arguments of a constabulary nature. In a sense, Nathman was, in Morgan's words, also "shooting ahead of the duck."[79]

To Nathman, the Navy's high-end, blue-water capabilities were the nation's most effective and cost-efficient instrument to manage crises, deter war, and protect U.S. interests. What would the United States' big stick be after the wars? The B-2, which flew from its base in Missouri? The United States' intercontinental ballistic missiles? Even as the United States' focus was on Iraq and Afghanistan, carrier strike groups were steaming off China and North Korea with a view to deterring those countries from doing anything imprudent. Under no circumstances, Nathman argued, should the Navy exchange even one Super Hornet for a squadron of rubber riverine boats, which did little to deter regional powers. Passionately, Nathman fought back at every opportunity. He argued that there was no reason why the three smaller circles of the Bear Paw should be anywhere but inside the larger circle. He even got OPNAV to admit one should not be concerned with the size or the positions of the three circles.[80] He scrambled to ensure other senior admirals understood what was going on and what was at stake.

In the end, Clark did not sign the "3/1 Strategy." He was due to retire in July 2005 anyway, and it was clear that Admiral Mullen, who had been announced as Clark's successor in March 2005, had his own ideas about where he wanted to take the Navy. Although Morgan got his strategic dialogue, for all practical purposes Nathman won the skirmish. What Nathman did not know was that this would prove to be the first in a series of clashes between him and Morgan that would color the landscape of American naval strategy for the next two years.

Conclusion

The Bush foreign policy was an unusually aggressive strain of Wilsonianism, the belief that U.S. security interests are best served by increasing the number of liberal democracies.[81] The administration had an unfailing belief in the centrality of military power in international politics and in its ability to bring real change, which was buoyed by the promises of decisive revolutionary technologies. After Iraq exposed the American way of war and the self-indulgent quest to realize the revolution in military affairs, the administration shifted its approach. The new one portrayed the United States as the principal guardian of the international order, which worked with and on behalf of those that enjoyed the fruits of the U.S. system. From that practical point of view, the administration's portrayal of a threat that endangered not only the United States, but also its allies and trading partners, ensured material and conceptual support for the global war on terror.

The approach did not marginalize considerations for a maritime strategy: just the opposite, it invited them.

For his part, Morgan was emboldened with the knowledge that he understood in a way that other senior Navy leaders did not that the emerging strategic environment and the new direction in U.S. strategy would be advantageous to the Navy. Given the poor state of institutional strategic thinking, he believed the Navy had failed utterly to comprehend the implications of shifts in the political and economic order caused by globalization. Unlike Art Cebrowski, Archie Clemins, Jerry Tuttle, and Bill Owens, John Morgan was an institutional critic of a different sort. He was not a technological visionary, but rather was a strategic one. Unlike the initiatives of these admirals, however, Morgan's initiatives cut across the grain of institutional thinking. Consequently, although Morgan got his dialogue, it admittedly raged out of his control, which diverted attention away from his primary arguments about how the United States' vital interests and military should be viewed in terms of the system and how the Navy had a unique relationship with the system.[82]

Moreover, Morgan did not make these arguments clear enough. By their nature, these arguments were abstract and their essential points were not self-evident to a corps of officers whose backgrounds did not lend themselves to an understanding of what globalization meant, let alone what a maritime strategy is, how emerging trends were buoying considerations for a maritime strategy, or how such a strategy would further institutional (and national) interests. What was abundantly clear to Navy leaders, however, was that Morgan was attempting to rebalance the fleet and alter how it was to be deployed. Since the fleet's composition and use go to the core of how Navy officers see the Navy's purpose, the ensuing debate should have been of no surprise. The appointment of Mullen as CNO in July 2005 provided Morgan with an opportunity to apply the lessons learned from the "3/1 Strategy" and, with the new CNO's guidance, launch a wave of strategic concepts and strategic statements that would provide the conceptual stepping-stones for "A Cooperative Strategy."

Chapter 11

The 1000-Ship
Navy, 2005–6

Mullen Tasks the "Navy Strategic Plan"

C NO Mullen moved decisively after taking over. He immediately tasked the development of a Navy strategic plan that aimed to determine the fleet's composition, stabilize the shipbuilding budget, and set the number of ships required.[1] He intimated that he would change the composition, noting in his assumption-of-command message that among his principal challenges was "the need to build a fleet for the future, [which] . . . will be different from the one we have today."[2] He publicly fired Vice Admiral Sestak, deputy CNO for N6/N7, a protégé of CNO Clark, for having maintained a poor command climate, the result of Sestak's ill temper and habit of working his subordinates around the clock.[3] These decisions, all of which happened within a week of taking over, served notice that Mullen was now in charge and change was coming.

Mullen wanted the "Navy Strategic Plan" to provide his guidance to the resource sponsors, who were expected in turn to show the CNO how their programmatic decisions reflected his guidance.[4] The CNO saw the "Navy Strategic Plan" as the primary document of the planning phase of the Navy's Planning, Programming, Budgeting, and Execution process. Mullen wanted the document to examine the future security environment, identify required high-end capabilities, and develop a global concept of operations. He also wanted it to serve as the cornerstone for a family of follow-on strategies. As noted, the "Navy Strategic Plan" would provide the CNO's "risk guidance" (e.g., "take more risk in anti-submarine warfare capabilities") and "desirable effects guidance" (e.g., the "Navy operates across the full maritime spectrum—open ocean, littoral, coastal, and internal water—and influences events ashore").[5] However, Mullen did not task N8 or N6/N7 to develop it as one might expect. Instead, he tasked Vice Admiral Morgan to do it in collaboration with other OPNAV elements, the Navy component commands, the Office of the Secretary of the Navy, and Admiral Nathman's U.S. Fleet Forces Command. To influence the Navy's 2008 budget submission and the 2006 QDR, both of which were nearing completion, Mullen wanted the "Navy Strategic Plan" to be completed within a few weeks.[6] Given the bureaucratic nature of OPNAV, not to mention the need to form consensus, this was a tight timeline.

The 1000-Ship Navy

In September 2005 Mullen introduced the 1000-ship Navy concept, which was very favorably received by President Bush.[7] It argued that maritime security was an international problem that called for an international solution. The maritime security environment had grown too complex, its threats too diffused, for one navy to handle. As Morgan argued, "The process of globalization has inextricably linked nations together in a de facto security arrangement that has resulted in increased interdependence and reliance on international cooperation as a prerequisite for national prosperity."[8]

As envisioned by Morgan, the 1000-ship Navy was a self-organizing, self-governing, come-as-you-are cooperative global maritime security network that coordinated the activities of volunteer nations' navies, coast guards, and constabulary units. The goal was to protect ports and harbors, territorial waters, the high seas, and international straits, and to address the common threats of terrorism, piracy, illegal immigration, human smuggling, drug trafficking, environmental exploitation, and the proliferation of weapons of mass destruction.[9] The 1000-ship Navy, later renamed the Global Maritime Partnership, demonstrated the ability of the world's only globally deployed Navy to knit together the interests of like-minded states in ways that air forces and armies could not.

Morgan also helped develop the concept of a global fleet station. It was the brainchild of Capt. Wayne Porter, who had brought the idea over from Europe where he had worked for Mullen. As the head of CNO Mullen's N00Z, Porter further developed the idea with Strategy and Policy's (N5's) N5SC.[10] A global fleet station was a self-sustaining home base comprising one or more large amphibious ships that would steam off the coast and play host and coordinate the activities of U.S. small-craft and riverine boats, helicopters, mobile training teams, Seabees, Army engineers, explosive ordnance personnel, salvage divers, medical and dental teams, and so on.[11] Global fleet stations were to operate in cooperation with host nations and the ships of others, and would provide basing facilities for U.S. federal agencies and nongovernmental organizations. The global fleet station, which also proved popular with Secretary of Defense Rumsfeld, was conceived as a way to shape regional security by using capabilities that would normally have been considered support functions. Morgan also promoted the idea of maritime domain awareness, another concept that sought to leverage international cooperation by pooling and redisseminating information accumulated from shipborne identification systems, radar, and port security systems, for example, in order to track ships at sea and produce actionable intelligence on terrorists and criminals.

These initiatives reflected how the Navy was adapting conceptually to the emerging demands of the global war on terrorism and to the rash of natural disasters at this same time (notably the Indonesian tsunami in December 2004 and Hurricane Katrina in August 2005), to which Navy units had been called to respond. They reflected the Navy's growing experience in more population-centric missions, which were intended not simply as humanitarianism, but as a contribution to the war on terror, and which highlighted the Navy's ability to modulate force and bring about strategic effects at the local level without the need for a large American footprint on shore.

The National Strategy for Maritime Security

In September 2005 President Bush signed *The National Strategy for Maritime Security*.[12] The document, which remains the only national strategic statement of its kind, supported Mullen's and Morgan's argument about the relationship between sea power, collective maritime security, and global prosperity. It was the product of a collaborative effort between the Departments of Defense and Homeland Security.

The National Strategy for Maritime Security related maritime security to the prosperity and security of the United States and the international system generally. It argued, "The safety and economic security of the United States depend in substantial part upon the secure use of the world's oceans. The United States has a vital national interest in maritime security. . . . The oceans, much of which are global commons under no State's jurisdiction, offer all nations, even landlocked

States, a network of sea-lanes or highways that is of enormous importance to their security and prosperity."[13] Because of the global economy's reliance on the oceans, it asserted, all participatory nations have a common interest in sustaining the maritime-based commerce that undergirds economic security and in protecting it from terrorists, piracy, environmental degradation, and illegal seaborne immigration.

Overall, *The National Strategy for Maritime Security* reflected and expounded on the ideas of the "3/1 Strategy" and the 1000-ship Navy and provided another national-level handhold for Mullen and Morgan to reverse the Navy's slipping relevance. In speeches they began offering a simple and compelling formula that related and bound collective economic interests in a more interdependent, globalizing world with United States–led international sea power. As Mullen noted in London in December 2005, "Virtually every nation is touched in some way, shape, or form by globalization, and most nations understand the prosperity that comes from participating in global markets." He then related prosperity and sea power: "In this context, the case for Seapower becomes very clear: economic prosperity is the goal of most nations—or put more simply: I want my children to live a better life than I; this prosperity can best be achieved by embracing globalization and international market forces." He continued, "globalization and international markets require trade—in fact, 90% of the world's trade moves by sea; to trade by sea, the world needs a safe and secure maritime domain; and, to ensure the security of this vast domain, most nations need effective maritime forces. In our global and interconnected world, every Navy, coast guard, and maritime force matters."[14]

Mullen and Morgan were widening the dialogue beyond the Pentagon. They were appealing not only to the White House but also to a worldwide audience. At a time when the rest of the world saw the United States' conduct as increasingly unilateral, preemptive, and militarized, they were also advancing a contrasting approach. They were essentially repudiating the United States' recent strategic behavior, particularly in Iraq, in favor of behavior based on collective prosperity and coordinated global security, and on stabilizing the United States–managed system. The rebellious nature of their approach and its implications for the future direction of U.S. strategy were, surprisingly, lost on the Pentagon's leaders. Mullen and Morgan's defensive, systemic, and collective-managerial outlook was not lost on other governments and navies around the world, however.

Pushback: Part II

By the late fall of 2005 it was clear that CNO Mullen had fanned the flames of the smoldering debate between Morgan and Nathman, a debate that the CNO had hoped to avoid (though, in practical terms, he did little to referee). In August 2005 Mullen noted in a speech at the Naval War College that while Marines argue issues before the commandant makes a decision, in the Navy the "CNO makes a decision, and everybody goes, 'Holy Cow, he's serious, we'd better have a debate.'" "I'm not going to do that," Mullen stated, "I don't have the time."[15] He did not have much choice, however. Nathman, who was reportedly shocked that Mullen's agenda had gotten as much traction as it had, formed an opposition with other like-minded admirals, mostly aviators like Nathman, many of whom had also spent much of their careers in the Pacific.

Nathman and his supporters saw themselves as back-stoppers against both Morgan's soft-power concepts and the Bush administration's argument that the irregular threats were proportional to those encountered in the Cold War and after in the case of regional powers, most particularly China. They were not convinced that the trends that were being extrapolated from the world's present state were permanent to the extent that they required a departure from tradition or that they could not be handled by a traditional force structure and worldview that, from their perspective, had always proven to be flexible and adaptable enough.[16]

Nathman's camp believed the Navy should not squander its funds or prematurely erode the service lives of the fleet's ships and aircraft on disaster relief efforts or chasing terrorists. Instead, the Navy should keep its powder dry and organize to deter and fight a major war with China, North Korea, or Iran; these were the three states that headed the list of likely adversaries for the foreseeable future, wars that would see the Navy play a leading role. They believed that the Navy should present itself in those terms, because it was in the realm of major combat operations that they believed the greatest risks to U.S. security continued to be found. Moreover, focusing on them was the safest and surest way to secure the next generation of advanced warships and aircraft.

In contrast, Mullen and Morgan sought a broader, less-militarized understanding of sea power. They were not necessarily convinced that the threat of international terrorism was proportional, either, or that irregular war would define the strategic environment over the next generation and U.S. strategy with it. But failing to catch the broader, more long-term trend toward global economic integration—and, ideally, security cooperation—would not be good for the Navy's institutional health nor the nation's interests. Defining the Navy in the terms of major interstate conflict did little to highlight its unique role in underwriting global prosperity or to differentiate it from the other U.S. military services.

From Mullen's view, neither the Navy's identity nor its carrier-centric fleet was being directly threatened politically as they had been in the late 1970s. From Mullen and Morgan's perspective, then, Nathman was being overly sensitive as to the implications of Mullen's approach. Mullen had noted soon after taking over that he saw no need to trade high-end for low-end capabilities, which was a change from what the "3/1 Strategy" had asserted.[17] In essence, Mullen and Morgan thought that, relative to their costs, more-specialized capabilities required for local stability and shaping operations and counterterrorism would bring about disproportional results in terms of their systemic effects.[18] "When you think about what it takes to build a capital ship versus what it takes to develop this kind of capabilities," Mullen noted, "it's a relatively inexpensive investment."[19] But Nathman was having none of it. To him, Mullen was not trying to expand the fleet's capabilities: he was trying to rebalance the fleet.

Mullen and Nathman presented their respective views in the January 2006 issue of *Proceedings*. In his article, Mullen stated that his own discussion was not about programs or policies, but about developing a "framework" to "make sense of the world," implying that a small-minded Navy had utterly failed to understand what was happening at the strategic level. "My point is this," he continued, "it is time to elevate the discussion of sea power. For far too long and in far too many ways, it has been about big-ship battles and high-tech weapons systems. Life is just not that simple anymore. . . . We face entirely new challenges."[20] Mullen stated that while the Navy still required lethal warfighting capabilities, it needed much more than that. Taking aim at what he no doubt thought were the perspectives of leaders like CNO Clark and Nathman, Mullen noted, "The Navy cannot meet the threats of tomorrow by simply maintaining today's readiness and requirements."[21]

In his article, Nathman pushed back against the Bush administration's presentist mindset and argued for forward presence and for a "powerful," "flexible," and "responsive" power-projecting fleet that could "strike quickly and strike deep," which—by virtue of its ability to be used by U.S. leaders as a "diplomatic rheostat"—would prevent the kinds of costly wars the nation now confronted. "Today's principal struggle pits the United States and its partners against radical Islamists," he noted, "but if the past is prologue, America will again find itself confronting an aggressive state." He stated that as the "Navy expands its capabilities to promote maritime security and pursue terrorists abroad, it will continue to prepare for major combat operations. Prudence, custom, and history dictate that we be ready to deliver that level of power. . . . The Navy's ability to respond . . . [cannot be] handicapped by . . . the wavering commitment of a coalition member."[22]

Over the next year and a half, the bitter clashes between Morgan's N3/N5 and Nathman's U.S. Fleet Forces Command over three high-level strategic statements, the last of which was "A Cooperative Strategy," grew fiercer as the relationship between the two organizations descended into outright rancor. As one admiral in N5 remarked to the author in March 2006, the battle was "nothing less than a struggle for the heart and soul of the Navy."[23]

The 2006 QDR

Admiral Mullen's arguments received a boost with the 2006 QDR, which Rumsfeld signed in February 2006.[24] This influential and rather threat-centric document focused on countering an increasing number of threats to U.S. security. The 2006 QDR assumed the long war thesis, meaning that the future of U.S. security would be dominated by the demands of warfare against enemies employing irregular approaches over the next generation. Signaling a radical shift in U.S. strategy, it argued that the military's primary purpose should not be viewed so much in terms of traditional interstate conflict, but rather in terms of counterterrorism, counterinsurgency, and stability, transition, and reconstruction. Accordingly, the QDR argued that the military needed to shift its capability portfolio. "The United States' experience in the Cold War," it noted, "still profoundly influences the way that the Department of Defense is organized and executes its mission."[25]

Specifically, to defeat terrorist networks, defend the homeland, shape states that were at strategic crossroads, and prevent hostile states and nonstate actors from acquiring weapons of mass destruction, it argued, as had the "3/1 Strategy," that the military's capability sweet spot needed to be shifted toward irregular warfare and other forms of asymmetrical and disruptive threats.[26] (See figure 11.1.) The Department of Defense, it noted, needed a shift in emphasis "from nation-state threats—to decentralized network threats from non-state enemies"; "From responding after a crisis starts (reactive)—to preventive actions so problems do not become crises (proactive)"; and "From major conventional combat operations—to multiple irregular, asymmetric operations," among others.[27]

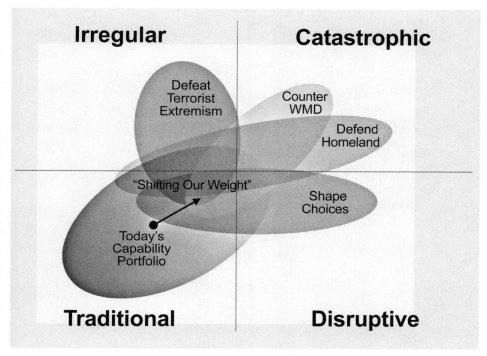

Figure 11.1. The 2006 Quadrennial Defense Review's Shift of Focus
Source: Quadrennial Defense Review Report of 2006, *19.*

The QDR also introduced a new force-planning construct, which replaced the 2001 QDR's 1-4-2-1 construct. The new construct divided the Department of Defense's activities into three areas: (1) homeland defense; (2) war on terror/ irregular (asymmetric) warfare; and (3) conventional campaigns. Each of these was further divided between continuous day-to-day steady-state and episodic surge operations (see figure 11.2). The QDR used a Venn diagram of slightly overlapping ellipses to represent the construct, which was colloquially known as the "Michelin Man" due to its resemblance to the cartooned figure in Michelin tire advertisements. The QDR, like the "3/1 Strategy," argued that the missions of homeland defense and war on terror/irregular warfare were not subsets of traditional, conventional campaign-oriented challenges and thus required unique capabilities. For homeland defense, steady-state operations included globally integrated missions that deterred attacks on the homeland, while surge operations meant responding to attacks that used weapons of mass destruction or to other catastrophic events like Hurricane Katrina.[28]

Figure 11.2. The 2006 Quadrennial Defense Review's New Force Planning Construct
Source: Quadrennial Defense Review Report of 2006, *38.*

War on terror/irregular warfare's steady-state operations included deterring transnational terrorists' attacks, particularly through forward presence, and assisting allies and partners and building their capabilities and capacities through security cooperation. A surge campaign meant large-scale and potentially protracted operations like those in Iraq that included counterinsurgency and security, stability, transition, and reconstruction operations. Steady-state for conventional campaigns meant using forward-deployed forces to deter regional interstate conflict with day-to-day presence missions and security cooperation efforts. Surging meant fighting two "nearly simultaneous conventional campaigns" or one conventional campaign plus one protracted, large-scale irregular war.[29]

In what was a radical shift in U.S. strategy, the 2006 QDR argued that the United States needed to be as competent in waging irregular war as it was in waging conventional war.[30] No longer could the services afford to ignore those modes of warfare that were not associated with their respective identities or that they were not comfortable with waging. The QDR also argued that steady-state operations— and not surge operations—would be the primary determinant used to size the U.S. military.[31] Reflecting Morgan's thinking, it called for developing "dynamic" cooperative partnerships with allies to help them defend themselves and police their own regions.[32] "Consistent with the QDR's emphasis on prevention," it noted, "guidance must place greater emphasis on forces and capabilities needed for deterrence and other peacetime shaping activities."[33] This was music to the ears of Navy leaders, who sought to highlight the steady-state abilities of a forward-deployed, combat-credible fleet that worked to deter conflict.

The "Navy Strategic Plan": The Means

The "Navy Strategic Plan" was not finished within a few weeks as the CNO had hoped. In fact, it took seven months. CNO Mullen signed the classified version in April 2006 and the unclassified version a month later. N5SC, which handled the document, had to reorganize the draft written by Rear Admiral Martoglio, who transferred in the fall of 2005, to accord with the QDR.[34] But the primary reason for the delay was that Mullen wanted his resource-allocation guidance to be the result of a collaborative effort between Morgan's N3/N5 and the three-stars and four-stars that led the Navy's component commands. Forging consensus on any Navy strategic statement was bound to be a time-consuming process, particularly a process that involved Nathman's U.S. Fleet Forces Command, which asked for and was granted extensions to turn in what would be pages on pages of critical, well-argued comments on OPNAV's drafts.[35]

The "Navy Strategic Plan" started out by explaining the CNO's overall vision: Americans secure at home and overseas; the sea and air lines of communication open to facilitate international commerce; enduring naval relationships and increased cooperation with emerging partners' navies; and "a combat-ready Navy—forward-deployed, rotational and surge capable—large enough, agile enough, and lethal enough to deter any threat and defeat any foe as part of the Joint Force."[36] Its view of the strategic landscape mirrored the QDR's and its vision of a future was rife with a variety of threats. It noted that, like the Cold War, the long war would "be punctuated by spikes of intense warfighting activity, not unlike those against North Korea and North Vietnam."[37] It highlighted how the Navy's recent concepts and initiatives like the 1000-ship Navy, Global Maritime Domain Awareness, and Global Maritime Security Cooperation supported the QDR. It asserted the virtues of forward-deployed naval forces and described how such distributed, networked forces operated across the spectrum of warfare and how they could aggregate rapidly for conventional campaigns and disaggregate for steady-state operations in support of the war on terror.[38] But the "Navy Strategic Plan" lacked any language about the relationship between sea power, free markets, and collective prosperity.

At its core, the "Navy Strategic Plan" was simply a reapplication of the force structure argument presented in the "3/1 Strategy." In its opening paragraph, it noted that the Navy "must implement a strategy that balances the enduring requirements for traditional naval capabilities integral to the conduct of conventional campaigns with those needed to squarely confront and influence the highly dynamic security environment of the 21st Century."[39] The "Navy Strategic Plan" leveraged the 2006 QDR to the hilt. It stated up front that the CNO's guidance was "directly and deliberately linked" to the QDR's force planning construct, which "suggests that 'non traditional' missions sets such as counter-terrorism, humanitarian affairs, disaster relief, counter-piracy, peace-keeping, and peace enforcement, *are no longer appropriately considered* lesser included subsets of the mission sets associated with major regional conflicts or major combat operations." It noted that it "suggests . . . [that] there are unique capabilities that the Joint Force must develop that fall outside of the rubric of conventional warfighting capabilities."[40] Like many of the Navy's strategic documents of the period, the "Navy Strategic Plan" inserted and referenced the Michelin Man diagram, which of course resembled the Bear Paw graphic from the "3/1 Strategy."

As noted in an unclassified brief presented by Morgan in June 2006, the "Navy Strategic Plan" sought to accept more risk where naval capabilities overlapped with those of the other U.S. military services and where "joint" efficiencies could be found, and less risk on those capabilities that only the Navy could provide. Taking aim at the institution's highly conservative approach to force structure decisions, Morgan noted that the Navy needs to "steer [the] best course, not just [the] safest."[41]

If the QDR bolstered Mullen and Morgan's force structure arguments, the *National Security Strategy*, which was signed by Bush in March 2006, supported their arguments about the need to relate the U.S. military to broader, more systemic goals. Bush stated that the strategy was founded on two pillars. The first, in his words, was about "promoting freedom, justice, and human dignity—working to end tyranny, to promote effective democracies, and to extend prosperity through free and fair trade" because "peace and international stability are most reliably built on a foundation of freedom." The second pillar, Bush stated, "is confronting the challenges of our time by leading a growing community of democracies."[42]

Rhetorically, at least, the Bush foreign policy was still Wilsonian.[43] As the *National Security Strategy* stated, "The goal of our statecraft is to help create a world of democratic, well-governed states that can meet the needs of their citizens and conduct themselves responsibly in the international system. This is the best way to provide enduring security for the American people." Democracies were noted to be the "most responsible members" of the international political and economic system. Thus, increasing them was viewed as the most effective way to ensure international stability, reduce regional wars, combat terrorism, and spread peace and prosperity.

The elephantine nature of the Pentagon's force structure development process made it difficult for the CNO to change the fleet's composition in anything less than five years. For the present, however, Mullen did not have to trade high-end for low-end capabilities. The Navy used its comparatively small portion of the Department of Defense's supplemental budget that paid for the ongoing wars to fund programs that could be rationalized in terms of counterterrorism, counter-insurgency, and stability, transition, and reconstruction operations.

Still, even though the "Navy Strategic Plan" was not completed in time to influence the Navy's 2008 POM development, other flag officers in OPNAV viewed it as useful enough to be repeated in subsequent years.[44] For their part, those in N5 finally had a CNO-mandated process that ensured they could shape the Navy's POM development instead of the other way around, compliments of a CNO whose background was profoundly programmatic.

The "Naval Operations Concept": The Ways

As the "Navy Strategic Plan" neared completion, another was already in the works. This was the "Naval Operations Concept," which Morgan set in motion after the Navy–Marine Corps Warfighter Talks in December 2005.[45] CNO Mullen wanted Morgan to update the "Naval Operating Concept for Joint Operations," which had been signed by CNO Clark and the commandant, Gen. Michael Hagee, in 2003. In a memo to Morgan, Mullen stated that he wanted it to identify the "guiding principles" of naval operations and the "operational methods" of how U.S. naval forces would balance homeland defense, global deterrence, war on terrorism/irregular warfare, conventional campaigns, and security and stability operations.[46] He wanted it to highlight the ability of U.S. naval forces to aggregate and disaggregate to shape the environment to prevent strife, conduct the steady-state war on terror mission, and provide "combat credible power" across the spectrum of warfare with "strategic speed." Moreover, he wanted it to align with national-level guidance as well as with the Marine Corps operating concept, which was in the works, and otherwise link strategic guidance to operations in a way that would be understood by every sailor and Marine.

Morgan and Lt. Gen. James N. Mattis, the commanding general of Marine Corps Combat Development Command (who later commanded U.S. Central Command in 2010–13), oversaw the effort. Rear Adm. Philip H. Cullom, who had been the branch chief of N513 in 1999, took the project with him when he left Deep Blue (which now was in N3/N5) and reported in March 2006 as the director of N51. While there were the usual differences of opinion between the two services, which were represented by two three-person writing teams, the effort was not nearly as contentious as past projects had been, apparently owing to the fact that the Marines saw similarity between Mullen's and Morgan's ideas and those in the "Marine Corps Operating Concepts for a Changing Security Environment," which Mattis signed in March 2006.[47] Still, the document took all summer to complete. Despite the objections of Nathman and U.S. Fleet Forces Command, Mullen and Hagee signed the thirty-six-page, pocket-sized booklet in September 2006.

The "Naval Operations Concept" characterized the strategic environment in terms of OSD's four challenges: (1) traditional, (2) irregular, (3) catastrophic, and (4) disruptive.[48] It stated that to achieve the nation's strategic objectives— which were to secure the homeland from attack, ensure strategic access and global freedom, solve problems with allies and partners, and bring about "favorable security conditions" by countering aggression—the United States needed distributed, forward-deployed forces to "assure" allies and friends, "dissuade" potential foes, "deter" aggression, and "defeat" foes if necessary.

It noted that U.S. naval forces had to change the way they operated to accord with *The National Strategy for Maritime Security*'s three broad, free-market-oriented guiding principles: (1) preserving freedom of the seas, (2) facilitating and defending commerce, and (3) facilitating the movement of goods and people across U.S. borders while screening out dangerous goods and people.[49] Otherwise, however, the "Naval Operations Concept," like the "Navy Strategic Plan," was devoid of the lofty language that related American sea power to collective prosperity and U.S. security.

It also repeated the QDR's argument that homeland defense and war on terror/ irregular warfare were not subsets of traditional conventional campaigns, and that they needed specialized capabilities. It interpreted the 2006 QDR as having five strategic missions: (1) homeland defense, (2) war on terror/irregular (asymmetric) warfare, (3) conventional campaigns, (4) deterrence, and (5) shaping and stability operations.[50] It argued that although forward presence, deterrence, sea control, power projection, and crisis response were their core capabilities, the Navy and Marine Corps would continue to be engaged in missions that were not subsets of traditional combat operations. The challenge was thus to remain proficient in traditional missions while improving their ability in nontraditional missions so as *"to ensure that naval power and influence can be applied at and from the sea, across the littorals, and ashore, as required."*[51]

The "Naval Operations Concept" then listed and briefly explained the Navy's and Marine Corps' naval missions, guiding naval principles, methods, and desired strategic objectives and outcomes. Some of the naval missions—like deterrence, forward presence, sea control, and power projection—were long familiar. A few, like civil-military operations, had come to the fore in the 1990s. The rest reflected the Navy's and Marine Corps' respective post-9/11 operational experiences. The document highlighted the role of U.S. naval forces in humanitarian assistance and disaster relief operations and the value of global fleet stations. The strategic objectives and outcomes list—which included "establish favorable security conditions," "secure strategic access and retain global freedom of action," and "strengthen alliances and partnerships"—reflected a broader understanding of the naval services' strategic effects and elevated the Navy's constabulary role in comparison to its warfighting and diplomatic roles.[52] The least that can be said for the "Naval Operations Concept," whose practical impact on the fleet was minimal, was that it did get all of OPNAV on one page. The Marines used it to inform follow-on strategic statements, as did those in the Navy who developed "A Cooperative Strategy."

Conclusion

The 2006 *National Security Strategy* was another in a growing number of systemically oriented national strategic documents. By arguing that U.S. security and prosperity depended on free markets and the spread of democracy, they addressed the broad ends of U.S. strategy. For its part, the 2006 QDR focused more on the ways and means required to address a broader set of more irregular-minded threats and only indirectly answered how the U.S. military would go about achieving those ends. Mullen's and Morgan's desire to expand the understanding of American sea power in a way that related U.S. military force to the promotion of democracy and free and open markets was, at least initially, more in line with the White House's thinking than it was with the Pentagon's. By implicitly repudiating the United States' recent strategic behavior and calling for a multilateral effort to maintain a stable United States–managed system, Mullen was enabling the White House's change in the U.S. strategic approach more than it probably knew, certainly more so than those in OSD understood at the time.

What is clear, at least in retrospect, is that for the first time since the Cold War the Navy had a CNO who was prepared to articulate and defend the maritime, as distinct from the purely naval, dimensions of U.S. strategy. Mullen's actions flew in the face of Secretary Rumsfeld's high-handed, Goldwater-Nichols–inspired decree that the services had no business writing strategy, a decree that only drained the well from which creative strategic concepts and strategic options could be drawn, this at a time when the United States was sorely in need of such.[53]

In many ways, the debate between Admirals Mullen and Morgan on the one hand and Admiral Nathman on the other was more structural than personality driven. It was not unusual for the Navy's component commands, which were commanded by three- and four-star admirals, to challenge OPNAV. Goldwater-Nichols had increased the power of the CINCs/combatant commanders and undermined the services' stature, which bred a dismissive attitude among the more warfighting- and operational-focused combatant commands and their respective component commands toward the service chiefs and their staffs. In this respect,

Goldwater-Nichols made it more difficult for U.S. naval leaders and their staffs to take the ideas and initiatives of the strategy section of OPNAV seriously.

Their debate reflected differences in how OPNAV and U.S. Fleet Forces Command interpreted their own purpose and that of the other. Regardless of which CNO held office, OPNAV saw its purpose in terms of its Title 10 responsibility, which was to ensure the Navy is organized, trained, and equipped for combat operations. From OPNAV's perspective, the CNO was responsible for understanding the political winds of U.S. policy and articulating the Navy's purpose in a way that convinced American leaders and society of the Navy's institutional necessity and of the validity of its budgetary claims. In other words, to OPNAV strategy encompassed how the Navy should be rationalized for purposes of preparing the Navy's budget submission or for the next QDR, for example.

In contrast, U.S. Fleet Forces Command saw its purpose as determining the Navy's warfighting requirements and ensuring the fleet was trained and ready for a range of operational contingencies. It was tasked with determining how the fleet should be trained and composed, and was a major player in determining the requirements that drove the Navy's programs. These requirements were based on inputs from the Navy component commands, which, in turn, had been based partly on the requirements of the regional combatant commanders' major combat operations campaign plans and attendant warfighting requirements. Those warfighting requirements were then passed from U.S. Fleet Forces Command to OPNAV's N6/N7 and N8.

Admiral Nathman's and U.S. Fleet Forces Command's entitled sense of ownership of the fleet and brazen attempts to take over the Navy's strategy development process was a byproduct of CNO Clark's tenure. The task of organizing, training, and equipping the Navy had become so complicated that Clark had seen fit to create a separate command outside of OPNAV's control as his executive agent. Nathman, a protégé of Clark, was simply carrying out what he thought were the responsibilities of U.S. Fleet Forces Command, which, by virtue of those operational and warfighting-focused responsibilities, saw the Navy's purpose in terms of the ways of naval operations and the means of the Navy's force structure. It is little wonder that Nathman argued that the responsibility for writing the "Naval Operations Concept" should not lie with OPNAV but with U.S. Fleet Forces Command, an argument whose merits should not be too readily dismissed.

In short, the creation and elevation of U.S. Fleet Forces Command only reinforced the Navy's narrow focus on operations and resource management and attempt to hold the locus of how the Navy was rationalized to the operational context. At the same time, Clark had not seen fit to expand OPNAV's capability and capacity for strategic thinking. As a consequence, Mullen and Morgan were now struggling to provide a strategic conceptual counterweight to the operation-focused mass that was U.S. Fleet Forces Command and indeed OPNAV itself, of which 80 percent of its billets were programming and budgeting oriented. In this sense, Mullen's "Navy Strategic Plan" was a new tool of governance. It allowed the CNO to broaden the analytical basis on which programmatic deci-sions were made beyond operational-level capability gaps, most of which were in terms of the geographic combatant commanders' campaign plans and opera-tional requirements, to include trends in the strategic environment and in U.S. declaratory strategy. These trends were not drawn up by the resource-oriented N8 or the warfighting-focused U.S. Fleet Forces Command, but by Morgan's N3/N5.

Controlling the development of the "Naval Operations Concept" also pro-vided Mullen and Morgan with a way to expand on how the Navy defined the fleet. How the Navy understood what "the fleet" meant was based on the institu-tion's operational experiences, which had been changing since 9/11, particularly for those smaller communities that were deployed about the world in population-centric missions and those of the surface community who dealt with local authorities and peoples to a far greater degree than did aviators and submariners. A concept of naval operations that embraced these grassroots experiences vali-dated the need for more-specialized constabulary capabilities. It demonstrated how the Navy was adapting operationally and politically, and captured how the very idea of sea power was changing.

So, while the "Navy Strategic Plan" described the means and the "Naval Operations Concept" described the ways, the project that would advance the Navy's broader claims about its strategic effects and link sea power, collective pros-perity, and U.S. security, one that defined the ends, in other words, was already under way at the Naval War College.

Chapter 12

A Cooperative
Strategy, 2007

Mullen Tasks a New Maritime Strategy

In June 2006, at the Naval War College's annual Current Strategy Forum, Admiral Mullen called for a new maritime strategy.[1] He noted that the Maritime Strategy of the 1980s had guided the Navy in uncertain times, but today's uncertainties and threats—rooted as they were in the "unrelenting pace of globalization" and the collapse of the Berlin Wall—were of an altogether different sort. Like Vice Admiral Morgan, Mullen believed that globalization was the primary reason for a new maritime strategy. In particular, the CNO cited three of its effects: first, the increasing interdependencies among nations, corporations, and societies brought about by expanding global markets and economies; second, the increasing demands for energy; and third, the unfettered flow of information across previously resilient cultural barriers. "So I am here to challenge you," Mullen emphasized. "First, to rid yourselves of the old notion—held by so many for so long—that maritime strategy exists solely to fight and win wars at sea, and the rest will take care of itself. In a globalized . . . world the rest matters a lot."

By way of support for a classical maritime strategy, Mullen invoked the most famous American navalist, Alfred Thayer Mahan, whose ideas about decisive battle, Mullen argued, distracted from his more fundamental concern with how naval forces spread the benefits derived from expanding free markets and open societies.

Where the old Maritime Strategy [i.e., the 1980s' Maritime Strategy] focused on sea control, the new one must recognize that the economic tide of all nations rises—not when the seas are controlled by one—but rather when they are made safe and free for all. Today, the globalization of the world economy is truly an engine of hope for our children for all people. Globalization has driven down trends in hunger and poverty while sharply enhancing standards of living across the globe. In just half a century, free markets and representative governments have spread from less than 20 percent to benefit more than 60 percent of the world's people.[2]

Echoing the 2006 *National Security Strategy*, Mullen was identifying U.S. naval power—if not American power generally—with the advancement of democracy and prosperity.

The CNO tasked Morgan to develop the strategy.[3] Morgan was to gather inputs from a wide variety of sources and coordinate with component and fleet commanders. He was to draw up a comprehensive process to develop the strategy, which would be executed over the next year and would support the *National Security Strategy* and *The National Strategy for Maritime Security*. He also was tasked to develop a strategic communications plan to "introduce, educate, and disseminate" the strategy.

Morgan's Campaign to Educate

Morgan wanted to start a dialogue, the purpose of which, as he noted, was to cohere institutional thinking around a new mental map from which Navy officers could discern the need to change the course of U.S. naval strategy and otherwise to catalyze strategic thinking beyond the requirements of naval combat.[4] He sought to expand the perspectives of Navy admirals and get them, as he put it, "to rethink" the Navy's purpose in broader terms of global trade, capital flows, and the expansion of prosperity and conflict-dampening democratic ideals, for example.

To that end, Morgan gave a series of extraordinary presentations to Navy admirals throughout the summer of 2006.[5] He explained how economics determined the fate of nations, and why globalization was changing the security calculus. In a globalizing era, the dominant features of international relations were economics and interdependency, and a nation's prosperity depended more and more on a stable and functioning world system and on the universal acceptance of the United States' stabilizing role. During the Navy's Three- and Four-Star

Flag Officer Conference and the All-Flag Officers' Symposium in June 2006, for example, he showed a video clip from a Public Broadcasting Service series called *The Commanding Heights: The Battle for the World Economy*, which was based on the book of the same name by Daniel Yergin and Joseph Stanislaw.[6] The series told what it called the epic story of the global economy's birth and recounted how gaining the "commanding heights" of trade, capital flows, and resources shaped the destinies of the great powers. To help them understand the rationale for a maritime strategy, Morgan quoted Samuel Palmisano, then the head of IBM: "Among the most urgent of the challenges facing emergent global institutions in all spheres of society," Palmisano noted, "is global security and order. Without them, nothing is possible. Companies will only invest in global systems of production if they believe that the geopolitical relationships that enable their investments will be stable and lasting. Without such confidence, investment will collapse."[7]

Morgan demanded that the admiral, in his words, "elevate the discussion" about the Navy's purpose and think hard about how the navies of liberal states in the past had underwritten their nation's financial success.[8] He asked the audience to think about the "moral consequences of naval force to the world order," which was a reference to Benjamin Friedman's *The Moral Consequences of Economic Growth*.[9] As Morgan noted, Friedman argued that economic growth has positively shaped social and political behavior around the world, implying that U.S. leaders should consider high living standards and other indicators of progress, for example, to be strategic goals. Morgan asked the admirals to think about how U.S. naval forces contributed to the perception of U.S. legitimacy around the world and implored his listeners to reflect on three fundamental questions that Mahan had posed: (1) What are the responsibilities of world power? (2) What are the enduring strengths of naval power? and (3) How have the strengths and weaknesses of naval forces shaped the history of nations and peoples?[10] Morgan proclaimed that this was the Navy's moment, its test. He noted that "our noble endeavor [is to] avert a global economic catastrophic crisis; localize and limit conflict; and arise to our commanding heights [to] influence history."[11]

Morgan also explained that the CNO wanted the strategy's development to be defined by a "competition of ideas." The CNO wanted an "inclusive," "open," transparent, and collaborative process, partly, perhaps, to ward off accusations that he or Morgan had shanghaied the process.[12] To explain Mullen's rationale, Morgan quoted James Surowiecki's *The Wisdom of Crowds*: "Groups are remarkably intelligent, and are often smarter than the smartest people in them. . . . The best collective decisions are a product of disagreement and contest, not consensus and compromise. . . . Crowds often make the best judgments because they aggregate a wide range of opinions and diverse information, cancelling out bias and emotion."[13]

By structuring a more inclusive process, Morgan was ensuring that the basis of knowledge that would inform the strategy's development would be broader, and more historically and theoretically oriented, than that of most U.S. naval leaders.

Organizing for the New Maritime Strategy

The project to develop the new maritime strategy was by far the most comprehensive, inclusive, organized, and expensive of any of the Navy's post–Cold War era efforts to devise a strategic statement. Its venues included war games, conferences, seminars, and symposia with the Naval War College, the Naval Postgraduate School, the Center for Naval Analyses, Lockheed-Martin, and Johns Hopkins University and its Applied Physics Laboratory, for example. Others included high-level warfighter talks between the senior leaders of the Navy, Marine Corps, and Coast Guard, international maritime security conferences, and the Navy's and Marine Corps' Three- and Four-Star Flag Officer Conferences and All-Flag Officers' Symposiums. The venues included bimonthly discussions with those in OSD, the Joint Staff, the Office of the Secretary of the Navy, the mentors that supported N00K, and even bloggers. Still other venues included visits to the leaders of the combatant commands, naval component commands, fleet commands, and of allied and partner navies. There was also a series of public outreach forums called Conversations with the Country.

A tri-service executive committee oversaw the project. The committee consisted of Morgan; Lt. Gen. James F. Amos, commanding general, Marine Corps Combat Development Command (commandant, 2010–14); and Rear Adm. Joseph L. Nimmich, USCG, the assistant commandant of the Coast Guard for Policy and Planning. In September 2006 the tri-service core writing team assembled under Cdr. Bryan G. McGrath, who was the coordinator and lead author of the strategy. He was the head of Morgan's Strategic Actions Group (not to be confused with the CNO's Strategic Actions Group, which was N00Z).

Morgan's group was an elite branch of officers that Morgan had handpicked, only a few of whom were members of the Navy's strategy community. The Strategic Actions Group represented the Navy's contribution to the core writing team.

McGrath's counterparts were Capt. Sam O'Neill, USCG, and Col. Douglas M. King, USMC, the latter a veteran of numerous efforts to develop Navy–Marine Corps documents, most recently the "Naval Operations Concept."

The Naval War College would run the first of the project's three main phases. The purpose of Phase I, which consisted of seminars, war games, and workshops, was to develop a set of maritime strategy options that the executive committee would prune in March 2007. The core team took over for Phase II and III. Phase II would see the options refined and would end in June 2007 when the executive committee selected one option to forward to the three service chiefs for their approval. Phase III would see the core team write the actual document for presentation to the three chiefs for their signatures.

Phase I: Developing the Maritime Strategy Options

Rear Adm. Jacob L. Shuford, the president of the Naval War College, oversaw Phase I, which was led by Robert C. "Barney" Rubel, a retired Navy captain and attack aviator who was the chairman of the war college's war-gaming department. Two weeks after the CNO's visit, Morgan had gone to the war college to provide detailed guidance. He reiterated the CNO's guidance that the war college would start with a clean slate; its efforts would not be constrained by existing U.S. strategic guidance or assumptions about the fleet's size or shape.[14] Rubel explained, "Consider our situation—the project was undertaken at the end of the Bush administration and our requirement was to look ahead twenty years. We could not responsibly make the assumption that current U.S. security strategy would remain in place, and there was no adequate way to predict the direction of the next administration's policies." As Rubel acknowledged, in a period of uncertainty that had come to surround America's place in the world during the waning years of the Bush administration, the CNO's guidance that the Naval War College should start with a clean slate created a sense of intellectual freedom that directly shaped "A Cooperative Strategy."[15]

The centerpiece of Phase I was the Strategic Foundations War Game. It ran from early September to mid-October 2006. The war game was to produce a body of knowledge from which a variety of maritime strategy options would be derived. Four Blue teams represented different U.S. strategic approaches that might be adopted over the next twenty years. These were (1) primacy, in which the United States would seek to maintain its hegemony; (2) selective engagement, which focused on preventing large-scale conflict among the major powers; (3) cooperative security, which saw the United States turn to international and multilateral institutions to provide security; and (4) offshore balancing, in which a semi-isolationist United States withdrew from alliances and balanced major powers from offshore.[16] Each of the U.S. teams played against five Red teams: North Korea, Iran, China, Pakistan, and al-Qaeda. Each Red team, which developed its own grand strategy in advance, was instructed to demonstrate hostility to the United States only if American actions threatened to prevent it from achieving its own objectives. As Rubel noted, the approach was unusual since most war games are based on worst-case scenarios.[17]

As the game progressed through four turns of play, with the U.S. teams going first each time, it became apparent to the organizers that all the state actors, including China and North Korea, had an abiding interest in a smoothly functioning system.[18] Only the likes of al-Qaeda thought otherwise. Rubel, who had been looking for an organizing principle, a kernel on which to base the new maritime strategy, something like containment was for the Cold War, had found it. This was the idea of defending the American-designed system of global trade and security. As Rubel noted, the game "produced the 'big idea' that the protection of the existing global system of trade and security (as opposed to the process of globalization) provided both the context for the new strategy and the intellectual glue that tied together all regions of the world."[19]

Given the lack of hostility on the part of other states in the game, it was difficult for the U.S. teams to contemplate a threat-based strategic approach. "Instead," Rubel noted, "we realized we had opportunities to disrupt the flow of events toward war. . . . What I call 'opportunity based' planning—positioning the maritime services to take positive actions to prevent war, protect the global system, and create a better peace."[20] Also on their minds was the CNO's guidance. Apart from his desire to elevate the discussion, Mullen had indicated that the new strategy would not discuss force structure, a decision backed by the commandants of the Marine Corps and Coast Guard.[21]

To guide the development of the maritime strategy options, the organizers drew up four what they called "National Security Objectives" and eight "Geo-Strategic Assumptions."[22] The four objectives were to (1) protect the U.S. homeland, (2) prevent the proliferation and use of weapons of mass destruction, (3) hedge against the emergence of near-peer competitors, and (4) maintain the free flow of commerce, including energy. The eight assumptions were these: (1) The global commons (sea, air, space, cyberspace) remain important for U.S. national security and economic prosperity. (2) Not all threats to the United States are strategic. (3) China's relative importance in global politics will increase because of economic and military growth, making it the only credible potential near-peer competitor. (4) The threat of attack from terrorists will be low in terms of probability, but high in terms of costs should an attack occur. (5) Access to Persian Gulf energy resources is essential for the global economy. (6) Potential foes will seek to counter the United States' conventional superiority. (7) States will seek weapons of mass destruction to address regional threats or to neutralize U.S. military advantages. And (8) U.S. maritime forces will maintain a strategic deterrence capability. After the game, the organizers spent two months sifting through the data before coming up with five options, Options Alpha through Echo.

Option Alpha: Maintain Winning Combat Power Forward

Option Alpha was called "Maintain Winning Combat Power Forward," which accorded with the primacy strategic approach. It represented the status quo of U.S. naval strategy and mainstream institutional thinking. In analyzing this option, however, one has difficulty understanding how it could be construed as a maritime strategy as classically understood. It did not view the world or locate U.S. vital interests in systemic terms, nor did it admit to the centrality of globalization. In fact, it essentially argued that globalization did not matter, either because it was not fundamentally changing the security calculus or because it was not durable enough to require a drastic change in the direction of U.S. naval strategy.

Option Alpha saw the world as a collection of independent regions, each filled with distinct potential foes.[23] It saw the purpose of sea power to be the following: coercively shape states' behavior, overcome anti-access strategies, and prevail in major combat operations. These high-end scenarios highlighted the virtues of joint warfighting from the seas and in the littoral, and aimed to keep a power such as China from cordoning off areas of the sea for its own economic use. Option Alpha maintained that the Navy's two major hubs of operations, the north Arabian Sea/Persian Gulf and northeast Asia, would be preeminent. In terms of U.S. naval operations, the other theaters would be characterized by an economy of force. In terms of means and capabilities, Option Alpha's areas of emphasis were, in priority order (1) forward maritime presence, (2) power projection, and (3) sea control.

Option Bravo: The High-Low Force Structure

Option Bravo was inserted late in the process by Wayne Hughes, a highly respected professor at the Naval Postgraduate School and author of the seminal *Fleet Tactics and Coastal Combat*, which examined historical and contemporary fleet tactics from a broad operational analysis perspective.[24] Hughes' high-low approach argued for the need to address both emerging high-end state-based threats and low-end irregular threats.[25] Specifically, the approach sought to enhance high-end capabilities needed to defeat emerging anti-access strategies (of the Chinese, for example) while trading legacy platforms designed for major combat operations for new capabilities that were designed to address the emerging low-end threats. These new capabilities included a fleet of small littoral warfighting ships and networks that could tie the world's navies and coast guards together. Hughes argued for improving constabulary functions and building partnership capacity to counter low-end threats, which highlighted the Coast Guard's role. If Option Alpha's approach was unilateralist, hegemonic, and offensive minded, Hughes' Option Bravo was internationalist, systemic, and defensive minded, at least in terms of defending the status quo of the United States–managed system. Its areas of emphasis were (1) sea control, (2) forward maritime presence, (3) homeland defense/security, and (4) power projection.

Option Charlie: Offshore Balancing

Option Charlie was called "Offshore Balancing," which reflected the war game's strategic approach of the same name.[26] Here, U.S. naval forces would be deployed only to the Persian Gulf. The rest of the fleet would be recalled and maintained in readiness to surge when required. It assumed that no Eurasian state would rise to a peer or near-peer status for at least ten to fifteen years, and, with the exception of energy crises, that regional crises would be resolved in ways that the United States could tolerate. It further assumed, "Peace is best assured by encouraging traditional allies to take more responsibility for their own defense. . . . Diplomatic, political, and economic outreach will often prove more influential than military engagement."[27]

Option Charlie was a minimalist strategy from the Navy's perspective, one that relied heavily on the United States' ability to wield skillfully its diplomatic and economic instruments.[28] It assumed that the system was largely able to maintain itself and reconcile interstate differences without forcible U.S. intervention. At the same time, with the exception of the Persian Gulf, Option Charlie was

all about (surged) warfighting, and not coercive diplomacy or constabulary operations. Savings gained by garrisoning the fleet would be used to retain the force
structure in the face of budget cuts, improve the fleet's surge capability, and invest
in advanced technology that would be needed in the future. As it stated, its areas
of emphasis were (1) strategic deterrence (including air and missile defense), (2)
forward maritime presence, (3) maritime security cooperation, (4) crisis response,
and (5) power projection.

Option Delta: Securing the Global Commons

Option Delta was called "Securing the Global Commons," which the authors
stated was the Navy's primary mission.[29] This option, which reflected Barney
Rubel's outlook, stated that the United States could not assume maritime suprem-
acy in every situation in every part of the world. In other words, the ability of
the United States to control the seas was diminishing in the face of technological
developments such as ballistic antiship missiles, a shrinking force structure, and
new legal norms of a political and economic nature that governed control of the
oceans. It assumed that nonstate actors would attempt to use the seas for their
own purposes, and that maritime choke points and trade routes were still strategically significant enough to warrant a strong focus on sea control and sea denial.
Option Delta sought to integrate other navies into the United States' sea control
and sea denial operations. It also sought to improve the ability of developing
nations to police their own areas.

In many ways, Option Delta was operationalizing the 1000-ship Navy and
Maritime Domain Awareness concepts. It was internationalist and defensive
minded, while recognizing the continued reality of U.S. hegemony. In essence, it
was less an overarching maritime strategy than it was the operational embodiment
of Option Echo, "Global System," which sought to organize how that strategy
was to function in peace and war.[30] Clearly, it was systemic in nature. Its areas of
emphasis were (1) sea control, (2) forward maritime presence, (3) homeland
defense/security, and (4) power projection.

Option Echo: Global System

Option Echo was called "Global System." It was almost certainly inserted into
the process by McGrath, probably with the concurrence of Rubel and Morgan.
Of the five options, Option Echo had the broadest perspective, and was the
one most reflective of a holistic maritime strategic approach. If Option Alpha

faithfully represented Admiral Nathman's views, then Option Echo came about as close as any to representing Morgan's and Mullen's. Option Echo probably reflected more the thinking of McGrath, though, whose thinking focused less on promoting economic and political integration for its own sake than it did on preventing major wars like World War I that had brought about the collapse of the international system.

Option Echo and Option Alpha represented two fundamentally different approaches. Option Echo was associated with the war game's selective engagement strategic approach, which saw the world in terms of continents, trade, capital flows, and alliances. According to Option Echo, the United States drew most of its power and influence from its role as the system's manager and protector.

Option Echo argued that the greatest threat to the stability and the continuation of the United States–managed global system was great power war. Consequently, it argued, "Avoiding great power war assumes the same priority as fighting and winning wars."[31] Option Echo argued that maritime forces have a unique role in preventing the kind of wars that might bring about the system's collapse. These forces deterred great power war by forward deploying credible combat power to keep local and regional wars from expanding, and by working to establish trust and confidence in American protection through "persistent, culturally-aware shaping operations."[32]

Reflecting emerging thinking at the time, Option Echo was arguing for a broader and less-coercive-minded understanding of deterrence. The emergence of this broader preventive approach stemmed partly from the realization that actually deterring martyrdom-bent terrorists was problematic, and hence one needed to address the underlying environmental conditions from which these jihadist motivations sprang. As Geoffrey Till noted, "The coercive approach of demonstrating denial capabilities against, or promising punishment for, prospective wrongdoers has been absorbed into a much wider concept of working against the social, environmental, and economic conditions that make wrongdoing more likely."[33]

Option Echo also argued that maritime forces knitted multilateral interests together and prevented small wars from escalating in ways that armies and air forces could not. It subscribed to the belief, articulated by Daniel Moran, that "large and small wars now seem to encircle and engender each other, to the point where there is little reason to be good at the first if you are not also good at the second."[34]

Option Echo blended and otherwise put into broader perspective Option Alpha and Option Delta. It blended the former's need for forward-deployed combat power to deter conflict and build confidence in U.S. management of the system with the latter's need to ensure U.S. access and protect the maritime-based infrastructure on which global markets depend. Option Echo's areas of emphasis were (1) strategic deterrence (including missile and air defense), (2) forward maritime presence, (3) maritime security cooperation, (4) crisis response, and (5) power projection.

In mid-January 2007 Shuford and Rubel pitched the five options to the executive committee, which gave them two months to refine. The mid-March meeting saw the elimination of Hughes' option, whose high-low mix was thought to be inherent in the surviving options, along with Option Charlie, whose rejection of forward deployment did not comport with the need to differentiate the Navy from the Army and the Air Force. It also did not accord with Mullen's desire to base a strategy on Mahan's three enduring naval strengths of the ability to influence events abroad; to anticipate and respond flexibly to events; and to cultivate partnerships and friendships.

Conversations with the Country

Meanwhile, the forums called Conversations with the Country were getting under way. Round one started in November 2006 and ended in June 2007. The Conversations were Mullen's idea.[35] They took the form of a series of one-day public forums whose speakers were senior flag officers from the Navy, Marine Corps, and Coast Guard, professors from the Naval War College, and members of the core team. Round one consisted of seven large-scale symposia (which averaged 175 attendees each) and three smaller senior executive seminars (which had fifteen to twenty participants from Fortune 100–level corporations).

Ostensibly, this extensive outreach program was designed to bring together a cross section of Americans—almost invariably business leaders, civic leaders, retired military, interested citizens, and college students—in order to expose them to the issues of maritime security, engage them in dialogue about U.S. security, and encourage them to continue their involvement after the event. As McGrath noted, "We never wavered from the central proposition that we were there to listen."[36]

In practice, however, Conversations sought to make the case that sea power was important to the nation's prosperity and security. This was particularly true with the second round, which started after the release of "A Cooperative Strategy" and ended in September 2008. The Navy was making its case at a time when the wars in Iraq and Afghanistan dominated the headlines and when, according to Gallup, Americans believed the Navy and Coast Guard to be irrelevant.[37]

From their interactions, Morgan and the core writing team learned three things. As noted in the preface of "A Cooperative Strategy," they learned that Americans "want us to remain strong; they want us to protect them and their homeland, and they want us to work with partners around the world to prevent war."[38] Some, however, learned more. At first, McGrath did not see much value in the effort. But increasingly he did, if for no other reason than it revealed how Navy officers suffer from a lack of knowledge about what Americans thought about their Navy and strategy in general.

> I've spent a goodly part of the past 21 years working the edges of the empire; I just naturally assumed that the American public knew what we were doing out there and that they had some appreciation for why we do it. I was shocked at how wrong I was. . . . [M]y strongest take-away from the early conversations was that Homeland Defense and National Defense were the exact same thing to most of the people in the audience. . . . I did not discern a great deal of understanding as to why we were forward deployed around the world. There was only a vague sense of the importance of the Navy.[39]

McGrath's assumption that Americans understood more than they actually did about the Navy was, of course, institutionally ingrained. Although he did not state it, McGrath had to reflect on how difficult it would be to explain the merits of a maritime strategy to a society that equated national security with protecting the homeland from threats.

Phase II: Refining and Narrowing the Options

After the executive committee meeting in mid-March 2006, McGrath emailed the remaining strategic options—Option Alpha, Option Delta, and Option Echo—to all of the Navy's three- and four-star admirals and combatant commanders for comment. After the core team members adjudicated their inputs, McGrath then asked the three- and four-star admirals to respond to four questions: "(1) Which [option] is closest to the way you think? (2) Of the other two, what ideas are most attractive to you? (3) Of the one you chose, what ideas would you like to de-emphasize or eliminate? And (4) What trends do you think are most like[ly] to influence maritime affairs in the next twenty years?" The admirals and their staffs had four or five days to respond, in contrast with the two or three weeks that was the norm for the Navy's strategic statements. As McGrath noted, their comments revealed that there were significant differences in opinion between the Navy's senior admirals.[40]

The differences were familiar. On one side were aviators with backgrounds in the Pacific, which meant they had spent years grappling with how to address the threats posed by China and North Korea. Foremost among these were Nathman, who would retire in May 2007, and Adm. Robert F. "Rat" Willard, a fighter pilot who had been vice CNO before taking over the U.S. Pacific Fleet in May 2007. On the other side were surface warfare officers with operational backgrounds in the European and Atlantic theaters like Adm. Henry G. "Harry" Ulrich III, the commander of U.S. Naval Forces Europe, and Adm. Jim Stavridis, the commander of U.S. Southern Command (and later of U.S. European Command), who was a long-standing member of the Navy's strategy community and was, at that time, its acknowledged leader.

In his *Proceedings* article, Lt. John Ennis, who worked for McGrath, described what he thought were the project's five most contentious issues. The first was whether the new strategy should address force structure. Those in OSD, the Joint Staff, and the Office of the Secretary of the Navy argued that it should. As Ennis pointed out, "The ends, ways, and means methodology of strategy development, so firmly ingrained in military minds, forced many to conclude that a strategy without resources is not a strategy."[41] But from the outset the CNO stated that the effort to develop a new strategy would not deal with force structure and essentially banned any such discussion.[42] As the Navy's core representatives understood it, Navy leaders intended to release an associated force structure plan within six months after the strategy's release.[43] To Mullen and Morgan, the lesson of the "3/1 Strategy" was clear: given the fundamental differences among the Navy leaders, consensus would not be achieved if the dialogue included how the fleet should be balanced.

The second issue was whether the new maritime strategy document should be Navy-only or tri-service.[44] As Ennis noted, "To categorize this issue as contentious would be an understatement and would minimize the intensity of the emotions of those involved." Those against a tri-service one worried about the force structure implications. As one unattributed senior Navy admiral noted, it would "deemphasize the Navy's role in the missions detailed in the document, which makes a case for reduced force structure at the very least." Given the CNO's guidance, it is difficult to understand why this issue was so contentious and why one Navy four-star admiral was adamant that it should be a Navy-only document.[45]

After the second round of comments was adjudicated in early May 2006, the writing team took the elements of each of the three options that appeared to command the greatest consensus and knitted a hybrid strategy. With such a wide divergence of opinion on which option was the best, it had become increasingly apparent that senior leaders would only approve a blended best of breed strategy. McGrath, for one, had foreseen this, which explains why he had asked the admirals to identify the most attractive elements in their preferred options as a way to locate areas of consensus.

The hybrid strategy was based on Option Echo. As McGrath noted, it took Option Echo's big idea of the system and the need to protect it, Option Alpha's status quo focus on regional conflict in the Persian Gulf and the Western Pacific, and Option Delta's need for sea control and collective security.[46] Unlike the unilateralist Option Alpha, however, the hybrid strategy was cooperative, which is, for all intents and purposes, a defining element of any maritime strategy. After one last round with the four-star admirals, the team forwarded its framework to the three service chiefs, who approved it in early June 2007, thus opening the way to start writing the document.

Phase III: Writing the New Maritime Strategy

There was one problem, however. In early June 2007 Secretary of Defense Robert M. Gates, who had replaced Donald Rumsfeld in December 2006, announced that on October 1, 2007, Admiral Mullen would become the chairman of the Joint Chiefs of Staff. This was unexpected because Gen. Peter Pace, USMC, had served only one of the traditional two two-year terms. The project was now up in the air. As McGrath noted, now "it would be left to his successor to determine *if* he would follow-through with the work ongoing and more importantly, stay to the time line we had been advertising—that was, a roll out at the International Seapower Symposium in Newport in October [2007]."[47] The team pressed on, however. The three primary writers, McGrath, King, and O'Neill, would individually go off and write, then gather the next day to edit each other's drafts. By all accounts, they got along remarkably well. Discussions were at times passionate, but they were not marked by the kind of rancor that had beset previous Navy–Marine Corps efforts.

The summer of 2007 saw the team vet the draft four or five times with the three services' leaders; during this time two more of Ennis' contentious issues arose. The first was about how the document should refer to what the Bush administration called the global war on terror. This was a politically charged term that the three services did not wish to haul uninvited into the next administration, which would be chosen in a year and a half. Selecting the right term was a delicate matter.

One Navy four-star admiral supported the term "Islamic extremists," as did all the Marine Corps generals.[48] Interestingly, as Ennis noted, "One Marine four-star . . . held his support of the entire document based on what he felt was the appropriate characterization of extremism." Ennis pointed out that the Navy preferred what he called a "mixed message," one that called "out Islamic extremism on one hand while seeking to cultivate relationships and alliances on the other." Clearly, several admirals were worried about the potential divisive effects of employing the term "Islamic" in a strategy that styled itself cooperative in nature. Finally, late in the summer, the team discovered that OSD had taken to using the more neutral term "terrorist networks," a term that all agreed on.

The second issue was whether the document should, in Ennis' words, "call out" China.[49] OSD had done so in several recent documents, notably the 2006 QDR. The Navy's supporters in Congress were also asking that the Navy itself be more cognizant of the emerging threat from China. China was again raising the ire of its neighbors and the United States by aggressively defending its expansive territorial claims in the international waters of the South China Sea. China also alarmed the United States and its allies by developing and resourcing an anti-access strategy that aimed to keep U.S. forces from projecting power in the Western Pacific and elsewhere. In the end, the three services' senior leaders agreed not to name China for two reasons: "The first," as Ennis noted, "was the centrality of the global system to the strategy and the critical cooperative relationships with like-minded nations in fostering and sustaining that system. Simply put, China has a huge stake in having the global system function smoothly. Crafting a strategy that invited them to maintain the system, rather than needlessly antagonizing them, seemed appropriate." As McGrath noted, "I believe the strategy presented the Chinese with an interesting dilemma; do they get with the program, recognize that the global system in place handsomely rewards their people, and pony up to the responsibilities of a first-rate nation in terms of contributing to that system's protection and sustainment, or do they remain neo-mercantilist free-riders, fattening their coffers due in no small part to the largess of the U.S. Navy (and subject to its continued forbearance)?"[50]

Second, as all agreed, the Chinese were sure to read themselves in the document anyway.[51] There were other reasons as well. As demonstrated in the Strategic Foundations War Game, a threat-centric strategy that framed China as a likely adversary was unpalatable for many U.S. allies and partners. Moreover, Congress would read the document as little more than a means to leverage more high-end weapons systems.

At this point another roadblock appeared, more serious than the rest. Secretary of the Navy Donald C. Winter (2006–9) had gotten wind of what was in the draft and reportedly threatened to shut down the project if the team did not downplay its soft power message. At issue was the ordering of the strategy's six strategic imperatives, which Ennis had identified as his fifth and last contentious issue. The ordering reflected Mahan's three enduring naval strengths: the abilities (1) to influence events abroad, (2) to anticipate and respond flexibly to events, and (3) to establish and maintain partnerships and friendships. As Ennis noted, the imperatives were keyed "to increasing levels of complexity and violence." The list was as follows: (1) "Foster and sustain cooperative relationships with more international partners"; (2) "Prevent or contain local disruptions before they impact the global system"; (3) "Limit regional conflict with forward-deployed, decisive maritime power"; (4) "Deter major-power war"; and (5) "Win our nation's wars"; as well as (6) "Contribute to homeland defense in depth" being woven through each.[52] The ordering was arranged along the gradient from peace to war, and was intended to reflect the logic of how the U.S. maritime services would protect American interests. However, such an ordering also implied priorities, which could be used to change the fleet's composition, size, and posture. A list that placed deterring and winning major power war near the bottom of the batting order was not going to be palatable.

According to Ennis, the order of the imperatives was based on two premises. First, "One of the fundamental strategic notions advanced in this document was to protect and sustain a global system with like-minded maritime nations. Placing this imperative at the top of the list reinforced a firm commitment to the idea."[53] The preeminence of that imperative, which was the strategy's backbone, acknowledged the fundamental reality of governance in a globalizing era. As Niall Ferguson observed, "The paradox of globalization is that as the world becomes more integrated, so power becomes more diffuse."[54] Second, the model reflected the unique ability of sea power to modulate force as a way to escalate and deescalate crises.[55] Nevertheless, this model was scrapped because, as Ennis noted, "Navy leadership became concerned that it overemphasized 'soft power.'"[56] It was replaced by a radically new model that reflected the views of the new CNO, Adm. Gary Roughead (2007–11).

Roughead's Model

Admiral Roughead was a surface warfare officer, the third successive one as CNO. He had spent much of his career in the Pacific. He had been the executive assistant to the commander of U.S. Pacific Command as a captain and its deputy commander as a three-star. Before he replaced the retiring Nathman in May 2007 as the head of U.S. Fleet Forces Command, he had commanded the U.S. Pacific Fleet for nearly two years. Roughead, who had entered the Navy in 1973, had served in the Office of the Secretary of the Navy, but had little experience in OPNAV, and, overall, had comparatively less time in the Pentagon than his predecessors.

It quickly became apparent that Roughead shared the belief of Secretary Winter (who later commissioned studies to refute the resource implications of "A Cooperative Strategy") about the need to emphasize the Navy's warfighting virtues.[57] Nevertheless, Roughead also believed in the new strategy and in the importance of low-end missions. In the two months before taking over, Roughead worked closely with McGrath's team. At one point, he described a Venn diagram that captured how he wanted the team to relate the six imperatives.[58] (See figure 12.1.)

Befitting its title of "Regionally Concentrated, Credible Combat Power," the top ellipse in the figure was about concentrating power in two key regions: the Western Pacific and the Persian Gulf/Indian Ocean. Its imperatives were those most closely associated with state-based threats and major combat operations: (1) deter major power war; (2) limit regional conflict with forward-deployed, decisive maritime power; and (3) win our nation's wars. The bottom ellipse, which was entitled "Globally Distributed, Mission-Tailored Maritime Forces," was about distributing the rest of the fleet to nontraditional areas to do nontraditional missions.

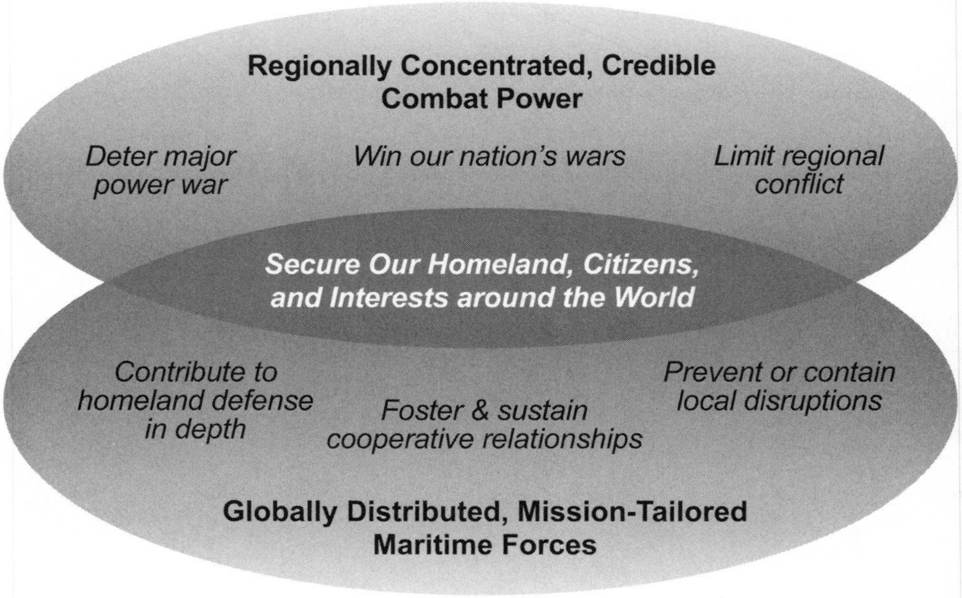

Figure 12.1. Admiral Roughead's Venn Diagram
*Source: Cdr. Bryan G. McGrath, USN, (Ret.) "The New Maritime Strategy"
(brief, Center for Naval Analyses, Arlington, VA, December 2007), slide 13.*

This straightforward division of labor reflected the perspective of the U.S. Pacific Fleet commander, which is what Roughead had been. The fleet's theater of operations, which stretches from California to Pakistan, contains many high-end threats, notably China, and much of the world's largest economies, while its engagement plan remains the most comprehensive of any of the Navy's component commands.

The model also reflected Roughead's understanding of what would be required to implement the strategy. Here one can see more clearly why he was selected as Mullen's successor. Winter wanted a CNO who would act on shared beliefs about the high end, while Mullen, the next chairman, wanted someone with the motivation and skills to move the strategy beyond the declaratory stage. Both were looking for a CNO whose skills were of an eminently practical sort. Roughead fit the bill. As a former Navy component commander, he understood how to link strategy to operational effects. As the former head of the Navy Department's Office of Legislative Affairs, he was adept at working with Congress. As a surface warfare officer with a Pacific background, he saw both sides of the internal debate and had the skills to establish and maintain a consensus.

The force structure implications of Roughead's model were clear. By placing the warfighting and coercive diplomacy ellipse above the systemic constabulary one, Roughead's model implied that high-end resource requirements came first, and, given the overlap between the ellipses (which was entitled "Secure Our Homeland, Citizens, and Interests around the World"), that such capabilities could serve the bottom imperatives to some extent. Still, the mere presence of the lower ellipse, which was identically sized, argued for platforms specifically intended to serve its imperatives. For his part, McGrath expected that the forthcoming resource plan would resource the bottom ellipse with smaller, lightly armed, and cheaper, more-mass-produced ships, which should not come at the expense of the high-end capabilities.[59] All of which is to say, from Roughead's perspective, that the previous model had not been clear enough about how the fleet should be employed, balanced, and rationalized, which of course is how Navy officers understand naval strategy.

"A Cooperative Strategy": The Ends

Finally, in October 2007, "A Cooperative Strategy for 21st Century Seapower" was released. It was signed by Admiral Roughead, the commandant of the Marine Corps, Gen. James T. Conway (2006–10), and the Coast Guard's commandant, Adm. Thad W. Allen (2006–10). The sixteen-page, 4,700-word pamphlet was filled with pictures of Navy, Marine Corps, and Coast Guard forces engaged in activities that ranged across the spectrum of military operations. In its introduction, "A Cooperative Strategy" asserted the revolutionary strategic assumption on which it was based: "Our Nation's interests are best served by fostering a peaceful global system comprised of interdependent networks of trade, finance, information, law, people and governance." This system, it stated, is susceptible to disruptions from major power wars, regional conflict, terrorism, and natural disasters, all of which potentially threatened U.S. security and collective prosperity.[60]

"A Cooperative Strategy" noted that in an era defined by increasing competition for influence and one in which the United States and its partners will find themselves neither fully at war nor fully at peace, the challenge was how "to apply seapower in a manner that protects U.S. vital interests even as it promotes greater collective security, stability, and trust," and that "*preventing wars is as important as winning wars.*"[61] Reflecting Mullen's desire to "elevate the discussion" and change the understanding that "maritime strategy exists solely to fight and win wars at sea," the strategy argued for a broader, more systemic understanding of

American sea power.[62] It noted, "While defending our homeland and defeating adversaries in war remain the indisputable ends of seapower, it [seapower] must be applied more broadly if it is to serve the national interest."[63]

In the next section, the future security environment was explained exclusively in terms of globalization.[64] Reflecting Mullen's comments about the system's ability to increase collective prosperity, it noted, "Expansion of the global system has increased the prosperity of many nations. Yet their continued growth may create increasing competition for resources and capital with other economic powers, transnational corporations and international organizations." It pointed out the importance of seaborne trade and noted that the world's sea-lanes are the "lifelines of the modern global economy." In a sentence that implicitly fingered the Chinese, it noted, "Heightened popular expectations and increased competition for resources, coupled with scarcity, may encourage nations to exert wider claims of sovereignty over greater expanses of ocean, waterways, and natural resources—potentially resulting in conflict."

The section also addressed how the proliferation of advanced anti-access weapons systems was improving the ability of state and nonstate actors to keep U.S. forces from projecting power overseas. It discussed how climate change would open new trade routes through the Arctic and foster or exacerbate natural disasters, regional crises, and social instability. Highlighting the growing importance of information as a source of strategic leverage, it asserted that "attacks on legal, financial, and cyber systems can be equally, if not more, disruptive than kinetic weapons."[65] Reflecting the writings of Frank Hoffman, a retired Marine Corps officer and strategic thinker, it noted how conflict was evolving into hybrid warfare, in which state and nonstate actors used a blend of traditional and irregular tactics and sophisticated and basic technologies, and decentralized planning and execution to achieve their political ends.[66]

The next section, which was entitled "Maritime Strategic Concept," explained Roughead's model, a graphical representation of which was not included, however.[67] At five pages, it was the document's longest section. Its one-page introduction highlighted the virtues of a globally deployed U.S. maritime forces. It stated that the ability of those forces to use the seas as a vast maneuver space and expand or contract U.S. power off-shore—thereby avoiding or mitigating the frictions of U.S. overseas bases—gave the United States an "asymmetric advantage." It highlighted how the "speed, flexibility, agility and scalability" of its forces gave the combatant commanders a range of flexible options and a rheostat to manage crises.

As usual, it argued for forward deployment: "*United States seapower will be globally postured to secure our homeland and citizens from direct attack and to advance our interests around the world.*"

This section also saw the document's core statement, in which the national interests of the United States were identified explicitly with the stability of global trade, finance, and politics. "As our security and prosperity are inextricably linked with those of others," it noted, "U.S. maritime forces will be deployed to protect and sustain the peaceful global system comprised of interdependent networks of trade, finance, information, law, people and governance."[68] Unlike the Navy's previous post–Cold War strategic statements, this one did not frame the Navy's raison d'être in terms of its operational virtues and power-projecting doctrine, but rather in the broader strategic context for which these were applied.

However, where the language up to this point was insistently systemic, the tone changed dramatically on addressing Roughead's model. In the previous six pages, for example, the word "system" had been used ten times. In the four pages that described the model, it was used only once. The top ellipse, which was "Regionally Concentrated, Credible Combat Power," was covered first. Here, the term "credible combat power" would be continuously employed in the Western Pacific and the Arabian Gulf and Indian Ocean to protect U.S. vital interests, demonstrate to "friends and allies" that the United States was committed to regional security, and deter and dissuade potential foes and "peer competitors."[69] Like the "3/1 Strategy," however, "A Cooperative Strategy" did not mention carriers or naval strike warfare (or amphibious assault or antisubmarine warfare for that matter). Given the centrality of such capabilities in the Navy's previous strategic statements, one can understand why many Navy leaders were worried about the strategy's resource implications. In response, Morgan would say that "A Cooperative Strategy" was about the ends of U.S. naval strategy, while the "Navy Strategic Plan" addressed the means and the "Naval Operations Concept" the ways.

The section then addressed the bottom ellipse, "Globally Distributed, Mission-Tailored Maritime Forces."[70] If everything that came before was marked by clear language and a lively tone, the discussion about the bottom imperatives was presented in language crafted to drain them of whatever energy they might possess. The discussion focused on establishing a persistent worldwide presence that was organized by missions ranging from humanitarian relief, counterterrorism, and irregular warfare, to peacetime activities in the increasingly important areas of Africa and the Western Hemisphere. In many respects, here—as so often in the past—

the Navy's systemic role was reduced to a recitation of the advantages of forward deployment. U.S. maritime forces would contribute to homeland defense by identifying and neutralizing threats as far from American shores as possible, and integrate their efforts with the joint force, the interagency, and international partners. Sustaining cooperative relationships was also something that could not be done at a distance. "Although our forces can surge when necessary to respond to crises," it noted, "*trust and cooperation cannot be surged.* They must be built over time so that the strategic interests of the participants are continuously considered while mutual understanding and respect are promoted."

Building relationships in turn required "cultural, historical, and linguistic expertise," which for the Navy meant its new Foreign Area Officer community, which consisted of four hundred officers.[71] It stated that the regional combatant commanders' theater security cooperation plans needed to focus on increasing partnerships and cooperation and capacities, preparing for humanitarian assistance missions, establishing regional structures to enhance maritime governance, and enforcing the rule of law on the seas. It explained how initiatives like the Global Maritime Partnership (formally the 1000-ship Navy) provided the cooperative structures needed to address the bottom ellipse's threats. "Maritime forces will work with others to ensure an adequate level of security and awareness in the maritime domain," it noted. "In doing so," it continued, "transnational threats—terrorists and extremists; proliferators of weapons of mass destruction; pirates; traffickers in persons, drugs, and conventional weapons; and other criminals—will be constrained."

The next section was "Implementing the Strategy."[72] This section argued that U.S. maritime forces had to expand their core capabilities and blend them to address both major combat operations and peacetime engagement. In order, the six core capabilities were (1) forward presence, (2) deterrence ("conventional, unconventional, and nuclear"), (3) sea control, (4) power projection, (5) maritime security, and (6) humanitarian assistance and disaster response. The ordering was telling. Arguably, even including constabulary missions like maritime security and humanitarian assistance and disaster response in the same list with sea control and power projection was a dramatic step, although some would say that the Navy had always been doing those missions anyway, and had merely found advantage in drawing attention to that fact. Be that as it may, placing sea control before power projection also signaled the increased importance of maritime security. It represented at least a tacit admission that the era in which the United States could project power unilaterally wherever it wished was over. The strategy had not become cooperative because the United States wished the world well, but because Washington required cooperation with allies and security and economic partners in order to achieve U.S. interests, which included maintaining American leadership of its system.

Conclusion

In calling for a new maritime strategy, CNO Mullen had noted that Mahan's ideas about decisive battle had distracted from his larger premise, which was about how naval forces uniquely shape the history of nations. One would be hard pressed to find a comment by a post–Cold War CNO that was more institutionally damning than Mullen's "Rid yourselves of the old notion—held by so many for so long—that maritime strategy exists solely to fight and win wars at sea, and the rest will take care of itself."[73] He was, in effect, revealing a missing dimension in American naval (and military) thinking that had caused the United States to neglect for too long the full range of political and economic effects that military power can achieve.

Morgan's campaign to broaden the thinking of Navy admirals was an indication of the sorry state of American naval thinking in the post–Cold War era. That he saw the need to present a basic brief on political economics, the security implications of globalization, and the systemic effects of sea power to a group of extraordinarily smart and busy Navy leaders speaks volumes about their pinched sensibilities and limited basis of knowledge. He aimed to inform them, but also to show them the narrowness of their thinking, which was in itself an act decidedly at odds with the Navy's institutional culture. But Morgan was not satisfied to leave it at that. The process that he developed with Mullen's concurrence, a process that was managed superbly at the beginning by the Naval War College to great effect, ensured that the knowledge that informed the strategy was much broader, and more systemically aware, than mainstream institutional thinking. Since the Naval War College reported directly to the CNO, other Navy leaders could not manipulate at least the first phase of the process, nor was the Naval War College subject to consensual decision making.

With Mullen gone, however, Morgan could not avoid the end-game politics. Like the Navy's first major post–Cold War strategic statement, " . . . From the Sea," "A Cooperative Strategy" had in the weeks leading up to its release been altered by the Navy's most senior leaders. To an extent, their changes reflected the pragmatic needs of implementing the strategy in operational terms. To a greater extent, the changes also reflected deeply held beliefs about the Navy's purpose, and specifically how the fleet should be balanced. The changes owed much to the realities of domestic politics. Like Secretary O'Keefe and CNO Kelso in 1992, Secretary Winter and CNO Roughead were undoubtedly worried that justifying the Navy in terms that extended much beyond high-end power and major combat operations was politically dangerous. "While raising the prevention of war to the same level as the conduct of war was intentional," Ennis noted, "any sense that hard power was *less* important was unintentional." He admitted that "although the writing team found this change [i.e., the replacement of the old model with Admiral Roughead's] hardest to swallow, the amount of criticism aimed at raising the stature of soft power in the document as it was released reinforced the wisdom of making this change."[74]

One can thus understand why, as McGrath noted, the internal debates about the new maritime strategy were defined by the tension between warfighting and everything else.[75] As McGrath saw it, Roughead's reordering of the six imperatives disrupted the document's flow and logic, but it was worth beefing up the high end as it took much of the criticism of the strategy off the table.

In terms of weighing military capabilities, the phrase "*preventing wars is as important as winning wars*," which Mullen often repeated as the chairman, was revolutionary.[76] The phrase implied that the skills and capabilities needed to prevent wars were not the same as those required to win wars. In the military, the capabilities needed to win wars are generally understood to be the same as those needed to deter war. In the Pentagon, it was understood that the capabilities to deter and win war were the only capabilities the military needed to accomplish its purpose of winning the nation's wars. So, if preventing included addressing the underlying social and economic conditions that enabled the rise of (particularly nonstate) threats, then the skills and platforms required to prevent conflict would not only be different from those needed to deter and win wars, but they also would be of equal importance. Apart from Mullen's phrase, however, discussions about prevention and a broader, and less coercive-minded, understanding of deterrence did not find their way into "A Cooperative Strategy."

To Winter and, to a lesser extent, Roughead, the safest, surest route to asserting the Navy's relevance and supporting its budget submission was to justify the Navy principally in terms of major combat operations. Winter, for one, was adamant that the strategy would not alter the fleet's composition or size. "Let there be no mistake," he noted at the 18th International Seapower Symposium held at the Naval War College shortly after the release of "A Cooperative Strategy," "we are not walking away from, diminishing, or retreating in any way from those elements of hard power that win wars or deter them from ever breaking out in the first place." Emphatically, he noted, "Our 30-year shipbuilding program . . . and our end strength targets will not change as a result of our new strategy."[77] Winter's promise was borne out. The force structure plan that was to follow within six months of the release of "A Cooperative Strategy" never materialized.

Like all of the Navy's strategic statements, "A Cooperative Strategy" reflected the limitations imposed by the requirements of consensus. As the "3/1 Strategy" demonstrated, agreement could not be obtained if force structure was to be included in the discussion. How the fleet was balanced went to the heart of how Navy officers understood strategy. By the same token, taking force structure off the table allowed a deeper, more fruitful discussion about the ends of sea power. Granted, the wide variance of opinion—which is inevitable as an institution attempts to redefine its purpose—required both sides to make considerable compromises.[78] Clearly, however, how Morgan and McGrath managed the competition sharpened both sides' respective arguments and, as a result, made for a better document. The success of Morgan and McGrath in reconciling diverse opinions (and Roughead in keeping it so) was perhaps the most remarkable aspect of the new maritime strategy.

So, while systemic thinkers like Mullen and Morgan got their maritime strategy, how it would be implemented and resourced ultimately accorded more with the preferences of traditionalists like Nathman. By itself, "A Cooperative Strategy" implied that while the ends of U.S. naval strategy had changed fundamentally, with the adoption of the goal to protect the system, the means would not be altered. Although the ways in which those means were to be used promised to change, the extent of the change remained to be seen. Broadly speaking, the best way to protect and maintain the system appeared to be to focus on deterring wars from starting in the first place, and then from escalating to the point where they threatened global stability. Forces not required for that fundamental purpose could be spread around on constabulary missions whose increased importance was acknowledged, but not to the extent that they came at the expense of warfighting and coercive diplomacy as normally understood. Viewed in a somewhat uncharitable light, "A Cooperative Strategy" essentially admitted that the Navy, the Marine Corps, and the Coast Guard had been protecting and sustaining the system all along, but were only now starting to understand that.

Regardless, however, a new—the true—maritime strategy had finally been developed. It had taken a number of implausible events for it to emerge. It had taken the shock of an impending defeat in Iraq in 2004–7 to bring about a systemically oriented U.S. strategic approach, one more aware of the perils of unilateralism, the need to sustain U.S. systemic leadership, and the requirement of allies and partners to work toward that shared end. It had taken two costly, protracted, and irregular ground campaigns that called into question the relevance of the Navy and its strike warfare approach, which effectively narrowed avenues by which the Navy could justify itself. It had taken a systemic threat in the form of al-Qaeda, which endangered the flow of petroleum and trade, and new institutional experiences borne from post-9/11 operations. Finally, it had taken the implausible arrival of two maritime-minded Navy leaders to shift the terms of the strategic debate.

Conclusion

The Reviews of "A Cooperative Strategy"

The reaction to "A Cooperative Strategy" was predictable. Whether in articles, the defense blogosphere, or in email debates among defense and naval analysts, critics found fault on foreseeable grounds.[1] Many argued that a strategy without a resource plan is not a strategy at all, evidently having forgotten that in the 1980s the Navy's goal of a 600-ship Navy came before and was a separate effort from the Maritime Strategy. Some argued that a strategy that did not explain how the fleet was going to be employed was not much of a strategy either. Others argued that it was too nuanced, and that it did not tell the Navy's story in a way that Congress and Americans could understand, which made it more difficult to justify its force structure. All of these arguments indicated that the document did not explain what a maritime strategy was as distinct from a naval strategy. This is unfortunate because the arguments also indicated that these critics, many of whom were well-known naval analysts or former naval officers (some of whom currently hold senior positions in the Defense Department), did not understand the difference between the two, having little idea of what a maritime strategy actually was.

Many charged that "A Cooperative Strategy" was not relevant to addressing what they saw as the greatest threat to U.S. security: China. They were upset that the strategy did not call out China. Along with the strategy's soft-power message, they thought that defining the Navy as something as opaque as a system manager only made it more difficult for the Navy to obtain advanced weaponry. They saw the Navy's purpose only in terms of warfighting; what mattered was high-end combat power, which was thought to deliver a higher quality of deterrence. Their arguments would have had more merit had they argued, for example, that globalization did not matter either because it had not fundamentally changed the U.S. security calculus or it was not durable enough to require a drastic change in U.S. naval strategy and, by implication, U.S. strategy. However, there was no indication that they grasped what globalization was, let alone the logic of a systemic approach within that context. Absent such arguments, a kind of strategic schizophrenia emerges from such thinking: on one hand, according to these critics, the United States is supposed to be in the opening stage of a cold war with China. On the other hand, these critics argue that an alliance-based maritime strategic approach to sustain U.S. leadership of its system in the face of the attempt by a continental foe in the form of China to carve out a regional hegemonic area is inappropriate.

Of the few historical analyses, some argued that "A Cooperative Strategy" suggested the Navy is in the midst of an identity crisis, which is true enough. As Geoffrey Till noted, navies in general and the U.S. Navy in particular are struggling with whether to define and rationalize themselves in terms of a traditional modern model of naval development or a postmodern model. The traditional model is based on peer competition, "when navies view each other as the benchmark for naval development."[2] The postmodern model, which has a Mahanian-inspired "internationalist, collaborative and almost collective world outlook," sees its role as defending the system.[3] Till notes that neither globalization nor the collective system-defense role of navies is new, and that both models have existed alongside each other for centuries. Which model to adapt depends on one's attitudes toward globalization: an understanding of its endurance and the furtherance of the forces of disintegration will see a continuation of the shift from the modern to the postmodern model, while an understanding of its impermanence or irrelevance compels a movement back to the modern model.[4] Ostensibly, which direction one takes has obvious implications for the fleet's composition. In general, the ever-conservative Navy has elected to maintain itself in accord with the modern model, while explaining and justifying itself, at least for the present, in the postmodern model, hence its identity crisis.

Notwithstanding Till's astute analysis, most observers did not seem to grasp the document's revolutionary nature. If the discussions surrounding its development revealed anything, it was that a realist, statist, and narrow operational and threat-centric view, as opposed to a broader systemic perspective, is still dominant in the Navy and defense establishment. More generally, the discussions revealed that the U.S. defense community is far from having mastered its Cold War experience. This is not to say that its Cold War experience is irrelevant to today's challenges—far from it—only that the fact that it continues to influence strategic thinking has escaped the notice of most in the U.S. defense community. As Sun Tzu advised, self-knowledge is critical for success in strategy.[5] Few in that community and fewer in the Navy have appreciated the need for strategic introspection.

Beyond the circle of established naval thinkers, "A Cooperative Strategy" did catch the eye of some systemically oriented scholars, who warmly greeted it.[6] These included Anne-Marie Slaughter and Michèle Flournoy, both of whom were later appointed to high-level positions in the first administration of President Barack H. Obama II. "A Cooperative Strategy" has also proved popular and influential among U.S. allies and partners, to an extent that has escaped Washington's notice.[7] The leaders of other nations have been ready to concede the need to sustain U.S. leadership over the system, because that leadership has brought them prosperity and high standards of living. Operationally speaking, "A Cooperative Strategy" has provided the leaders of many of the world's lesser navies with political top-cover that has allowed them to cooperate more with the U.S. Navy, particularly in working together in local constabulary missions and a range of cooperative actions and exercises, and creating maritime domain awareness systems.[8]

Much of the appreciation of U.S. allies and partners of "A Cooperative Strategy" stems from their understanding that, strategically, it is a defensive, status quo strategy; it seeks to sustain and maintain U.S. leadership of the system. From their perspective, "A Cooperative Strategy" frames the United States not as a unilaterally preemptive hegemon, but as a consolidating power that is managing the system with and on behalf of others. America's allies and partners see in the strategy an attempt to reconcile the demand for stability, which is necessary for economic growth, with the American drive to spread free market and democratic ideals, an acceptable balance between the United States as cop-on-the-beat and the United States as revolutionary. They have identified, as Daniel Moran noted, "the paradox at the heart of U.S. foreign policy, which has long sought to transform the world in line with American moral and ideological preferences, while simultaneously reaching out for the stability required by our material and power-political interests."[9]

To U.S. allies and partners, the strategy emphasizes stability and adopts a laissez-faire approach to advancing free market and democratic ideals, which globalization seems to facilitate by itself. The naval leaders of U.S. allies and partners view "A Cooperative Strategy" as a contract of sorts, one that completely changed their outlook from one hostile to the United States—much of which was owed to the United States' invasion of Iraq in 2003 and its inability to quell the insurgency—to one of embracing the U.S. Navy and its maritime strategy.[10]

Predictably, "A Cooperative Strategy" fell on deaf ears in Congress. "It's a nice, really slick brochure—[but] at the end of the day, it didn't do so much for our country," noted Congressman Gene Taylor (D-MS), then chairman of the House Armed Services Committee's Sea Power and Expeditionary Forces Sub-committee.[11] When the Navy failed to deliver the expected resource plan, Congress dismissed it. From its perspective, a strategy without a resource plan is simply a piece of paper. Not surprisingly, Congress missed the message that the government needs to think systemically and make the organizational changes necessary to enable a whole of government approach that is required in a highly interconnected globalizing world where the military, economic, and political spheres now overlap as to be indistinguishable. Such actions would go a long way in preventing the enemies of the United States from exploiting the legal, jurisdictional, and institutional cultural seams that exist between the federal agencies of a U.S. government that structurally has yet to adapt to the realities of a conflict in a globalizing world. Like most of the actors on the stage of U.S. postwar naval strategy, Congress has yet to emerge from the shadow of the Cold War.

In terms of the Navy's subsequent resource decisions, the strategy really was just a piece of paper. The Navy balked at linking the strategy to its programs or force levels. According to its thirty-year shipbuilding plans, the fleet's composition has not changed appreciably since the fall of 2005 even as the goal of a 313-ship Navy, a goal that CNO Mullen determined in 2006, has given way to the goal of a 306-ship Navy.[12] Navy leaders did not testify about the risks of not having a budget that could, for example, populate Admiral Roughead's lower ellipse with the twenty-first-century equivalent of the ubiquitous Victorian gunboat.[13] True, the U.S. Pacific Fleet, for one, was anxious to deploy the new littoral combat ship, which was developed during CNO Clark's tenure and resembles the constabulary-oriented gunboat of old. Although the Navy has given some thought to specialized constabulary platforms, the fleet's structure is squarely centered on major combat operations.

However, the Navy component commands and the numbered fleets have, in general, worked hard at operationalizing the strategy. For example, they are working closely with the staffs of the geographic combatant commanders to develop plans that shape the region to prevent conflict. They are improving other navies' abilities to undertake local constabulary missions, particularly to fill the Navy's own capability gaps as it continues to structure its own fleet around the require-ments for major combat operations. For its part, OPNAV N3/N5 has, at least initially, focused on developing partnerships and metrics and quantitative models to measure the fleet's local and regional effects. Much of the credit for all this goes to Roughead and his successor, Adm. Jonathan W. Greenert (2011–15), whose understated leadership and determination to implement the strategy in real terms were instrumental in shifting the Navy toward a new consensus. Given the flex-ibility of naval platforms, it is far easier to change the ways of naval strategy than it is to change the means.

Recurrent Themes in U.S. Naval Strategy in the Post–Cold War Era

Before addressing the prospects of "A Cooperative Strategy," it might be instruc-tive to summarize the recurrent themes that run through the evolution of U.S. naval strategy in the post–Cold War era. The direction of U.S. strategy shaped that of U.S. naval strategy. Not aligning in some fashion to the administration's foreign and defense policies (which sometimes were not well aligned themselves) risked marginalization and raised fears that the Navy Department's share of the defense budget would decrease, a product of the services' zero-sum mentality. There remained, however, a limit to how much the Navy could and would change. Structurally, the Navy cannot change the fleet's composition or posture in a rapid fashion. Ideationally, the Navy sought to maintain the flexibility that comes with a forward-deployed, and balanced, carrier-centered fleet, an institutional demand that was reinforced by the direction of U.S. strategy and short-term operational requirements through most of the era.

Another theme was the relationship between Congress and U.S. naval strat-egy. The surest and safest route to success in the budget wars was to justify the Navy and its preferred weapons systems in terms of the threat and in the context of war, not peace. Congress saw its purpose as supplying the means of warfare and—like Americans in general—saw the military's purpose as deterring and fighting and winning wars. Arguments about how U.S. naval forces help to under-write the political, commercial, and security conditions necessary for global pros-perity, which, by their nature, are abstract, simply do not resonate in Congress or with Americans in general, both of whom are threat sensitive. What did reso-nate with Americans and their representatives (apart from ensuring that defense-related jobs remained in their districts) were those culturally enabled advanced and airpower-enabled weapons systems and associated concepts that promised swift, decisive, and otherwise cost-effective victories on the battlefield.

How Goldwater-Nichols was institutionalized by Department of Defense leaders influenced U.S. strategy and U.S. naval strategy in the post–Cold War era. The power of the chairman of the Joint Chiefs of Staff and the combatant commanders was raised at the expense of the services'. Turning inward, the services saw their purpose more and more as exclusively supplying forces to the geographic combatant commanders. Goldwater-Nichols further shaped an understanding of strategy such that the White House, the secretary of defense, and the chairman of the Joint Chiefs of Staff determined the ends, the geographic combatant commanders determined the ways, and the CNO and OPNAV focused on the means. CNOs did not think that they were responsible for anything other than equipping, training, and organizing the Navy. Strategy was someone else's job. Ostensibly, the responsibilities of understanding how operational goals realized global U.S. interests and grand-strategic goals belonged to OSD and the geographic combatant commanders. Yet OSD's focus was not on strategy as much as it was on organizing and managing the immense bureaucracy that is the Department of Defense; the combatant commanders' focus was on their particular region, which did little to promote a global understanding of how to use military power to achieve broader, grand-strategic goals.

The need to cater to the geographic combatant commanders also influenced U.S. naval strategy. By virtue of Goldwater-Nichols, they now had a major hand in determining what kinds of capabilities the services needed to field, many of which were based on the requirements of the services' ongoing operations and campaign plans, the latter of which were kinetically oriented. As a result, the Navy's new decision-making process focused even more on what warfighting capabilities were required. The process did not lend itself to examining what constabulary and diplomatic capabilities might be needed or, in a larger sense, to understanding the Navy's strategic effects. OPNAV's means-centric focus meant that any strategic statement coming out of OPNAV had to hew to the Navy's current messages about its programmatic and budget decisions. To preserve its preferred force structure and style of warfare, the Navy aligned itself with OSD's and the geographic combatant commanders' focus on warfighting, regional conflict, jointness, and strike warfare, which shifted the Navy's operational outlook—not toward global and systemic requirements, but rather toward the problems of warfighting on land.

The Department of Defense's more centralized strategic decision-making process and OSD's mandate that the services are not supposed to do strategy restricted opportunities for Navy leaders to represent the maritime dimensions of U.S. strategy. This was unfortunate because, as Colin Gray noted, despite being the "world's greatest naval power," the United States "is neither a natural sea power nor does a maritime perspective and precepts dominate its strategic culture."[14] The changes wrought by Goldwater-Nichols further distracted the Navy from exploring its purpose in broader terms and relieved it from the more difficult task of understanding how achieving operational goals would lead to grand-strategic results. Despite a history that speaks of a close relationship between foreign and economic policy, trade, and the U.S. Navy, the Navy's admirals bore no responsibility to think in systemic terms or to represent the maritime dimensions of U.S. strategy. In short, no one was minding the strategy store.

Another related recurrent theme was the pernicious effects of the ever-narrowing backgrounds of Navy leaders. In response to budget cuts, downsizing, and the need to find cost-efficiencies amid the rising costs of weapons systems, the Navy promoted officers with backgrounds in programmatics and manpower. More than ever, Navy officers now assumed leadership positions devoid of anything but operational and programmatic experience and technical-technological expertise, none of which required a deep understanding of the Navy's purpose. Their experiences shaped an understanding of U.S. naval strategy that was limited to how the fleet should be balanced, rationalized, and employed. Within the Navy, the word "strategy" had more to do with the Navy's relationship with Congress, OSD, the combatant commanders, and the other U.S. military services than its relationship to the larger world. Their experiences did little to lend an understanding of the Navy's systemic effects or, inexcusably, how the effects of globalization were fundamentally altering the U.S. security calculus and ability of the United States to manage its system. As J. C. Wyle noted, "The Navy has, to a reasonable degree, isolated itself from the general cultural developments which bear directly upon modern strategy," a statement made in 1951 that is equally applicable to the post–Cold War Navy.[15]

Apart from the above, there were other factors at work that explain why the Navy's strategic statements took a narrow, more operationally focused and politically expedient route: Navy leaders needed a conceptual framework that could align the activities of a complex warfighting organization and provide a sense of purpose to its members about their activities. To be successful, those statements needed to be accessible and acceptable to those in the fleet. Those statements had little effect on longer-ranged programmatic decisions because the Navy lacked an integrated strategic process by which declaratory strategy shaped resource strategies, which, in turn, shaped operational strategies. In reality, these are separate processes. Declaratory strategy was simply the medium by which Navy leaders articulated the service's purpose to internal and external audiences.

Most of the Navy's strategic statements lacked a long-term follow-up plan that could shape programmatic decisions. But such a plan treads on the command prerogatives of the next CNO, whose appointment was only a few years away, and who invariably had different ideas and needs. One of those needs was to offer something new. In the political climate of Washington, a place that demands constant change and where only new ideas can be ensured a hearing, strategic statements have a shelf life. Navy leaders have to replace or update their ideas or risk being seen as too slow in responding to changes in the domestic political or international security environments.

The requirements of the Navy–Marine Corps relationship were yet another factor. The post–Cold War era saw the Marine Corps reach institutional parity with the Navy, the result of Goldwater-Nichols and the disappearance of the Soviet navy as a threat. The disappearance of that threat brought about a shift in U.S. naval strategy from blue-water operations to operations on shore, a move that benefited both services institutionally, at least initially. However, the Navy–Marine Corps strategic statements were subject to consensus. The backgrounds of the Marine Corps' leaders were similarly narrow (if not more so), and were shaped by the Marine Corps' identify, which is all about warfighting. The Marines did not understand or tolerate for that matter global thinking on the part of the Navy. As a result, the partnership bent the direction of U.S. naval strategy from a global perspective toward the Marines' focus on the operational art of warfare and the battlefield, neither of which required a deeper understanding of the Navy's purpose.

The institutional requirement for a consensual strategy-development process and the decreasing demand for strategic thinking were also at play. The requirement for consensus among the Navy's senior admirals only reinforced conventional thinking and marginalized the ideas of those few admirals who had strategic backgrounds and of those officers in the Navy's strategy community who developed those statements. As the demand for strategic thinking dropped off, so did the community's cohesiveness and intellectual abilities. For all their brilliance, neither Vice Admiral Morgan nor his successors did much to arrest the community's decline. Morgan's reliance on handpicked officers, most of whom were not from the community, meant that after he departed there were too few to extend his thinking to the next round of strategic statements. The community's (and therefore the Navy's) ability to think strategically continued to atrophy to such a degree that CNO Roughead's successor, Admiral Greenert, a submariner and self-professed "recovering budget officer," took notice.[16] The CNO, who had been frustrated at the lack of progress and strategic thinking after he tasked OPNAV to update "A Cooperative Strategy," took an extraordinary step. For the first time in the post–Cold War era, a CNO recognized the inability of the Navy to think strategically and set a course to improve it.

The Prospects of "A Cooperative Strategy"

"A Cooperative Strategy" has influenced or at least reinforced the systemic direction of U.S. strategy. As chairman, Admiral Mullen continued the effort to think systemically, as did his successor, Gen. Martin E. Dempsey, USA. Systemic thinking on the part of the White House and Pentagon has continued despite the change from the Bush administration to the Obama administration. At least in terms of U.S. declaratory strategy, systemic thinking is prominent, for example, in the 2012 Defense Strategic Guidance and its more budget-focused companion, the 2014 QDR, and the 2015 *National Security Strategy*.[17] In general, Department of Defense leaders seem to be casting off Cold War vestiges. They are starting to understand what the United States' position as leader of the world system means and the implications for the nation's security and prosperity should it lose that position. Even if a systemic-based strategic approach is an idea the Navy has not fully taken to heart, the Navy is at least the first and only U.S. military service to take it seriously as a strategic concept.

However, the defense budget continues to be cut, and the predations on the nondiscretionary part of the federal budget will continue. Herein lies the crux for the Navy. Overall, the direction of U.S. strategy promises to continue to be systemic. But as a strategic statement, "A Cooperative Strategy" has not been successful in generating the fiscal support needed to afford the next generation of warships and aircraft. In the end, it may not matter if "A Cooperative Strategy" or its recently signed update "A Cooperative Strategy for 21st Century Seapower: Forward, Engaged, and Ready" aligns with or informs U.S. strategy.[18] The number of ships in the fleet, which stands at 285, continues to decrease to levels not seen since 1916.[19] In an era defined by budget cuts and the desperate need to recapitalize the fleet, the prospects of "A Cooperative Strategy" will ultimately rest on the Navy's ability to secure the numbers and types of warships it needs to respond to an enormous diversity of challenges.

The temptation for Navy leaders to define and justify the Navy in terms of traditional great power conflict may prove irresistible for budgetary reasons alone. As Colin Gray noted, "The characteristic twenty-first-century perils tend not to carry the kind of implications for military posture that are easily explained to sceptical taxpayers."[20] Such a course would simplify the Navy's acquisition problems and would probably represent the path of least resistance toward obtaining the necessary budgetary support for a fleet that, while ostensibly designed to address a notional Chinese threat, could be employed to sustain U.S. leadership of the system, much as the present one does. An adversary like China—which seems to be implementing a long-term systemic strategy of its own—brings its own clarity and theatrics that can more easily animate congressional support.

There are indications that the Navy is already heading in this direction. While the updated version of "A Cooperative Strategy" retains a maritime outlook and offers a clearer and more comprehensive explanation of American naval power than the original, it is also more threat-centric, seen particularly in the explicit calling out of China, and more attendant to the requirements of high-end warfare and budgetary battles. Reflecting the more traditional approach of the Navy's post–Cold War strategic statements, the update takes a narrower and more operationally focused and politically expedient route than the original. As noted on the update's signature page, "This maritime strategy describes how we will design, organize, and employ the Sea Services . . . [and] it also sets maritime priorities in an era of constrained budgets, while emphasizing warfighting capabilities and forward presence."[21] If one were looking for an elaboration or expansion of maritime-systemic thought in the update, which, at twelve thousand words and forty pages is thrice the size of the original, one would be disappointed. Undoubtedly, to gain support in Congress and to provide the fleet with a conceptual framework, the update has framed the three services' purpose primarily in terms of their operational virtues and how those virtues are aligned with national policy.

The updated version of "A Cooperative Strategy" leveraged the 2012 Defense Strategic Guidance and the 2014 QDR. Both are systemic in their rationale and highlight the need for cooperation and building partnership capacity. Apart from highlighting the challenges set by proposed congressionally mandated budget cuts, the documents also call for sustaining a global approach to counter the rising threat from Islamist terrorists and the increasing use of hybrid (conventional and irregular) warfare and proxies by state and nonstate actors. But both documents also mandate that the U.S. military will rebalance to the Asia-Pacific region and address the challenges posed by cyber and space warfare and anti-access and area-denial technologies and strategies. It is chiefly in light of the above considerations—budget cuts, the focus of recent national strategic statements, and high-end and high-tech challenges like cyber warfare and anti-access and area denial—that "A Cooperative Strategy" was revised. These considerations explain why China commands such attention in the update, and why it has introduced a fifth function—"all domain access"—to what it calls the traditional four functions of deterrence, sea control, power projection, and maritime security. As the update notes, "This function assures appropriate freedom of action in any domain—the sea, air, land, space, and cyberspace, as well as in the electromagnetic (EM) spectrum."[22] Such considerations also explain why the document details plans to increase the presence of U.S. warships postured in the Indo-Asia-Pacific region and in the Middle East and calls for a fleet of more than three hundred ships.[23]

Because the Asia-Pacific region is fundamentally a maritime- and aerospace-oriented theater, as well as one that highlights the need to address an increasingly aggressive China, its naval expansion into the Indian and Pacific oceans, and its sobering cyber and space warfare and anti-access and area-denial capabilities, the mandate to pivot to East Asia stands to elevate the importance of the Navy and Air Force and to increase those services' share of the budget in an era of fiscal retraction. With a growing, farther-ranging, and increasingly capable fleet designed for sea denial and nuclear retaliation, the Chinese are, at least in the Indio-Asia-Pacific region, challenging the United States for control of the seas. For the first time since 1989, the Navy is faced with the prospect of having a bona fide rival at sea.

Navy leaders may very well use the broad cover provided by "A Cooperative Strategy" and its updated version for a few years before they unmask at some point what promises to be an explicit threat-centric strategic approach. Among others, such a move signals a return to Till's traditional modern model of naval development and, presumably, the return of maritime ideas to the margins of official consideration. The result might be a tactical victory for the Navy as an institution in competition with the other U.S. military services. But surely it is shortsighted to believe that the ends of maritime strategy should be limited to obtaining the means to employ naval power. Regardless of which course the Navy chooses, it would do well to remember, as Dan Moran noted, "The surest path to victory in any global conflict, 'hot' or 'cold,' is to conduct yourself so as to insure that the rich countries and critical resource areas of the world end up on your side. This has been the essence of maritime strategy since the Age of Sail, and there is no reason to expect the pattern to change anytime soon."[24]

Recommendations

Overall, the Navy will need to do much more if it wants to make its maritime strategy the focus of its institutional identity, as the 1980s Maritime Strategy was, and otherwise become more strategically proficient. The Navy needs to ask questions that require its leaders to put aside their in-baskets and reflect on strategy and the implications of globalization. As James Billington noted, "We ought to be seeking tentative answers to fundamental questions, rather than definitive answers to trivial ones."[25] One need not be an alarmist to recognize that, left to themselves, there is no reason to assume the decentralized forces that are reshaping the world system will unfold in ways favorable to the interests the Navy exists to defend; these are interests that, as "A Cooperative Strategy" insists, are not merely American, but rather are global. Regardless of how globalization proceeds, the Navy still needs to understand and represent the maritime-systemic dimensions of U.S. strategy in a manner that is befitting of the world's only global Navy. Who else can realistically be expected to do so?

Foremost, the Navy needs to improve the quality of its strategic thinking. As CNO Greenert admitted in a June 2014 speech at the Naval War College's annual Current Strategy Forum, strategic thinking is a capability the Navy simply cannot "buy." "We need to nurture a strategic cadre," he noted, essentially admitting that the Navy let its strategy community wither and die. "We need to position strategic subspecialists carefully; keep them in the mainstream, make sure they're moving on, and track the maritime strategists and assign them so you're going to get some sort of return in investment."[26] The high-level effort to address the Navy's ability to think strategically, which was initiated by Rear Adm. James G. Foggo III, the deputy N3/N5 and long-standing member of the strategy community, was highlighted in the update of "A Cooperative Strategy": "We will . . . cultivate strategic thought and intellectual capital through Service initiatives such as . . . the establishment of the Navy Strategic Enterprise to create synergy between the Navy Staff and other strategically-minded institutions, and the development of a cadre of Navy strategic thinkers."[27] Not since the 1970s has a CNO demanded a wholesale improvement of the Navy's ability to think strategically.

All of this is required, but insufficient. Apart from questioning how it should manage and employ its strategists, the Navy should question the type of degrees held by its strategists. These have largely been in international relations, which tend to promote a realist, state-centric outlook, and not ones that see the world in terms of trade, capital flows, and economic history, for example. The cadre needs a breadth of knowledge, which might include postgraduate degrees in economics, political economics, international finance, security or strategic studies, and history, among others. It needs a breadth of experiences that might include fellowships with U.S. federal agencies like the Department of the Treasury and investment firms.

To close the gap between American scholarship and maritime affairs, the Navy should establish an institute for maritime research and chairs for maritime studies at select civilian universities and at the Naval Postgraduate School. Given the historic relationship between U.S. prosperity, security, and sea power, that gap is too wide. As Colin Gray noted, "Despite a glittering record of strategic accomplishment in the twentieth century, sea power has not attracted the balanced appreciation that it deserves."[28] In historiographic terms, navies have always attracted but a fraction of scholarship compared to armies. In general, political scientists, economists, and political economists have not admitted navies into their research. They have not much explored how military or naval issues interact with economic and political issues in peacetime. Nor have they immersed themselves deeply enough in maritime affairs to advance theories. In comparison to the claims of airpower theory, the indirect effects of maritime strategies rarely yield the types of information that make it more amenable for study by the nomothetic disciplines of political science and economics, for example.

In this vein, the Navy might also consider establishing a more pragmatically oriented in-house strategic analytical organization. Its purpose would be to study the Navy's strategic effects and, with the combatant commanders and their naval component commands, work toward developing ways to link operational goals to strategic effect. In support, the Navy might contemplate creating a strategic analysis curriculum at the Naval Postgraduate School, which would be the strategic-level version of its heralded operational analysis curriculum.[29]

Overall, the Navy will need to admit more theory into its thinking and accept that operational flexibility and readiness and programmatic expertise are no substitute for analytic rigor of a strategic sort. Despite possessing unique importance in the U.S. state-global market relationship, the Navy's understanding of how it functions within that relationship has always been superficial. The need for such an understanding has become more acute given the world's increasing interdependencies and the nexus between U.S. economic power and security.

The Navy needs to explore further the implications of the argument that, as noted in Admiral Mullen's 2011 *National Military Strategy*, "preventing wars is as important as winning them, and far less costly."[30] This is not a new or novel idea, but it has never gained much institutional traction. There is no institute to study the prevention of conflict inside the Navy, or for that matter inside the Department of Defense. The Department has think tanks that have studied prevention during and after the Cold War, but those think tanks study prevention from a coercive-deterrent perspective. The act of exerting influence in peacetime should receive as much analytical attention as that spent on fighting war. Yet no service has more to gain than the Navy from demonstrating that its forces do prevent war, whether by shaping the environment to improve economic and political conditions, building alliances, or dissuading or coercively deterring foes.

The Navy needs to explain in clearer and more compelling terms the merits of a maritime-systemic strategic approach. It needs to provide the broader political, economic, and historical context that was missing in "A Cooperative Strategy" and its update. If nothing else, Conversations with the Country indicated the need for a long-term comprehensive strategic communications plan. The lack of long-term follow-through to expound on those merits means that, at least at the present, Americans, U.S. officials, and even members of the U.S. Navy know only marginally more about the implications of globalization for American security than they did before "A Cooperative Strategy" was released.

There has been a growing acceptance in the Navy of the need for the kind of global thinking that undergirds the Navy's new maritime strategy. As Colin Gray noted, "An education in strategy should inoculate against undue fascination with means and processes as ends in themselves."[31] But little has changed since the 1960s in terms of the career track of an average Navy officer. The Navy still expects its officers to earn master's degrees before becoming commanders, but opportunities for in-residence programs are disappearing, at least partly because the Navy's operating tempo is as high as it has ever been in the post–Cold War era. Officers now have less time for postgraduate education of any kind, let alone the kind of education that could put their operational and programmatic experiences in broader perspective.

Culturally then, not much has changed since the end of the Cold War. "The seafaring and scientific technique of the naval profession," as Winston Churchill once observed, "makes such severe demands upon the training of naval men, that they have very rarely the time or opportunity to study military history and the art of war in general."[32] To ensure the United States maintains its leadership of the system, and otherwise understands how to wield the full range of military power to serve its interests and those of its key security and economic partners, the Navy will have to work hard to reverse or at least mitigate the corrosive effects of such institutional beliefs. As Bernard Semmel noted, "No community can long survive profound disharmonies in its ideology, interests, and instruments of power."[33] Regardless of where globalization may lead, there is only one institution on earth currently capable of conceiving and executing a maritime strategy. The fact that the U.S. Navy cannot do so alone does not relieve it of the requirement to exercise strategic leadership.

Notes

INTRODUCTION

1. Adm. Gary Roughead, Gen. James T. Conway, and Adm. Thad W. Allen, "A Cooperative Strategy for 21st Century Seapower" (Washington, DC: OPNAV, October 2007).
2. Ibid., 2.
3. NATO is the North Atlantic Treaty Organization, which was named, appropriately, for the ocean that separated and, from a naval perspective, unified the allies.
4. Colin S. Gray, *The Navy in the Post–Cold War World: The Uses and Value of Strategic Sea Power* (University Park: Pennsylvania State University, 1994), 190.
5. Henry Kissinger, *Diplomacy* (New York: Simon & Schuster, 1994), 608.
6. Colin S. Gray, "Strategy in the Nuclear Age: The United States, 1945–1991," in *The Making of Strategy: Rulers, States, and War*, ed. Williamson Murray, MacGregor Knox, and Alvin Bernstein (Cambridge, UK: Cambridge University, 1994), 582.
7. The fleet was balanced in the sense that it included air, surface, and subsurface forces.
8. David A. Rosenberg, "Process: The Realities of Formulating Modern Naval Strategy," in *Mahan Is Not Enough: The Proceedings of a Conference on the Works of Sir Julian Corbett and Admiral Sir Herbert Richmond*, ed. James Goldrick and John B. Hattendorf (Newport, RI: Naval War College, 1993), 145.
9. Bernard Brodie, *War and Politics* (New York: Macmillan, 1973), 452.
10. Sean O'Keefe, Adm. Frank B. Kelso II, and Gen. Carl E. Mundy Jr., U.S. Marine Corps, " . . . From the Sea: Preparing the Naval Service for the 21st Century," U.S. Naval Institute *Proceedings* 118, no. 11 (November 1992): 93–96.
11. These free market economies were established by democratic governments, which transferred much of the governments' economic decision making to the market.
12. David Held and Anthony McGrew, "The Great Globalization Debate," in *The Global Transformations Reader*, ed. Held and McGrew, 2nd ed. (London: Polity Press/Blackwell Publishing, 2003), 14.
13. Ibid., 12–14.
14. Vice Adm. John G. Morgan Jr., USN (Ret.), discussion with the author, March 10, 2010, Arlington, Virginia.
15. Herbert A. Simon, *Administrative Behavior*, 3rd ed. (New York: Free Press, 1976), xvi.
16. Rosenberg, "Process," 145.
17. David A. Rosenberg, "American Naval Strategy in the Era of the Third World War: An Inquiry in the Structure and Process of General War at Sea, 1945–90," in *Naval Power in the Twentieth Century*, ed. N. A. M. Rodger (New York: Macmillan, 1996), 243.

18. There are two types of CINCs/combatant commanders: geographic (e.g., U.S. Pacific Command) and functional (e.g., U.S. Transportation Command).

CHAPTER 1. THE COLD WAR

1. Fleet Adm. Ernest J. King, quoted in Thomas B. Buell, *Master of Sea Power: A Biography of Fleet Admiral Ernest J. King* (Boston: Little, Brown, 1980), 236.
2. Colin S. Gray, "Seapower for Containment: The U.S. Navy in The Cold War," in *Navies and Global Defense: Theories and Strategy*, ed. Keith Neilson and Elizabeth Jane Errington (Westport, CT: Praeger, 1995), 188.
3. Gray, "Strategy in the Nuclear Age," 602.
4. George W. Baer, *One Hundred Years of Sea Power: The U.S. Navy, 1890–1990* (Stanford, CA: Stanford University, 1994), 3, 276.
5. Daniel J. Moran, "Geography and Strategy," in *Strategy in the Contemporary World: An Introduction to Strategic Studies*, ed. John Baylis, James Wirtz, Colin S. Gray, and Eliot Cohen (Oxford: Oxford University, 2007), 125.
6. Colin S. Gray, *Explorations in Strategy* (Westport, CT: Greenwood Press, 1996), 94.
7. John Shy, "Jomini," in *Makers of Modern Strategy: From Machiavelli to the Nuclear Age*, ed. Peter Paret (Princeton, NJ: Princeton University, 1986), 164.
8. John B. Hattendorf, John R. Wadleigh, and B. Mitchell Simpson, *Sailors and Scholars: The Centennial History of the United States Naval War College* (Newport, RI: Naval War College, 1984), 119. Emphasis added.
9. Ibid., 119, 137.
10. Adm. Arleigh A. Burke, USN (Ret.), "Reminiscences of Admiral Arleigh A. Burke, USN (Ret.)": Special Series on Selected Subjects, 4 vols. (Annapolis, MD: Naval Institute Press, 1979–83), 3: 146, 4: 472–84; quoted in Baer, *One Hundred Years of Sea Power*, 278.
11. Adm. Richard L. Conolly, USN, letter to CNO Forrest P. Sherman, USN, May 1, 1951; quoted in John B. Hattendorf's introduction to Rear Adm. J. C. Wylie, USN, *Military Strategy: A General Theory of Power Control* (Westport, CT: Greenwood, 1989), xxii.
12. Fred M. Kaplan, *The Wizards of Armageddon* (Stanford, CA: Stanford University, 1991), 11.
13. As Colin S. Gray noted, "Much of the frenzied preoccupation in developing a theoretical approach to the three most central ideas of nuclear-age American strategic theory— deterrence, limited war, and arms control—for example, could have been avoided as each has very considerable pre-nuclear analogues." Gray, *Strategic Studies: A Critical Assessment* (Westport, CT: Greenwood, 1982), 18–19.
14. See Campbell Craig and Fredrik Logevall, *America's Cold War: The Politics of Insecurity* (Cambridge, MA: Belknap, 2009).
15. John Lewis Gaddis, *Strategies of Containment: A Critical Appraisal of American National Security Policy During the Cold War* (New York: Oxford University, 2005), 96.
16. Gray, "Strategy in the Nuclear Age," 599. Emphasis in the original.
17. Marc Trachtenberg, *History and Strategy* (Princeton, NJ: Princeton University, 1991), 46.
18. Geoffrey Till, "Maritime Power and the Twenty-First Century," in *Seapower: Theory and Practice*, ed. Geoffrey Till (Portland, OR: Frank Cass, 1994), 196–97.
19. H. P. Willmott, *Sea Warfare: Weapons, Tactics and Strategy* (Chichester, UK: Antony Bird, 1981), 10, quoted in Gray, *The Navy in the Post–Cold War World*, 86.
20. Capt. J. C. Wylie, USN, "Why a Sailor Thinks Like a Sailor," *U.S. Naval Institute Proceedings* 83, no. 8 (August 1957): 813.
21. Rosenberg, "Process," 152.
22. The demands of transitioning to jet aircraft were such that in 1954 alone mishaps claimed the lives of 535 Navy and Marine Corps aviators and destroyed 776 aircraft—

compared to a current annual average of roughly fifteen to twenty deaths and destroyed aircraft combined. Robert C. Rubel, "The U.S. Navy's Transition to Jets," *Naval War College Review* 63, no. 2 (Spring 2010): 52.

23. Rosenberg, "Process," 153.

24. John F. Lehman Jr., *Command of the Seas* (New York: C. Scribner's Sons, 1988), 25–26.

25. Unless otherwise indicated, paragraph is based on Hattendorf, Wadleigh, and Simpson, *Sailors and Scholars*, 179–180 and 257–259.

26. Lehman, *Command of the Seas*, 26.

27. Rosenberg, "Process," 168.

28. Vice Adm. James L. Holloway Jr., USN, letter to Vice Adm. Lynde D. McCormick, USN, president, Naval War College, April 5, 1956, quoted in Hattendorf, Wadleigh, and Simpson, *Sailors and Scholars*, 235. Holloway's use of the word "line" refers to those in the Navy's unrestricted line community—surface warfare, aviation, submarines, and Navy Special Warfare (SEALs)—who, unlike those in the restricted line or staff corps communities like supply officers, lawyers, chaplains, and doctors, are eligible for operational command.

29. Hattendorf, Wadleigh, and Simpson, *Sailors and Scholars*, 235.

30. Geoffrey Till, *Seapower: A Guide for the Twenty-First Century* (London: Frank Cass, 2004), 74.

31. As David Rosenberg noted, the Cold War's most important naval innovation, the SSBN, was the brainchild not of the RAND-styled civilian theorists, but of Navy leaders. Rosenberg, "Process," 173.

32. See John B. Hattendorf, "Recent Thinking on the Theory of Naval Strategy," in *Maritime Strategy and the Balance of Power: Britain and America in the Twentieth Century*, ed. John B. Hattendorf and Robert S. Jordan (New York: St. Martin's, 1989), 137–41.

33. Capt. J. C. Wylie, USN, letter to Rear Adm. C. J. Moore, USN, July 13, 1951, quoted in Hattendorf, Wadleigh, and Simpson, *Sailors and Scholars*, 201.

34. In fiscal years 1961–63 the SSBN-Polaris program took up a staggering 13 percent of the Navy's budget. Baer, *One Hundred Years of Sea Power*, 356.

35. Jerry L. McCaffery and L. R. Jones, *Budgeting and Financial Management for National Defense* (Greenwich, CT: Information Age, 2004), 89, 92. Program budgeting means organizing capital expenditures into functional programs like the *Sturgeon*-class fast attack submarine rather than budget line-items spread over different programs. Organizing around programs facilitates comparative analysis and policy decisions.

36. Robert S. McNamara, testimony to the House Armed Services Committee, *Statement of Secretary of Defense Robert S. McNamara on the Fiscal Year 1963–67 Defense Program and 1963 Defense Budget*, 87th Congress, 2nd Session, January 24, 1962, quoted in Richard E. Hegmann, "In Search of Strategy: The Navy and the Depths of the Maritime Strategy" (doctorate dissertation, Brandeis University, 1991), 385.

37. Carl Kaysen (Deputy National Security Adviser, 1961–63), interview by Bruce Kuklick, March 27, 2004, quoted in Kuklick, *Blind Oracles: Intellectuals and War from Kennan to Kissinger* (Princeton, NJ: Princeton University, 2006), 20.

38. Adm. Arleigh A. Burke, USN, letter to Rear Adm. Walter G. Schindler, USN, May 14, 1958, quoted in David A. Rosenberg, "Arleigh Albert Burke," *The Chiefs of Naval Operations*, ed. Robert W. Love Jr. (Annapolis, MD: Naval Institute Press, 1980), 287. Emphasis in the original.

39. Wylie, "Why a Sailor Thinks Like a Sailor," 811.

40. Jeffrey G. Barlow, *From Hot War to Cold: The U.S. Navy and National Security Affairs, 1945–1955* (Stanford, CA: Stanford University, 2009), 87, 89.

41. Lawrence Korb, "George Whalen Anderson Jr.," in Love, *Chiefs of Naval Operations*, 324.

42. Ibid., 323, 324, 329–30.

43. Thomas C. Hone, *Power and Change: The Administrative History of the Office of the Chief of Naval Operations, 1946–1986* (Washington, DC: Naval Historical Center, 1989), 51–53.

44. Adm. David L. McDonald, USN (Ret.), interview by John T. Mason Jr., 1976, U.S. Naval Institute Oral History Program, quoted in Hone, *Power and Change*, 129.

45. Robert McNamara, "Recommended FY 1964–1968 General Purpose Forces," draft presidential memorandum, December 2, 1962, 27, quoted in Hegmann, "In Search of Strategy," 405.

46. Gray, "Seapower for Containment," 188.

47. N. A. M. Rodger, "Introduction," in Rodger, *Naval Power in the Twentieth Century*, xxi.

48. Lehman, *Command of the Seas*, 128.

49. OPNAV Fleet Operations (OP-03G), memo to Director, Navy Program Planning (OP-090), September 23, 1970, quoted in Hone, *Power and Change*, 86.

50. Rosenberg, "Process," 153.

51. Elmo R. Zumwalt Jr., *On Watch: A Memoir* (New York: Quadrangle, 1976), 337–38.

52. See "Project SIXTY," in *U.S. Naval Strategy in the 1970s: Selected Documents*, ed. John B. Hattendorf, Newport Paper 30 (Newport, RI: Naval War College, 2007), 1–30.

53. Vice Adm. Stansfield M. Turner, "Missions of the U.S. Navy," *Naval War College Review* 26, no. 5 (March-April 1974): 2–17.

54. Ronald O'Rourke, "Navy Force Structure and Shipbuilding Plans: Background and Issues for Congress" (Washington, DC: Congressional Research Service, October 2, 2008), 28.

55. Unclassified executive summary of "SEA PLAN 2000," dated March 28, 1978, in Hattendorf, *U.S. Naval Strategy in the 1970s*, 119.

56. Gray, *Explorations in Strategy*, 113.

57. Baer, *One Hundred Years of Sea Power*, 412–15.

58. Robert W. Love Jr., *History of the U.S. Navy*, 2 vols., vol. II 1942–1991 (Harrisburg, PA: Stackpole, 1992), 679.

59. Gray, "Seapower for Containment," 189.

60. Ibid., 190–91.

61. See "SEA PLAN 2000" in Hattendorf, *U.S. Naval Strategy in the 1970s*, 103–24; and Adm. Thomas B. Hayward, "The Future of U.S. Sea Power," *U.S. Naval Institute Proceedings* 105, no. 5 (May 1979): 66–71.

62. See John B. Hattendorf and Peter M. Swartz, eds. *U.S. Naval Strategy in the 1980s: Selected Documents*, Newport Paper 33 (Newport, RI: U.S. Naval War College, 2008); and John B. Hattendorf, *The Evolution of the U.S. Navy's Maritime Strategy, 1977–1986*, Newport Paper 19 (Newport, RI: U.S. Naval War College, 2004).

63. O'Rourke, "Navy Force Structure and Shipbuilding Plans" (2008), 28–29.

64. Gray, "Strategy in the Nuclear Age," 582–84.

65. Ibid., 594.

CHAPTER 2. MARITIME STRATEGY FOR THE 1990s, 1989

1. George H. W. Bush and Brent Scowcroft, *A World Transformed* (New York: Knopf, 1998), 149.

2. George H. W. Bush, quoted in Robert Ajemian, "Where Is the Real George Bush?," *Time* Magazine, January 26, 1987, 20.

3. Lorna S. Jaffe, *The Development of the Base Force 1989–1992* (Washington, DC: Joint History Office, Office of the CJCS, July 1993), 19.

4. Leslie Lewis, Roger Allen Brown, and C. Robert Roll, *Service Responses to the Emergence of Joint Decisionmaking* (Santa Monica, CA: RAND, 2001), 14.

5. Molly Moore and Patrick E. Tyler, "Secretary Cheney—Still the Skeptic—Grim View Complicates Task of 'Building Down' Defense," *Washington Post*, March 21, 1990.

6. Jaffe, *Development of the Base Force*, 21. The name denoted a floor beneath which the force structure should not be allowed to drop.

7. Ibid., 11–15, 21–22.

8. Ibid., 18, 35.

9. Don M. Snider, *Strategy, Forces, and Budgets: Dominant Influences in Executive Decision Making, Post-Cold War, 1989–91* (Carlisle Barracks, PA: U.S. Army War College, February 1993), unpaged, PDF, 5, 22. http://www.strategicstudiesinstitute.army.mil/pubs/display.cfm?pubID=346.

10. Jaffe, *Development of the Base Force*, 18, 35.

11. Snider, *Strategy, Forces, and Budgets*, 22.

12. Ibid., 18. Snider ascribed this quote to Wolfowitz (see ibid., fn48).

13. Jaffe, *Development of the Base Force*, 21.

14. Ibid., 23.

15. Ibid.

16. James J. Tritten, *Our New National Security Strategy: America Promises to Come Back* (Westport, CT: Praeger, 1992), 7; and Jaffe, *Development of the Base Force*, 23.

17. Snider, *Strategy, Forces, and Budgets*, 17. Snider noted that this quote was intentionally unattributed (see ibid., fn44).

18. Adm. Carlisle A. H. Trost, USN, "Maritime Strategy for the 1990s," U.S. Naval Institute *Proceedings* 116, no. 5 (May 1990): 92–100.

19. Ibid., 92, 94, 95. Emphasis in the original.

20. Adm. Carlisle A. H. Trost, U.S. Navy (Ret.), interview by Don M. Snider, February 8, 1993, Washington DC, in Snider, *Strategy, Forces, and Budgets*, 16.

21. Ibid.

22. Trost, "Maritime Strategy for the 1990s," 94.

23. Trost, interview; Snider, *Strategy, Forces, and Budgets*, 16.

24. Ibid.

25. Adm. Carlisle A. H. Trost, USN (Ret.), letter to John B. Hattendorf, September 2, 2007, quoted in Hattendorf's introduction to "Maritime Strategy for the 1990s," in Hattendorf and Swartz, *U.S. Naval Strategy in the 1980s*, 309.

26. Capt. Peter M. Swartz, USN (Ret.), discussion with the author, June 19, 2009, Alexandria, Virginia. Swartz was General Powell's special assistant in 1990–92 and one of the developers of the Maritime Strategy.

27. Colin L. Powell and Joseph E. Persico, *My American Journey* (New York: Ballantine, 1996), 425.

28. Gen. Colin Powell, quoted in Rear Adm. J. C. Wylie, USN (Ret.), "Heads Up, Navy," U.S. Naval Institute *Proceedings* 117, no. 5 (May 1991): 17.

29. Ibid.

30. Trost, "Maritime Strategy for the 1990s," 94.

31. Ibid.

32. Adm. Carlisle Trost, quoted in Fred H. Rainbow and Fred L. Schultz, "Interview: Admiral Carlisle A. H. Trost, Chief of Naval Operations," U.S. Naval Institute *Proceedings* 116, no. 6 (June 1990): 69.

33. Trost, "Maritime Strategy for the 1990s," 92–93.

34. Ibid., 93.

35. Adm. Carlisle A. H. Trost, USN, "Army Doesn't Have to Compete with Marines; Why We Need a Navy," letter to the editor, *New York Times*, January 1, 1990.

36. Trost, "Maritime Strategy for the 1990s," 98.

37. See Richard Halloran, "Navy Chief Says Lehman Was Not 'Balanced,'" *New York Times*, April 30, 1987; Peter Grier, "Lehman's Navy," *Christian Science Monitor*, January 9, 1989; and Lehman, *Command of the Seas*, 481.

38. See Frederick H. Hartmann, *Naval Renaissance: The U.S. Navy in the 1980s* (Annapolis, MD: Naval Institute Press, 1990), 44–45.

39. Lehman helped draft the Republican Platform for the 1980 presidential election, of which the 600-ship Navy was a plank. Lehman, *Command of the Seas*, 100–101.

40. Michael R. Gordon, "John Lehman: The Hard Liner Behind Reagan's Buildup," *National Journal*, October 3, 1981, 1765.

41. John Lehman, quoted in Donald Loepp, "Navy Brass Scorn Lehman Proposal," *Daily Press*, April 5, 1990.

42. Rainbow and Schultz, "Interview," 70.

43. In 1990, for example, the Army's reserves made up 58 percent of its total personnel compared to the Navy and Marine Corps' 29 percent. Harry G. Summers, *On Strategy II: A Critical Analysis of the Gulf War* (New York: Dell, 1992), 73.

44. Adm. Carlisle Trost, quoted in Loepp, "Navy Brass Scorn Lehman Proposal."

45. Adm. Carlisle A. H. Trost, USN, "Looking Beyond the Maritime Strategy," U.S. Naval Institute *Proceedings* 113, no. 1 (January 1987): 15.

46. Lehman, *Command of the Seas*, 144–47.

47. Trost, "Maritime Strategy for the 1990s," 100.

48. Trost, "Looking Beyond the Maritime Strategy," 15.

49. Snider, *Strategy, Forces, and Budgets*, 16–17.

50. Elaine Sciolino, "Washington at Work; Stoic, Stubborn Admiral Is Guiding Navy in a Stormy Time of Changes," *New York Times*, December 5, 1989.

51. Snider, *Strategy, Forces, and Budgets*, 17.

52. Intentionally unattributed, quoted in ibid., 17, fn44.

53. Lewis, Brown, and Roll, *Service Responses*, 81.

54. Jaffe, *Development of the Base Force*, 22.

55. Secretary John Lehman, quoted in Gordon, "John Lehman," 1765.

56. Capt. E. Richard Diamond Jr., USN (Ret.), discussion with the author, March 25, 2011, Washington, DC. Diamond was the head of the Strategic Concepts Branch (OP-603) from February 1990 to July 1991.

57. All three quotes in this paragraph from Sciolino, "Washington at Work."

CHAPTER 3. THE WAY AHEAD, 1990

1. Adm. Frank B. Kelso II, USN, testimony to the Senate Armed Services Committee, *Hearings on the Confirmation of Admiral Frank B. Kelso to the Chief of Naval Operations*, 101st Congress, 2nd Session, June 14, 1990.

2. Capt. Peter M. Swartz, USN (Ret.), discussion with the author, November 20, 2009, Alexandria, Virginia.

3. Adm. William A. Owens, USN, *High Seas: The Naval Passage to an Uncharted World* (Annapolis, MD: Naval Institute Press, 1995), 123–24.

4. See Hone, *Power and Change*, 114–22.

5. Ibid., 116.

6. Tom Hone, quoted in ibid., 114.

7. Lehman, *Command of the Seas*, 417–18.

8. Diamond, discussion.

9. Ibid.

10. George H. W. Bush, "Remarks at the Aspen Institute Symposium in Aspen, Colorado" (speech, Aspen, CO, August 2, 1990), http://bushlibrary.tamu.edu/research/public_papers.php?id=2128&year=1990&month=8.

11. Paragraph based on Jaffe, *Development of the Base Force*, 39–41

12. Lawrence Garrett III and Adm. Frank B. Kelso II, USN, Memorandum, Subject: The Way Ahead. Navy Department: Office of the Secretary and the CNO. OPNAV Ser 00/0U500222, 1. Photocopy. August 23, 1990. Emphasis in the original.

13. Jaffe, *Development of the Base Force*, 40.

14. Garrett and Kelso, Memorandum, 1.

15. Paragraph based on Diamond, discussion.

16. Its official name was the Strategic Planning and Political-Military subspecialty community. Subspecialties are disciplines that are in addition to an officer's primary warfare specialty and require postgraduate education and experience in the respective field.

17. Lehman, *Command of the Seas*, 129.

18. The vast majority of the community's members came from the surface warfare community and, to a lesser extent, the Navy's land-based maritime patrol aviation community. The route to command for submariners and carrier aviators was far less accommodating, more narrowly prescribed, and institutionally less forgiving if one deviated. Fewer than six of the ninety or so Navy officers that served in the Strategic Concepts Branch during its heyday—1978 to 1991—were carrier aviators or submariners. Peter M. Swartz, "The Maritime Strategy of the 1980s: Threads, Strands and Line" (unpublished; photocopy, draft date: February 12, 1996), 179–81.

19. Diamond, discussion.

20. Paragraph based on ibid.

21. Unless otherwise noted, paragraph based on ibid.

22. Laura M. Zabriske, "New Maritime Strategy Will Elevate Marine Corps' Role in Naval Operations," *Inside the Navy* 3, no. 51 (December 24, 1990).

23. Diamond, discussion.

24. Swartz, discussion, November 20, 2009.

25. Paragraph based on ibid., and Terry Terriff, "'Innovate or Die': Organizational Culture and the Origins of Maneuver Warfare in the United States Marine Corps," *Journal of Strategic Studies* 29, no. 3 (June 2006): 486–94 passim.

26. Fleet Marine Force Manual 1 "Warfighting" (Washington, DC: Headquarters Marine Corps, 1989).

27. Jaffe, *Development of the Base Force*, 38.

28. Powell and Persico, *My American Journey*, 425.

29. Paragraph based on Capt. E. Richard Diamond Jr., USN, "Memorandum for the Record," Headquarters Marine Corps, September 7, 1990," 1, 3; quotes on p. 3.

30. Ibid., 2.

31. Ibid., 3.

32. H. Lawrence Garrett III, Adm. Frank B. Kelso II, USN, and Gen. Alfred M. Gray Jr., USMC, "The Way Ahead," U.S. Naval Institute *Proceedings* 117, no. 4 (April 1991): 36–47; *Marine Corps Gazette* 75, no. 4 (April 1991): 19–27.

33. "Global Reach–Global Power" (Washington, DC: Office of the Secretary of the Air Force, June 1990).

34. Garrett, Kelso, and Gray, "The Way Ahead," quotes on 38, 36, and 38, respectively. Emphasis added.

35. Ibid., 39.

36. Richard Meinhart, *Strategic Planning by The Chairmen, Joint Chiefs of Staff, 1990–2005* (Carlisle Barracks, PA: U.S. Army War College, April, 2006), 17.

37. Garrett, Kelso, and Gray, "The Way Ahead," 41.

38. Ibid.

39. Ibid., 46.

40. Rear Adm. Riley D. Mixson, USN, "Where We Must Do Better," U.S. Naval Institute *Proceedings* 117, no. 8 (August 1991): 38.

41. Diamond, discussion.
42. Sciolino, "Washington at Work."
43. Swartz, discussion, November 20, 2009.
44. Ibid.
45. Gen. Charles C. Krulak, USMC (Ret.), interview by Terry Terriff, March 10, 2004. Terriff, "Innovate or Die," 483.

CHAPTER 4. . . . FROM THE SEA, 1991–92

1. Richard Hallion, *Storm over Iraq* (Washington, DC: Smithsonian, 1992), 1.
2. See Snider, *Strategy, Forces and Budgets*, 28–29.
3. Paragraph based on Diamond, discussion.
4. See John M. Broder and Melissa Healy, "Allied Ground Push in 20 Days Foreseen," *Los Angeles Times*, February 3, 1991; Jeffrey Record, "AF's Future Bright after Stellar Gulf Showing," *Air Force Times*, March 11, 1991; and Molly Moore, "War Exposed Rivalries, Weaknesses in Military," *Washington Post*, June 10, 1991.
5. Nora Zamichow, "Unsung Heroes?," *Los Angeles Times*, March 17, 1991.
6. Melissa Healy, "Navy Riding Out Storm of Criticism of Gulf War Role," *Los Angeles Times*, April 28, 1991.
7. See Marvin Pokrant, *Desert Storm at Sea: What the Navy Really Did* (Westport, CT: Greenwood, 1999), 283–85.
8. Ibid., 273–74.
9. Zamichow. "Unsung Heroes?"
10. Paragraph based on Diamond, discussion; quote is from that discussion.
11. Littoral refers to two hundred miles on either side of the shoreline.
12. "Final Report of the Naval Force Capabilities Planning Effort": Enclosure (2), "Briefing Slides and Text" (Center for Naval Analyses, Arlington, VA, March 23, 1992), slide 6.
13. Samuel P. Huntington, "National Policy and the Transoceanic Navy," U.S. Naval Institute *Proceedings* 80, no. 5 (May 1954): 483–93.
14. Ibid., 483.
15. Ferd V. Neider and Thomas P. M. Barnett, "Memorandum for the Record," cover letter to "Final Report," 1.
16. Edward A. Smith Jr., "' . . . From the Sea': The Process of Defining a New Role for Naval Forces in the post–Cold War World," in *The Politics of Strategic Adjustment: Ideas, Institutions, and Interests, New Directions in World Politics,* ed. Peter Trubowitz, Emily O. Goldman, and Edward J. Rhodes (New York: Columbia University, 1999), 270–71.
17. Thomas P. M. Barnett, *The Pentagon's New Map: War and Peace in the Twenty-First Century* (New York: G. P. Putnam's Sons, 2004), 65.
18. Smith, "Process of Defining a New Role," 297.
19. Ibid., 269.
20. Paragraph based on Barnett, *Pentagon's New Map*, 63–70; and Capt. William H. J. Manthorpe Jr., USN (Ret.), "A Review and Personal Reflections On: *The Pentagon's New Map: War and Peace in the Twenty-first Century*," Parts I and II, *Naval Intelligence Professionals Quarterly* 22 (Fall 2005): 25–28; and 23 (Winter 2006): 50–54, respectively.
21. The subsections "The Transitioneers," "The Big Sticks," and "Cold Worriers" are based on Barnett, *Pentagon's New Map*, 63–70, 98–106; and Thomas P. M. Barnett and Henry H. Gaffney, "It's Going to Be a Bumpy Ride," U.S. Naval Institute *Proceedings* 119, no. 1 (January 1993): 23–26.
22. Barnett, *Pentagon's New Map*, 76.
23. Paragraph based on Smith, "Process of Defining a New Role," 269–80; quote is on p. 278.
24. Ibid., 279.

25. Ibid., 280.
26. "Final Report": Enclosure (5), "The Global Economy," 1.
27. Ibid., 8.
28. Smith, "Process of Defining a New Role," 270.
29. Ibid., 287.
30. Ibid., fn9.
31. Capt. Bradd C. Hayes, USN, "Keeping the Naval Service Relevant," U.S. Naval Institute *Proceedings* 119, no. 10 (October 1993): 59.
32. Congressman Leslie Aspin Jr. (D-WI), "National Security in the 1990s: Defining a New Basis for U.S. Military Forces" (speech, Atlantic Council, New York, January 6, 1992), quoted in Hayes, "Keeping the Naval Service Relevant," 59.
33. Hayes, "Keeping the Naval Service Relevant," 59.
34. Smith, "Process of Defining a New Role," 287–88.
35. Paragraph based on Adam B. Siegel, "The Use of Naval Forces in the Post-War Era: U.S. Navy and U.S. Marine Corps Crisis Response Activity, 1946-1990" (Alexandria, VA: Center for Naval Analyses, February 1, 1991), http://www.cna.org/research/1991/use-naval-forces-post-war-era-us-navy-us-marine; "Final Report": Enclosure (6), "The Use of U.S. Naval Forces for Crisis Response, 1977–91," 1–4, which was based on research that was later published in Thomas P. M. Barnett and Lt. Cdr. Linda D. Lancaster, "Answering the 9-1-1 Call: U.S. Military and Naval Crisis Response Activity, 1977-1991" (Alexandria, VA: Center for Naval Analyses, August 1, 1992), http://www.cna.org/research/1992/answering-9-1-1-call-us-military-naval-crisis.
36. Barnett, *Pentagon's New Map*, 71.
37. Ibid., 73.
38. Peter M. Swartz with Karin Duggan, "U.S. Navy Capstone Strategies and Concepts (1981–1990): Strategy, Policy, Concept, and Vision Documents" (Alexandria, VA: Center for Naval Analyses, December 1, 2011), 27, slide 53, http://www.cna.org/research/2011/us-navy-capstone-strategies-concepts-1981-1990.
39. Barnett, *Pentagon's New Map*, 73.
40. Hayes, "Keeping the Naval Service Relevant," 59.
41. "Final Report": Enclosure (2), slide 14.
42. *The National Military Strategy of the United States* (Washington, DC: U.S. Department of Defense, Government Printing Office, January 1992), 4.
43. "Final Report": Enclosure (2), slide 22. Emphasis in the original.
44. Paragraph based on ibid., 21–38.
45. "Final Report": Enclosure (2), slide 36.
46. Paragraph based on "Final Report": Enclosure (2), slides 67–86.
47. "Final Report": Enclosure (1), "White Paper," 17. Emphasis in the original.
48. Ibid. Emphasis in the original.
49. Hayes, "Keeping the Naval Service Relevant," 59.
50. Owens, *High Seas*, 123.
51. O'Keefe, Kelso, and Mundy, " . . . From the Sea."
52. Ibid., 93.
53. Maj. F. G. Hoffman, USMC Reserve, "Stepping Forward Smartly: 'Forward . . . From the Sea,' The Emerging Expanded Naval Strategy," *Marine Corps Gazette* 79, no. 3 (March 1995): 33.
54. See Owens, *High Seas*, 101–2.
55. O'Keefe, Kelso, and Mundy, " . . . From the Sea," 94.
56. As President George H. W. Bush noted, "By God, we've kicked the Vietnam syndrome once and for all." George H. W. Bush, quoted in Ann Devroy and Guy Gugliotta, "Bush to 'Move Fast' on Mideast Peace," *Washington Post*, March 2, 1991.

57. See Gray, *Explorations in Strategy*, 83–94.
58. Colin S. Gray, *The Sheriff: America's Defense of the New World Order* (Lexington: University Press of Kentucky, 2004), 45.
59. Burke, "Reminiscences," 3: 146, 4: 472–84; quoted in Baer, *One Hundred Years of Sea Power*, 278.
60. John B. Hattendorf, "The Uses of Maritime History In and For the Navy," *Naval War College Review* 56, no. 2 (Spring 2003): 13.
61. Wylie, "Why a Sailor Thinks Like a Sailor," 811.

CHAPTER 5. FORWARD . . . FROM THE SEA, 1993–94

1. Owens, *High Seas*, 123.
2. Ibid., 126–27.
3. In the post–Cold War era, it is not uncommon for the deputy CNOs of OPNAV's N-codes (e.g., N8, N3/N5) to change the title of their respective N-code. The author uses the titles that apply to that particular time.
4. These were Surface Warfare (N86), Submarine Warfare (N87), and Air Warfare (N88), which were joined by CINC Liaison (N83) and Expeditionary Warfare (N85), the latter of which was headed by a Marine two-star.
5. Owens, *High Seas*, 127.
6. Ibid., 131.
7. Ibid. Emphasis added.
8. Lewis, Brown, and Roll, *Service Responses*, 54, 49.
9. Secretary of Defense Leslie Aspin Jr., "Report of the Bottom-Up Review" ("Bottom-Up Review") (Washington, DC: U.S. Department of Defense, Government Printing Office, October 1993), iii.
10. Les Aspin, quoted in Bill Gertz, "Aspin Plan Envisions 'Lean, Mobile' Military–Powell's Support not Enthusiastic," *Washington Times*, September 2, 1993.
11. See Robert J. Caldwell, "The Pentagon Drifts as Clinton Fumbles Defense Policy," *San Diego Union-Tribune*, January 23, 1994.
12. See Eric V. Larson, David T. Orletsky, Kristin J. Leuschner, "Defense Planning in a Decade of Change: Lessons from the Base Force, Bottom-Up Review, and Quadrennial Defense Review" (Santa Monica, CA: RAND, 2001), 41–42.
13. O'Rourke, "Navy Force Structure and Shipbuilding Plans" (2008), 24.
14. Ronald O'Rourke, quoted in John Lancaster, "Navy Plans Cutback of 117 Ships," *Washington Post*, May 8, 1993.
15. Art Pine, "Navy Officials Propose Deep Cuts in Fleet," *Los Angeles Times*, May 17, 1993.
16. Les Aspin, quoted in Barton Gellman, "Rumblings of Discord Heard in Pentagon," *Washington Post*, June 20, 1993.
17. Amphibious ships made up 11 percent of the fleet in the 1990s, which was the same percentage as that in the 1980s. Peter M. Swartz with Karen Duggan, "The U.S. Navy in the World (1991–2000): Context for U.S. Navy Capstone Strategies and Concepts" (Alexandria, VA: Center for Naval Analyses, March 2012), 77, slide 154, http://www.cna.org/research/2012/us-navy-world-1991-2000-context-us-navy-capstone.
18. Derek H. Chollet and James M. Goldgeier, *America between the Wars, 11/9 to 9/11: The Misunderstood Years between the Fall of the Berlin Wall and the Start of the War on Terror* (New York: BBS Public Affairs, 2008), 58–59, 91; Hal Brands, *From Berlin to Baghdad: America's Search for Purpose in the post–Cold War World* (Lexington: University Press of Kentucky, 2008), 105; and David Halberstam, *War in a Time of Peace: Bush, Clinton, and the Generals* (New York: Scribner, 2001), 245–47.
19. Halberstam, *War in a Time of Peace*, 246–47.

20. Les Aspin, quoted in Brands, *From Berlin to Baghdad*, 107. See also Brands, *From Berlin to Baghdad* 105, 107; and Halberstam, *War in a Time of Peace*, 247.

21. Chollet and Goldgeier, *America between the Wars*, 71.

22. Brands, *From Berlin to Baghdad*, 110, 134–35.

23. See Anthony Lake, "From Containment to Enlargement" (speech, Paul H. Nitze School of Advanced International Studies, Johns Hopkins University, Washington, DC, September 21, 1993), http://www.mtholyoke.edu/acad/intrel/lakedoc.html.

24. Warren M. Christopher, testimony to the Senate Foreign Relations Committee, *Hearing on the Nomination of Warren M. Christopher to be Secretary of State*, 103rd Congress, 1st Session, January 13, 1993, http://dosfan.lib.uic.edu/ERC/briefing/dispatch/1993/html/Dispatchv4no04.html.

25. Leslie Aspin Jr., testimony to the Senate Armed Services Committee, *Hearing on the Consideration of Leslie Aspin Jr. to be Secretary of Defense*, 103rd Congress, 1st Session, January 13, 1993, quoted in Brands, *From Berlin to Baghdad*, 110. The Weinberger-Powell Doctrine was a reaction against President Reagan's interventions in the Middle East, which saw the suicide bombing of the U.S. Marine barracks in Beirut airport in 1983 that killed 241 Marines and sailors, as well as the United States' Vietnam experience.

26. Lake, "From Containment to Enlargement."

27. Madeleine Albright, quoted in Elaine Sciolino, "Madeleine Albright's Audition," *New York Times Magazine*, September 22, 1996; see also Powell and Persico, *My American Journey*, 561.

28. Powell and Persico, *My American Journey*, 561.

29. Gray, *Explorations in Strategy*, 236.

30. Brands, *From Berlin to Baghdad*, 120–22.

31. Anthony Lake, "The Limits of Peacekeeping," *New York Times*, February 6, 1994.

32. Monica Borkowski, "Chronology of a Scandal that Tarnished the Navy," *New York Times*, February 9, 1994.

33. Paragraph based on Eric Schmitt, "Senior Navy Officers Suppressed Sex Investigation, Pentagon Says," *New York Times*, September 25, 1992; Michael R. Gordon, "Pentagon Report Tells of 'Debauchery,'" *New York Times*, April 24, 1993; and Eric Schmitt, "Investigation of Sex Assaults by Pilots Had to Beat Wall of Silence in Navy," *New York Times*, May 2, 1993.

34. Mark Thompson, "Up From the Depths: Why Is the Navy Off Course?," *Time*, February 28, 1994.

35. See John H. Dalton, "The Navy After Next," U.S. Naval Institute *Proceedings* 120, no. 8 (August 1994): 9.

36. William J. Clinton, "Statement on the National Security Strategy Report," July 21, 1994, http://www.presidency.ucsb.edu/ws/index.php?pid=50525.

37. Dalton, "The Navy After Next," 9.

38. Capt. Sam J. Tangredi, USN (Ret.), email message to Peter M. Swartz, November 25, 2005.

39. Nick Kotz, "Breaking Point," *Washingtonian*, December 1996, 98.

40. See Adm. Jeremy M. Boorda, USN, "Time for a ' . . . Sea' Change," U.S. Naval Institute *Proceedings* 120, no. 8 (August 1994): 9–10.

41. Boorda, "Time for a ' . . . Sea' Change," 9.

42. Adm. Mike Boorda, quoted in Otto Kreisher, "Navy's New Strategic Doctrine Is on Deck," *San Diego Union-Tribune*, July 1, 1994.

43. Capt. Joseph F. Bouchard, USN (Ret.), email message to John B. Hattendorf, July 17, 2006. Bouchard relieved Sestak in early 1995 and served as the branch chief until 1997.

44. Larson, Orletsky, and Leuschner, "Defense Planning in a Decade of Change," xx.

45. See Philip Gold, "The Military Frets Over the Absence of 'Presence,'" *Washington Times*, October 25, 1994.
46. Capt. Joseph F. Bouchard, USN (Ret.), email message to Peter M. Swartz, April 8, 2005.
47. John H. Dalton, Adm. Jeremy M. Boorda, USN, and Gen. Carl E. Mundy Jr., USMC, "Forward . . . From the Sea," U.S. Naval Institute *Proceedings* 120, no. 12 (December 1994): 46–49.
48. Ibid., 46.
49. Ibid., 48.
50. Ibid., 47.
51. Ibid., 46.
52. Ibid., 47. See *National Security Strategy of Engagement and Enlargement* (Washington, DC: Department of Defense, Government Printing Office, July 1994).
53. Sentence and the rest of the paragraph based on Bouchard, emails, April 8, 2005, and July 17, 2006.
54. Peter M. Swartz with Karin Duggan, "U.S. Navy Capstone Strategies and Concepts (1991–2000): Strategy, Policy, Concept, and Vision Documents" (Alexandria, VA: Center for Naval Analyses, March, 2012), 95, slide 189 -190, http://www.cna.org/research /2012/us-navy-capstone-strategies-concepts-1991-2000.
55. Colin S. Gray, *Strategy and History: Essays on Theory and Practice* (London: Routledge, 2006), 77.
56. Chollet and Goldgeier, *America between the Wars*, 84.
57. Gordon R. England, Adm. Vernon E. Clark, USN, and Gen. James L. Jones, USMC, "Naval Power 21 . . . A Naval Vision" (Washington, DC: Department of the Navy, October 2002), 1, http://www.au.af.mil/au/awc/awcgate/navy/navpow21-2002.pdf.

CHAPTER 6. 2020 VISION, 1995–96

1. See Brands, *From Berlin to Baghdad*, 192–97.
2. Ibid., 195–96.
3. Carl P. Leubsdorf, "Why Bosnian Quagmire Bedevils Clinton," *Dallas Morning News*, August 3, 1995.
4. See Halberstam, *War in a Time of Peace*, 350, 354.
5. Richard Holbrooke, quoted in Richard P. Hallion, "Precision Guided Munitions and the New Era of Warfare," Working Paper 53 (Fairbairn, Australia: Air Power Studies Centre, 1995), http://fas.org/man/dod-101/sys/smart/docs/paper53.htm.
6. John F. Harris, *The Survivor: Bill Clinton in the White House* (New York: Random House, 2005), 221.
7. See Bradley Graham, "Battle Plans for a New Century," *Washington Post*, February 21, 1995.
8. Cdr. Michael C. Vitale, USN, "Jointness by Design, Not Accident," *Joint Force Quarterly* 9 (Autumn 1995): 25. Emphasis in the original.
9. Gen. Henry H. Shelton, USA, "Operationalizing Joint Vision 2010," *Airpower Journal* 12, no. 3 (Fall 1998), http://www.airpower.maxwell.af.mil/airchronicles/apj/apj98/fal98 /shelton.htm.
10. Douglas C. Lovelace Jr. and Thomas-Durell Young, *Strategic Plans, Joint Doctrine, and Antipodean Insights* (Carlisle Barracks, PA: U.S. Army War College, 1995), 5.
11. See Bradley Graham, "Military Services to Propose More Standardized Munitions," *Washington Post*, March 22, 1995.
12. James Blaker, "How the Pentagon Designs Its 21st Century Strategy," *Christian Science Monitor*, January 30, 1996; Chris Black, "Joint Operations Called Trend for Armed Services Savings, Improved Readiness Drive Move," *Boston Globe*, December 31, 1994.

13. Jeffrey R. Cooper, *Another View of the Revolution in Military Affairs* (Carlisle Barracks, PA: U.S. Army War College, 1994), 13.
14. Gen. John Shalikashvili, quoted in Graham, "Battle Plans for a New Century."
15. O'Keefe, Kelso, and Gray, " . . . From the Sea," 96. Emphasis in the original.
16. See Capt. Wayne P. Hughes Jr., USN (Ret.), *Fleet Tactics and Coastal Combat* (Annapolis, MD: Naval Institute Press, 2000), 29–33.
17. Lovelace and Young, *Strategic Plans*, 3.
18. Memorandum (MCM-90–94), Director of the Joint Staff, Office of the Chairman of the Joint Chiefs of Staff, Pentagon, Washington, DC, July 28, 1994, quoted in ibid.
19. Swartz, "U.S. Navy Capstone Strategies and Concepts (1991–2000)," 73, slide 146.
20. Rebecca Grant, "Closing the Doctrine Gap," *Air Force Magazine* 80, no. 1 (January 1997): 48.
21. Paragraph based on Capt. Robert M. Zalaskus, USN (Ret.), email messages to John Hattendorf and Peter M. Swartz, August 10, 2006; and to the author, May 6 and 7, 2013. Zalaskus was the primary writer for three of the five naval doctrine publications.
22. The six doctrine publications were *Naval Warfare:* NDP-1, *Naval Intelligence:* NDP-2, *Naval Operations:* NDP-3, *Naval Logistics:* NDP-4, *Naval Planning:* NDP-5, and *Naval Command and Control:* NDP-6.
23. Zalaskus, emails.
24. *Naval Warfare:* NDP-1 (Washington, DC: Department of the Navy, March 28, 1994).
25. Ibid., 33.
26. James J. Tritten, email message to Peter M. Swartz, April 11, 2005.
27. Hughes, *Fleet Tactics and Coastal Combat*, 310.
28. *Naval Warfare:* NDP-1, 51.
29. James J. Tritten, email message to Peter M. Swartz, May 21, 2005.
30. Zalaskus, emails; *Naval Intelligence:* NDP-2 (Washington, DC: Department of the Navy, September 30, 1994); *Naval Logistics:* NDP-4 (Washington, DC: Department of the Navy, January 10, 1995); *Naval Planning:* NDP-5 (Washington, DC: Department of the Navy, January 15, 1996); *Naval Command and Control:* NDP-6 (Washington, DC: Department of the Navy, May 19, 1995).
31. Zalaskus, emails.
32. Ibid.
33. Ibid. The Naval War College remained on the sidelines during the development of the other NDPs.
34. Swartz, "U.S. Navy Capstone Strategies and Concepts (1991–2000)," 72, slide 143.
35. At issue was the command relationship between the commander, amphibious task force; and the commander, landing force, which has been at the heart of some of the bitterest disagreements between the Navy and Marine Corps dating back to at least the Guadalcanal campaign in 1942. Zalaskus, emails to the author.
36. See Capt. Sam J. Tangredi, USN, "Who's Afraid of the NETF?," U.S. Naval Institute *Proceedings* 125, no. 11 (November 1999): 45.
37. Zalaskus, emails.
38. Boorda, "Time for a ' . . . Sea' Change," 9–10.
39. Bouchard, email, April 8, 2005.
40. Capt. Joseph F. Bouchard, USN (Ret.), email message to Peter M. Swartz, June 27, 2005.
41. "Operational Maneuver from the Sea" (Washington, DC: Headquarters Marine Corps, January 4, 1996).
42. Bouchard, email, April 8, 2005.
43. Ibid.
44. Paragraph based on ibid.
45. Paragraph based on ibid.

46. "Naval Operational Concept Project: Final Report Draft," unpublished, prepared by the U.S. Navy, U.S. Marine Corps, and Systems Research and Applications Corporation, Arlington, VA, January 19, 1996, 1-3.

47. Ibid., 1-5.

48. Ibid., 1-3.

49. Ibid., 1-4.

50. Bouchard, email, April 8, 2005.

51. Paragraph based on ibid.

52. Paragraph based on ibid.

53. Rest of paragraph based on Adm. Jeremy M. Boorda, USN, testimony to the Senate Armed Services Committee, *U.S. Department of Defense Authorization for Appropriations for FY97*, 104th Congress, 2nd Session, March 12, 1996, 313.

54. Sentence and rest of paragraph based on Adm. Jeremy M. Boorda, USN, testimony to the Senate Armed Services Committee; Dale Eisman, "Draft Report Makes a Case Against Further Navy Cuts," *Virginian-Pilot*, March 6, 1996.

55. Eisman, "Draft Report Makes a Case Against Further Navy Cuts."

56. Adm. Mike Boorda, quoted in Eric Schmitt, "Aircraft Carrier May Give Way To Missile Ship," *New York Times*, September 3, 1995; David Lerman, "Bush Calls for Revival of Arsenal Ship," *Daily Press*, April 9, 2000.

57. John Mintz, "New Ship Could Be Next Wave in Warfare," *Washington Post*, June 23, 1996.

58. Dale Eisman, "Arsenal Ship Wouldn't Replace Carriers," *Virginian-Pilot*, September 11, 1995.

59. Eisman, "Draft Report Makes a Case Against Further Navy Cuts."

60. Mintz, "New Ship Could Be Next Wave in Warfare."

61. Edward J. Rhodes, "'. . . From the Sea' and Back Again: Naval Power in the Second American Century," *Naval War College Review* 52, no. 2 (Spring 1999): 40–41.

62. Norman Polmar, quoted in Mintz, "New Ship Could Be Next Wave in Warfare."

63. Eisman, "Arsenal Ship Wouldn't Replace Carriers."

64. Lerman, "Bush Calls for Revival of Arsenal Ship."

65. Andrew Krepinevich, quoted in Mintz, "New Ship Could Be Next Wave in Warfare."

66. Rhodes, "'. . . From the Sea' and Back Again," 41.

67. Ibid.

68. Andrew Krepinevich, quoted in Schmitt, "Aircraft Carrier May Give Way To Missile Ship."

69. Capt. Joseph F. Bouchard, USN (Ret.), email message to Peter M. Swartz, March 20, 2006.

70. See Dale Eisman, "In First Year, CNO Steadies the Crew, and Stays the Course," *Virginian-Pilot*, May 31, 1997.

71. See Otto Kreisher, "Pentagon Proposes to Renovate Navy's Carrier Air Program," *San Diego Union*, April 27, 1991.

72. Barry Posen, quoted in Healy, "Navy Riding Out Storm."

73. Adm. Jay Johnson, quoted in John Diamond, "New Versions of F-18 Cheapest of Contenders," *Fort Worth Star-Telegram*, March 30, 1997.

74. Ibid.

75. William Flannery, "On the Line: McDonnell and the Navy are Counting on the Super Hornet," *St. Louis Post-Dispatch*, September 25, 1995.

76. John F. Lehman Jr., "Most Anti-Navy Budget in 14 Years," *St. Louis Post-Dispatch*, February 20, 1991.

77. Swartz, discussion, June 19, 2009.

78. Colin S. Gray, "Strategic Thoughts for Defence Planners," *Survival* 52, no. 3 (June–July 2010): 160.

79. Frederick W. Kagan, *Finding the Target: The Transformation of American Military Policy* (New York, NY: Encounter Books, 2006), 321.

80. Bouchard, email, March 20, 2006.
81. Both quotes unattributed, quoted in Tom Philpott, "Full Speed Ahead," *Washingtonian*, July 1999, 94.

CHAPTER 7. ANYTIME, ANYWHERE, 1996–97

1. Gen. John M. Shalikashvili, *Joint Vision 2010* (Washington, DC: U.S. Department of Defense, July 1996).
2. Philip Gold, "The Army's Fancy PR and Glossy Pictures," *Washington Times*, August 13, 1996. The word "purple" is a synonym for jointness, a symbolic mixture of the services' institutional colors.
3. Lewis, Brown, and Roll, *Service Responses*, 23.
4. Ibid., 23, 24.
5. Shalikashvili, *Joint Vision 2010*, i. Emphasis added.
6. Ibid., 4.
7. Ibid., 8–9.
8. Kagan, *Finding the Target*, 229.
9. Quotes in this paragraph from Shalikashvili, *Joint Vision 2010*, 13, 13 (emphasis in the original), 11, 13, respectively.
10. Kagan, *Finding the Target*, 230. For Kagan's description of Dominant Battlespace Knowledge and Shock and Awe, see pp. 212–22. The outstanding work on Dominant Battlespace Knowledge is Stuart E. Johnson and Martin C. Libicki, eds., *Dominant Battlespace Knowledge: The Winning Edge* (Washington, DC: National Defense University, 1995). Shock and Awe is based on Harlan K. Ullman and James P. Wade with L. A. Edney, Fred M. Franks, Charles A. Horner, and Jonathan T. Howe, *Shock and Awe: Achieving Rapid Dominance* (Washington, DC: Center for Advanced Concepts and Technology, 1996).
11. Paragraph based on Bouchard, emails, April 8, 2005, June 27, 2005, and March 20, 2006.
12. Paragraph based on Bouchard, email, March 20, 2006. Adm. Jay L. Johnson, USN, "The Navy Operational Concept: Forward . . . From the Sea," *Seapower* 40, no. 5 (May 1997): 15–22.
13. See James R. Blaker, *Transforming Military Force: The Legacy of Arthur Cebrowski and Network Centric Warfare* (Westport, CT: Praeger Security International, 2007), 18–19.
14. Ibid., 14.
15. Paragraph based on Bouchard, emails, April 8, 2005, March 20, 2006.
16. *National Military Strategy of the United States of America, 1995: A Strategy of Flexible and Selective Engagement* (Washington, DC: U.S. Department of Defense, February 1995), i–ii.
17. Johnson, "The Navy Operational Concept," 16.
18. Ibid., 15, 16.
19. Ibid., 17–18.
20. Ibid., 21.
21. Ibid., 18, quote on 17.
22. Ibid., 20.
23. Ibid., 19.
24. Ibid.
25. Ibid., 16, 19.
26. Ibid., 21.
27. Bouchard, email, March 20, 2006.
28. George C. Wilson, *This War Really Matters: Inside the Fight for Defense Dollars* (Washington, DC: Congressional Quarterly, 2000), 39.
29. Bouchard, email, March 20, 2006, both points this paragraph.

30. Paragraph based on Bouchard, email, April 8, 2005.

31. "Global Engagement: A Vision for the 21st Century Air Force" (Washington, DC: Department of the Air Force, 1996); "Army Vision 2010" (Washington, DC: Department of the Army, 1996).

32. *The National Military Strategy: Shape, Respond, Prepare Now* (Washington, DC: Department of Defense, May 1997); *National Security Strategy for A New Century* (Washington, DC: White House, May 1997).

33. Ronald O'Rourke, "Navy Force Structure and Shipbuilding Plans: Background and Issues for Congress" (Washington, DC: Congressional Research Service, July 15, 2009), 29, 33, 34.

34. Adm. Donald Pilling, quoted in Wilson, *This War Really Matters*, 57.

35. Eisman, "In First Year, CNO Steadies the Crew."

36. Paragraph based on Swartz, "U.S. Navy Capstone Strategies and Concepts (1991–2000)," 126, slide 252.

37. Adm. Jay L. Johnson, USN, "Anytime, Anywhere: A Navy for the 21st Century," U.S. Naval Institute *Proceedings* 123, no. 11 (November 1997): 48–50.

38. Bouchard, email, March 20, 2006.

39. Operational primacy was one of CNO Johnson's guiding stars, with the others being leadership, teamwork, and pride. See Johnson, "The Navy Operational Concept," 15.

40. Johnson, "Anytime, Anywhere," 48, 49.

41. Ibid., 49.

42. Ibid., 48, 50.

43. Paragraph based on Gen. Charles C. Krulak, USMC, "The Strategic Corporal: Leadership in the Three Block War," *Marines Corps Gazette* 83, no. 1 (January 1999): 18–22, http://www.au.af.mil/au/awc/awcgate/usmc/strategic_corporal.htm.

44. Swartz, "U.S. Navy Capstone Strategies and Concepts (1991–2000)," 128, slide 255. See Vice Adm. Stansfield Turner, USN, "Missions of the U.S. Navy," *Naval War College Review* 26, no. 5 (March–April 1974): 2–17.

45. Johnson, "Anytime, Anywhere," 50; quote on 49.

46. Ibid., 49.

47. Swartz, "U.S. Navy Capstone Strategies and Concepts (1991–2000)," 132, slide 263. Even in the issue of *Proceedings*, "Anytime, Anywhere" did not receive top billing. It was buried in the middle of an issue that had a Marine Corps theme, which was a bit puzzling as few CNOs published articles, particularly Johnson.

48. Gray, *Explorations in Strategy*, 90.

49. Owens, *High Seas*, 96.

CHAPTER 8. THE NAVY STRATEGIC PLANNING GUIDANCE, 1998–2000

1. Brands, *From Berlin to Baghdad*, 202.

2. Ibid., 224.

3. See Bradley Graham and Eric Pianin, "Military Readiness, Morale Show Strain," *Washington Post*, August 13, 1998.

4. Ibid.

5. Philpott, "Full Speed Ahead," 91.

6. Otto Kreisher, "Pentagon Insider Is Likely Choice for Navy Secretary," *San Diego Union-Tribune*, June 30, 1998.

7. See Wilson, *This War Really Matters*, 39–42.

8. See Kagan, *Finding the Target*, 234.

9. Kreisher, "Pentagon Insider Is Likely Choice for Navy Secretary."

10. See Bradley Graham, "Cohen Cautions Hill on Military Pay Hike," *Washington Post*, February 2, 1999; and Alison Mitchell, "Clinton Signs Military Budget Bill, Avoiding Split Among Democrats," *New York Times*, October 26, 1999.

11. Richard Danzig, quoted in Philpott, "Full Speed Ahead," 92.

12. Ibid.

13. Paragraph based on and quote found at Philpott, "Full Speed Ahead," 92, except as noted.

14. Ibid., 94.

15. Roman Schweizer, "Navy Hopes to Deliver New 'Maritime Strategy' This Summer," *Inside the Navy*, 12, no. 24 (June 21, 1999), 5.

16. "A Maritime Strategy for the 21st Century" (unpublished; photocopy, OPNAV White Paper; draft date: November 1999).

17. Ibid., 5.

18. Ibid.

19. Ibid.

20. Ibid., 12.

21. Sentence and rest of paragraph based on "A Maritime Strategy for the 21st Century," 5–8. Quotes on p. 7, p. 6.

22. See "A Maritime Strategy for the 21st Century," 8–12.

23. Ibid., 3. Emphasis in the original.

24. Robert Holzer, "U.S. Navy Envisions Broad Influence Over Land Combat," *Defense News*, June 21, 1999.

25. Ronald O'Rourke, quoted in ibid.

26. Swartz, discussion, November 20, 2009.

27. Gen. Chuck Krulak, quoted in Philpott, "Full Speed Ahead," 94.

28. Paragraph based on Swartz, discussion, November 20, 2009.

29. Paragraph based on ibid.

30. Paragraph based on Bouchard, email, April 8, 2005, except as noted.

31. Peter M. Swartz with Michael C. Markowitz, "Organizing OPNAV (1970–2009)" (Alexandria, VA: Center for Naval Analyses, January 2010), 60, http://www.cna.org/research/2010/organizing-opnav-1970-2009.

32. Ibid., 59.

33. "Navy Strategic Planning Guidance: Long Range Planning Objectives" (Washington, DC: OPNAV, April 2000).

34. Ibid., 5.

35. Ibid., 5, 13.

36. Ibid., 3.

37. Ibid., 42. Emphasis in the original.

38. "A Capstone Concept for Naval Operations in the Information Age" (Newport, RI: Naval War College, 2000).

39. "Navy Strategic Planning Guidance," 29–38.

40. Ibid., 31. Emphasis in the original.

41. Ibid., 34–36.

42. Ibid., 36–37. Emphasis in the original.

43. Ibid., 40.

44. Ibid., 79.

45. Swartz, "U.S. Navy Capstone Strategies and Concepts (1991–2000)," 149, slide 297.

46. Ibid.

47. William Cohen, quoted in Jack Dorsey, "Norfolk-Based Admiral Tapped for Top Navy Post," *Virginian-Pilot*, March 1, 2000.

48. Swartz, "Organizing OPNAV (1970–2009)," 71.

49. Capt. Peter M. Swartz, USN (Ret.), discussion with the author, February 18, 2010, Arlington, Virginia. Swartz was the Center for Naval Analyses' support analyst for N51 off and on for much of the post–Cold War period. Passim.

50. Peter M. Swartz with Karin Duggan, "U.S. Navy Capstone Strategies and Concepts (2001–2010): Strategy, Policy, Concept, and Vision Documents" (Alexandria, VA: Center for Naval Analyses, December 1, 2011) 4, slide 7, http://www.cna.org/research/2011 /us-navy-capstone-strategies-concepts-2001-2010.

51. Adm. Vern Clark, quoted in Scott C. Truver, "The U.S. Navy in Review," *U.S. Naval Institute Proceedings* 129, no. 5 (May 2003): 88.

52. Adm. Vernon E. Clark, USN, foreword to "Vision . . . Presence . . . Power: A Program Guide to the U.S. Navy 2002 Edition" (Washington, DC: OPNAV, 2003), http://www .Navy.mil/Navydata/policy/vision/vis02/contents.html.

53. Truver, "The U.S. Navy in Review," 88.

54. Swartz, "Organizing OPNAV (1970–2009)," 85.

55. Ibid., 73.

56. Chollet and Goldgeier, *America between the Wars*, 249.

57. Robert J. Art, "Congress and the Defense Budget: Enhancing Policy Oversight," *Political Science Quarterly* 100, no. 2 (Summer 1985): 227.

58. President Bill Clinton, quoted in Chollet and Goldgeier, *America between the Wars*, 247.

59. Bouchard, email, March 20, 2006.

60. "Navy Strategic Planning Guidance," 42.

CHAPTER 9. SEA POWER 21, 2000–2004

1. See Chollet and Goldgeier, *America between the Wars*, 275–77, 326; quote on 277.

2. George W. Bush, "A Period of Consequences" (speech, The Citadel, Charleston, SC, September 23, 1999), http://www.citadel.edu/pao/addresses/pres_bush.html.

3. See Brands, *From Berlin to Baghdad*, 272–83.

4. George W. Bush, "Post-9/11 Address to a Joint Session of Congress" (speech, Washington, DC, September 20, 2001), http://www.americanrhetoric.com/speeches/gwbush911joint sessionspeech.htm.

5. Bob Woodward, *Bush at War* (New York: Simon & Schuster, 2002), 43; quote is from Bush, "Post-9/11 Address."

6. Kagan, *Finding the Target*, 252.

7. *Quadrennial Defense Review Report of 2001* (Washington, DC: U.S. Department of Defense, Government Printing Office, September 30, 2001), 29.

8. George W. Bush, "Commencement Address at the United States Naval Academy" (speech, Annapolis, MD, May 25, 2001), http://www.presidency.ucsb.edu/ws/index.php?pid =45908&st=&st1=.

9. Bush, "A Period of Consequences."

10. Thomas E. Ricks, "For Rumsfeld, Many Roadblocks," *Washington Post*, August 7, 2001.

11. Loren Thompson, quoted in Richard Whittle, "War Speeds Up Pace of Change for Military," *Dallas Morning News*, December 5, 2001.

12. Richard Cheney, quoted in Ricks, "For Rumsfeld, Many Roadblocks."

13. Unidentified Rumsfeld political appointee, quoted in ibid.

14. Vernon Loeb and Thomas E. Ricks, "1's and 0's Replacing Bullets in U.S. Arsenal," *Washington Post*, February 2, 2002; Bill Keller, "The Fighting Next Time," *New York Times Magazine*, March 10, 2002.

15. The George W. Bush administration adopted the phrase "global war on terror" soon after 9/11 to describe in general terms the U.S.-led campaign to eliminate al-Qaeda and other Islamist terrorist organizations. Specifically, before a joint session of Congress on

September 20, President Bush stated, "Our war on terror begins with al Qaeda, but it does not end there." Bush, speech, "Post-9/11 Address to a Joint session of Congress." The phrases "global war on terror," "global war on terrorism," and "war on terror," for example, were used interchangeably by the administration without any real difference of meaning. In general, the author applies the term that the respective source material uses.

16. Kagan, *Finding the Target*, 290, 296.
17. See Ron Martz, "War on Terrorism: Backgrounder: U.S. Military Strategy," *Atlanta Journal-Constitution*, December 8, 2001.
18. George W. Bush, "Remarks at the Citadel: 2001" (speech, The Citadel, Charleston, SC, December 11, 2001), http://www.presidency.ucsb.edu/ws/index.php?pid=73494.
19. Vice Adm. Arthur K. Cebrowski, USN (Ret.), "Special Briefing on Force Transformation" (brief, Pentagon, Washington, DC, November 27, 2001), http://www.au.af.mil/au/awc/awcgate/transformation/t11272001_t1127ceb.htm.
20. Andrew Krepinevich, quoted in Whittle, "War Speeds Up Pace of Change for Military."
21. Loren Thompson, quoted in ibid.
22. Benjamin S. Lambeth, *American Carrier Air Power at the Dawn of a New Century* (Santa Monica, CA: RAND Corporation, 2005), 28.
23. Rebecca Grant, *Battle-Tested: Carrier Aviation in Afghanistan and Iraq* (Washington, DC: IRIS, 2005), 38.
24. Lambeth, *American Carrier Air Power*, 22.
25. Grant, *Battle-Tested*, 38.
26. Lambeth, *American Carrier Air Power*, 22
27. Ibid., 23.
28. Vice Adm. John B. Nathman, USN, "'We Were Great': Navy Air War in Afghanistan," *U.S. Naval Institute Proceedings* 128, no. 3 (March 2002): 95.
29. Swartz, "U.S. Navy Capstone Strategies and Concepts (2001–2010)," 35, slide 69.
30. Capt. C. Will Dossel, USN (Ret.), email message to Peter M. Swartz, June 23, 2005. Dossel, who was the deputy for N51, took over as the Strategy and Concepts Branch chief from September 2001 to the fall of 2003.
31. Based on author's experience while serving in Joint Staff J5 Strategic Plans and Policy, December 2000–December 2002.
32. Cdr. Paul N. Nagy, USN (Ret.), discussion with the author, March 4, 2010, McLean, Virginia. Nagy served in N513/N5SC from December 2001 to September 2007, which included several long stints as its branch chief.
33. Dossel, email; Nagy, discussion.
34. Dossel, email.
35. Swartz, discussion, November 20, 2009.
36. Paragraph based on Nagy, discussion.
37. Lt. Cdr. Mark W. Lawrence, discussion with the author, March 3, 2010, Arlington, Virginia. Lawrence served in the Strategy and Concepts Branch (N513/N5SC) from the fall of 2003 to 2005.
38. Dossel, email. Also killed were Cdr. William H. Donovan, Cdr. Patrick Dunn, and Lt. Cdr. David L. Williams, USN. Lt. Kevin Shaeffer, USN, survived, but suffered severe burns.
39. Discussions between the author and Naval Postgraduate School administrators and professors, May 2008, Monterey, California; unattributed. (The author is a 1998 graduate of the Naval Postgraduate School's strategic planning master's degree program.)
40. By 2008 Robby Harris, Peter Swartz, and Dick Diamond had revived the Strategy Discussion Group, which meets at least monthly to host talks by high-ranking U.S. officials (including the CNO), analysts, and scholars.
41. *Quadrennial Defense Review Report of 2001*, 17–21.

42. Cdr. Paul N. Nagy, USN (Ret.), email message to Peter M. Swartz, June 22, 2005.

43. Adm. Vernon E. Clark, USN, "Sea Power 21: Projecting Decisive Joint Capabilities," U.S. Naval Institute *Proceedings* 128, no. 10 (October 2002): 32–41.

44. Adm. Vernon E. Clark, USN, "Sea Power 21: Operational Concepts for a New Era" (speech, Current Strategy Forum, Naval War College, Newport, RI, June 12, 2002), quoted in Peter J. Dombrowski and Andrew L. Ross, "Transforming the Navy: Punching a Feather Bed?," *Naval War College Review* 56, no. 3 (Summer 2003): 111.

45. Swartz, "U.S. Navy Capstone Strategies and Concepts (2001–2010)," 15, slide 30.

46. Clark, "Sea Power 21: Projecting Decisive Joint Capabilities," 33.

47. Capt. Joseph F. Bouchard, USN (Ret.), email message to Peter M. Swartz, July 25, 2006.

48. Clark, "Sea Power 21, Projecting Decisive Joint Capabilities," 34.

49. Ibid., 35.

50. Vice Adm. Charles W. Moore Jr., USN, and Lt. Gen. Edward Hanlon Jr., USMC, "Sea Basing: Operational Independence for a New Century," U.S. Naval Institute *Proceedings* 129, no. 1 (January 2003): 80.

51. Clark, "Sea Power 21, Projecting Decisive Joint Capabilities," 36–37.

52. Swartz, "U.S. Navy Capstone Strategies and Concepts (2001–2010)," 28, slide 56.

53. See Dombrowski and Ross, "Transforming the Navy: Punching a Feather Bed?," 116–18.

54. See Cdr. Jeff Huber, USN (Ret.), "Invasion of the Transformers," U.S. Naval Institute *Proceedings* 129, no. 10 (October 2003): 74–76; and Lt. Cdr. Jon R. Olson, USN, "An Alternative Vision of Sea Power 21," U.S. Naval Institute *Proceedings* 129, no. 10 (October 2003): 80–83.

55. Dave Ahearn, "Report Assails LCS Program as Unwise, Hits CNO on Fleet Growth," *Navy News Now*, May 1, 2003.

56. Adm. Michael G. Mullen, USN, "Sea Enterprise: Resourcing Tomorrow's Fleet," U.S. Naval Institute *Proceedings* 130, no. 1 (January 2004): 60. The Systems Commands were Naval Air, Naval Sea, Naval Supply, Naval Facilities, and Space and Naval Systems Warfare.

57. Clark, "Sea Power 21, Projecting Decisive Joint Capabilities," 40.

58. "Six Sigma" refers to a program to find efficiencies in processes. It uses quantitative methods to find duplicative or prohibitively time-consuming steps in production or repair, for example.

59. Based on author's experience as a commanding officer of Carrier Airborne Early Warning Squadron One One Two (VAW-112) deployed on the USS *Carl Vinson* in support of Operation Iraqi Freedom in 2005.

60. Gordon R. England, Adm. Vernon E. Clark, and Gen. James L. Jones, "Naval Power 21 . . . A Naval Vision"(Washington, DC: Department of the Navy, October 2002), http://www.Navy.mil/Navydata/people/secnav/england/navpow21.pdf.

61. "Marine Corps Strategy 21" (Washington, DC: Headquarters Marine Corps, November 3, 2000); "Expeditionary Maneuver Warfare" (Washington, DC: Headquarters Marine Corps, November 10, 2001).

62. Swartz, "U.S. Navy Capstone Strategies and Concepts (2001–2010)," 33, slide 65.

63. "Naval Power 21," 1. Emphasis in the original.

64. Ibid., 4.

65. Swartz, "U.S. Navy Capstone Strategies and Concepts (2001–2010)," 44, slide 88.

66. Dossel, email, and Cdr. Paul N. Nagy, USN (Ret.), email message to Peter M. Swartz, April 12, 2005.

67. Nagy, email, April 12, 2005.

68. Dossel, email.

69. Adm. Vernon E. Clark and Gen. Michael W. Hagee, USMC, "Naval Operating Concept for Joint Operations," (Washington, DC: OPNAV, October 2003), signature page.

70. Ibid., 2.

71. Swartz, "U.S. Navy Capstone Strategies and Concepts (2001–2010)," 56, slide 111.

72. *The National Security Strategy* (Washington, DC: White House, September 2002), 29.

73. Ibid.

74. See Jason Sherman, "10-30-30 Strategic Plan Could Steer Future Force," *Army Times*, April 26, 2004.

75. Capt. Joseph F. Bouchard, USN (Ret.), email message to Peter M. Swartz, August 25, 2003.

76. David Chu, quoted in Vince Crawley, "Chu Says Readiness Reports are Result of Services' Differences," *Navy Times*, June 24, 2002.

77. See Swartz, "U.S. Navy Capstone Strategies and Concepts (2001–2010)," 66–68, slides 131–36.

78. Thom Shanker and Eric Schmitt, "Critics and Fans Alike As Navy Chief Steps Down," *New York Times*, July 17, 2005.

79. Adm. William J. Fallon, USN, testimony to the House Armed Services Committee, Subcommittee on Military Readiness, 108th Congress, 1st Session, March 18, 2003.

80. Bouchard, email, June 27, 2005.

81. Andrew Hoehn, Deputy Assistant Secretary of Defense (Strategy), "DoD Security Cooperation Guidance" (brief, Security Cooperation Agency Conference, Washington, DC, October 28, 2003), slide 3.

82. Hoehn, "DoD Security Cooperation Guidance," slide 4.

83. "Admiral: Fleet Response Plan Does Not Mean Less Presence Worldwide," *Inside the Navy* 17, no. 9 (March 1, 2004).

84. Adm. Vernon E. Clark, USN, "Remarks to the Defense Writers Group" (speech, Washington, DC, March 2, 2004).

85. Bob Woodward and Dan Balz, "'We Will Rally the World'," *Washington Post*, January 28, 2002.

86. Kagan, *Finding the Target*, 310.

87. Ibid., 321, 322.

88. Ibid., 355.

89. Ibid., 358.

90. Wylie, "Why a Sailor Thinks Like a Sailor," 811.

CHAPTER 10. THE 3/1 STRATEGY, 2005

1. Condoleezza Rice, "Remarks by National Security Advisor Condoleezza Rice on Terrorism and Foreign Policy" (speech, Paul H. Nitze School of Advanced International Studies, Johns Hopkins University, Washington, DC, April 29, 2002), https://repositories.lib .utexas.edu/bitstream/handle/2152/13089/Rice_Hopkins_FP.pdf.

2. Donald Rumsfeld quoted in Bob Woodward, *Plan of Attack* (New York: Simon & Schuster, 2004), 41.

3. Paragraph based on Grant, *Battle-Tested*, 141, 155, 163, 164, 182.

4. Kagan, *Finding the Target*, 358.

5. Rest of paragraph based on Jason Sherman, "Pentagon Readies New Planning Points," *Defense News*, May 3, 2004; and OSD's Quad Chart, of which there were various versions. See, for example, the one in Vice Adm. Arthur K. Cebrowski, USN (Ret.), "Trends in Security Cooperation" (brief, Washington, DC, June 15, 2004), slide 6, http://www.au.af .mil/au/awc/awcgate/transformation/oft_cebrowski_security_challenges.pdf.

6. *The National Defense Strategy of the United States of America* (Washington, DC: U.S. Department of Defense, Government Printing Office, March 2005).

7. Ibid., 1.

8. See Chollet and Goldgeier, *America between the Wars*, 275–77, 326; quote on 277.

9. *National Defense Strategy*, 5.
10. Ibid.
11. Ibid.
12. Ibid., 6–7. Emphasis added.
13. See Dale Eisman, "Navy's Changing Tide," *Virginian-Pilot*, March 7, 2005; and Loren Thompson, "Triage Time for Military Modernization," *Defense News*, March 29, 2004.
14. O'Rourke, "Navy Force Structure and Shipbuilding Plans" (2009), 34.
15. William Matthews, "U.S. Service Secretary Nominees Face Challenges, Tight Budgets," *Defense News*, October 10, 2005.
16. Robert A. Hamilton, "Mullen Seen as Extending Olive Branch to the Submarine Force," *Day*, September 14, 2005.
17. Eisman, "Navy's Changing Tide."
18. Otto Kreisher, "New Navy Leader Sees Bigger Role for Sailors on Shore," *State Journal-Register*, October 14, 2005; O'Rourke, "Navy Force Structure and Shipbuilding Plans" (2009), 33.
19. Ronald O'Rourke, "Navy Force Structure and Shipbuilding Plans: Background and Issues for Congress" (Washington, DC: Congressional Research Service, August 17, 2010), 31.
20. Adm. Vern Clark, quoted in Shanker and Schmitt, "Critics and Fans Alike as Navy Chief Steps Down."
21. Paragraph based on Shanker and Schmitt, "Critics and Fans Alike as Navy Chief Steps Down"; Eisman, "Navy's Changing Tide"; and Gina Cavallaro, "A Different Stripe: Some Sailors Are Jumping Ship to Save Their Careers," *Navy Times*, October 4, 2004, except as noted.
22. Vice Adm. Lewis Crenshaw, quoted in Gopal Ratnam, "Weapons Win Out: As QDR Nears Completion, Services Plan Personnel Cuts to Save Cash," *Navy Times*, December 26, 2005.
23. Bart Jansen, "A New Threat to BIW's [Bath Iron Works] Future?," *Portland Press Herald*, October 27, 2005; and David S. Cloud, "Navy Plans to Expand Fleet, With New Enemies in Mind," *New York Times*, December 5, 2005.
24. Adm. Vernon E. Clark, USN, testimony to the Senate Appropriations Committee, Subcommittee on Defense, *Hearings on Navy and Marine Corps Appropriations*, 108th Congress, 2nd Session, March 10, 2004.
25. Gregory Platt, "Carrier Viewed as Old and in the Way," *Florida Times-Union*, January 16, 2005.
26. Adm. Vernon E. Clark, USN, testimony to the Senate Armed Services Committee, *Hearing on the Fiscal Year 2006 Department of Defense Budget*, 108th Congress, 2nd Session, February 10, 2005.
27. Ratnam, "Weapons Win Out."
28. Jeremiah J. Gertler, quoted in Eisman, "Navy's Changing Tide."
29. Gallup Poll, "Which Branch of the Armed Forces Is Most Important?," Gallup News Service, May 27, 2004, www.gallup.com/poll/1666/Military-National-Defense.aspx.
30. See Shanker and Schmitt, "Critics and Fans Alike as Navy Chief Steps Down."
31. Ratnam, "Weapons Win Out."
32. Vice Adm. Charles Moore, quoted in Michael Fabey, "Military Chiefs Looking to Organize, Cut Costs," *Daily Press*, October 28, 2003.
33. James W. Crawley, "Navy Rethinking Deployment Strategy," *San Diego Union-Tribune*, May 16, 2003.
34. Paragraph based on Vice Adm. John G. Morgan Jr., USN (Ret.), discussion with the author, March 10, 2010, Arlington, Virginia.
35. Ibid.

36. Swartz, discussion, February 18, 2010.
37. Anthony D. McIvor, ed., *Rethinking the Principles of War* (Annapolis, MD: Naval Institute Press, 2005).
38. Paragraph to here based on Nagy, discussion; and Lawrence, discussion. Rest of paragraph based on the notes of Cdr. Paul N. Nagy, USN, on the comments by Vice Adm. John G. Morgan Jr., USN, during the Global N5 Conference, Washington, DC, April 7–8, 2005.
39. Morgan, discussion.
40. Lawrence, discussion.
41. Ibid.
42. Morgan, discussion.
43. Nagy, discussion; Lawrence, discussion.
44. Lawrence, discussion.
45. The rest of section "Morgan and the Lack of Strategic Perspective" based on Morgan, discussion.
46. Morgan, discussion.
47. Ibid.
48. Nagy, discussion.
49. Nagy, notes of Morgan's comments.
50. Lawrence, discussion.
51. Nagy, discussion.
52. Swartz, discussion, February 18, 2010.
53. "Soft power" is understood as shaping the behavior of other states via more indirect and less kinetic means. See Joseph S. Nye Jr., *Soft Power: The Means to Success in World Politics* (New York: PublicAffairs, 2004), 5–11.
54. Adm. Mike Mullen, quoted in "Mullen Nominated for CNO," *U.S. Fed News*, March 2, 2005.
55. Nagy, discussion.
56. Paragraph based on "Navy's 3/1 Strategy: The Maritime Contribution to the Joint Force in a Changing Strategic Landscape," draft paper, version April 12, 2005, 6–7.
57. Ibid., 7.
58. Ibid.
59. Ibid., 4. Emphasis added.
60. Ibid., 2.
61. Ibid., 35.
62. Ibid., 2, 32, 34.
63. Ibid., 4–5.
64. Ibid., 13.
65. Paragraph based on ibid., 16. Of note, the Navy prefers the term "Arabian Gulf" over "Persian Gulf." The use of the latter lends credence to Iran's claim that the Persian Gulf is its domain.
66. Ibid., 10.
67. Paragraph based on ibid., 15.
68. Ibid., 16.
69. Ibid., 23.
70. Ibid.
71. Ibid.
72. Paragraph based on and quotes drawn from ibid., 19, 22.
73. Ibid., 19.
74. Morgan, discussion.

75. See "Humanitarian Assistance Key to Favorable Public Opinion in World's Three Most Populous Muslim Countries: Results from New Polls of Indonesia, Bangladesh and Pakistan," a study conducted by Terror Free for Tomorrow, Inc., in 2006, http://www .terrorfreetomorrow.org/upimagestft/Indonesia%20Bangladesh%20TFT%20Final %20Poll%20Report.pdf.

76. Paragraph based on and quotes taken from "Navy's 3/1 Strategy," 21–22, 44–45; quote on 44–45.

77. Nagy, discussion.

78. Rest of section "Pushback: Part I" based on Adm. John B. Nathman, USN (Ret), discussion with the author, May 5, 2010, Alexandria, Virginia, except as noted.

79. Morgan, discussion.

80. Nagy, notes of Morgan's comments.

81. Jonathan Monten, "The Roots of the Bush Doctrine: Power, Nationalism, and Democracy Promotion in U.S. Strategy," *International Security* 29, no. 4 (Spring 2005): 141.

82. Morgan, discussion.

CHAPTER 11. THE 1000-SHIP NAVY, 2005–6

1. Adm. Michael G. Mullen, USN, memo to Vice Adm. John G. Morgan Jr., USN, deputy CNO for Information, Plans, and Strategy (N3/N5), Subject: "Navy Strategic Plan," July 29, 2005.

2. Adm. Michael G. Mullen, message to the Navy, Subject: "All Ahead Full," date time group: 231853Z JUL 05 (July 23, 2005), 1.

3. See Christopher P. Cavas, "Deputy CNO Sestak Is 'Reassigned': New CNO Reportedly Makes Move Because of 'Poor Command Climate,'" *Navy Times*, July 25, 2005; and Thomas Fitzgerald, "Sestak's Tough Fight for Senate Seat," *Philadelphia Inquirer*, April 11, 2010.

4. Mullen, memo, "Navy Strategic Plan," 1.

5. Ibid.

6. Ibid.

7. Christopher P. Cavas, "'1,000-Ship Navy' Plan Draws Mixed Reviews: President Is Reportedly Among Backers," *Navy Times*, October 9, 2006.

8. Vice Adm. John G. Morgan Jr., USN, and Rear Adm. Charles W. Martoglio, USN, "The 1,000-Ship Navy Global Maritime Network," U.S. Naval Institute *Proceedings* 131, no. 11 (November 2005): 14.

9. Ibid., 15.

10. The author was the branch chief for OPNAV N5's N5SC from February to June 2006, a position he filled temporarily before reporting to the Naval Postgraduate School as the first officer selected for OPNAV N3/N5's then-new PhD program in security studies, a program that was established in 2005 by Rear Admiral Martoglio and the previous branch chief, Capt. Thomas E. Mangold Jr.

11. "White Paper on Global Fleet Stations," unpublished draft (Washington, DC: OPNAV, March 20, 2006).

12. *The National Strategy for Maritime Security* (Washington, DC: White House, Government Printing Office, September 2005).

13. Ibid., 1.

14. Adm. Michael G. Mullen, USN (speech, Royal United Services Institute's Future Maritime Warfare Conference, London, December 13, 2005), http://www.Navy.mil/Navydata /cno/mullen/speeches/mullen051213.txt.

15. Adm. Mike Mullen, quoted in Christopher J. Castelli, "Navy Proceeds with Reviews on Readiness, Organization, Shipbuilding," *Inside the Navy* 21, no. 37 (September 15, 2005).

16. See Geoffrey Till, "'A Cooperative Strategy for 21st Century Seapower': A View from Outside," *Naval War College Review* 61, no. 2 (Spring 2008): 25–26.

17. Castelli, "Navy Proceeds with Reviews."

18. Daniel J. Moran, "Stability Operations: The View from Afloat," in *Naval Peacekeeping and Humanitarian Operations: Stability from the Sea*, ed. James J. Wirtz and Jeffrey A. Larsen (New York: Routledge, 2008), 15.

19. Adm. Mike Mullen, quoted in Castelli, "Navy Proceeds with Reviews."

20. Adm. Michael G. Mullen, USN, "What I Believe: Eight Tenets That Guide My Vision for the 21st Century Navy," U.S. Naval Institute *Proceedings* 132, no. 1 (January 2006): 13.

21. Ibid., 16.

22. Adm. John B. Nathman, USN, "Shaping the Future," U.S. Naval Institute *Proceedings* 132, no. 1 (January 2006): 20–21.

23. Quote is intentionally left unattributed.

24. *Quadrennial Defense Review Report of 2006* (Washington, DC: U.S. Department of Defense, Government Printing Office, February 6, 2006).

25. Ibid., 83.

26. Ibid., 19.

27. Ibid., vi, vii.

28. Ibid., 37.

29. Ibid., 38.

30. Colin S. Gray, "Document No. 1: The Quadrennial Defense Review (QDR), 2006, and the Perils of the Twenty-First Century," *Comparative Strategy* 25, no. 2 (April–June 2006): 142.

31. *Quadrennial Defense Review Report of 2006*, 36.

32. Ibid., vii.

33. Ibid., 36.

34. Nagy, discussion.

35. Ibid.

36. "Navy Strategic Plan in Support of Program Objective Memorandum 08," 3–4.

37. Ibid., 7.

38. Ibid., 16–18.

39. Ibid., 3.

40. Ibid., 8–9, 12. Emphasis added.

41. Vice Adm. John G. Morgan Jr., USN, "Navy's Maritime Strategy" (brief, All-Flag Officers' Symposium, Annapolis, MD, June 20, 2006), slide 12.

42. George W. Bush, signature page, *The National Security Strategy of the United States* (Washington, DC: U.S. Department of Defense, Government Printing Office, March 2006), ii.

43. Paragraph based on and quotes taken from ibid., 1, 3.

44. Swartz, "U.S. Navy Capstone Strategies and Concepts (2001–2010)," 99–101, slides 198–202.

45. Adm. Michal G. Mullen, USN, and Gen. Michael W. Hagee, USMC "Naval Operations Concept," (Washington, DC: OPNAV, June 2006).

46. Rest of paragraph based on and quotes taken from Adm. Michael G. Mullen, USN, memo to Vice Adm. John G. Morgan Jr., USN, deputy CNO for Information, Plans, and Strategy (N3/N5), Subject: "Naval Operating Concept," January 6, 2006.

47. "Marine Corps Operating Concepts for a Changing Security Environment," Marine Corps Combat Development Command, Quantico, VA (March 2006), http://www.dtic.mil/dtic/tr/fulltext/u2/a446044.pdf.

48. Paragraph based on Mullen and Hagee, "Naval Operations Concept," 6–7; quote on 7.

49. Ibid., 7–8.

50. Ibid., 10.
51. Ibid., 11. Emphasis in original.
52. Ibid., 7.
53. For a strident argument on Goldwater-Nichols' deleterious effects, see Cdr. Bryan G. McGrath, USN (Ret.), "The Unbearable Being of Jointness," U.S. Naval Institute *Proceedings* 136, no. 5 (May 2010): 40–43.

CHAPTER 12. A COOPERATIVE STRATEGY, 2007

1. Adm. Michael G. Mullen, USN (speech, Current Strategy Forum, Naval War College, Newport, RI, June 14, 2006), quotes on 3, 5, http://www.navy.mil/navydata/people /cno/Mullen/CNO_CSF140606.pdf.
2. Ibid., 6.
3. Paragraph based on Adm. Michael G. Mullen, USN, memo to Vice Adm. John G. Morgan Jr., USN, deputy CNO for Information, Plans, and Strategy (N3/N5), Subject: "New Navy Maritime Strategy," July 17, 2006. Quote from p. 1. In the margin, on page 1, Mullen had hand-written "This is a *very high priority* and should be given the time and resources to complete with all due speed." Emphasis in the original.
4. Morgan, discussion.
5. Paragraph based on Morgan, "Navy's Maritime Strategy"; "Rethinking America's Maritime Strategy: Why, Why Now and How?" (brief, Three- and Four-Star Flag Officer Conference, February 2007), except as noted.
6. Morgan, "Navy's Maritime Strategy," slide 17. See Daniel Yergin and Joseph Stanislaw, *The Commanding Heights: The Battle for the World Economy* (New York: Simon & Schuster, 1998); and "The Commanding Heights: The Battle for the World Economy" (film series, WGBH, Boston, 2006), http://www.pbs.org/wgbh/commandingheights/.
7. Samuel Palmisano, quoted in Morgan, "Navy's Maritime Strategy," slide 20. The quote is from Samuel J. Palmisano, "The Globally Integrated Enterprise," *Foreign Affairs* 85 (May/June 2006): 135.
8. Morgan, discussion.
9. Morgan, "Navy's Maritime Strategy," slides 45, 58. See Benjamin M. Friedman, *The Moral Consequences of Economic Growth* (New York: Alfred A. Knopf, 2005).
10. Ibid., slide 45.
11. Ibid., slide 58.
12. Cdr. Bryan G. McGrath, USN (Ret.), "Maritime Strategy 2007: The Team Leader Speaks," *Steeljaw Scribe* (the blog of Capt. C. Will Dossel, USN [Ret.]), October 21, 2007, http://steeljawscribe.com/2007/10/21/maritime-strategy-2007-the-team-leader -speaks.
13. James Surowiecki, quoted in Morgan, "Navy's Maritime Strategy," slide 46. See James Surowiecki, *The Wisdom of Crowds* (New York: Anchor, 2005), xi–xxi.
14. Paragraph based on Capt. Robert C. Rubel, USN (Ret.), "The New Maritime Strategy: The Rest of the Story," *Naval War College Review* 61, no. 2 (Spring 2008): 70.
15. Ibid.
16. Ibid.
17. Ibid., 71.
18. Ibid.
19. Ibid., 71–72. At an earlier seminar, several developers of the 1980s' Maritime Strategy had remarked that the Navy's post–Cold War strategic statements lacked an intellectual glue that related naval operations in the Western Pacific to those in the Middle East, hence Rubel's "glue" reference. Captain Robert C. Rubel, U.S. Navy (Ret.), discussion with the author, February 17, 2011, Newport, RI.

20. Ibid., 72.
21. Lt. John Ennis, USN Reserve, "Inside the New Maritime Strategy," U.S. Naval Institute *Proceedings* 135, no. 12 (December 2009): 69.
22. Paragraph based on Rear Adm. Jacob L. Shuford, USN, and Capt. Robert C. Rubel, USN (Ret.), "Maritime Strategy Options" (brief, Executive Committee, Washington, DC, March 20, 2007), slides 3–6.
23. Paragraph based on Rubel, "The New Maritime Strategy," 76; Shuford and Rubel, "Maritime Strategy Options," slides 7–16; McGrath, "Team Leader Speaks"; and Rubel discussion.
24. Hughes, *Fleet Tactics and Coastal Combat.*
25. Rest of paragraph based on Rubel, "The New Maritime Strategy," 76; Shuford and Rubel, "Maritime Strategy Options," slides 17–27; McGrath, "Team Leader Speaks"; and Rubel discussion.
26. Paragraph based on Rubel, "The New Maritime Strategy," 76; Shuford and Rubel, "Maritime Strategy Options," slides 28–38; McGrath, "Team Leader Speaks"; and Rubel discussion.
27. Shuford and Rubel, "Maritime Strategy Options," slides 30, 31.
28. Paragraph based on Rubel, "The New Maritime Strategy," 76; Shuford and Rubel, "Maritime Strategy Options," slides 28–38; McGrath, "Team Leader Speaks"; and Rubel discussion.
29. Paragraph based on Rubel, "The New Maritime Strategy," 76; Shuford and Rubel, "Maritime Strategy Options," slides 39–50; McGrath, "Team Leader Speaks"; and Rubel discussion.
30. Paragraph based on Rubel, "The New Maritime Strategy," 76–77; Shuford and Rubel, "Maritime Strategy Options," slides 51–62; and McGrath, "Team Leader Speaks."
31. Shuford and Rubel, "Maritime Strategy Options," slide 52.
32. Ibid.
33. Till, "A View from Outside," 28.
34. Moran, "Stability Operations," 16.
35. Morgan, discussion.
36. McGrath, "Team Leader Speaks."
37. Gallup, "Which Branch of the Armed Forces Is Most Important?"
38. Roughead, Conway, and Allen, "A Cooperative Strategy," 1.
39. McGrath, "Team Leader Speaks."
40. Ibid.
41. Ennis, "Inside the New Maritime Strategy," 69.
42. Ibid.
43. Cdr. Bryan G. McGrath, USN (Ret.), discussion with the author, February 14, 2011, Arlington, Virginia.
44. Paragraph based on and quotes taken from Ennis, "Inside the New Maritime Strategy," 69.
45. Mullen's direction was captured in a memorandum signed by Vice Adm. John G. Morgan Jr., USN, Lt. Gen. James F. Amos, USMC, and Rear Adm. Joseph L. Nimmich, USCG; Memorandum, Subject: "Terms of Reference for Maritime Security Development," unpublished photocopy, undated (which the author believes was signed in October 2006 or January 2007).
46. McGrath, "Team Leader Speaks."
47. Ibid. Emphasis added.
48. Paragraph based on and quotes taken from Ennis, "Inside the New Maritime Strategy," 70.
49. Paragraph based on and quotes taken from ibid., 71, except as indicated.
50. Cdr. Bryan G. McGrath, USN (Ret.), "Thoughts on 'A Cooperative Strategy for 21st Century Seapower' Two Year's Later: Author's Response," *Steeljaw Scribe* (the blog of

Capt. C. Will Dossel, USN [Ret.]), October 21, 2009, http://blog.usni.org/2009/10/21
/thoughts-on-a-cooperative-strategy-for-21st-century-seapower-two-years-later-authors
-response.

51. Ennis noted that Andrew Erickson, from the Naval War College's China Maritime
Studies Institute, later confirmed that the Chinese did read themselves into the document. The Chinese liked the document's painting of a multipolar world, but worried
about the purpose of all the talk about cooperation. Ennis, "Inside the New Maritime
Strategy," 71.

52. Ibid., 70.

53. Ibid.

54. Niall Ferguson, *Colossus: The Price of America's Empire* (New York: Penguin, 2004), 298.

55. Ennis, "Inside the New Maritime Strategy," 70.

56. Ibid.

57. One of these studies was Jerome Burke, Grant Sharp, Alfred Kaufman, and Patricia
Cohen, "Assessment of Naval Core Capabilities" (Alexandria, VA: Institute for Defense
Analyses, January 2009).

58. McGrath, discussion.

59. McGrath, "Thoughts on 'A Cooperative Strategy for 21st Century Seapower' Two Years
Later." As he noted, "What I considered essential . . . was a ship that could be built in
numbers—not 55, but more like 155, which we could send out around the world to the
very edges of the empire to work the issues of global system protection." Cdr. Bryan G.
McGrath, USN (Ret.), " . . . In Which I Respond to Professor Farley et al.," entry on the
blog *Information Dissemination*, December 4, 2009, http://www.informationdissemination
.net/2009/12/in-which-i-respond-to-professor-farley.html.

60. Roughead, Conway, and Allen, "A Cooperative Strategy," 2.

61. Ibid. Emphasis in the original.

62. Mullen, speech, Current Strategy Forum.

63. Roughead, Conway, and Allen, "A Cooperative Strategy," 2.

64. Paragraph based on and quotes taken from ibid., 3, 4.

65. Ibid., 5.

66. Ibid., 4. See, for example, Frank G. Hoffman, "Complex Irregular Warfare: The Next
Revolution in Military Affairs," *Orbis* 50, no. 3 (Summer 2006): 395–411; "Conflict in
the 21st Century: The Rise of Hybrid Wars" (Arlington, VA: Potomac Institute for
Policy Studies, 2007); and "Hybrid Warfare and Challenges," *Joint Force Quarterly* 52
(First Quarter 2009): 34–39.

67. Paragraph based on and quotes from Roughead, Conway, and Allen, "A Cooperative
Strategy," 6. Emphasis in the original.

68. Ibid.

69. Ibid., 7.

70. Paragraph based on ibid., 8, 9; quote on 9. Emphasis in the original.

71. Paragraph based on and quotes taken from ibid., 9–10.

72. Paragraph based on ibid., 10–12; quote on 11.

73. Mullen, speech, Current Strategy Forum.

74. Ennis, "Inside the New Maritime Strategy," 70. Emphasis in the original.

75. Paragraph based on McGrath, discussion.

76. Roughead, Conway, and Allen, "A Cooperative Strategy," 2. Emphasis in the original.

77. Donald C. Winter (speech, International Seapower Symposium, Naval War College,
Newport, RI, October 18, 2007), quoted in *Report of the Proceedings of the Eighteenth
International Seapower Symposium, 17–19 October 2007*, ed. John B. Hattendorf with
John W. Kennedy (Newport, RI: Naval War College, 2007), 85.

78. Till, "A View from Outside," 32.

CONCLUSION

1. The most impressive debates were in the blogosphere, particularly on three blogs—Raymond Pritchett's (whose blogger name is Galrahn) *Information Dissemination*, http://www.informationdissemination.net/; Will Dossel's *Steeljaw Scribe*, http://steeljawscribe .com/; and *CDR Salamander*, http://cdrsalamander.blogspot.com/.

2. Geoffrey Till, "Maritime Strategy in a Globalizing World," *Orbis* 51, no. 4 (Fall 2007): 570. For other efforts that examine "A Cooperative Strategy" in historical context, see John B. Hattendorf, "The United States Navy in the Twenty-first Century: Thoughts on Naval Theory, Strategic Constraints and Opportunities," *The Mariner's Mirror* 97, no. 1 (February 2011): 285–97; Martin Murphy, "Forward to the Past," *Armed Forces Journal* 144 (December 2007): 27–29; and Geoffrey Till, "New Directions in Maritime Strategy, Implications for the U.S. Navy," *Naval War College Review* 60, no. 4 (Autumn 2007): 29–43.

3. Till, "Maritime Strategy in a Globalizing World," 571.

4. Ibid., 573.

5. Sun Tzu, *The Art of War*, trans. Samuel B. Griffith (London: Oxford University, 1963), 84.

6. See, for example, Michèle Flournoy and Shawn Brimley, "The Contested Commons," U.S. Naval Institute *Proceedings* 135, no. 7 (July 2009), http://www.usni.org/magazines /proceedings/2009–07/contested-commons.

7. Rubel, discussion.

8. Ibid.

9. Moran, "Stability Operations," 14.

10. Rubel, discussion.

11. Congressman Gene Taylor, quoted in Michael Bruno, "New Maritime Strategy Plan Meets Congressional Doubts," *Aviation Week's* Aerospace Daily and Defense Report, December 14, 2007.

12. Ronald O'Rourke, "Navy Force Structure and Shipbuilding Plans: Background and Issues for Congress" (Washington, DC: Congressional Research Service, August 1, 2014), 1.

13. Cdr. Bryan G. McGrath, USN (Ret.), "On One Year Out of the Navy," entry on his blog *Conservative Wahoo*, April 1, 2009, http://conservativewahoo.blogspot.com. (The entry was later removed.)

14. Gray, "Strategy in the Nuclear Age," 594.

15. Wylie, letter.

16. Adm. Jonathan W. Greenert, USN (speech, Current Strategy Forum, Naval War College, Newport, RI, June 17, 2014), https://www.usnwc.edu/About/News/June-2014/CNO -Kicks-off-65th-Annual-Current-Strategy-Forum.aspx.

17. The title of the Defense Strategic Guidance is "Sustaining U.S. Global Leadership: Priorities for 21st Century Defense" (Washington, DC: U.S. Department of Defense, Government Printing Office, January 5, 2012); *Quadrennial Defense Review Report of 2014* (Washington, DC: U.S. Department of Defense, Government Printing Office, March 4, 2014); *The National Security Strategy* (Washington, DC: White House, February 2015).

18. Adm. Jonathan W. Greenert, USN, Gen. Joseph F. Dunford Jr., USMC, and Adm. Paul F. Zukunft, USCG, "A Cooperative Strategy for 21st Century Seapower: Forward, Engaged, and Ready" (Washington, DC: OPNAV, March 2015).

19. The 285 figure is from O'Rourke, "Navy Force Structure and Shipbuilding Plans" (2014), 59. As CNO Roughead testified, "Having 288 ships today [March 9, 2011], it's the smallest we've been since 1916." Adm. Gary Roughead, testimony to the House Appropriations Subcommittee on Defense, *Hearing on the Proposed Fiscal 2012 Appropriations for the U.S. Navy and Marine Corps*, 112th Congress, 1st Session, March 9, 2011.

20. Gray, "Strategic Thoughts for Defence Planners," 172.
21. Greenert, Dunford, and Zukunft, "A Cooperative Strategy," iii.
22. Ibid., 2.
23. Ibid., 11, 13, 27.
24. Moran, "Stability Operations," 17.
25. James H. Billington, quoted in Ann Geracimos, "New Librarian Called Fundamental Scholar," *Washington Times*, September 14, 1987.
26. Greenert, speech.
27. Greenert, Dunford, and Zukunft, "A Cooperative Strategy," 31.
28. Gray, *The Navy in the Post–Cold War World*, 3.
29. Strategic analysis students might study how U.S. ambassadors and geographic combatant commanders would use U.S. naval forces to increase foreign direct investment in key developing partner nations or regions. Or they might examine the relationship between U.S. naval presence and overseas markets. For an example of the latter, see Robert E. Looney, "Market Effects of Naval Presence in a Globalized World: A Research Summary," in *Globalization and Maritime Power*, ed. Sam J. Tangredi (Washington, DC: National Defense University, 2002), 103–31.
30. *The National Military Strategy of the United States: Redefining America's Military Leadership* (Washington, DC: U.S. Department of Defense, Government Printing Office, February 2011), 7.
31. Colin S. Gray, *War, Peace, and Victory: Strategy and Statecraft for the Next Century* (New York: Simon & Schuster, 1990), 23.
32. Winston Churchill, quoted in Philip Ziegler, *Mountbatten* (New York: Alfred A. Knopf, 1985), 220.
33. Bernard Semmel, *Liberalism and Naval Strategy: Ideology, Interest, and Sea Power during the Pax Britannica* (Boston: Allen and Unwin, 1986), 181.

Index

A-12 carrier attack jet, 116–17
Afghanistan, 10, 31, 150, 151–52, 156
Air Force, U.S.: air campaign management,
  65; analysis of worth of tactical air forces,
  27; bomber project funding, 115; Cold War
  role of, 16–17; command authority and
  structure, 25; conventional forces to deter
  Soviet threat, 30–31; Enduring Freedom
  joint operations, 151–52; force strength and
  structure, 98; Gulf War role, 64, 66, 83–84;
  operational doctrine and naval aviation,
  119; regional powers, capabilities for conflict
  against, 10, 65; relevance of, 6–7, 32, 178;
  sea-lane access during wars, 29; systems
  analysis to rationalize purpose, 26; theorist
  and outlook of, 24
aircraft carriers: arsenal ship threat to, 115;
  attack jet program, 116–17; balanced
  carrier-based fleet, 6, 7, 15, 118, 170–71;
  Desert Storm role of, 58, 59–60; Enduring
  Freedom and carrier-based strike missions,
  151–52, 156; funding for supercarriers, 24;
  as hedge against political unknowns, 29–30;
  mission of under Kennedy, 24; missions for,
  24, 29–30, 32; nuclear conflict and vulnerability of, 24; strike warfare focus and, 9, 85,
  156; surge capability, 166–68; twelve-carrier
  fleet, 91, 98, 117, 127; versatility of, 7, 15,
  29–30
airpower, 5, 16–17, 24, 33, 64, 105, 126
Albright, Madeleine J. K., 93
Alignment, 144–45
Amphibious Warfare Strategy, 54–55
"Anytime, Anywhere," 127–30, 268n47
arms/weapons, 35, 40, 129, 254n13
Army, U.S.: analysis of worth of ground forces,
  27; command authority and structure, 25;

conventional forces to deter Soviet threat,
  30–31; expeditionary warfare mission, 55;
  force strength and structure, 98; Gulf War
  role of, 64, 66, 83–84; maritime strategy and,
  11; overseas deployments and funding for,
  132–33; regional powers, capabilities for
  conflict against, 10, 65; relevance of, 6–7,
  10, 32, 178; reserve forces, 42, 258n43;
  sea-lane access during wars, 29; theorist and
  outlook of, 24; written doctrine, 107–8
"Army Vision 2010," 127
arsenal ships, 114–15, 118
Aspin, Leslie "Les," Jr., 73, 90, 91, 92, 95,
  101, 104

Baker, Edward "Ted," 66, 68, 74–75, 98
Barnett, Thomas P. M., 68–69, 72, 74
Base Force plan, 36–41, 44–47, 50–51, 55–56,
  86, 257n6
Battlespace Attack, 136, 158
Battlespace Control, 136, 158
Battlespace Sustainment, 136, 158–59
Big Sticks, 69, 70
Boorda, Jeremy M. "Mike": career and
  experience of, 95–96; death of, 115, 119;
  "Forward . . . From the Sea" strategy, 96–97;
  naval forces, missions for, 110; Naval
  Operational Concept development, 111–12;
  Tailhook scandal and appointment of,
  95–96, 115; "2020 Vision" role, 113
Bosnia, 91, 93, 95, 105, 106, 112, 117, 151
"Bottom-Up Review," 90, 99–100, 101–2
Bouchard, Joseph F., 111–13, 122–24, 125,
  139–40, 152, 158, 159, 167, 263n43
budgets and funding: Base Force plan and
  budget cuts, 37, 39, 44–47, 50–51, 55–56,
  60, 65; budget submission as strategy, 144;

283

Bush budgetary environment, 149–50; Clinton budgetary environment, 91, 132–33; congressional role in, 44; defense budget cuts, 247; defense budget increase, 133; fleet modernization, funds for, 28, 30; funding for Air Force, 19, 115; funding for Marine Corps, 99, 119, 134; funding for Navy, 13, 26–27, 99, 112–13, 114–15, 116–17, 119, 127, 132–33, 146, 176–78, 247–48; military programming and budgeting processes, changes to, 5–7, 25–27, 37, 38, 255n35; POMs, funding of, 50; QDR and budget decisions, 125–26, 127, 132, 138–39, 142, 197, 247, 248; Reagan budgetary environment, 32; resource apportionment process under Kelso, 51, 87–89; slash-and-burn approach, 37; SSBN-Polaris funding, 24, 28, 255n34; strategy to shape programmatic decisions, 138–43, 182; supercarriers, funding for, 24

Burke, Arleigh A., 18, 21, 22, 25, 27, 84, 123, 144

Bush administration and George H. W. Bush, 35, 42, 44, 46, 47, 48, 50, 55–56, 65, 78, 83, 93, 261n56

Bush administration and George W. Bush: election of, 148; foreign policy, 168–70, 194–95, 207; global war on terror, 150, 168–69, 186, 198, 270–71n15; national security team, 148; strategy and defense policy, 165; transformation defense policy goals, 149–51, 169–70, 173

Carter, Jimmy, 30–31

Cebrowski, Arthur K. "Art," 89, 122–24, 127, 128, 136, 150, 158, 159, 170, 195

Center for Naval Analyses, 68, 74

Cheney, Richard, 36–37, 44, 45, 116, 148, 150, 169

Chief of Naval Operations (CNO): authority and influence of, 9, 26, 27; careers and experience of, 22, 29, 41–42, 48, 96, 116, 143–44, 178; length of tenure, 143–44, 155; McNamara and role of, 26–27

Chief of Naval Operations (CNO), Office of (OPNAV): authority and control over, 26–27, 89; balance of power in, 89; development of strategic statements and policies by, 12–13; focus of on budgetary and management process, 27, 244; force structure, focus on reshaping, 52; "Navy Strategic Plan" development role, 197; QDR decision-making process and preparations for, 138–39, 142; reorganization of, 87–89, 102, 144–45, 146, 262nn3–4; role in and

influence on U.S. strategy, 9, 210–11; strategic education, lack of need for, 23; Strategy and Policy Division, 32; strategy to shape programmatic decisions, 138–43; strategy-making structure, reorganization of, 152–53

China, 193, 194, 200, 218, 227–28, 232, 239–40, 248–49, 280n51

Clark, Vernon E.: appointment of, 143–44; atrophy of strategic thinking capabilities under, 153–55, 212; Bear Paw initiative, 184; career and experience of, 143–44; Fleet Forces Command establishment, 161–62; garrisoning of fleet, 178–79, 183; legacy of, 162; OPNAV reorganization under, 144–45, 146; OPNAV strategy-making structure, reorganization of, 152–53; priorities of, 144–45, 177–78; retirement of, 194; "Sea Power 21" roadmap, 157–58, 160–61; strategy, opinion about, 144, 155, 170; strategy development role of, 162, 164, 165, 180, 208; success of, 170; "3/1 Strategy," 194

Clinton administration and Bill Clinton: "Bottom-Up Review" of military under, 90, 99–100, 101–2; defense budget under, 91, 132–33; domestic agenda focus of, 91, 94; foreign policy of, 93–94, 101–2, 104–5, 117–18, 130, 132–33, 145–47; interventionist enlargement, 91–94, 97, 101; national security team, 91–92; political skills of, 104; regional conflict policies, 94, 97

Coast Guard, U.S., 2, 220, 224

Cold War: airpower role during, 16–17; end of, 35, 44; focus of, 2–3; identity, purpose, and strategic outlook of Navy, 6–8, 20–24; influence on strategic thinking, 241; naval strategy during, 5–8; Navy role during, 16–17, 46–47; threat-centric strategy during, 19–20, 45–46; winning of, 3, 31–32, 44

Cold Worriers, 69, 70–71, 82, 90, 100, 102

command of the sea, achieving versus using, 75–78

commanders in chief of the unified commands (CINCs)/combatant commanders: force structure and weapons decisions, responsibility for, 36; force structure, focus on reshaping, 50; force structure to advance foreign policy, 145–46; role in and influence on U.S. strategy, 9; stature and authority of, 8, 80–82, 85, 102, 210–11; strategic statements and policies for, 13; types of, 254n18

Congress, U.S.: "A Cooperative Strategy," reaction to, 242; defense planning and spending role, 44, 65, 145; "Forward . . . From the Sea," response to, 100; military programming and budgeting processes, changes

to, 5–7; POMs, funding of, 50; relevance of Navy and justification of spending by, 62–63; strategic statements and policies for, 13; understanding about purpose of military, 44, 46, 62–63, 73, 75
containment, 15–16, 35, 92
"A Cooperative Strategy for 21st Century Seapower": changes to, 235–36; as classic maritime strategy, 3; Conversations with the Country forums, 216, 223–24, 252; debate about and roadblocks in development, 227–29, 236; development and writing of, 195, 216–23, 224–31; focus and provisions of, 1–2, 210, 231–38, 250; influence and prospects of, 247–49; Mullen call for new strategy, 213–14, 235, 278n3; operational-ization of, 242–43; Phase I, 217–23; Phase II, 224–26; Phase III, 226–29; reaction to and reviews of, 239–43, 281n1; release of, 1, 231; Roughhead model, 229–31, 242, 280n59; timing of development and release of, 2–4
"A Cooperative Strategy for 21st Century Seapower: Forward, Engaged, and Ready," 247–49, 250
counterinsurgency mission, 58, 61, 173, 174, 190, 192, 202–5, 207
crisis management and crisis response team mission, 39–41, 47, 55–60, 67, 71–72, 73–74, 75–78, 97–98, 102–3, 118, 130–31

Dalton, John H., 95, 96, 111, 126, 133, 134
Danzig, Richard J., 96, 133–35, 138, 140, 143
Deep Blue, 152, 162, 167
Defense, Department of, 5–7, 13, 25–27, 37, 38, 144, 255n35
Defense Reorganization Act (1958), 26
Defense Strategic Guidance, 247, 248, 281n17
Deliberate Force, Operation, 105, 119
Deming, W. Edward, 49, 87
deterrence, 5, 16–17, 21, 22, 24, 30–31, 32–33, 129, 254n13
Diamond, E. Richard, 53–54, 56, 60, 66–67, 271n40
diplomacy: coercive diplomacy, 21, 29–30, 40, 118; gunboat diplomacy, 24, 32, 71; nuclear bomb and need for skills, 5, 33; power pro-jection and, 56
Dossel, C. Will, 153, 162, 163–64, 271n30
Dur, Philip A., 98–99

economics: economic security concept, 19; free-market economies, 11, 253n11; global-ization, security, and, 10–11, 135, 145–47, 181–83, 194–95, 197–99

Eisenhower, Dwight, 18–19, 21
enabling force, Navy–Marine Corps team as, 54, 56–62, 246
Enduring Freedom, Operation, 150, 151–52, 156, 169
England, Gordon R., 162, 177, 179
enlargement/interventionist enlargement, 91–94, 97, 101
Ennis, John, 225, 227, 228–29, 236, 280n51
the Enterprise, 162, 272n59
Europe, 30–31, 35, 38, 39–40
expeditionary warfare mission, 67, 77–78, 81–83, 85, 86, 97, 107, 130, 260n11

F-22 aircraft, 116
F-35 Joint Strike Fighter, 116
F/A-18C Hornet, 116
F/A-18E/F Super Hornet, 112, 113, 116–17, 127, 143, 173
fleet: analysis of worth of, 27; balanced fleet, 253n7; capabilities of smaller fleet, 59; combat flexibility, reorganization for, 156; composition of, 7; force strength and struc-ture, 28, 29, 32, 37, 90–91, 97–98, 118, 127, 170–71, 176–78, 195, 236–37, 247, 262n17, 281n19; force structure decisions, changes in, 86; force structure, reshaping of, 50–51, 52; garrisoning of, 178–79, 183; half the fleet as reserve forces, 42–43; littoral-oriented fleet, 91; modernization of, funds for, 28, 30; modernization of to counter Soviet sea-denial threat, 28–29; plan for fleet under Owen, 89–91; reorganization of, 144–45; restructuring of, 3; sea power and, 7, 15; support of by rest of Navy, 16. *See also* aircraft carriers
Fleet Forces Command, U.S., 162, 211–12
Fleet Response Plan, 165–68, 179
flexible response doctrine, 24, 27
Force 2001, 90, 91, 103
ForceNet, 159, 164
foreign policy: Bush policy, 168–70, 194–95, 207; Clinton policy, 93–94, 101–2, 104–5, 117–18, 130, 132–33, 145–47; convention-al land and air forces to deter Soviet threat to, 30–31; interventionist enlargement, 91–94, 97, 101; interventionist policy under Reagan, 55; naval forces as instrument for, 99, 102–3; regional conflict policies, 94, 97; U.S. foreign policy, trade, and naval power, 4
"Forward . . . From the Sea": development and writing of, 98–99; end of Navy–Marine Corps partnership, 103; expeditionary war-fare and, 111; focus and purpose of, 96–98,

99–101, 103, 127; no replacement for, 126; opinions about and response to, 100–101, 111; success of, 101

forward presence: Air Force orientation for, 98, 100–101; Army orientation for, 98, 100–101; conflict deterrence and, 73–74, 75–78; definition of, 100–101; fleet orientation for, 6–8, 37, 41, 58–59, 97–98, 99–101, 118, 129, 131, 189–91; forward presence approach instead of overseas base structure, 38, 71–72; mission and purpose of, 124–25, 131; sea power and, 7, 15; strategy to focus on, 96–98, 99–101; surge capability and, 164–68

4 x 4 concept, 134–35

". . . From the Sea": decision on title of, 78; development and writing of, 78–79, 90; fleet orientation for, 91, 110; focus and purpose of, 9–10, 78–83, 85–86, 89, 99, 103, 107, 130; OPNAV changes to, 87–89; update to, 96–98

Gang of Five, 68, 74–75

Garrett, Henry L. "Lawrence," III, 50, 56–57, 58, 71, 95

Global Concept of Operations, 155–56, 164

"Global Engagement," 127

global fleet stations, 197–98, 209

Global Maritime Partnership, 197–98, 234

"Global Reach–Global Power," 57

global threats and operations: fleet orientation for, 37, 97–98, 99–100, 103, 118; interval between conflicts and crises, 68–71. *See also* forward presence

globalization: Bush administration opinion about, 148; concept and definition of, 11, 135; economics, security, and, 10–11, 135, 145–47, 181–83, 194–95, 197–99; end of Cold War and expansion of free world, 3; maritime strategy development and, 10–12, 135, 145–47, 181–83, 210, 213–14, 232, 250–52; Navy mission, 147; spread of, drive behind, 10–11; systemic strategy and, 11; threat-centric strategy and, 11

Goldwater-Nichols Defense Reorganization Act (1986): focus of and changes under, 8–9, 80–82, 86, 244–45; Gulf War and validation of, 64–65; influence of Navy and, 9–10, 210–11; timing of enactment, 45; U.S. strategy, responsibilities for, 9, 36–37, 44–45

Gray, Alfred M. "Al," Jr., 55–57, 58, 60–61, 66

Gulf War (1990–1991): air campaign management, 65; airpower and winning of, 64, 105; casualties of, 173; command arrangements,

65; daily Air Tasking Order, 66; Goldwater-Nichols and, 64–65; identity and purpose of Navy and, 9, 63; lessons from, 83–84, 86, 261n56; Navy role during, 58, 59–60, 66; operations during, 64, 83, 151; "The Way Ahead" submission timing and Desert Storm, 59; winning of, 64–65, 66, 84, 117

Hagee, Michael W., 164, 208

Haiti, 91, 94

Harris, R. Robinson "Robby," 127–28, 271n40

Hayward, Thomas B., 29, 31, 53, 116

Holloway, James L., III, 29–30, 31

Holloway, James L., Jr., 255n28

humanitarian assistance mission, 29–30, 58, 61, 93, 94, 129, 133, 162, 185, 187, 191, 206, 209, 233–34

international economic and political system: crisis management and international stability through naval forces, 39–41, 47, 55–60, 67, 71–72, 73–74, 75–78, 97–98, 102–3, 118, 130–31; design of, 1–2; economics, security, and globalization, 10–11, 135, 145–47, 181–83, 194–95, 197–99; guardian of the system, U.S. as, 11–12, 174–76, 181, 194–95; interventionist enlargement, 91–94, 97, 101; protection of by maritime services, 2, 41, 71–72, 145–47, 188–91, 194–95, 199; regional stability, 71–72; U.S. leadership role in, 1–2, 3, 33–34; vital U.S. interests in, 1–2

interventionist enlargement/enlargement, 91–94, 97, 101

Iraq: cruise missile attack on, 105; democratic government in, installation of, 172; insurgency in, failure to counter, 10; invasion of and U.S. strategy, 10, 84, 172–74, 180; invasion of Kuwait by, 50, 58, 59, 83; Iraqi Freedom operation, 167, 169; loss of war in, 4–5, 11; Southern Watch campaign, 119; threat-centric strategy in, 11; UN sanctions against, enforcement of, 60. *See also* Gulf War (1990–1991)

Johnson, Jay L.: appointment of, 115–16; career and experience of, 116; funding for aircraft program, 117; funding for Navy, 127, 133; institutional thinking changes, difficulty of, 134; maritime strategy, opinion about, 138; naval doctrine, development of, 122–25; naval doctrine, signing of, 118; "Navy Strategic Planning Guidance," signing of, 140; retirement of, 143; strategic statements, opinion about, 126, 144; vision to define purpose of Navy, 127–28, 268n39, 268n47

Joint Chiefs of Staff, chairman of: force structure and weapons decisions, responsibility for, 36–37; Mullen appointment, 226; presidential adviser role, 36; role in and influence on U.S. strategy, 9, 36–37, 44–45; stature and authority of, 8, 36–37, 44–45, 244; vision to define purpose of military, 8–9

Joint Resource Oversight Council, 106

Joint Vision 2010, 120–22, 123, 124, 126, 127, 128, 130, 136

jointness/joint warfare: authoritative publications, 108; coordinated versus integrated view of, 110; definition of, 105; doctrine for, 106–8; integrated air campaigns, 119; Joint Mission Areas, 88, 141; land-centric focus of, 108; military services reorganization for and focus on, 8–9, 85–86; Navy–Marine Corps joint doctrine, 111–13, 118–19; new vision for military, development of, 105–7; purple color and, 120, 267n2; resource decision priorities based on, 88; strike warfare and, 126; support for, 105–6, 117; trend toward jointness and corporateness trend in Defense Department, 144

Jomini, Antoine-Henri, 5, 17, 130

Jones, James L., 111–12, 162

Kelley, P. X., 54–55

Kelly, Robert J., 52, 54, 65–66, 67

Kelso, Frank B., II: Base Force plan, support for, 50–51; career and experience of, 48; consensus-building process under, 51, 139; force structure decisions, changes in, 86; managerial process efficiency under, 49, 51, 60, 87, 102; naval doctrine development, role in, 107, 108, 109; naval policy, interest in, 48–49, 51, 54; opinions about, 60; OPNAV reorganization under, 87–89, 145, 262nn3–4; purpose of Navy, concerns about defining, 80; relationship with Lehman, 48, 49; relationship with Miller, 50, 54; resource apportionment process under, 51, 87–89, 102; retirement of, 95, 119; roadmap to reshape Navy, 50–51; strategy definition, 48–49; Tailhook scandal and, 95; vision to define purpose of Navy, meeting about, 66–67; "The Way Ahead," 56–57, 58, 63

Kennedy, John, 24

King, Douglas M., 217, 226–27

King, Ernest J., 16, 85

Knowledge Superiority, 136, 159

Korean War, 18, 24–25, 151, 152

Krulak, Charles C., 111, 112–13, 129, 138

Kuwait, 50, 58, 59, 83. *See also* Gulf War (1990–1991)

Lake, W. Anthony K. "Tony," 93, 94

Lehman, John F., Jr.: activist viewpoint of, 133; aircraft for carriers, cancellation of program for, 117; career and experience of, 42; half the fleet as reserve forces, 42–43; Maritime Strategy purpose, 49; officers, education of, 23; opinions about, 42, 49; relationship with Kelso, 48, 49; Republican Platform and the 600-ship Navy, 258n39; resource apportionment process under, 49; strategic thinking group, relationship with, 53; threat-centric strategy and spending, 45–46

limited war, 24, 254n13

littoral environment: command structure for naval expeditionary force, 110, 265n35; definition of, 260n11; expeditionary warfare in, 67, 77–78, 81–82, 85, 86, 97, 107, 130, 260n11; fleet orientation for operation in, 91, 262n17; ". . . From the Sea" and focus on, 81–83; opinions about warfare mission in, 67, 96–97; shift in strategy from blue water to, 78

Mahan, Alfred Thayer, 4, 17–18, 23, 24, 34, 130, 213–14, 235

Mangold, Thomas E., Jr., 276n10

Manthorpe, William H. J., Jr., 68–69

Marine Corps Combat Development Command, 110, 111, 112

"Marine Corps Strategy 21," 162

Marine Corps, U.S.: amphibious warfare mission, 55, 61; crisis management and international stability through naval forces, 55–60, 67, 71–72, 73–74, 75–78, 102–3, 118; doctrine development for, 110; enabling force, Navy–Marine Corps team as, 54, 56–62; expeditionary warfare mission, 55, 77–78, 81–83, 85, 86, 97, 107, 130; Gulf War role, 66; institutional culture and partnership with Navy, 62; institutional thinking in, 133–34; jet aircraft, transition to, 254–55n22; maritime strategy and efforts of, 11; mission and purpose of, 54–56, 60–61, 81–83, 85, 138; operational concepts, 111, 112, 122, 136; paranoia in, 62; partnership with Navy, end of, 103, 119, 130; relevance of, 10, 178; reserve forces, 258n43; Three Block War, 128–29; warfighting philosophy and manual, 55, 57, 62, 85; written doctrine, 107–8

maritime research, institute for, 251
Maritime Strategy: Amphibious Warfare
    Strategy, 54–55; defense of and support for,
    41–44; development of, 42, 52, 89, 257n26;
    focus and purpose of, 32–33, 40, 41–44,
    46–47, 48–49, 213–14; officers to act as
    strategic thinkers for development of, 32;
    replacement of, 51–54, 57, 62–63; 600-ship
    Navy and, 42–43, 63; success in shifting
    national debate, 32
maritime strategy: decisions and factors in
    development of, 4–5, 10–12; development
    of, education about, 214–16; experience of
    officers and capacity to develop, 8; focus
    and purpose of, 3, 181, 210–12; globaliza-
    tion and strategy development, 10–12, 135,
    145–47, 181–83, 210, 213–14, 232, 250–
    52; Morgan strategy goals, 180–83; naval
    strategy and, 5; post–Cold War era, why
    did Navy not develop a strategy earlier in, 4,
    5–10; pushback about Mullen and Morgan
    goals, 200–202; recommendations, 249–52;
    strategic thinking and development of, 4;
    strategy development, education about,
    214–16, 235
"A Maritime Strategy for the 21st Century":
    development and writing of, 134–35; focus
    and organization of, 135–38, 158–59;
    opinions about, 137–38
"Maritime Strategy for the 1990s," 38–41,
    59, 63
Maritime Strategy mafia, 52–53
Martoglio, Charles W., 184, 205, 276n10
massive retaliation doctrine, 18–19, 21
McGrath, Bryan G., 216, 221–22, 224–25,
    226–28, 229, 231, 236, 280n59
McNamara, Robert S., 6, 24–27, 36
"Meeting the Challenges of a Changing
    World," 54
Middle East, 39–40, 263n25
military services: Base Force plan and cuts in,
    37, 39, 44–47, 50–51, 55–56, 60, 65, 86;
    "Bottom-Up Review," 90, 99–100, 101–2;
    civilian control over, 150; congressional
    understanding of purpose of, 44, 46, 62–63,
    73, 75; conventional forces, relevancy of,
    18–19; downsizing of, 8; force structure and
    weapons decisions, responsibility for, 36–37,
    44–45; forward presence approach instead of
    overseas base structure, 38, 71–72; jointness
    and reorganization of, 8–9, 85–86; military
    force, understanding use of, 91–92, 93;
    mission and focus, 2006 QDR and shift in,
    202–5, 206, 209, 210; morale in, 132–33;
    new vision for, development of, 105–7;

programming and budgeting processes,
    changes to, 5–7, 25–27, 37, 38, 255n35;
    purpose of military, Powell opinion about,
    93, 101; service-specific strategy, 144; tacti-
    cal and operational success and success in
    war, 10; unification of roles and missions,
    16–17; vision to define purpose of, 8–9;
    winning wars as primary mission of, 94
Miller, Paul David, 50, 54, 57, 58, 61, 65, 90
"Missions of the U.S. Navy," 28
Morgan, John G., Jr.: appointment as deputy
    CNO, 11; career and experience of, 179–80;
    globalization and maritime strategy develop-
    ment, 10–12, 181–83, 213–14; maritime
    strategy goals of, 180–83, 210; maritime
    strategy goals, pushback about, 200–202;
    The National Strategy for Maritime Security,
    198–99; "Naval Operations Concept,"
    208–10, 212; "Navy Strategic Plan," 207;
    "Navy Strategic Plan" development role,
    197; new maritime strategy, development
    and writing of, 216–23; opinions about,
    179–80; strategic initiative development,
    183–86, 195; strategic thinker reputation of,
    179–80, 195; strategy development, educa-
    tion about, 214–16, 235; strategy to shape
    programmatic decisions, 182; "3/1 Strategy,"
    183–94, 195
Mullen, Michael G. "Mike": appointment
    of, 194, 195; career and experience of,
    184–86; chairman of Joint Chiefs of Staff
    appointment, 226; conversion to maritime
    perspective, 11, 185–86; the Enterprise,
    role of, 161; Global Concept of Operations
    concept to support shipbuilding program,
    156; globalization and maritime strategy
    development, 10–12, 210, 213–14, 232;
    institutional thinking of, 134; maritime
    strategy goals, pushback about, 200–202;
    The National Strategy for Maritime Security,
    198–99; "Naval Operations Concept," 208–
    10, 212; "Navy Strategic Plan," 196–97,
    205–8, 212; new strategy, call for, 213–14,
    235, 278n3; opinions about, 184; prevent-
    ing wars as important as winning wars, 231,
    236, 251–52; systemic thinking by, 247
multilateral intervention, 91–94
Mundy, Carl E., 66, 79, 96, 97, 109

Nagy, Paul N., 184, 271n32
Nathman, John B. "Black," 152, 192–94, 197,
    200–202, 210, 211, 222, 225
National Defense Policy, 189
National Defense Strategy, 174–76
National Military Strategy, 75–76, 124, 127, 251

national security: Bush defense policy, 165; Bush national security team, 148; Clinton crises and U.S. interests, 93–94, 101–2; Clinton national security team, 91–92; economics, security, and globalization, 10–11, 135, 145–47, 181–83, 194–95, 197–99; interventionist enlargement, 91–94, 97, 101; overseas interventions and, 78; transformation defense policy goals, 149–51, 169–70, 173

National Security Strategy, 100, 165, 207, 210, 214

National Security Strategy for A New Century, 127

The National Strategy for Maritime Security, 198–99, 209, 214

NATO (North Atlantic Treaty Organization), 31, 253n3

Natter, Robert J., 143, 167

Naval Academy, U.S., 22–23, 48, 115

naval aviation: adoption of Air Force operational doctrine, 119; careers and experience of officers, 22, 27, 259n18; jet aircraft, transition to, 254–55n22

naval doctrine: development and writing of, 108–10, 118, 122–27, 265n21, 265n33; end of interest in, 119; Navy–Marine Corps joint doctrine document, 111–13, 118–19; opinions about doctrine, 107–8, 122; publications on, 108–10, 265n22

Naval Doctrine Command, 107, 108, 109, 110, 112–13, 119

Naval Force Capabilities Planning Effort, 67–78; command of the sea, achieving versus using, 75–78; consensus on operational concept and resource allocation, 79, 90; disagreements during Phase II, 74–75; final report, 72, 78, 79–80, 85; force structure reorganization, 77–78, 85; global economics section of final report, 72; naval power, understanding of, 85; Phase I, 68–72; Phase II, 72–75; Phase III, 75–78; purpose of, 67; review process, 67–68

naval maneuver warfare, 123–24, 125–26

"Naval Operating Concept for Joint Operations," 163–65, 208

Naval Operational Concept, 111–13, 118–19

Naval Operations, 109, 110, 119

"Naval Operations Concept," 208–10, 212

naval policy, 48–49, 51, 54

Naval Postgraduate School, 154–55, 216, 251, 271n39, 276n10

naval power: advancement of democracy and prosperity through, 214; command of the sea, achieving versus using, 75–78; understanding of, 85; U.S. foreign policy, trade, and, 4; U.S. interests and, 1

"Naval Power 21 . . . A Naval Vision," 162–63

naval purpose, theory of, 28–29

Naval Reserve, U.S., 42–43, 258n43

naval strategy: Cold War strategy, 5–8; contingent and implicit outlook, 20–21; maritime strategy and, 5; Navy belief system and, 12; process for making, 12–13; recurrent themes and, 243–47

Naval War College, U.S., 16, 17, 23, 85, 109, 154–55, 212, 213, 216, 217, 235, 265n33

Naval Warfare, 108–10, 164

Naval Warfare Development Command, 163–64

Navy, U.S.: backstop to shortsighted policies, 21, 33; battle-centric purpose and identity, 34; belief system in and naval strategy, 12; Cold War role of, 16–17, 46–47; command authority and structure, 25–27; conventional capabilities, restoration of, 32; enabling force, Navy–Marine Corps team as, 54, 56–62, 246; foreign policy, trade, and naval power, 4; Goldwater-Nichols and influence of on U.S. strategy, 9–10, 210–11; Gulf War and rationalization of, 65; historical insight, interest in, 85; identity, purpose, strategic outlook, and the Cold War, 6–8, 20–24; identity and purpose post–Cold War, 9–10; institutional culture and partnership with Marine Corps, 62; institutional thinking in, 4, 12, 133–34; managerial process efficiency, 49, 51, 60, 102; mission and purpose of, 3, 34, 39–41, 45–47, 58, 62–63, 110, 130–31, 147, 181–83, 210–12, 249–52, 268n39; missions of and theory of naval purpose, 28–29; morale, readiness, and retention issues, 132–33; naval power and U.S. interests, 1; nuclear weapons and relevance of, 15; operational analysis, 26; operational concept and resource allocation, consensus on, 79; operational concept of, lack of, 111; operations-based identity and purpose of, 6–8, 15–18, 22–24; partnership with Marine Corps, end of, 103, 119, 130; rationalization of, 13, 240; relevance of, 1, 5, 6–7, 10, 16–17, 32, 84–86, 178, 224; relevance of, defense of, 62–63; resource apportionment process, 49, 51, 87–89, 102; restricted line/staff corps communities, 255n28; roadmap to reshape, 50–51; Soviet sea-denial threat, reorganization of Navy around, 28–29; technical-technological focus of, 7, 9–10, 17–18, 22–24, 34; unrestricted line community, 23, 255n28; vision to define purpose of, 51–54, 61, 66–67, 127–30, 268n39, 268n47. *See also* fleet; officers

"The Navy Operational Concept," 24, 122–27, 128, 130

"Navy Strategic Plan," 196–97, 205–8, 212

"Navy Strategic Planning Guidance": background and development of, 138–40; focus and provisions of, 140–43, 147

Navy Strategy Discussion Group, 155, 271n40

Navy Warfare Development Command, 119

network-centric warfare, 123–24, 125–26, 131, 152, 169

North Korea, 97, 193, 194, 206, 218

nuclear bombs/weapons: Cold War and use of, 16–17; deterrence and, 5, 16–17, 21, 22, 24, 30–31, 32–33, 129, 254n13; flexible response doctrine, 24; nonnuclear defense of NATO-Europe, 31; nuclear-age strategic theory, 19, 254n13; planning for nuclear war, 18–19; proposal for cuts in number of, 35; relevance of Navy and, 15; retaliatory or preemptive strikes, planning for, 18

Nunn, Sam, 43–44

officers: career path changes under McNamara, 27; career paths and length of careers, 23; careers and experience of, 6–8, 12, 16, 22–24, 245, 252, 259n18; careers and professional experience of officers, 102; education and training of, 22–24, 27, 102, 250–51, 252, 282n29; experience of officers and capacity to develop maritime strategy, 8; flag officers, 27; technical-technological knowledge of, 7, 17–18, 22–24, 34

O'Keefe, Sean C., 79, 80

Olsen, Eric T., 163–64

1-4-2-1 construct, 155, 157, 163, 165–66, 202–5

1000-ship Navy concept, 197–98, 199, 206, 234

O'Neill, Sam, 217, 226–27

"Operational Maneuver from the Sea," 111, 112, 122, 136

operations: generic operational flexibility, 20–22, 30; officer education and experience to support, 22–24; operations-based identity and purpose of Navy, 6–8, 15–18, 22–24; primacy of, 15–18

Owens, William A. "Bill": authority and influence of, 89; career and experience of, 89; consensus-building process under, 139; ". . . From the Sea" development role, 90; Joint Resource Oversight Council role, 106; maritime strategy development role, 158, 159; naval doctrine, role in development of, 123; new vision for military, development of, 105–7; operational concept and resource allocation, 79; OPNAV reorganization and

authority of, 87–89; plan for fleet, 89–91; promotion of, 91; relationship with Aspin, 91; resource apportionment process under, 87–89, 102, 106; technologies, enthusiasm for, 99, 170, 195; unified battlespace concept, 158

Pacific Campaign, World War II, 6, 15, 23, 29

Pandolfe, Frank C., 152, 157–61

peacekeeping mission, 58, 61, 94, 129, 187, 190

Persian Gulf, 41, 275n65

Petrea, Howard "Rusty," 78–79

population-centric missions, 198, 212

Porter, Wayne, 197–98

Powell, Colin: authority and influence of, 36, 37, 44–45, 78, 86, 93, 150; Bush national security team, 148, 169; Clinton national security team, opinion about, 91–92; defense structure proposal, 39–40; force structure, focus on reshaping, 50, 52; Gulf War role, 65; military force, understanding use of, 93; purpose of military, opinion about, 93, 101; strategy and Base Force plan, 36–41, 44–47, 55–56, 60, 86; successor of, 91; understanding of Navy, 39

"Power from the Sea," 78. See also ". . . From the Sea"

power projection, 56, 58, 61–62, 81, 118, 129, 147

presence. See forward presence

Program Objective Memorandum, 50, 153, 182

"Project SIXTY" action plan, 28–29

Qaeda, al-, 11, 149, 150, 151, 168–69, 181–82, 218, 270–71n15

Quadrennial Defense Review (QDR): 2006 QDR, 197; 2014 QDR, 247, 248; budget decisions and, 125–26, 127, 132; military mission and focus, 2006 QDR and shift in, 202–5, 206, 209, 210; OPNAV decision-making process and preparations for, 138–39, 142; requirement for, 126; transformation defense policy goals, 149–50

Reagan administration and Ronald Reagan, 31–32, 46–47, 55, 263n25

regional powers: capabilities for conflict against, 9–10, 65; crisis management and international stability through naval forces, 41, 47, 55–60, 102–3, 118, 130–31; forward-deployed, combat-ready fleet to counter threats, 58–59; Powell strategy, 36–37; regional stability, 71–72; strategy to focus on regional threats, 37, 65, 85–86, 94, 97

Rickover, Hyman G., 22–23, 49, 102

Roughhead, Gary, 229–31, 236, 242, 281n19

Rubel, Robert C. "Barney," 217, 218, 278n19
Rumsfeld, Donald H., 148, 150, 153, 156, 162, 169, 177, 198, 210, 226

Sea Basing, 158–59, 160, 163, 164
"SEA PLAN 2000" study, 29–30, 31
sea power: command of the sea, achieving versus using, 75–78; destruction of Soviet naval forces and control of the sea, 32–33; forward-deployed, offensive-minded fleet and, 7, 15; long term phenomenon of, 21; sea control, 24, 56, 129; Soviet challenge for control of the seas, 28; U.S. strategy and, 34; victory at sea, 15; war from the sea, 15, 75–78
"Sea Power 21," 157–61, 162, 164, 170, 180
"Sea Power and Global Leadership," 54
Sea Shaping, 191
Sea Shield, 158, 160, 164
Sea Strike, 158, 160, 164
Secretary of Defense, Office of (OSD): authority of, 26–27, 36; force structure and weapons decisions, responsibility for, 36–37, 44–45, 60; strategy development role of, 144, 244–45
Sestak, Joseph A., Jr.: career and experience of, 98; firing of, 196; relief of, 263n43; strategy development role, 98, 135–38, 152, 153, 158–59, 165; strategy to shape programmatic decisions, goal of, 138–43; "3/1 Strategy," opinion about, 192; transfer of, 143; vision to define purpose of Navy, role in development of, 54
Shalikashvili, John M., 91, 104–7, 108, 120–21, 127
600-ship Navy, 32, 41, 42–43, 55, 63, 258n39
Smith, Edward A. "Ed," Jr., 68, 71, 73–74, 78–79, 113, 128
Smith, Leighton W. "Snuffy," Jr., 65–66, 67, 68, 91
soft power, 185, 200, 228, 275n53
Somalia, 91, 94, 97, 104
Soviet Union: Afghanistan invasion by, 31; capabilities, intentions, and naval force expansion, 38; collapse of, 33, 78; conventional land and air forces to deter, 30–31; destruction of Soviet naval forces and control of the sea, 32–33; fleet deployment and containment, 15–16; prestige, power, and presence of, 28–33; retaliatory or preemptive strikes against, 18, 21–22; threat from and end of Cold War, 35, 44; threat from and Navy's purpose, 9; threat from and U.S. strategy, 5, 19–20; withdrawal of army, 35, 38
stability operations, 189–91

Stavridis, James G. "Jim," 79, 152, 162, 225
Strategic Air Command, 19
strategic concept, 67, 81
Strategic Concepts Branch, 52, 97, 152, 259n18
Strategic Planning and Political-Military sub-specialty community, 259n16
Strategic Planning Guidance, 174
strategic thinking: atrophy of capabilities under Clark, 153–55, 212; career paths of members of strategic thinking group, 102, 259n18; Cold War influence on, 241; community of Navy strategists, 52–54, 259n16, 259n18; defense policies and need for, 31; forces that shape how the Navy thinks, 4; formative years of, 18–24; lack of need for, 48–49, 60, 63, 144, 146–47, 153–55, 170; lack of proficiency in, 18, 24, 34, 53, 84, 246–47; Mahan tactics and lack of need for, 17–18, 24, 34; maritime strategy development and, 4; officer education and training for, 23–24, 27, 154–55, 250–51, 282n29; officers to act as strategic thinkers for strategy development, 32; quality of, improvement in, 250–51; recommendations, 249–52; strategic statements, opinion about, 126
strategy: concept of, 9; declaratory U.S. strategy, 21; globalization and U.S. strategy, 10–12, 135, 145–47, 232; nuclear-age strategic theory, 19, 254n13; process for making, 12–13; regional powers, capabilities for conflict against, 9–10; regionally-focused strategy, 37, 65, 85–86, 94, 97; responsibility for development of, 144; Soviet threat and U.S. strategy, 5, 19–20; strategy to shape programmatic decisions, 138–43, 182; U.S. strategic culture, 34; U.S. strategy, responsibilities for, 9–10, 36–37, 44–45. *See also* maritime strategy
Strategy and Concepts Branch, 97, 102
strike warfare: aircraft carriers and, 9, 85, 156; aircraft for, 103; decisive victory with, 86, 105; Enduring Freedom joint operations, 151–52, 156; fleet orientation for, 91, 97, 112–13, 118, 125–26; focus of Navy on shore adversaries, 9–10, 85–86; Iraq invasion, 172–74; jointness and, 126; precision strike warfare, 131
submarines: attack submarines and sea control, 24, 129, 136; attack submarines, funding for, 112; careers and experience of officers, 22, 27, 102, 259n18; cruise missiles on SSBN, 115; development and deployment of SSBN, 21, 22, 255n31; force strength of, 91; *Ohio*-class submarines, 48, 115, 156;

Soviet SSBNs, destruction of, 32–33; SSBN and deterrence, 21–22; SSBN and nuclear retaliation, 24; SSBN-Polaris funding, 24, 28, 255n34

surge capabilities and campaigns, 58–59, 61, 165–68, 204–5

systemic strategy: Cold War and, 20; development of, 4–5, 101–2, 247; economic and political goals and, 2, 3, 33–34, 146–47; globalization and, 11; guardian of the system, U.S. as, 11–12; merits of, 252

systems analysis and the science of management, 25–27

Systems Commands, 161, 272n56

Tailhook Association scandal, 94–96, 115, 143

technology: decisive victory and, 117–18; development of and the Cold War, 22; focus of Navy and Navy officers, 7, 9–10, 17–18, 22–24, 34, 170; "Forward . . . From the Sea" and, 99; network-centric warfare, 123–24, 125–26, 131; transformation defense policy goals and use of, 149, 169–70, 173

10-30-30 concept, 165–66

terrorists and terrorism: Cold War approach to after 9/11 attack, 148–49; counterterrorism mission, 58, 61, 182, 187, 189, 190, 192, 201, 202–5, 207, 233–34; generational struggle against Islamist terrorist threats, 4–5; global war on terror, 150, 168–69, 186, 198, 270–71n15; strategy development and, 4–5

threat-centric strategy and outlook, 2, 11, 19–20, 45–46, 148–49

Three Block War, 128–29

"3/1 Strategy": Bear Paw, 184, 185, 186, 194; development of, 183–86; focus and purpose of, 186–91, 195, 199, 206; opinions about, 192–94

Tomahawk cruise missiles, 60, 115, 116, 118

Total Quality Leadership, 49, 51

Total Quality Management, 49

trade, 2, 3, 4, 41

transformation defense policy, 149–51, 169–70, 173

Transitioners, 69–70, 82–83, 90, 101

Trost, Carlisle A. H.: Base Force plan and, 37–41, 44; career and experience of, 41–42, 48; competition for resources, opinion about, 51, 145; "Maritime Strategy for the 1990s," 38–41, 59, 63; Maritime Strategy purpose, 49; Maritime Strategy, support for, 41–44; naval reserve forces, 42–43; opinions about, 46–47, 60; relationship with Warner, 44; relevance of Navy, defense of, 62–63; resource apportionment process under, 51

Truman, Harry, 15–16, 41

Turner, Stansfield M., 28–29, 129

"2020 Vision," 113–15, 118

Vietnam War, 24–25, 28, 36, 64, 65, 83, 93, 206, 261n56

warfighting: continentalist approach to, 34; decisive victory, 17, 117–18; departure from focus on, 2; focus of U.S. strategy on, 9; Jomini approach to, 5, 17, 130; Marine warfighting philosophy and manual, 55, 57, 62, 85; peacetime versus warfighting requirements, 72–75; preventing wars as important as winning, 231, 236, 251–52; sea-lane access during wars, 29; separate sea and land warfare realms, 15; tactical and operational success and success in war, 10, 17–18; Three Block War, 128–29; winning wars as primary mission of military, 94

"Warfighting" Fleet Marine Force Manual 1, 55, 57, 62

Warner, John, 43–44

Watkins, James D., 49, 53, 54–55

"The Way Ahead," 56–60, 63

Weinberger-Powell Doctrine, 92–93, 263n25

Wilkerson, Thomas L. "Tom," 74–75, 98–99

Winter, Donald C., 228, 229, 230, 236–37

Wolfowitz, Paul D., 37, 65, 148

"Won if by Sea," 54

Zalaskus, Robert M., 108, 109, 265n21

Zumwalt, Elmo R. "Bud," Jr., 28–29, 30, 96, 116, 145

About the Author

Capt. Peter D. Haynes, USN, is the deputy director, Strategy, Plans, and Policy (J5), U.S. Special Operations Command. A carrier aviator, decorated combat veteran, and former squadron commander, he has served four tours in strategy positions on several senior staffs. He has a PhD in security studies, an MA in strategic planning (both from the Naval Postgraduate School), and a BA in history from the University of Notre Dame.